"It Shocked Even Us!"
And More Crazy Stories Covering Local News

BY: FRANK CIPOLLA

Published by Taryn Vinik © 2011
Edited by Andy Caploe and Taryn Vinik
Assistant Editor: Elinore Schochet
All images courtesy of Frank Cipolla

Cover and interior design copyright © 2011 by
EMAIL: tvinik@yahoo.com

Published in the United States.
ISBN: 978-0-578-08140-3

Dedicated to the lovely Bride Lauren, my loving children Charles and Taryn and our Yorkie Max, the prince of the house.

Table of Contents

PROLOGUE

For someone whose business it is to deal in sound and image, I most remember the smell.

I know that sounds unusual but it's the truth. For the past thirty years, I have spent most of my time reporting stories in cities big and small.

Anchoring a newscast alone in a stuffy radio studio – or trying to concentrate on a TV camera lens while sixteen things are going on just beyond its unblinking eye.

But for this city kid "the smell" is both vivid and comforting. And it always brings a smile.

Leaving my first on-air radio job interview in the summer of 1980 I breezed through a landscape as alien to me as the surface of Mars. I knew I had gotten the job and was floating on-air. As I drove the eighty-eight miles home from one of the most rural areas of New Jersey to my block in Howard Beach, Queens – there it was! In every direction there were corn stalks and cows. Horses and hay. Plants and blossoming flowers. It was the smell of the Earth in full bloom.

It is forever etched in my mind and will always connect me to a certain time of my life. A time and place where it all began and in looking back, among the most carefree and exhilarating times of my life.

Every once in a while I smell it again. I'll be driving home late in the evening after visiting friends or family somewhere far away, and there it is.

I always open my sunroof and slide the windows down hoping like a time machine it will take me back to the first time I smelled it. I can count on one hand the times it has happened and I know this sounds crazy – but I cherish each one.

For an instant I am the young kid. The cub reporter. Anxious and ambitious. Passionate and excited. Cocksure of where I am – and absolutely certain of where I'm going. I have tried to convey to my kids and close friends what that smell means to me but it's just too personal a thing.

I wish that moment for everyone.

Maybe this book will help you understand.

Chapter 1
SHOCKING!

It was idiotic video. Footage of a not-so-bright wannabe thief who thought he could make a few dollars robbing a convenience store. The plan was to enter at night – through the ceiling.

We've all seen something like it. One of those video moments that end up with you scratching your head or laughing your ass off.

The crook in this video didn't realize the small drop ceiling panels that covered the store's swirl of wires could never support his weight. He came falling into the store with a thud, a groan and the crash of a food rack.

And guess what?

It was caught on tape!!

In our newsroom, the surveillance video was heralded as "Startling" and "Amazing!"

It was promo-ed regularly ahead of the newscast and expertly edited to leave out the exact moment the poor bastard came crashing to the floor. The money shot would have to wait until the top of the *Ten O'Clock News*.

I remember shaking my head as I passed the edit bay where this "startling" and "amazing" video was being cut up into small digestible pieces.

At ten on the dot the wild newscast effects swished and swirled. Another snippet of Mr. Stupid falling through the ceiling. The anchor spoke, more carnival barker than newsperson.

"Tonight – startling video! A man tries to rob a Kansas City convenience store. It's video that's so startling… so amazing … *it shocked even us!*"

What shocked me at that moment was that this was actually considered "news." War raged thousands of miles away in Iraq and Afghanistan. In the halls of Congress decisions were being made that would change the size and shape of Medicare. A former vice president had just raged against the current administration. What was so shocking – "that it shocked even us" – shocked me instead.

It was clear that a new guard had quietly staged a palace coup. Idiotic video and hot, young blondes were more important than cold, hard facts.

For me it was an epiphany.

It reminded me of a live shot in lower Manhattan several nights before.

I was about a half hour from going on the air live when my photographer Dave Rosenfeld and I were approached by a young, tall, pretty blonde. In a voice made so familiar by all those "Valley Girl" parodies she alerted us that she had been watching what we were doing and wanted us to know that she also wanted to be a journalist.

A good reporter asks the obvious question first.

"Why do you want to be a journalist?" I said.

"Because people think I'm pretty… and I look good on camera… "

I glanced at Dave and he just shrugged. I thought, *Okay I'll play along and see where this ends up.*

"They're right," I said, trying to be nice. "You surely are pretty but why do you want to be a journalist?"

She looked puzzled. Hadn't the question been asked and answered?

At that point you could hear the gears in her pretty little head grind harder as she tried to process what I was asking her.

"Well," she said. "People say I talk good and I'm very tall…"

Another pause, another quick glance at Dave, another shrug. Again I tried, "Yes – but why do you want to be *a journalist*?"

"Because I look good on TV and I'm pretty… " she said in a huff.

A good reporter knows when it's time to move on. I shook her hand, wished her well and sent her on her way.

Turning to Dave I said, "You know, some people just don't get it."

He turned toward me even more puzzled than our pouty-lipped; blue eyed future news Twinkie and said. "No…. maybe *you* don't get it."

He was right. One day this twenty-five-year-old would be batting her eyes on some cable news network while really good reporters would be fighting to air stories that mattered.

"IT SHOCKED EVEN US!"

Chapter 2
FLYING THROUGH QUEENS

She was as big as a Buick and smelled like hell. She was also my first customer. Rose Skip, her husband and her daughter were grotesquely obese. They walked around their house casting gigantic shadows on the walls and furniture. For a boy of eight it was an early lesson in how large bodies orbit each other. Only at Rose's house the people seemed larger than the planets.

There was not much real news to report on 118th street in South Ozone Park, Queens. It was just another block in a universe of blocks like it – but damned if I wasn't going to find something!

Maybe the father of eight next door was drunk again. Or maybe the World War II combat vet two houses down was having another one of his scary flashbacks. And what about Tony the mailman?

Tony was always late. Turns out he was making a daily "special delivery" to Mrs. Catalano around the block. Often we'd see Tony racing around the neighborhood late in the day, hair mussed up, tongue hanging out, jamming letters into whatever box was in front of him.

One day we got our mail at 6:15 p.m.!

Knowing and gossiping about what might have been happening with Tony, Mrs. Catalano, Rose Skip and everyone else on the block was a delightful little diversion for the neighbors, a delicious way to make themselves feel better.

Seeing it in black and white was another story.

I knew a good story when I saw one so I published the five-cents-a-copy *118th Street Gazette*. I pecked away in my basement on some ancient typewriter and with the help of carbon paper made about fifteen copies. I sold twelve, the first to Rose Skip. I was left with plenty of money for candy and patted myself on the back for a job well done.

Then the phone rang.

Rose Skip wasn't happy with everyone on the block knowing about her new diet. We also heard from the remaining relatives of the family of Mrs. Pilot, a concentration camp survivor who lived across the street. The day before I published my newspaper, she had been swinging her broom at the kids on the block. It was actually a great lead. Her relatives didn't think so. And as for Tony the mailman – we never saw him again.

When the *Gazette* hit the street my Mom – who took the calls – put an end to it. She explained to me that this was private stuff. It was not to be printed – even if I had the First Amendment on my side.

When this lesson was learned she pulled me aside again. "And by the way Frank," she said. "If you're going to put this kind of gossip out there in black and white for everyone to see, you have to charge more than five cents a copy."

Mom – what a businesswoman!

My mother, Mary Cipolla, actually got me interested in the news business. She was a single mom even before the term was invented. Working as a saleswoman for a syrup company, she'd bounce around from pizzeria to pizzeria throughout Queens and Long Island selling syrup to Italian immigrants who made their living with dough, sauce and cheese.

As she put on her makeup every morning she asked me to read the New York *Daily News* to her, imitating my TV news anchor idols like Jim Jensen and Rolland Smith. I was a little kid, thick Queens accent, reading about New York's Mayor Lindsay and President Nixon.

My mom listened to me read the newspaper and was pleased. And that made me feel special. Mom was making up for the time when she was too busy to read to me or help me with my homework – what family therapists now call "quality time."

Sometimes after school Mom would pick me up and together we'd go on her sales calls. The old Italian pizzeria men loved her. While they flirted with her she bumped up their syrup orders. She was a very successful saleswoman and it was a great lesson for me in the art of the "schmooze."

My mother was also a ham – an actress and a singer. One of my earliest memories is of my mom rehearsing a play at the local school while I sat on the floor near the stage playing with my toy trucks. She had a great voice.

If I got my personality, outgoing nature and sales skills from my mom, I got my discipline from my dad. Vincent Cipolla Sr. served honorably in the Army Air Force during World War II. He was stationed on the island of Guam, and came back from that experience in early 1946 with two things that never changed: military discipline and a lifelong disdain for hot weather.

Once in a while he'd plan something for us and then tell my brothers, sister and me, "Okay, we'll all get up exactly at oh-five-hundred hours." I'd look at my brothers and think, *What the hell is oh-five-hundred hours?*

If we answered him quickly or correctly we'd get a snappy, "Roger that."

My favorite was when we'd pulled up in front of the house, or the bagel store, or the ice cream place and he would stop the car, look back at my brothers and sister and me and say, "Okay, bail out!"

He was a Fred Flintstone type – small and solid with a low rumbling voice and Fred's perpetual five o'clock shadow. Before he and my mom separated when I was ten, I'd watch him head off every weekday to the giant train yards in Brooklyn or Queens or sometimes to the tunnels below Manhattan. He worked for the New York Metropolitan Transit Authority, the agency that runs and maintains New York's subways and buses. Having worked on the engines of the mighty B-29s that lumbered over Japan and won the war in the Pacific, tinkering with the brakes of an F-Train was child's play. My dad knew everything mechanical. What he didn't know he read in *Popular Mechanics*. Within the family – and well beyond it – his ability to fix anything, and I mean anything, was legendary. His precise nature and focus rubbed off on me, not with tools, but with the discipline to see the job through.

You also crossed him at your peril. My brothers Sal and Vincent and our sister Ginger all knew this. But he wasn't always the tough disciplinarian. One summer weekend my brother Sal returned from a giant rock concert in the Catskills.

He left his mud-caked boots in the hallway and when he woke up he had tons of stories about something called "Woodstock." My dad was reading the newspaper on the couch downstairs. In it were photos of this out-of-this-world, one of a kind concert including shots of topless women bathing in the lakes and ponds near the concert site.

My dad's eyebrows went up as he scanned the photos. Just as he was finished taking it all in my brother came down the stairs looking the image of a Sixties hippie.

"Sally?" my dad roared in that low body shaking voice.

"Yeah," my brother said half-asleep.

"You mean to tell me this was going on up there?"

"Yeah," my brother grunted.

My dad looked up and said, "Why didn't you call me?"

●●●

At the age of thirteen I got a paper route delivering the New York *Daily News*. Every morning I'd get up at dawn rain or shine. I'd wrap up the newspapers in front of my house, squeeze them into my metal bicycle basket and then speed through the neighborhood slinging them with expert precision.

Boy, this was great! Not only was I learning what was going on in the world before anyone even got up but now I was bringing the news to my customers. The folks at the afternoon paper called once in a while to ask if I would consider delivering for them. Heck no! I wanted to be the first to know – not the last.

The Sixties was also an eventful decade filled with all sorts of news stories. There were the assassinations of President John F. Kennedy, Martin Luther King and Robert F. Kennedy. I remember vividly as a kid coming home from school the afternoon JFK was shot and seeing grown men and women crying as they walked past me on the street.

The biggest news story of the decade though was man's landing on the moon. Being a space geek, I was hunkered down in my basement watching our brand new color TV. I will never forget that summer afternoon of July 20, 1969 when the Lunar Module 'Eagle' touched down on the moon's surface.

I wish I could say that was my only memory of this historic event but it wasn't.

When the landing happened I was so excited that I ran out to tell the first person I saw. The only person around was the elderly man next door known to us only as "Nono" – or Grandpa, in Italian.

"Nono… Nono", I said, "Man has landed on the moon. People are on the moon!"

Nono, who was born in the late 1800's, could not comprehend that this was possible. I insisted but he waved me off. When I insisted some more he stood up from his usual perch on the front steps of his house and starting swinging his cane at me. He then charged me and for a time we struggled. It was quite a wacky scene: an eighty five year old man mixing it up with a ten-year-old kid. He got his cane back but not before I was able to twist off the rubber nib at the bottom of it.

Later that evening when my mom found out I was ordered first to apologize to Nono and then return his nib.

Till this day man's landing on the moon – for me at least – is always followed by terrifying images of an old Italian man chasing me with his cane.

My paper route customers loved me and in short order I had imitations down of some of my favorites, like the old lady in the apartment building and her husband who probably fought in World War I. No matter when I came it was always a surprise to her. She'd shuffle around apartment while I waited at the door saying, "Bill, give the kid a buck… BILL! *Give the kid a buck.*" I never saw Bill but when the handoff was made in some back room it took forever for the woman to penguin walk her way back up to the front door. Sometimes I'd ring the doorbell to collect for the paper delivery, and then disappear for a half-hour, coming back just in time to meet her at the door with my buck.

There was also the playboy. Every time I'd show up some scantily clad woman would be flitting back and forth behind him while he reached into his pocket, or robe, to pay me.

Sometimes I'd ring the bell for ten minutes before he was able to finish up and come to the door. As I got older, I figured out why it was taking him so long. The bell then became an instrument of torture. My friend Charlie Degliomini (who occasionally joined me on my collections) and I would ring the bell ten or twelve times and then disappear. We'd work the rest of the building – go back to the playboy's apartment, frantically ring the bell again and then disappear.

We invented "newspaper interruptus."

The 1960's and early 70's were a whole different world. Those who grew up then can tell you we did stuff that today would land our parents in front of a judge. Mom or Dad would say, "Go out and play." The only rule – be back by five for dinner. This meant that the entire neighborhood was ours for the picking. Whatever mischief we could get into – or whatever stunt we could imagine – we did.

One time my childhood buddy Teddy Aurora and I decided to find our way from one end of the block to the other by sneaking through everyone's backyard. That meant jumping fences, tiptoeing through backyard tomato patches, shimmering up stockade fences to meet our "objective." When that got old we kicked it up a notch, going from one end of the block to the other – jumping from garage rooftop to garage rooftop. It was crazy and could have gotten us killed.

Early on we got wind of some weird chick several blocks away with crazy colored hair. It ended up being Cyndi Lauper. Not too far away the actress and singer Bernadette Peters grew up. But I didn't even have to look that far. All I had to do was look out my front window. I lived right across the street from the McCann family. The eldest son Jimmy now owns 1-800-FLOWERS. Later on in my career I interviewed Jimmy's sister. She came on a TV show I was hosting to talk about Jimmy's company and how it was so easy to order flowers. We laughed and reminisced. When we came back on the air she couldn't resist looking into the camera and saying, "Hey Jim, look who I found, Little Frankie."

New York back then was a tasty stew of street games like Saluggi, Johnny On A Pony, War, Skully, ice cream and the occasional pony ride. Twice, sometimes three times a year, an old Italian man used to come down the block with a horse pulling a small cart. It was straight out of Sicily. For a nickel you sat in the cart and got a ride around the block. Today the poor bastard would probably need fifteen permits from the city and get run over by some souped-up Chevy blasting hip hop.

As I got older and my mom got busier, my Italian immigrant grandmother Millie Messina was pressed into duty. Instead of going home for lunch from school every day I walked a few blocks in the opposite direction to my grandmother's house. It was the best diner in the world! I'd make a request the day before and – bingo! – my hot lunch was waiting for me when I got there at twelve-thirty. She'd make anything I wanted.

My grandmother was also a religious sort. Back then Sunday Mass was the rule. No if, ands or buts. Women back in the Sixties and Seventies could not enter church unless they had something on their heads. This sign of respect for the Almighty usually came in the form of a hat, kerchief, or sometimes a small scarf.

One day, in a rush, Grandma and I headed off to church. As she walked she was simultaneously digging through her pocketbook. She had left the house with nothing to cover her head and now late for church she had to produce *something*.

So there I stood next to my grandmother – giant fans circulating the air of the stuffy church – and bobby-pinned to her head sat a grocery store receipt fluttering in the breeze.

Sometimes my mother would ask my grandmother *and* my grandfather Sam Messina to watch me while she worked overtime or on the weekends. One day they decided to take me to the movies. Easy pick right? Make the kid happy. Bring him to some animated movie or G-rated flick. I don't know who made the selection, but there I was 12 years old, sitting between my seventy-two-year-old-grandmother and seventy-three-year-old grandfather watching *2001: A Space Odyssey*.

My grandmother would occasionally look over to me and say in Italian – "What the hell is going on?" As a twelve-year-old, the symbolism and conceptual nature of the Stanley Kubrick's classic was lost on me.

Finally in desperation – and for some guidance – I looked over to my grandfather.

He was snoring.

Chapter 3
BENDING THE RULES

In 1972 I started my first year at Christ the King High School in Middle Village, Queens; exposing me to theater, radio, TV and lifelong friends. Christ the King was a great school with a terrific reputation.

Life coaches will tell you that if you really desire something the universe will present it to you. High school was my first real test of that theory. In the years that followed, the universe would work its magic with amazing regularity. It was a great lesson for a young mind in the power of visualization.

At Christ the King High I built a great network of friends. From there we instinctively understood we'd have fun first and foremost.

Part of our dream was to make a movie. The idea percolated for a while and then hit us. We would go where no man has gone before. We would film – there wasn't any consumer videotape back then – a *Star Trek* movie.

It started when one of our gang working after school scouted out a semi-circular storage room in the basement of the school. It had the exact shape of the bridge of the Star Ship Enterprise. We called our movie *Star Trip*.

My friend Gene and I worked on a *Star Trip* script for days. Both of us laughing and giggling the whole way while friends hanging out near by smoked pot. After an hour of second hand pot smoke everything seemed funny to Gene and me! Say what you want about pot, but son of a gun, we wrote one hell of a script. Even though I did stand-up comedy later in life it remains, with the help of Gene, one of the funniest things I've ever written.

The pot also seeped into the script. In our movie Captain Kirk is abducted and taken prisoner on Cannabis 4. Spock, McCoy and Sulu beam down to save him while the Enterprise orbits above. Those orbiting scenes were campily recreated with a model of the Enterprise and a hand whishing it back and forth on a black background covered with white chalk stars.

In our script the leader of Cannabis 4 is played by a fellow student in a robe, scepter and hat. He looks like a manic magician. In an example of monumental miscasting, I was Scotty – the Scottish engineer who lives for the Enterprise. Here I was a short, dark skinny Italian kid with a Queens accent doing the best Scottish imitation I could. Saying things like, "Captain – I gotta leak in the engine room." To which Kirk responded, "Permission granted."

With the room selected, the script done, and the key clandestinely secured from a sympathetic teacher – we now had frequent and easy access to the "bridge" of the Enterprise.

We were working under the radar and in debt to a teacher friend we never identified. This "Deep Throat" instructor of Christ the King encouraged us to be creative. The nickname oddly fit him. Shortly after we graduated, he left his uptight wife and opened his own business making a bundle single-handedly creating the body paint industry and then selling his company for millions.

My jaw dropped when I saw a profile of him years later on the Playboy Channel. There he was dancing with Playboy bunnies at the mansion and chitchatting with Hef.

As word seeped out about the movie other students volunteered to help. After the school day, we'd haul plywood and furniture into the room to build the set. The captain's chair was swiped off the curb in front of a home in Glendale, Queens. The controls on the console were flickering Christmas lights poking out of painted black plywood. Small risers were taken from the school theater to give the set some depth. Another large piece of wood became the sliding door to the bridge, dutifully whisked back and forth by an ever-expanding crew of stagehands.

The transporter control panel, the device Scotty was to use to beam us back and forth to Cannibus 4, was going to be a problem. We had a line on a piece of furniture with the exact dimensions we needed, but it was hidden in a room offstage in the school auditorium. We had to get the key.

With all the planning, coordination and intrigue of a Nazi prison break, we secured the key and after school dragged what we needed down the hallway and onto our set.

Monday morning we were summoned to the principal's office. Had any of us seen the "transporter console"? Apparently, over the weekend the priests at Christ the King had a special mass to honor one Saint or another. Parents attended, as did the Monsignor from a nearby parish.

It was a big deal. There was one hitch. The priests couldn't find the portable altar.

They frantically scoured the building. Little did they know it had been 'appropriated' and left in the transporter room aboard the Enterprise orbiting the Glock galaxy – or whatever spot in the cosmos we had been visiting when we wrapped up Friday's shoot.

I had a lot of time to think about revisions in the script while in detention. It could have ended there but we were determined to finish the project. Production started up again slowly, with proper scheduling and lookouts to make sure the priests didn't catch us.

The crew of the Enterprise "beamed" down to the backyard behind the school, using the tricorder to see if there was intelligent life just beyond the parking lot. All we had to do though was look behind us. In one scene you see a jogger running by in the distance. In another a plane roars overhead.

One tricky scene required a small room. The only rooms that size onsite were up on the fourth floor of the school. That was the priests' residence and an area strictly forbidden to all students, but accessible. We hatched a plan: We were going to slip into the priests' fourth floor living quarters late Friday before a long holiday weekend and be out within an hour or so. It didn't go as smoothly as we predicted.

Between the flubbed lines, giggling, and technical problems – not to mention some pot smoking by my friends – we were quickly behind schedule and rushing to wrap things up. Then, as if on cue, one of the priests came home, startling us in the middle of a key scene. The lighting guy swung around. In an instant, Father Joe's retinas were seared, blasted by countless watts of light from a belt-mounted contraption to which we had attached two-dozen floodlights.

It was the last scene we shot. We were forced to shut down production. Somewhere on Super 8 film is the original and only print of *Star Trip*.

My mom had high hopes for me and I certainly did not want to let her down. At one point she thought it would be nice to have a lawyer in the family. I took a few classes to see if I would like it. Most of my time though was spent trying to stay awake. Lawyers work in the intricacies of case law and precedent. It was all too arcane and stupefying for me.

The straw that broke the camel's back came during a springtime high school class on law. The weather was perfect, the air light, temperature in the seventies. A zephyr danced through the classroom curtains now and again and one by one the lids of my classmates descended. Before I drifted away to a peaceful sleep, I glanced around the class and took a head count. Of the twenty-eight of us, twenty were either asleep, sitting up, or had their heads down. Just before I slipped away, I spotted my friend Gene. His body was slumped, but he was still awake. A closer look presented a logical explanation.

Gene – a prolific artist – had anticipated what was coming and painted eyes on his eyelids.

High school was also the first place I appeared on camera and in front of the mic. At the start of my sophomore year our teachers went on a strike. It dragged on for a few weeks. With my ham of a personality, I quickly assumed the role of official student spokesman. On cue, I would rally the students to protest outside the school; lead chants and shamelessly throw myself in front of whatever news crew showed up.

I had it down to a science. The TV crew would show up and look for the administrators who were still working, even though the school was closed. I would run toward the crew and say something like, "It's not fair. All we want to do is learn, right everybody?" And whoever was around would cheer.

The reporter would inevitably say, "Okay, wait here. I want to talk with you." I liked being on TV and it just reinforced my desire to be seen and heard. Somewhere in the archives of my local TV stations is video of a fourteen-year-old Frank Cipolla being interviewed and mugging for the camera.

The other opportunity that presented itself came courtesy of Mr. Veltri. In the spring of my junior year, he was given the assignment of finding someone to make the morning announcements on the school public address system. Maybe he saw something in me – maybe not.

Whatever the case, he sought me out.

It's funny because I had secretly imagined myself doing just that. During trips to the principal's office I would peek into the room just near the main desk. It was a very small with a microphone on a table. I was visualizing again – seeing myself sitting there saying something to everyone in the school.

I came in early as directed the next day and with sweaty palms delivered my first over-the-microphone announcement.

"Class will be dismissed at two P.M. tomorrow for a teacher's meeting. Mr. Mitchell, please report to the office. Thank you."

Okay, it wasn't much, but for a high school sophomore, it was pretty cool.

This went on for a while. I used to practice on the bus in the morning. Between my earlier TV appearances during the strike and later the "announcer" gig, I was positively sure that this is what I wanted to do. Being on TV or radio gives you an "aura." People want to know you –

they want to be your friend. And even though I didn't lack for friends, I enjoyed being the king.

I was surrounded by a great group of friends who I still know and love. They include, in no particular order, Frank Demundo, Tony Massimini, Bart Manzella, Gene Grillo, Joe Schwerdt, Bernie Bosio, "Animal" Al Sporing, Reginald T.W. Ruecker, "Pistol" Pete Reinherdt and the Shirley Maclaine to our "Rat Pack," Bernadette Englert. All funny people and we gelled wonderfully.

Two of my very favorites are Rose Fabrizio and Lillian Cancemi. Both are married now and still live in Queens. They are also as caring and wonderful as they were when I first met them.

In the spring of 1976, a month or so before I was to graduate, I was told that I would be nominated for the "Most Outstanding Graduate" award. It was an award to honor the person whose fellow students considered "most likely to succeed". There was one catch. It had to be an overwhelming vote, something like sixty percent or more. Many students had come close over the years, but no one had won it in more than a decade.

The announcement came at the end of the last graduation rehearsal. I leapt to my feet. The award would be given to me the following day at graduation in front of my fellow students and their parents. '*Oh,*' I thought, '*another audience to impress.*'

The announcement left me just twenty-four hours to cook something up that would be remembered forever! '*Why receive the award,*' I thought, '*if in time it just fades away into the collective memories of your fellow classmates and parents?*'

I needed help to pull off my plan in case the teachers suspected something.

The accomplice would be the person sitting next to me Danny Cignigliaro – a tall lanky classmate who could hide something easily under his flowing graduation gown.

After the greetings by the salutatorian and the address by the valedictorian, it was time to announce the special award winners. As my name was about to be announced, I reached over to Danny who slowly passed me a Groucho Marx fake nose, mustache and eyeglasses.

Announcer: "And this year's honoree and winner of the Most Outstanding Graduate Award, Frank Cipolla."

I put on the Groucho glasses, stood up and waved to the crowd of about six thousand people. The place went nuts: students laughing, parents laughing, everyone pointing. I had tipped off my sister who was in perfect position to snap a picture. I jumped on stage, took a bow, grabbed the award and skipped away to screams of laughter. It was glorious!

Then it got ugly.

Following this beautiful stunt was a speech by the head of the science department. To say she was not the most exciting person on two feet is an understatement. She began speaking in a monotone about how life is like the light spectrum.

It went something like this: '*red is for passion, orange for curiosity, yellow for envy*' – you get the picture. With the excitement of my stunt still working its way from one end of the auditorium to the other, she was all but drowned out by waves of residual laughter and chatter by the time she got to indigo.

She rushed through the speech and ended it with a muffled sob. Any other time, those who had to sit through such a speech would have offered up a polite applause, or taken the opportunity to hit the head. But there was too much post-Groucho craziness bouncing around.

Following the graduation, the faculty needed a target for her embarrassment. They blamed me for getting the crowd riled up. They also attempted to strip me of my award and for a long time after that I was forbidden from returning to my high school. But it was worth it.

In fact, in 2005 I was inducted into the Christ the King Hall of Fame. My friend Joe Schwerdt flew in from Florida to make the introduction speech. He brought a fake nose, mustache and eyeglasses and talked about what I had done all those years before. Several teachers approached me later to say they still remembered.

My favorite post-stunt story comes from my friend Tony. Years later whenever Tony – who had a couple of friends named Frank – told his mom he was going to see Frank, she'd reply, "Which Frank? Frank Nose?"

COLLEGE

In the fall of 1976, I entered Saint John's University in Jamaica, Queens. The game plan was still the same: Build a network of friends, locate what it is you wanted and identify the people who pull the levers of power. Then schmooze, schmooze, schmooze.

I never read a book about how to schmooze, nor attended any kind of seminar. The art of the schmooze was learned by osmosis, taking it in as I watched my saleswoman mother work her clients in the pizzerias and also sell clothing out of our basement. There were a lot of "Hello my dear's" and "Hello my darling's".

I believe schmoozers are born, not made. I guess you could probably learn it, but there's a thin line between being properly schmoozed and knowing you're the target of a schmooze.

I have always rated schmoozing by several standards. The best of the best accomplish what I like to call the switchover. It's tough to do, but when it's done properly, it's magic! The schmooze switchover is performed when you are talking with someone at a party, mixer or other event and someone *more important* comes in.

The great schmoozers are able to terminate the conversation on a dime and disappear from view without making you feel the least bit insulted. Let's face it, just about anyone can strike up a conversation. The real pros know how to end it politely. Politicians are the best at this. Having worked for one and being around many, I have seen their skills up close.

I have also been both the victim and the benefactor of the schmooze switchover. I have come in contact with the really good ones only once or twice in my life. Sort of like the Haley's Comet of schmoozerism.

One of the greatest schmoozers I ever met was a local TV news anchor in New York named Ernie Anastos. I had been told about his superior schmooze abilities by my friend Wayne Cabot, but didn't quite believe it. I met Ernie at the top of a small parapet aside a building overlooking Ground Zero in New York City. It was the third anniversary of the 9/11 World Trade Center attack. There were reporters, producers, technicians, and politicians swirling everywhere. The roof was a hornet's nest of arms and elbows, not to mention all the sobering activity below.

As I walked to the men's room, Anastos and his co-anchor walked toward me. This was it. I was going to go mano-a-mano with the schmooze-meister.

"Hey, Ernie. Frank Cipolla. You know we have a mutual friend."

"Who?" Ernie said, locking eyes on me.

"Wayne."

I don't quite know what happened from that point on. It was the schmooze equivalent of an alien abduction. The world stopped. The din of the crowd whistled away. And for a brief minute, I was the most important thing in Ernie's world. More than his wife, his kids, his possessions – everything. He looked me in the eye. Listened to every word. It was wondrous. I stood there in complete amazement… and then he was gone.

Later, when I had shaken off the affects of the full frontal schmooze, I called our mutual friend Wayne. "

"Wayne, you're right. He's the Svengali of schmooze! If only I could learn from him."

Wayne said, "I told you."

My schmoozing abilities were still kind of raw in college. Saint John's University was the home of the famous *Redmen* basketball team. Well, that's what they were called then. Later, the very large and vocal Native Indian community in the heart of central Queens complained. The name was then changed to the *Red Storm*, whatever the hell that is. And yes, I'm kidding, there probably isn't one Native American in the city of New York.

My first day at Saint John's University I sat near a guy with curly brown hair named Dale. He seemed like me to be finding his way. I also met another student named Fred. The three of us hit if off and would become fast friends and the building blocks of my social network.

Within a few months, all three of us decided it was time to hit the road. We would drive to Florida in January, soak up some rays, sniff out some chicks, and pile on the 'yuks.'

First, we needed a car. Neither my car, a 1969 Chevy Impala, nor Fred's jalopy was up to the task. But have no fear; we would take Dale's AMC Matador, a blister-shaped car – more window than steel. His dad had gotten a great deal on it from a friend just before AMC went out of business.

It was the weird cousin of cars. We don't know what kind of friends Dale's dad had, but we did question the two bullet holes in the passenger side door.

As a bonus, our sunshine bound chick magnet was orange! *Orange!* Imagine that. A bright orange AMC Matador headed through the deep south in the dead of winter, with three Italian kids in it and the air whistling through a couple of bullet holes in the door.

I don't know how we didn't get stopped.

We took turns driving. We found the sun – but not the chicks. It didn't matter I had already found one. I just had to wait until I got back.

Just before we left for Florida Fred's mom insisted she meet Dale and me. At his house that night was his beautiful neighbor and Fred's childhood friend who lived across the street. She was a fetching Swedish-American blonde and – talk about luck – she was a twin! I was going to be around a couple of Swedish American twins. It was my very own beer commercial.

She was the complete physical opposite of me. I had my eye on her and made it clear I'd be back. When I did return she "happened" to be in Fred's kitchen. At that moment – as they say at Cape Canaveral – all systems were 'go.'

My sweet little blonde and I spent every waking moment examining each other's bodies. I was going to school, working at a florist after school and bumping ugly well into the night. I had everything I needed and she was happy to play the slot to my tab.

I don't remember specifics since I was a mere 18-years old, but it was a blur of nudity punctuated frequently by a moist tissue.

"IT SHOCKED EVEN US!"

Chapter 4
THE KNIGHTS OF THE NEWS TABLE

Spring of 1978 brought a new girlfriend. A classic Greek Mediterranean beauty named Elaine whom I spotted in marketing class. She looked like a young Isabella Rosselini, but with fuller facial cheeks. Fred and I spotted her on the first day of marketing class and instinctively sat on either side of her to get a closer look. Later that night we decided one of us would ask her out. As the discussion progressed, it got heated. After some pushing and shoving the deal was struck. I would get first crack at her.

She was gorgeous and much prettier than I was handsome. Another lesson learned: grab for something higher and don't be afraid to fail. Before long, she was mine!

With a growing social network, a beautiful new girlfriend and good grades it was time to turn my attention to my next conquest: the college radio station. I had seen it during orientation and I knew it was where I wanted to be.

The radio station itself was nothing more than a glorified public address system that was heard about a mile or so around the college - but it was cool! I auditioned for WSJU in the summer of 1977 and by fall, I was doing two shows. I was spinning country favorites as "Farmer Frank" in the mornings (the first of many morning gigs) and later in the day I was grooving as "Fast Frankie", doing top-40 music. Fred was my engineer.

After I got into radio, I never listened to radio the same way again. Dale (who was also now a disc-jockey on WSJU), Fred and I used to sit for hours breaking down radio formats and we were listening to the best New York City had to offer.

The number one radio and TV market was home to the best DJ's and news anchors in the country: jocks like Dan Ingram, George Michael, Cousin Brucie on Music Radio WABC, Zacherly, Carol Miller on WPLJ. On TV, the local news heroes shone. WCBS' Jim Jensen was the Cronkite of TV news in New York. He co-anchored the evening cast with Rolland Smith. Across town, WABC-TV offered up the "Rowan and Martin" of news, Bill Beutel and Roger Grimsby. Roger had a sarcastic delivery that got worse the longer he was in the business. One time he read a story about a ten-year-old John Kennedy Jr. on a shopping spree in the city with his mom Jackie Onassis. It went something like this: "Jackie-oh took John-John-oh shopping-oh. Why this is a story – I'll never know."

You had to love Grimsby. He was doing Jon Stewart's shtick while Stewart was learning to ride a bicycle.

As soon as I was able, I drove into Manhattan to get my third class radio broadcaster's license. Strange as this may seem, you had to have a license to be on the air back then. I don't think you needed one to be on a glorified public address system at your local college station, but having it meant you could show it off. You were in the fraternity of broadcasters. I laminated mine and carried it with pride.

In my junior year at college, we started taking radio and TV classes in earnest. One was held at the Hilton on Sixth Avenue. Radio personalities and radio executives visited our class to lecture. One radio reporter – Stan Brooks from 1010 WINS – served as an adjunct professor. Later, I would work by his side covering stories around the city.

During one class at the Hilton, an executive from WPIX radio came to speak to us. When she was done, she asked if anyone wanted to be an intern at the classic rock station. She needed two interns to help with paperwork and "other things." I clicked on the schmooze button. I approached her and told her of my credentials as the morning jock at WSJU 680-AM. I might have even showed her my third class FCC license.

A few days later I was bouncing out of Grand Central Terminal and walking the three blocks to the Daily News building, where WPIX occupied the 21st floor. Its lobby, with a giant silver globe, later served as a backdrop in a series of *Superman* movies as the home of the *Daily Planet*.

I was summoned upstairs to meet the local sales manager – the gracious woman who spoke to us that night at the Hilton. I was getting my first whiff of a hot radio studio and I wasn't going to leave until she let me hang around and do something – *anything*. I got the internship. WPIX was a loose operation. A prudish student might have begged off, but to me it was fascinating. The first thing I learned is that most jocks drank heavily and smoked pot.

The front door of the office opened to show the main studio. As you waited for assistance you could watch the show in progress. To the left of the studio were the administrative offices; to the right the jocks' offices, the jock lounge and their bong collections.

Often I'd come in for my internship and get smacked in the snout with a blanket of pot smoke. You could get stoned on the way to the men's room. The place reeked, but no one said anything. It was like someone farted and you were nice enough not to mention it.

It was also before substance abuse policies and the lawsuits that followed, so anything went. A famous disc jockey working there at the time had one heck of a problem with pot and booze. One day, he ended his morning shift and waved me into the studio. It was one of the few times I actually got to go into the studio.

When I got in there, his head was in his hands and he was mumbling.

I said, "Aaahhh… excuse me... I didn't hear what you said."

"You have to keep me company for a few hours.", he grumbled.

"I do have class later, but I'm sure I can help you out. You need something?"

"Yeah.", he said. "You have to make sure I don't leave the building because if I do I'm going to end up at the bar."

I hung with the disc jockey until he was sober enough to stagger home. I was getting an education, all right – an education in; what sitting in a dark studio, talking to your self all day long can do.

Meanwhile, the sales manager who gave me the internship had some "special" work for me.

"I've got a tour coming in.," she said sweetly.

"Would you like me to talk to them about the radio biz?"

"Not exactly." she answered with a smile. "I've got a costume in my office – you look about the right size. Could you jump into it and be the WPIX kangaroo for a half hour?"

I opened her office to find a crumpled costume you would find at a minor league baseball stadium. You know, the goofy mascot.

I pulled it on. She forgot to tell me not to talk, so when the kids showed up there I was a kangaroo with an attitude and a Queens accent.

"Oh, how cute." one girl said.

"Hey – how ya doin?" I said, "Wanna reach into my pouch?"

My job also included errands. What this had to do with learning the radio business I'll never know, but I was often called upon to go get the secretary's dry cleaning or some frozen yogurt. The usual gopher stuff. You know, go fer this... go fer that...

It was also at WPIX that I met Alan Colmes – now with Fox News. I secretly wanted to be him – he was a disc jockey/talk show host during the day and a stand-up comedian by night. Even then you could see he had the ability to connect with his listeners. I'm happy to say we remain friends today and later in my career would work together.

I also, like Alan, started doing some stand-up comedy. I have always seen the craziness in stuff. I put together about a half hour of wacky observations; mostly about TV commercials and the usual pop culture junk from my era. I also added a few sight gags.

Occasionally, I would venture out of the clubs in Queens and into Manhattan to do an open mic night at Catch a Rising Star – one of the premier comedy clubs of its day. I didn't know it at the time, but I was working with comic royalty. I shared the bill with Eddie Murphy and other future comedy stars. Years later, while redoing my basement, I came across an article I had saved about one of my performances.

Turns out, I had been on one night with Jerry Seinfeld. I joke to my friends, "Hey, *I'm* on TV – I have no idea what *he's* been doing." In fact, out of all I've achieved in my career, my niece Rosemarie is most impressed about the time I shared the bill with Jerry.

Even with all I was doing, I still had time to schmooze. A great guy name Ralph Garone was my next target at WPIX. He was the general sales manager and he seemed to like my ambition. One day, I went into his office and asked for exactly what I wanted.

"I know my internship here will be over soon – do you know anyone at WNBC radio? I want to work there as a news intern."

As luck would have it, Ralph had worked at WNBC and knew all the players. Toward the end of my internship at WPIX he called me into his office for a lesson in "networking." As I sat there, he had dialed up WNBC's operations manager.

There were a few "Yeah"–s, and "Hey, I've got someone here… "–s. He then hung up and handed me a piece of paper. "Go see Nell Basset. She takes care of hiring interns at WNBC radio."

Nell Basset was a pioneer of New York radio. One of the first female disc jockeys in the Sixties. She had broken in at WNEW-FM, which at the time was the premier rock station in the city. Now, she had moved into management.

Walking into 30 Rockefeller Center – the home of NBC – is an experience like no other. The walls are dripping with history. It is one of the most famous buildings in the world, and at that time, *the* place for any aspiring broadcaster. As soon as I told them I had an appointment with Nell Bassett, I was waved passed the guards, went up two floors and was ushered into the WNBC lobby. I was just shy of nineteen years old and I'd arrived in broadcast heaven.

When I got to Nell's office there was some small chitchat. She looked busy, so she just blurted out, "When can you start?" The internship interview was not an interview. Ralph Garone made sure of that. I was in. The meeting was just a formality.

If WPIX set the rocket in position, it was Ralph who lit the fuse. Sadly, he would never see it take off. A couple of years after he made that call, he died of cancer. I recently Googled him. Nothing. But I remember him well: a nice guy who made a difference in my life.

The internship at WNBC was a dream come true. I was up close and personal with all my radio heroes: "Imus in the Morning", Johnny Dark, Frank Reed, Alan Beebe, Scott Bingham and more. At WNBC, you would regularly wander into an elevator, glance over and say, "Shit, that's Garrett Morris" or, "singer, Dion Dimucci" or, "sports writer and author, Dick Schaap!" You'd also see many icons of the nightly newscast.

My job was morning news intern. I love mornings. I'd pop out of bed every morning at about four, drive my 1969 Chevy Impala to the Kew Gardens train station, hop on the F-train (trying to avoid the bums) and arrive at Rockefeller Center at about five-thirty.

The job was both simple and limited; I was to assist the radio newsmen. That meant running errands for them and not touching anything I was told not to touch. There was also a long list of union rules to abide by, which meant the scope of my tasks were extremely limited. The union shop steward made sure of that. If I ripped copy off the old Associated Press wire machine and place it on someone's desk, he'd file a union grievance. In fact, two: one for touching the copy, the other for placing it *on the desk*. It was embarrassing – a grievance would be posted in the newsroom listing the violation with my name on it.

The radio newsroom consisted of a long table in a large room surrounded by chattering news wire machines. At the head of the table sat Bill Maher Sr., the comedian's father. As funny as Bill Maher Jr. is, Bill Maher Sr. was not. He was the "Lou Grant" of the newsroom and did not suffer fools gladly. Many a time, half-asleep, worn out from an all-night study session or a round of nookie with my girlfriend the night before, I'd write and then hand Bill some copy and wait for him to growl at me.

He usually flung it back in my face, ordering me to change this, fix that, or correct the spelling. He was harsh, but always fair. I learned a lot about how to write news from Bill.

Nowadays, Bill would probably be forced to attend a meeting with me and the H-R person to discuss his "anger issues." Then there would be a follow-up meeting and a report. Back then you just watched, listened and learned.

Sadly, there aren't enough Bill Maher Seniors anymore in the news business. One friend of mine at a major New York City station told me he was assigned an intern to help him generate the evening weather forecast. When he gave her too much to do she started crying and ran out. She wasn't expecting the weather guy to be so demanding. She's part of a generation that grew up being told they were "special." Even if you come in twelfth in the soccer tournament you receive a "participation" award – What the hell is that supposed to teach you? That coming in twelfth is winning?

Sitting next to me were the mighty and faithful news knights of radio. Sam Hall, Jack Welch, Neil Seevey, Jim Eyer, and of course, Imus's sidekick Charles McCord. It took me about a week to stop staring at these guys. They were my heroes and I had been invited to their table… literally. I mustered the courage to meekly pick their brains for ideas about how I could write better.

Neil Seevey was one of my favorites, a super guy who was portrayed as the stuck up newsman in Howard Stern's movie *Private Parts*. In reality, he was as cool as cool could be. He would regularly play along with Stern's on-air stunts. One time, filling in for Robin Quivers, he inhaled helium and then read some news copy. It was cutting edge and hysterical. He was also very helpful to me, teaching me how to write copy better and schooling me in the nuances of storytelling.

Eventually, most of the radio reporters and anchors at WNBC got used to me being around and asking questions. But the news director, Meredith Hollaus, was someone whom I've never felt totally comfortable around – either in the office, or in her apartment.

I'll explain.

The New York subway strike of 1979 closed the city. People carpooled, walked and even bicycled to work. Mayor Ed Koch stood at the base of the Brooklyn bridge exhorting everyone to "tough it out." For me, that meant having to wake up extra early, bicycle to Queens Boulevard, find a passing minibus, throw my bike in the back and pay $5 to get a ride into Manhattan. That lasted one day. Meredith Hollaus decided the staff should be available around the clock to keep New Yorkers informed. Remember, this was the era before twenty-four-hour TV news stations. Meredith would stay at the station, or at a friend's apartment within walking distance of Rockefeller Center. When she heard about my commuting plight, she decided I shouldn't ride home to Queens because there was a chance I wouldn't make it in on time the following day. She declared that instead, I should stay in her apartment uptown. She handed me her keys with the address on a piece of paper and told me to make myself comfortable. Oh, and don't forget to feed her cat.

I rode the fifteen blocks or so to her apartment, jammed my bicycle into the milk crate-sized elevator and rode it up to Meredith's apartment. I jiggled her key and cracked open her door.

There I was. Nineteen years old and looking at my forty-ish, unmarried news director's studio apartment.

I could have done anything. Rifled through her panty drawer. Anything! But I was the perfect gentleman.

I made friends with her cat, watched a little tube in an uncomfortable chair and then decided it was time to go to sleep… but where? That's when it hit me. Since there was no couch I had to sleep in her bed! I slept between her sheets and thought nothing of it. It was just me sleeping in my boss's bed. Looking back of course it's inappropriate, at the very least.

How many of you reading this can say they have slept in your boss's bed?

Okay, hands down.

There was more inappropriate behavior back at WNBC. Just like WPIX, there was a special place for the jocks to get high. The jocks' lounge was a few steps from the main studio and a practiced jock could roll a joint there, light up and get a handful of tokes while the longest song in his collection spun on the turntable.

The place reeked of pot. The couch also had the familiar stains I had seen on some of the chairs at my college radio station. What police investigators would refer to as "male genetic material".

And of course, WNBC wasn't the only place for gratuitous disc jockey drugging and fucking. A friend of mine at the time told me the story of a station he was working at across town. There was so much sex going on in the production studio that management finally cracked down. Out went the memo. It read something like this:

"It has come to my attention that there has been some inappropriate activity involving staff members in this room. As many of the studio chairs have been soiled, which requires a lengthy and costly dry cleaning process, we are now asking all jocks and salespeople to refrain from giving and receiving blowjobs in the production studio.

Thank you."

Imagine working that memo through Human Resources today.

Radio wasn't as corporate then and wouldn't get like that for at least another decade. Long enough for me to enjoy some of the fun before giant companies gobbled up stations like so many Jujubes. WNBC also gave me my first real bite of corporate humble pie. One day, Bill Maher informed me that Bob Sherman wanted to see me. Now.

Bob Sherman was the WNBC general manager. The top guy at the station! I was somewhere between the lowest engineer and Hank the janitor. "Well," I thought, "this could only mean one thing: word has gotten up to the big guy that there was a true talent in his midst." Raw, granted, but talent nonetheless. I popped out of my chair at the end of long newsroom table with a satisfied smirk and swaggered away. I couldn't help but let slip to those I passed along the way that the big boss had summoned me.

I could hardly believe it. This was it – my big break – and how quickly it had come! I was running through the long list of possible co-hosts for my new show, when I arrived at Mr. Sherman's ante office and met his secretary.

She said sweetly, "Bob is looking for you."

As I grabbed the knob attached to his giant mahogany door, it finally dawned on me – maybe he *didn't* want to give this little pipsqueak kid from Queens his very own show WNBC.

I poked my head into his ginormous office and started stammering.

"You ca… ca… called for me, Mr. Sherman?"

The man himself stood up very slowly from behind his huge desk and looked right into my eyes. There was a short uncomfortable pause as he took the measure of me, reached into his pocket, pulled out a set of keys and tossed them my way.

"My car is parked illegally out front – drive it to the lot on Fifty-Third and Second…. and hurry!"

●●●

Substance abuse in radio was a big problem. Don Imus was in his darkest period and many a morning the show would start without him.

He'd do the first half hour, or forty-five minutes of it from the back of his limo – his sidekick Charles McCord bantering with him by phone as Imus sped to the station from his Manhattan apartment.

I sat quietly one day trying to take it all in as an inebriated Imus stumbled into the newsroom and started screaming at the top of his lungs at one of the news anchors, who then bolted out of his chair to confront him. There was some pushing and shoving before a few of the other anchors stepped in to break it up.

Ironically, I would return years later to anchor the news the same day Imus returned from one of his stints in rehab. On that day, he came into the newsroom to talk to me.

"Hey." he said.

"Welcome back, Mr. Imus."

"I'm thinking maybe you could come into the studio and join us today instead of sitting back here in the news booth."

It was a very gracious invitation. It was like Johnny Carson asking you to come sit on the couch after your first seven minutes of stand-up on the *Tonight Show*.

For some reason it got more complicated than he thought it would. He wasn't quite sure where I should sit. I asked questions. Finally he said, "Look Frank, I just got back from rehab. Please don't confuse me, 'cause you can send me right back over the edge." Classic sardonic Imus.

Imus also exposed me to the possibilities of making big bucks in broadcasting. One day as he went to get coffee, I watched as he chatted with one of the sales guys near the elevator bank.

"Come on, for me?"

"Can't do it… won't do it." Imus was adamant.

The salesman tried to make his case. He wanted Imus to make a special appearance at a local car dealership.

Finally, Imus said, "Tell him it's a thousand for one hour, otherwise forget it."

I gulped. A thousand dollars for an hour!

The salesman skipped away as if he had just won the sweepstakes. Sure, the car dealer would go for it. The elevator door opened and I stumbled into it in disbelief.

There was lots of money to be had in this industry for the talent and from upstairs. It was the late Seventies, but even then NBC corporate was trying on the idea of buying people out to save some money. A giant check could send a long time employee into retirement and with him all the benefits that NBC would pay for the rest of his tenure.

The union shop steward, whose grievances and union demands used to drive management crazy, was targeted for a buyout. He was only in his forties, but NBC had had enough of him. Short of a murder conviction, there was no way of getting him out unless you made him a nifty offer.

One day the engineer, whom I had befriended, started chatting with me. He was clearly thinking it over.

"These bastards want me out, but I won't go."

"Why not?"

"Not enough money."

So, there I am a kid thinking, '*Well maybe they offered him one or two years severance. Maybe some medical coverage for he and his family.*"

Really, what the hell did I know about severance packages?

As my gears are turning he says, "They told me they'll give me $600,000 dollars if I leave."

Remember, this is the late 1970's. Six hundred thousand dollars is like two million in today's money.

I stood there like a statue. He scanned my face for some feedback but I couldn't speak. He shrugged and walked off.

Back in the newsroom I kept on schmoozing. I made sure to smile and talk to everyone. I remembered to wish them a happy birthday if I knew it, to volunteer to go get breakfast at the NBC commissary and to tidy up the newsroom. I even made note of their kids' names and birthdays.

The elevator was a great spot to meet famous people. I chatted with sex doctor Ruth Westheimer one day, Dick Schaap and the venerable Tom Snyder. In the late Seventies, Snyder was at the top of his game, hosting the *Tomorrow Show* every night and in a lot of ways inventing the carefree, freewheeling talk show format. It was such a hit that Dan Aykroyd made his dead-on impression of Snyder a weekly staple in the early days of *Saturday Night Live*.

One day, I was waiting to take something downstairs as Snyder swung around the corner.

"Hey Tom." I said, making it sound like he and I had met many times before. It was just another trick I learned from my mom, as she found out the owner's name and then made it sound as if they had met before. "Hey." he responded. He was basically the same guy off the air as he was on. I continued, imitating him now, "Tom... now... now... how the hell do you do it? Ha!"

He knew immediately what I was doing and chuckled. So, I did some more to his delight. He finally said, "What's your name again?" I told him and he shook my hand, laughing as he got into the elevator. He had made a note of my name and I had made a "friend."

Snyder also gave me an opportunity to show off my stuff for the big folks at WNBC. Late in my internship, he announced on his show that he was going to hold a talent show. It was open to NBC employees only. I did some investigating and found out that it did not apply to NBC interns – *only* paid employees. I wasn't going to let that stop me. I made some calls, did a little begging and got an appointment to audition for Tom's talent show. I was escorted into a large studio at 30 Rockefeller Plaza and introduced to three talent show judges who were also *Tomorrow Show* producers.

"What do you do?" one of them said without looking up.

"I tell jokes… do imitations."

"Go ahead."

I was told I would have to keep my "act" down to five minutes. I had rehearsed again and again, so it would be five on the nose. I pulled out all the stops. A little Johnny Carson, some observations about popular TV commercials, even threw in my Tom Snyder impression.

I went back to my desk at WNBC radio and waited for the phone call that would change my life. It never came.

Back at the college radio station, I was on a roll. I listened to my radio heroes and did what I could to imitate them. Fred and I practiced again and again in the car, "hitting the post." That means talking over the musical intro of a song and ending your rap just as the vocals begin. Practicing that over and over again bit me on the rear one night.

I was disc jockeying the last show of the evening at WSJU. It ended at seven P.M. At that time, I would turn the station off the air while one floor below in the college cafeteria there was to be a memorial service for a student who had died unexpectedly at the age of eighteen.

As I was wrapping up the show, one of my friends came up to tell me about the crowd gathering for this somber service and asked if I wanted to come down and join those grieving the passing of this young man.

I didn't really know him, so I elected instead to stay in the studio and practice "hitting the post." As my show ended, I clicked the switch that turned off the radio station so it could not be heard on the college's public address system.

At least, I thought I did.

I then put another record on the turntable, jacked up the volume in my earphones and in the studio, turned the microphone on and pressed the button to start the turntable. Immediately, "Werewolves Of London" by Warren Zevon began blasting into my headphones.

As I grooved to Warren, I could hear a pounding through my heavily insulated earphones. Someone was racing up the stairs. The next thing I knew the door flew open and my friend Joe dove for the off button. Apparently, the memorial downstairs was just underway when the priest asked that all gathered – including family members – observe a moment of silence. And sure enough, Warren Zevon's "Werewolves Of London" starting blaring out of the cafeteria speakers at that very moment. Maybe now, Warren is up there laughing with the kid who died much too early in life. After all, he did make an appearance at his memorial.

I often skirted the rules at the station. It was a bad habit I had picked up as an intern. Watching the pros drink too much and blow off authority. A popular song of that day was Billy Joel's "Only the Good Die Young." It began with the lyrics, "Come out, Virginia/don't let me wait/you Catholic school girls start much too late…"

As St. John's was a Catholic university, the song was banned. We were told we would be immediately expelled if we played it. Just to be on the safe side the program director seized the album and put a piece of gaffer's tape across that particular cut. We could play the rest of the songs on the album, but not that one. The album remained in its sleeve with more warnings on the album cover. I thought I'd test this ban out.

The opening four or five seconds of the song were not covered by gaffer's tape. I set the album on the turntable, let it roll for the first few seconds, and faded it out; banging into a station jingle before the lyrics started. I did it once or twice a show, again and again. I wasn't technically breaking the rules, but I was walking a very fine line. I could only imagine having to explain to my mom that I had been kicked out of college for playing four bars of a Billy Joel song.

The station manager came down on me. He thought it was childish and dangerous. I thought it was damn funny and was kind of hoping the president of the college would challenge me on this silly rule. Whatever happened to the first amendment? The same one I tested out years before with my small newspaper in Queens?

The student run station administration also was peeved. Because of this and other minor infractions, the station manager had grown weary of me. He tried to give me the boot, but this is where my ace in the hole came in.

The station administration needed five votes to boot someone off the station. They could never get the last one. That's because my best friend Fred sat on the board. His vote saved me again and again.

College radio was exciting and freewheeling. It was also a learning experience. In time though, I got itchy. It was the kind of feeling everyone gets when they know it's time to move on; in this case, to graduate and get on the air for real.

In the spring of 1980, I was a senior. I remember distinctly staring out my classroom window. Like a horse in the gate, I was ready to bolt. I knew that in just a few months my commercial radio career would be underway and I couldn't wait.

Chapter 5
WARREN COUNTY'S RADIO VOICE

When I left college, I was extremely focused. Many of us wander up
the cliffs of life and get picked off along the way. Only a few reached
the pillbox. Now thirty years later, only three of us with whom I
worked in college radio are still employed on-air: Bill Buckner, who
has done radio in and around New York for many years, Mike
Salvatorelli at the Wall Street Journal Radio Network and me.

But, that's how this business works. It weeds out those who aren't
ready to sacrifice or aren't focused on success. Those who are not
prepared to endure years of crappy pay and moving from market to
market every few years. I was hell bent on being one of those who
would make it up the hill.

My strategy was simple: I would fill the funnel. Shoot out as many
resumes and tapes as I could and whoever wanted me at whatever
price, I was theirs. I was also ready to chuck New York City. The Big
Apple was in the throes of a serious fiscal crisis and seemingly on the
verge of going broke. So, I opted instead to head to the sun and fun of
Southern California.

I sent out sixty-five tapes and resumes. They hit all the small markets
on the outskirts of Los Angeles and San Diego. Places like Bishop,
San Luis Obispo and Beaumont; small stations that pumped out a
thousand watts. Then I waited. And waited. Aside from one short letter
expressing passing interest, there was nothing.

Seems my thick Queens accent was enough to dissuade a program
director to take a chance on hauling me all the way out there and then
letting me go when the listeners complained. Resigned to remaining
near home, I flooded the tri-state area. I employed the same strategy –
volume, volume, volume.

The first call came in early July of 1980. It was from a small station in
Princeton, New Jersey. The program director set up the interview, but
he was probably just bored. I drove my beat-up Dodge Dart to central

New Jersey. He brought me into a studio, listened to my tape in front of me and then talked about how bad I was. Thanks a lot. We could have done this by phone and saved the gas.

The next call was from a tiny country music radio station in the northwest corner of New Jersey. An NBC affiliate in Washington, Warren County – population 4,243 people. The owner had apparently been intrigued by my NBC connections. The station was ten miles from the Pennsylvania border and light years from my crowded city block in Queens. I remember being flabbergasted, as I drove farther and farther into northwest New Jersey for the interview in my girlfriend Elaine's Ford Capri.

I stared out the window. Are those really cows?

As the car rattled over a small wooden bridge along Route 31 in Warren Country, New Jersey something came over me. I don't know what, but I knew that this was going to happen. I was going to be a working journalist and a broadcaster.

I breezed through downtown Washington (one of six towns named Washington in the state). At quick glance, it looked to be three or four city blocks long. The station was about two miles north of the center of town. My heart was pounding. I spotted its pointy antenna from about a half mile away. It seemed to be beckoning me.

The station was nothing more than a small wood framed house alongside a two-lane highway. The antenna was in the backyard, surrounded by overgrown weeds and grass. I opened the door to the home's living room – which was the lobby – and waited. There I sat in a blue polyester leisure suit, listening to the strains of country music's Johnny Paycheck and George Jones.

One of the first things that caught my eye was a small sign on a back wall of the newsroom. It was one I had never seen before, but would see many more times in my career. It always gives me a laugh:

I work in radio. My father robbed a bank and is in prison. My mother is a drug addict. My sister dropped out of grade school and works turning tricks. No one seems to know why. My brother killed a man and is on the lam. Now I'm getting married. Here's my problem. How do I tell my fiancé I work in radio?

I waited until the owner emerged. He came from upstairs. It turned out this was not only his place of business – it was his home. His wife had thrown him out of his residence earlier that year, but he was okay for now. Besides his family, being at the station 24/7 was the most important thing to him.

Nick DeRienzo was short, stocky and built like a bowling pin. A "Weeble", with a ruddy face. His shirt was stained with some long, spilled morsel. He spoke with a lisp and his facial muscles near his right eye twitched now and again. I wondered how in the heck he was able to work in radio. He looked me up and down probably trying to make heads or tails out of me as well.

Nick was a news hound in every sense of the word. His red-hot desire to get to the story was the cause of his lisp and twitch. In the early Seventies, he was working as a reporter for a radio station in Morris County, New Jersey. They were lucky enough to have a small news plane. When an especially juicy story broke Nick grabbed the pilot and bounced into the passenger seat on their way to get a bird's eye view.

Nick's trench coat ended the journey prematurely.

Ten feet from the ground, the loop on the sleeve of his raincoat caught the plane's control stick. It came crashing down on its side. Nick sustained facial injuries and a lifelong lisp. He also made a ton of money. When the lawsuit against the plane's maker was settled he walked away with enough cash to buy his own station. He called it WCRV. It stood for "Warren County's Radio Voice."

My interview took place in the kitchen of this small, wood-framed house. There was a reason for that. One of Nick's favorite pastimes was eating. So, through a mask of steam fluffing up from his boiling hot cardboard soup bowl of Oodles-o-Noodles, he agreed to give me a shot. He couldn't pay me much – but at that point I wasn't listening. He needed a newsman, I needed a break and the money meant nothing.

I left grinning. I remember saying to myself, "I'm a news anchor! A journalist!" And since I was the only full time news employee, I was also the News Director! All for a whopping $140 a week.

Before I drove back home, Nick suggested I find a place to live. He recommended the Saint Cloud Hotel. Lucky thing he did, since on my salary it was all I could afford. The Saint Cloud was smack dab in the middle of Washington. A creaky, dilapidated building constructed in the early 1880's. It served two purposes: a flophouse for drunks to dry out and a place to shelter starving radio news people.

The owner Lynn Gulick cast a weary eye upon me when I asked to rent a room, but Nick had called ahead so I was good.

I was assigned room number 35. Third floor. It was just big enough for the bed, a small sink and a closet. The shower was down the hallway. Showing people around took anywhere between ten and twelve seconds: "This is the main area, this is the sink, and of course my closet."

The great part about the St. Cloud Hotel was the owner's mother. Every day, she'd go into all the rooms and tidy up. I'd come back from my shift and the bed was made, the dresser dusted, the floor swept.

The clientele at the Saint Cloud, however, wasn't as accommodating. Many times, I'd show up at night and hear someone yelling in the hallway. It was a couple of drunks dukin' it out, swinging wildly and crashing into the walls.

Oddly, after I started bringing girls up to my room they politely objected to the surroundings.

Frank: "I'd love to see you naked, baby."

(Down the hallway) "Where the fuck is my bottle? I…" SMASH!

Oddly, this proved to be a "turn off" for the ladies.

Later on I was able to make enough money to move into room number 2. We called it "The Presidential Suite." It was whopping $42 a week and a lot bigger. Same set-up though, with the shower *still* down the hallway.

The only room that had a full bathroom and shower was room number 1. Or as we called it, "The Bridal Suite". Joe Oliva, the morning jock at the station, was renting it and occasionally he would let me use it on weekends to "entertain" the ladies. Good thing, because some of my lady friends who stayed in my room began complaining – loudly – about having to run the gauntlet of strung out hoboes in the hallway to go to the "powder room."

My first day at the station turned out to be quite an eye-opener in how things worked in rural America. When I showed up at four-thirty A.M., the front door was ajar. Had it been left open all night? This was a small town – but could it be that small? I mean, no locks? I called out meekly into the darkness but no one answered.

Relying on my one and only memory of the place from my interview, I groped around for the banister. Once I latched on, I climbed up the stairs to Nick's bedroom and knocked on the door. It was an accordion style door that opened into a closet sized room. Nick always had the air conditioner running at full tilt. Even in winter. It was a perpetual forty-five degrees inside Nick's inner sanctum. I thought if there ever was ever a haunting that involved a ghost spinning off a cold spot or two, Nick would never feel it.

Nick was startled, but up in a flash. We got to work. His instructions in how to gather the news were given to me that day while he flopped around the newsroom in a brown cloth robe, matching slippers and under a mop of uncombed hair. That's the beauty of radio. No one can see you.

As an example of that beautiful camouflage that all radio people work under – one day, in the heat of summer, I showed up for work at WCRV in shorts and a t-shirt. Toward the end of the shift, a woman came in. The secretary was out, so she began to wander the small hallways of WCRV.

When she spotted me she said, "Excuse me, I am looking for Frank Cipolla." Pleased that she knew my name and was looking for me I replied, "I'm Frank Cipolla." She sized me up, stared and my outfit and gasped, "My God – I never would have guessed. When I listen to you – you sound like you have a suit on!"

It also worked in reverse, but not as well. I had been working at the station for a while when I received repeated calls from a very sensual sounding woman. She *loooved* my newscasts and wanted very much to meet me. For a few weeks we flirted on the phone until it was decided that we would take the next step. She'd meet me at the Saint Cloud Hotel, so we could get acquainted. And God knows, with the drunks and fistfights, the Saint Cloud was the perfect place for a first date.

I left the station anxious to see this lovely woman and raced back to the Saint Cloud. The front door of the hotel opened up to a large staircase that led straight to the second floor. When I got there, I opened the door and looked up. There she was at the top of the stairs. A mountain of a woman! The sun backlighting her rolls and creases which, in turn, cast odd shapes on me and everything behind me. I knew in an instant, I was had. Weeks of phone sex led me to a trap I should have seen miles away.

I had two choices. Run, or head up to my room. I remember thinking, *"Will I be able to squeeze by her gargantuan body?"* It was clear though, like Captain Ahab, I had to confront the beast. With each step up the stairs I struggled for an answer. What to do? What to do?

When I got to the top of the stairs, she said in that voice that could make you wet yourself, "Excuse me, do you know where Frank Cipolla's room is?"

I said, in a made up voice, "No – never heard of him," and scurried off to my room. She lingered in the hallway for about fifteen minutes and then pounded down the creaky old stairs of the St. Cloud Hotel. The boards of the building, constructed when Chester Alan Arthur was president, groaning with each monstrous step. I would never do that again.

Having a radio station in a quaint little house actually made it feel homier. Many times, I would come in morning, or at night to find Nick hammering out news about last night's township council meeting. He'd also occasionally wander into the kitchen to grab a snack. With Nick, radio news in the morning was always accompanied by the smells of bacon, eggs or his ubiquitous Oodles-o-Noodles.

Having a kitchen steps from the newsroom and news booth was a blessing for a hungry twenty-year old. But there was a down side.

The longer you stay in radio, the more your mind becomes a giant clock. To this day, I can sit quietly for a time and tell you exactly – probably within ten seconds or less – when a minute has passed, or two. For a long time, this wonderful ability – learned over years – served me well. In fact, I had the "Science of the Pop Tart" down flat. Through trial and error, I determined it took seven to eight minutes to toast an Apple Cinnamon Pop Tart to my personal specifications. That required putting it into the toaster oven just before I went to do my five-minute newscast and then heading straight back to the kitchen as soon as I stepped out of the booth.

All worked well, until the day we had a problem with the NBC Radio Network news feed that followed my local newscast. The connection was down. I threw it to the NBC newsroom and there was nothing. The jock on the air decided we'd fill time with some banter. I nervously glanced at my clock in the news booth. My mind clock, as well, was ticking away feverishly. As the jock chatted on about politics, interjecting various pearls of long forgotten wisdom and humor, I began to sweat. There was no easy way to break off the conversation. Alarms were going off in every corner of my skull.

At about ten minutes, the smoke started to waft into the lobby. Seconds later, I could smell it in the news booth. I gulped. Hastily wrapping up whatever I was saying, I raced into the kitchen. The toaster oven was ablaze. The paper towels and the dispenser hanging over the toaster oven were burning as well. I grabbed the teapot and frantically filled it with water. I somehow doused the blaze seconds from setting the kitchen cabinets on fire.

The smoke and commotion woke Nick up. In his brown robe and slippers, he flopped his way down the stairs, into the kitchen and bawled me out. The smoke finally cleared and he calmed down. That's when he looked me in the eye and asked if I had any more Pop Tarts. Apparently, the smell of burning cinnamon, paper, plastic and wood had triggered some kind of food alarm in his head.

The teapot also became the focus of many close calls and threats. In the couple of years I spent at WCRV, my colleagues and I destroyed at least three of them. Without the teapot there was no boiling water and without boiling water there was no "Oodles of Noodles" soup – and to Nick that was simply unacceptable.

Boiling water, like timing the Pop Tart, was pretty much the same drill. We'd put water in, set our mind clocks, and then get busy doing something. We'd return in four or five minutes and make some tea. Sometimes, though, we'd forget. The water would evaporate, leaving the metal skin of the teapot to suffer a brutal death. This was always followed by a spate of yelling from Nick and threats to take the teapot away forever.

After blackening two teapots in a row – one beyond repair – I was genuinely afraid of losing my job. That's where WCRV's newest employee and my friend of thirty years, Wayne Cabot, came in. Wayne has made a long career of being one of the top radio news anchors in New York City; a wonderfully gifted communicator who is a "natural" in every sense of the word. At that time, however, he was a seventeen-year-old high school kid with a commanding deep voice and pimples. He came to work every morning before school on a moped.

I was the twenty-one-year-old "veteran" and damned if I was going to take the rap for frying another teapot. When yet another was seared thanks to my negligence, I pulled Wayne aside. I made him familiar with a standing and relatively new station policy. It went something like this:
When bad things happened that made Nick mad, all of the employees took turns taking the blame. It was like a car's crumple zone. The impact was felt head on, but if the blame was shared the full force of

the impact was spread throughout the vehicle. In short, the passengers were saved. I invented a name for it on the spot – calling it "The Rotating Responsibility Policy." Of course, there was no such policy. It was something I cooked up on the fly to save myself from getting canned.

"Wayne," I said, "It's your turn."

"What do you mean?"

I explained "the policy" to him. Naively, he took the bait.

When Nick came looking for the culprit who issued the death sentence for Mr. Teapot, Wayne, to his credit, valiantly stepped into the breach. He took full responsibility. Nick then spun off into a blue rage. I slunk away.

As my dear friend Mizar Turdiu, whom you'll hear about later, likes to say, "It wasn't very nice, but it was damn funny."

Wayne and I laugh about it now, but I don't think he's ever forgiven me. It might seem cruel to set up my one of my friends at the station to be slaughtered by Nick, but then again I had seen Nick do the same – to me!

It was the week of December 7th, 1981. Nick decided on that week – and day – he would look back to one of the most important events of the Twentieth Century. Nick hosted a talk show everyday from eleven to noon, called "Comment." It was a freewheeling discussion of the issues facing Warren County and the state and would include listener phone calls. On this day, Nick planned a retrospective of the attack on Pearl Harbor. It would be a 40th anniversary special. There was one problem though. Nick couldn't find an audio copy of President Roosevelt's famous "date that will live in infamy" speech. Remember, this was before the internet and file sharing.
As luck would have it, Nick had a friend who had an album that contained the full speech. It was more than thirty years old and a family heirloom. His buddy hated like hell to part with it, so when he dropped it off, he made sure to tell Nick several times to take very

good care of it. It was a one-of-a-kind pressing. He even mentioned to Nick that he intended to leave it to his son.

On the appointed day, Nick got ready to head into the "Comment" studio. He would spend the hour talking about World War II. The show would open with the speech that hurled the U.S. into the conflict. Nick even purchased a special cloth to wipe the album down with before putting it on the turntable. From a distance, I watched this special ceremony. It was for Nick, who had served honorably in World War II *and* the Korean War, a special and private ritual. His wiped one side and then as he wiped the other, I heard a small crack. Like a precious vase slamming into a concrete wall, the album's brittle slate cracked into a thousand pieces.

I stopped cold! This irreplaceable album was now destroyed. It could never be salvaged or replaced.

Nick exploded. He launched into a temper tantrum, angry with himself for destroying this heirloom his dear friend entrusted him with – and concerned about how he was going to tell his friend that he had done the one thing he promised he would not do.

Nick didn't see me watching him, so when the time came it was easy for him to sell me out. Without consulting me, he applied the aforementioned "Rotating Responsibility Policy."

"You know," he told his friend, "I warned these kids, but they're rough. Frank was manhandling the album as he was putting it on the turntable and broke it into a million pieces."

When the man – holding back tears – left the station with the album cover and a small bag of jagged pieces, I railed on Nick. He sort of smirked and patted me on the back. He thanked me for taking the rap – and headed for the refrigerator.

WCRV's Associated Press machine was from another time. Nowadays, news people work with computers – pecking away quietly on slim keyboards and surfing the net for background information. Back then we had giant clattering news wire machines. Ours was ensconced inside a small closet next to the newsroom – sealed by two sliding doors. You'd slide these doors open, grab the wire copy paper, rip it off and write your radio stories from the information it dutifully spewed out. For me, it was a great thrill to report a story *to* the Associated Press and then see my name at the bottom of it. Being credited with breaking a story validated your existence in every other radio and TV newsroom around the state.

Our Associated Press machine was a chattering beast. It had to be fed regularly, with cumbersome rolls of blank paper. Often, my colleagues and I would show up for work to reams of paper all bunched up – all the nights' news in black and white. Sometimes, the paper would run out overnight. It didn't matter. The AP machine's mechanical typewriter continued to dutifully bang away even with no paper to talk to.

The Associated Press machine closet came with a little surprise. It was between the newsroom and the bathroom. For reasons that were never fully explained, the pipe that vented the excess methane gas from a thousand bowel movements ran along side the clanking AP machine and up to the roof. It had broken years ago and had never been fixed.

Every time Nick, guests, or any employee made a crap we sat in the smell for hours. The sliding doors strained to hold back the stench but it was too much. In short, it was unhealthy and something the Occupational Safety and Health Agency would have shut us down for had they known.

I suffered in silence. Holding my nose as I made a mad dash to grab the wire copy and slide the door closed, as not to get the shit smell on my clothes or up my nose. When the time came to change the paper – something that took more than just a few seconds – I cringed and groaned, overcome by the smell.

I didn't want to make waves. I was young and just starting out but the shit smell had to go.

After a year of enjoying the colonic fumes of my colleagues, I had had enough. I gathered my small part time staff on a Friday and we took a stand. The toilet-venting pipe had to be sealed, or we would not be back Monday morning. Nick blanched at the insurrection. He stomped his feet and tried to put it off for another time, then painfully gave in.

Later that day, the local plumber, who also served as the town's part-time mayor, came in to seal the pipe. Despite the repair, the smell lingered for weeks. It had found its way into the walls of the closet. I can still smell it years later.

Oh, and there was one other thing. The station's transmitter (a small Volkswagen Bug-sized electric unit) was placed in the basement right underneath the bathroom. One day, the toilet overflowed and water flowed down to the basement shorting out the transmitter. It might have been the only time in radio history a station was knocked off the air because the toilet backed up.

It took some doing to get used to the pace of life in Warren County. Wayne grew up there and Nick had lived in the area for years, so they understood it. For me, it was as rural as rural could get. You'd drive miles and see nothing but cornfields, cows and roadside tomato stands. They were all new experiences for me. The Warren County Farmer's Fair was one of these Mayberry RFD experiences. It was held every August in the small town of Harmony, New Jersey – a can kick from the Pennsylvania border.

It might as well have been Kansas.

There were contests for the biggest squash, the tallest cow, and the feistiest hen. It was famous for tractor pulls and trucks with giant wheels clawing over mountains of discarded cars.

WCRV was *the* station for the Warren County Farmer's Fair. Every year we'd dust off the WCRV van, load it up with WCRV tee shirts and other goodies and drive it to the fairgrounds. We'd broadcast live from the fair until closing every day and meet and greet our listeners. It also was a giant moneymaker for the station. Every business in Warren County wanted to advertise on the radio during the biggest fair in the county.

One afternoon, we were running late. We jumped into the WCRV van and turned the key. Nothing.

We were about twenty minutes from our first paid commercial live from the fair. We panicked. I called the gas station down the road and explained it was an emergency, but the owner of Big M's Service Station made it clear that it would be about an hour before he could come down.

That's when the light bulb went off. We raced into the station's production studio and rifled through the sound effects albums. Sure enough, Volume 7 had "State Fair Sounds." Kids laughing, people talking, carnival barkers, the sound of rides. It ran three minutes. We quickly made a continuous loop of the sound effects.

At the appointed time, we went on the air and for the next hour or so pretended we were at the fair. Describing the scene, spotting the mayor in the distance. Talking about what a wonderful day it was.

I could only imagine people at the fair looking for our van and seeing an empty WCRV tent. Luckily, the advertisers never caught on.

The Warren County Farmer's Fair was also a time for Nick to mingle with the listeners – which was both good *and* bad. Nick enjoyed the festive nature of the fair. It gave him a chance to combine two of his greatest loves – breaking news and food. One afternoon, I stood ten feet from Nick aghast as he attacked a local politician on live radio.

Nick conducted the interview just before *and while* gobbling down shelled roasted peanuts. Cracking them open in one hand and jamming them in his month, while balancing the mic in his other hand. It was quite a spectacle.

The politician was cornered. He tried mightily to evade Nick's questions, while periodically dodging the fusillade of incoming peanut pieces and shells. Nick demanded this poor bastard be more specific about how the Sheriff's Department had wasted money; a pressing issue in the county. But with Nick's lisp "specific instances" became *pa-cip-pic in-ten-tes.* The popping "P"–s and "T"–s working perfectly in ejecting BB sized peanut parts all over the politician's Sunday best.

With each demand to be more specific, Nick sprayed the politician. He could have walked away but it was live radio. There was no way out. He finally had to say something to get away from Nick before his suit was ruined. Nick, oblivious, crunched and spat away for the rest of the afternoon. It was culinary ambush journalism at its best.

Wayne and I also cooked up contests to get folks to come out and see us. One we worked out was the "Win A Date with Cabot and Cipolla" contest. Our listeners were intrigued. At the fair, we got a local camper dealership to lend us a camper to serve as our headquarters. We were also taking no chances on who might win the contest. To boost up the entries, Wayne came up with the brainstorm of an idea of cutting out two male model shots from a fashion magazine and put them on the poster on the camper with entry forms and a box underneath.

The old broads and homely listeners of Warren County's only Country Music station filled the contest box. Later in the week, the winners were announced and the date set. You can only imagine the look on the ladies faces when they didn't have dinner with some striking square-jawed models – but instead, two scrawny kids, twenty–five years their junior.

Even with the ad money from the fair and the cash generated from the November elections, Nick was always in the hole. He wasn't exactly the best of businessmen. He'd go into a bargaining session with a potential advertising client and get his ass kicked.

One afternoon, out of curiosity, the afternoon jock Bob Schultz took out pen and paper to work the numbers for one of our biggest advertisers – a clothing store called "Cohen's of Washington." Ten minutes later we heard him scream with laughter. When Bob divided the number of spots by the size of the client's yearly advertising contract the price came out to 45-cents a spot! That was even lower than the traditional "Dollar a Holler" small time radio advertising plan.

No wonder Nick was always bellyaching about money. One Friday, he came to us to say he couldn't meet payroll. Not one of us would get paid. You can imagine what happened next. We all worked long hours and now Nick said this week – he'd skip cutting checks.

He, however, was able to scrounge up a few bucks and bought us pizza. We ate the pizza and bitched. Even though we were still angry, for now he was off the hook. For all his shortcomings, you couldn't help but root for him.

Things seemed like they were always working against poor Nick. He had bills to pay at the station, child support for his three kids and the usual unexpected expenses. For a time, he owned a small percentage of a radio station in Blairstown, New Jersey; about fifteen miles north of WCRV and about a half mile from the Delaware River. It was an FM station, which meant he could charge more per spot. FM is much more attractive to advertisers because of its cleaner signal and younger following.

WFMV broadcasts from a converted train station. The setting was beautiful except for the occasional train rumbling by right outside the studio window. The few times I was pressed into duty there as a disc-jockey, I had to time everything to the train schedule so I wouldn't be opening the mic as the 4:53 rolled by hauling logs.

The building also abutted a large state forest. Every fire season, a state fire ranger was posted high above the trees to spot any fires. He would arrive at nine every morning and leave at five in the evening. It was great to have this added protection, but in Nick's "Rodney Dangerfield-like world", it didn't work out like that. Our trusty ranger suffered a heart attack. After he recovered and returned to his post, he claimed the radio waves from the nearby WFMV antenna were throwing off his pacemaker. Nick ignored him until he was sued.

Mr. Ranger wanted the station off the air while he manned his post. He sued and won. From that point on, every day at nine A.M. until five P.M. during the fire season, WFMV had to shut down and Nick lost eight hours a day of advertising revenue. Nick was ready to set the tower on fire with the ranger in it but thought better of it.

WCRV and WFMV were like so many small stations of that time and era. So small, that often they would be used in bizarre ways. The story goes that one night a new jock was doing a late night shift at a small station in Newton, New Jersey. The program director stuck around for the first hour or so to help the new jock get started and then headed home. Before he did, he told the jock, "If you need me call my house. I'll be home in about forty minutes." This was before cell phones.

Shortly after the PD left, something went haywire. Panicking and not knowing what to do, the jock did the only thing he could. Figuring the PD was listening to the station on the way home, the jock took the mic right after a song ended and said, *"That was Perry Como here on WSUS. Up next something from the great Ella Fitzgerald... and if you're listening, Tony, could you turn around and come back? I'm having trouble with the transmitter."*

Hit jingle.

Despite the obstacles thrown in front of him, Nick always had the capacity to dust himself off, get up and move ahead. It was his greatest attribute. One idea was especially imaginative and a terrific way to generate advertising revenue. During the Citizen Band radio craze of the 1970's, Nick came up with the "WCRV Convoy" promotion. It was based on the popular country trucker song of that decade, *"Mighty Convoy" by Brandt Paul*, and tied in with our country music format.

Nick would use the WCRV van to start a convoy and have listeners follow him to a giant parking lot where they would gather and profess their love for WCRV. The sponsors ate it up.

At the appointed time – and after weeks of promotion – Nick jumped into the WCRV van and started to lead the convoy. At its peak, there were dozens of vehicles following him. Nick though got lost. So there he was, leading a mile long convoy, making confused lefts and rights and going around in circles. Lost and flustered, Nick turned down a dead-end street in a residential area of tiny Phillipsburg, New Jersey. Traffic was tangled for more than a half hour, as everyone made a series of K-turns and waited for Nick to get back to the front of the line.

I was pulling down a hefty $140 a week for five and a half days of work. Nick promised me a ten-dollar weekly raise after three months. When the day came, I dutifully walked into the WCRV kitchen and asked Nick when I would be seeing the extra ten dollars in my paycheck. You'd think I had just told him they discontinued Oodles-o-Noodles. I think he was hoping I'd forget. We squabbled over the raise for about three days before Nick gave in. When the additional taxes were taken out, I netted an additional $7.33 a week.

Not being paid enough – or sometimes, not at all – led us to desperate measures. For a time, we had a small box of goodies in the station left by a local vendor. It was a cardboard box with various candies and chips and a slot for you to put in your money. The plan was the vendor would show up every two weeks to replenish the box with treats and collect his cash. It was based on the honor system.

When you're hungry, broke and working in small time radio, the honor system goes out the window. After two weeks, the vendor returned to find the box smashed and crumpled, all the treats gone and about 45-cents in the "honor" box.

We never saw him again.

Some of the cardboard was even ripped off. I'm not sure who ate that.

Because broadcasters in a small community could not demand much for an ad, Nick made the best with what he had and skirted FCC rules if need be. Two days before Christmas, one of the new disc jockeys interrupted Nick, Wayne and me in the newsroom. He pointed out that according to his calculations he was running 27 minutes of commercials each hour in violation Federal Communications Code 13, paragraph 4, which clearly states that a station is limited to a maximum of 22 minutes of commercials per hour and no more. Was Nick aware of this, he asked?

Nick looked at me as if to say, "Is this guy for real?" Then he looked at the jock and said, "Hell yeah!" and walked away laughing. I had to hand it to him. He wasn't going to say no to easy money.

Meanwhile, I was getting used to things back at the Saint Cloud. It wasn't the Waldorf Astoria, but it was a starting point. Through all the trials and tribulations at WCRV I was thankful to be on the radio and loved every second of it, but when my Queens friends visited, it was quite a culture shock.

First of course, I would give them the tour of my room. "This is the main area, this is the sink… " and so on. Then we'd hit the streets. Until I was able to hook up to the homely, but willing local female population, our entertainment consisted of the usual: dinner at the town's only diner, a tour of the station, and a drive around town.

Washington did, however, have a movie theater and it was a good one – showing first-run flicks. My friend Dale came one day in the middle of the week to hang out with me. We decided to see a movie.

It was a big time blockbuster. One that would have jammed the theaters in Queens. We paid for tickets to see the seven-thirty show and went in. Seven-thirty came and went… and nothing. We waited some more. At seven-fifty, the lights of the theater came on. That's when we noticed we were the only ones sitting there. Before we could talk a voice came from the projectionist's booth.

"Sorry fellas, you're gonna have to leave. You can get a refund at the front counter."

I looked at Dale puzzled. "What's he talking about?"

The disembodied voice continued, "We can't run the movie unless there are at least four people in the theater."

We were ready to walk out until I said, "Screw this." I told the projectionist we'd be right back.

I went outside and offered to pay for the first two people who would like to see the movie. There were no takers. There I was begging random passersby to join us. Nothing. We got a refund and walked out. In our speck of a town, even the movie theater couldn't get a crowd of four on a weekday night.

There were signs of that little town attitude wherever I went. I met a girl at the local convenience store and asked her out. She called shortly after we started dating and asked me to come over her house. I figured, *'I'm in!'* We'd do the slap and tickle and then "get busy."

When I arrived her mother greeted me at the door. I guessed we weren't going to be alone. Her mom showed me up to the den where my convenience store girl was waiting for me. Then shut the door and headed back downstairs.

Apparently, we were going to talk and maybe neck like the old days – Mom downstairs in case things got out of hand. It seemed kind of funny to me. It was right out of small town, USA. After snuggling with her a bit and watching TV there was a knock on the door.

Her mom was being courteous. She didn't want to catch us kissing. She entered with a tray of chocolate chip cookies and two glasses of ice-cold milk. I thought I had slipped back in time.

Then there was the cop on the beat. Every night, he walked down the street twisting the doorknobs of local businesses, making sure they were locked. I had never seen that before. The cops would also graciously cut me a break. Often when I was exhausted, I'd accidentally leave my car on Main Street overnight, in violation of the township's parking rules.

Sometimes there was note asking me not to do it again. One morning, though, there was a ticket. The fine was one dollar and I had to make a court appearance! My jaw dropped.
Anyway, there I was in court several weeks later. They had me sit around for several hours. When my time came I pled guilty, with an attitude.

I made my feelings known and paid the fine. Nick got a call from the judge about his nasty employee who wasted the court's time. Wasted my time? The judge threatened to throw me in jail if I ever acted up like that again. Can you imagine the headline?

<u>LOCAL RADIO NEWS ANCHOR DOING 2-5 YEARS IN CONNECTION WITH A ONE DOLLAR PARKING TICKET</u>.

By the way, His Honor would not accept cash. It had to be a one dollar check!

One of my faithful listeners showed up one day to chat with me between newscasts. She was a delightful, fifty-ish, God-fearing woman who had to drop something off. We chatted in the newsroom for a while and since there was a lot of noise outside in the hallway, I shut the door.

Being a young guy and enjoying the female body, I had taped the centerfold of a recent Playboy bunny to the back of the newsroom door. It was okay because I was the only one who ever saw it. I had forgotten about it and when I closed the door this big busted, curvaceous beauty was staring at both the middle-aged, uptight church lady and me.

She eyed the shapely model and then looked right at me. She seemed to be contemplating her next move.

"That's okay," she said, "I'm a nudist."

She told me about her and her friends going to the nudist colony up in Hackettstown, New Jersey and enjoying the wonders of walking around with no clothes on. She was cool with it and extended an invitation to me to come as her guest. From what I heard about people who walk around nudist colonies, I respectfully declined.

Many *employees* of WCRV were cool with nudity and there was a lot of it going on. We took our cues from Nick. Now separated and living upstairs, Nick enjoyed scoring using his "Funnel Theory."

Here's how it worked.

He'd ask every woman he would come in contact with if they'd like to go up to his room at the station and play station manager and naughty employee. Two would slap him, six would humor him, one would feign interest and the last one would say yes. You'd be surprised what volume, volume, volume did for Nick.

Sometimes, Nick wasn't the only one coming down the stairs the next morning in a robe and slippers.

Nick also looked the other way when the on-air talent and the saleswomen would hook up – as long as you cleaned up the mess when you were done.

The best place to go hunting for lovely ladies was in the sales department. Since no one saw us on-air jocks and newsmen didn't so much care about what we looked like at work. The saleswomen, though, always looked and smelled great.

They were impressed with saying to their friends that they knew or slept with the person they heard on the air – we were happy obliging their small time star fuck fantasies.

Nick had a severe predilection toward big busts and true to form, in early 1981, he hired a huge-breasted weekend disc jockey with waist length hair. Heidi took a liking to me and I returned the interest.

Fast forward to Election Day 1981. Heidi and I worked the results of the elections well into the night. It involved heading over to the courthouse in the Warren County seat of Belvedere and listening to fat guys with cigars hanging out of their mouths call out the numbers.

One town, Pahaquarry Township, had a grand total of six residents. They didn't vote at all. The four adults in the town would meet for coffee in early November and decide who would be mayor for the year. They also had one police officer. He worked weekdays eight to four.

If something happened after hours, you had to wait until help came from the next town 15 miles away or the following morning. If you had a heart attack while Officer Floyd was off duty, you were dead. I guess that meant everyone else had a better chance next year of being mayor.

When the voting was done, the votes tallied and the scripts written for the morning show following election night, this big breasted beauty and I decided we needed to get some sleep or we wouldn't be able to go on the air. WCRV was what was called a day-timer station. It could only broadcast during the day because at night its signal interfered with a station in Cincinnati. Since the station in Cincinnati was established first, we had to shut down. That night she and I were the only people at the station.

I threw a blanket on the floor of the main lobby, locked the front door and lay down. She lay down next to me. One thing led to another and before you knew it I was looking up at that long luscious hair and those big breasts. Best of all, we were still on the clock so it was one the only time I ever got paid for sex.

Another hottie soon arrived at the station and everyone's eyes popped up. She was a former dancer in Vegas who was trying her hand at deejaying. Everyone else was just trying his hand at grabbing her rear. She was cool though. A twenty-eight-year-old divorcee, she had been around the block a few times and liked what she liked. One of those likes, unexpectedly, turned out to be me.

One night, safely in my Oakland Raiders pajamas and set to go to sleep, I heard a knock on the door. It was nearly ten-thirty and my room was at the very end of the hallway. No one came down that way unless they made a wrong turn.

"Who the heck is this?" I said to myself. I opened my door to find this comely new disc jockey leaning against the doorjamb with a bottle of wine and two glasses in her hand.

I was both shocked and pleased. She wanted me. I obliged. And for several months we enjoyed each other's company. That is until she switched over to one of the weekend jocks and made his life that much better.

Sometimes I slept alone in my room and sometimes at the station. There were occasions when I would drive to WCRV Sunday night or early Monday morning and arrive at the Saint Cloud at about one-thirty A.M., only to find that I had forgotten my key to the front door of the hotel. At that point, I would ride on over to the station and wake up Nick who gave me a couple of blankets. Exhausted, I would go down to the main studio (which was usually the warmest one), throw the blanket under the console and try to sleep. One cold night I asked Nick for a blanket and he gave me a small towel. I huddled in the fetal position trying to stay warm until daybreak.

And winters in Washington were really cold! In fact, I spent my coldest night on the planet in Washington. It was February and I got up at 4:30 AM to make the ride to the station. It was 15 degrees below zero. As I got into my red Dodge Dart, I sneezed. A piece of mucus flew out of my nose, hit the steel dashboard and froze – on contact!

In a rush one Monday morning, I tried to make it to WCRV from Queens with what I thought was enough gas. The car sputtered to a halt a mile and a half from the station. I had no choice but to walk the rest of the way. I almost didn't make it. By the time I stumbled through the door, icicles were hanging off my mustache. The police called later. By then my car was a fixture on the country roads in and around Washington. Thankfully, I wasn't hit with another dollar fine.

Driving from Queens was always an interesting proposition. Either, I gave out – or, my car did. Most of the time it was me. After a weekend of partying in Queens, I would rumble the nearly ninety miles from my home to the Saint Cloud, sleep three or four hours and be up at four–thirty. To stay awake during the long ride I would often open my car windows, the ice-cold wind slapping my face. I also scored some caffeine candy pills from a truck stop and downed them two at a time to keep my eyes open.

Central New Jersey was not built up back then, so I would drive for miles and miles on unlit roads and not see anything.

One night, as the hum of the engine was lulling me to sleep, a deer jumped out in front of the car. I missed it by inches. Another time, I went back to WCRV in a pelting ice storm. The entire road was a sheet of ice. I crawled along at thirty-five miles an hour and watched another car going at least twice as fast speed by me. Two or three miles up the road I saw what looked like a giant trash dumpster in the left lane. It was that same car upside down, its wheels still spinning.

Another time I was nearly abducted by aliens.

It was one of the darkest of nights, on one of the darkest roads. And there it was – a flash of light!

It lit up the area for a mile. The flash had a greenish tinge and was so bright, I remember looking in my rear view mirror and seeing my silhouette flash across the back seats.

To make matters worse, this happened in an area of New Jersey where there had been rumors of UFO sightings and alien abductions. I was alone on the road and had not seen a car in any direction for a half hour. I figured this was it. I was resigned to the lost time phenomenon, the anal probe and a lifetime of freaking out every time I was alone in the dark. I slammed on the gas and raced as quickly as I could, periodically sticking my head out the window to see if anything or anyone was following me. My heart was pounding out of my chest.

It was only the next day that a fellow employee, who had lived in the area for years, concluded it was a meteorite tumbling through the atmosphere. The greenish light shone as its elements burned up in the atmosphere.

Some of WCRV's employees actually looked like aliens.
Nick hired women salespeople primarily, but when a salesman stood out, despite the size of his breasts, Nick hired him. One salesman did stand out with the emphasis on "stand." His name was Ernie Latterman.

Ernie was a radio advertising account executive by day – a professional clown on nights and weekends. Ernie's twist on the clown act was kind of perverse. Ernie was the one and only "Three Legged Clown." He had a prosthetic leg he attached to his waist and a pair of pants with three legs. When he walked the three legs moved in perfect sequence. It was quite the thing to see. He even had a business card with a photo of him standing there with his third leg. I often wondered how he drove to gigs. Did he hit the gas with the middle one?

I don't know what kind of parties Ernie was doing. I never found out. Shortly after Nick hired him, Ernie got the boot (with which leg I can't say). Apparently, Ernie was checking in at nine A.M. and then going home to sleep. He'd return at four in the afternoon for a sales meeting and that was Ernie's day. Nick thought he was selling. Ernie was pulling his leg.

Then there was T-Bone Tommy. Tommy was a World War II veteran who had made loads of money in the stock market. A former postal employee, he was in his late sixties when Wayne Cabot and I befriended him. Actually, he befriended us, first by calling the station requesting the 1981 Kim Carnes tune *"Bette Davis Eyes"* and then making regular visits, as many as four or five times a day.

Nick objected at first – but after Tommy started bringing donuts, Nick relented.

Tommy was a little off. He spent most of his day stopping in at the newly opened Dunkin' Donuts (the very first one for miles around) and buying boxes and boxes of donuts. He'd drop four or five boxes at the station, talk with the jocks and occasionally flick his cigarette ashes on the rug in the main studio when he thought they weren't looking. He'd also take his dentures out for us, sometimes while Wayne or I was on the air. Talk about keeping your composure. *You* try to do a serious newscast while five feet away an old guy is twirling his fake teeth in his mouth.

Tommy never could get our names right. Wayne became "Dwayne", Nick became "Dick", and I, for some reason, became "Doug". But, thank God for Tommy. He kept us in donuts and coffee forever. He also gave Wayne and me odd jobs at the home he shared with his three spinster sisters, paying us the then unheard of sum of ten dollars an hour.

It was that endless supply of donuts, though, that led to a story that still lives in New Jersey radio folklore. Often in talking with friends in the business, especially those who have worked in and around New York City, I have been asked if I have ever heard the "Jelly Donut Story."

"Heard it?!" I always reply. "My friend Wayne and I cooked it up!"

I wish I could say the jelly donut prank was planned for weeks, worked out like the great escape from Stalag 17. In reality, it was the brainchild of two bored guys knocking around the station one weekend afternoon.

Nick relied on the generosity of fill-in jocks to cover the Sunday morning and afternoon shifts. A couple of hours every Sunday were occupied, free of charge, by former state senator Wayne Dumont. An elderly, one-time gubernatorial candidate, Dumont spent two hours every Sunday mumbling into the mic about one or another real or perceived threat to democracy.

The late morning was the radio domain of Dave Kelber. Dave was the head of the communications department at a nearby high school. Dave was the consummate radio professional. He knew radio inside and out. On Sunday mornings, he'd attend church and then head straight over to WCRV to spin records. What he was paid didn't matter. He did it simply for the love of radio.

One lazy Saturday afternoon, Wayne and I were hanging around the main studio when we noticed that the earpieces on Dave's favorite pair of headphones looked eerily like donuts. Same shape. Same size. Same color. I mean they looked like two plastic jelly donuts. Those thoughts easily led us to the next step.

Why not yank the earpieces off the headphones and replace them with *actual* jelly donuts? We had everything we needed: the time, the headphones – and thanks to Tommy – plenty of donuts. Wayne and I thought this was ingenious. When we actually made the switch we sat back and laughed uncontrollably for about ten minutes. There the headphones hung. You could hardly tell the circular earpieces didn't belong. We even got an old wire and squeezed one end into the bottom of one of the donuts and plugged the jack on the other end into the console. We intended to switch everything back before we left, but something else pulled us away. We skipped out of the station that night forgetting about the "jelly donut" headphones in the main studio.

During our next Monday morning show we got "the call". What we know in the business as being "hot-lined". That's when the owner or manager calls you, *while you're on the air,* to let you know he has to see you right after the show. Wayne and I spent the last fifteen minutes of the show wracking our brains. Why in the world would Nick want to see us?

When the show ended Nick met us outside the studio, another bad sign. "Follow me." was all he said.

We were still scratching our heads as we walked up the stairs behind him to his office. That's when I caught a glimpse of something in Nick's right hand. It was a wire, at the end of which was the faint crusty remnants of what looked like jelly.

Nick told us Dave had experienced a problem on Sunday. The Mass he attended ran late and he'd come rushing into the station to start the show. He didn't have time to prepare, not even to look around. Instead he bounced into his seat and popped the headphones on. No sound in the headphones, but plenty of jelly down both sides of Dave's new suit.

We soiled Dave's best suit and in so doing, Nick almost lost his reliable Sunday morning jock. We almost got fired… but it was worth it.

The "Jelly Donut Story" lives on. No kidding, not more than three months before this book was published, Wayne called and said that he was talking to a radio consultant who said, "Did you ever hear the Jelly Donut story?"

Dave was involved in another incident that stays with me to this day. To get out of the studio and meet our fans, we created a softball team. In honor of our owner we called ourselves the WCRV "Nicks." It actually said "Nicks" on our uniform along with the NBC Network logo. We then produced a promo challenging all comers: The WCRV Nicks would take on every team willing to get their ass kicked. Or so, we thought.

Before you knew it, the phone lines were lighting up with challenges from some serious softball teams. Company teams with years under their belts and monster hitters who lived and breathed softball. We, on the other hand, were a bunch of scrawny kids with some delicate female disc jockeys and saleswomen thrown in.

Once we had lost a couple of games by the scores of 42-2, and 23-3, we figured we were in over our heads, but with twelve more games on the schedule there was no backing out. All efforts to try and play down the importance of the game with comments like, *"It's all for fun."* and *"Nobody gets hurt, right?"* were rebuffed.

Since I was among the fastest players on the team, I played shortstop. There, I was able to watch hit after hit sail over my head. The ones blasted near me were only detectable by a blur and a whistle. Dave Kelber, who had actually played softball regularly, was positioned at third base – the "hot corner" where many right hand-hitting players do business. Between ducking to prevent my head from getting knocked off and smiling weakly after yet another ball had whizzed past me, I would chat with Dave.

Once the game began, there was nothing we could do but stand out there and take it. By the end of the first inning it was over. The rest was some kind of sadistic treat for these hulks of the local company assembly lines. One of the teams that challenged us was a company called Elastimold. It was going to be a long day. The game started like all the others and before you knew it we were down something like 18-1. Dave and I watched the left side of the infield as best we could and actually got our gloves on one or two missiles launched from home plate – no outs, no catches, just a tip of the glove touching the ball as it continued its meteoric journey to the left field fence.

Then he came up… one of the best players on the Elastimold Team. A combination of Sasquatch and Mongo from *Blazing Saddles*. The very first pitch was creamed and headed straight for Dave. I watched in horror as the ball headed right for his chest. In a defensive move (one an assault victim would used to fend off a knife attack), Dave jutted his arm out and braced for the Saturn 5 rocket headed straight for the center of his glove.

Dave miraculously caught the ball! His long stiff-arm and elbow initially held up but something had to absorb the force of this whizzing projectile. I watched as first Dave's arm eventually crumpled. Then the sheer force of the ball worked its way up his body, through his upper chest and finally straight up to his baseball cap before rattling his eye glasses right off his face. The ball had been hit so hard that the force looking for an outlet had to claim something before swirling up to the heavens. I stood there agape as his glasses hit the ground and pledged, right there, not even to attempt to catch a ball. The 'WCRV Nicks' enjoyed one ignominious season before packing it in.

•••

At every radio station you will find at least one "laugher." He's the jock who can't keep his composure. Once you've determined what makes him laugh, you own him. He laughs when you do it. He laughs anticipating you'll do it. He laughs if he thinks you might do it. And if you're really good, he'll laugh if you just walk by.

The jock at WCRV who couldn't hold it together was Bill Scarato, a teacher at a local high school and the station program director and unofficial historian. All you had to do for Bill was to imitate Nick's distinctive facial twitch and he let out the biggest guffaw. For optimum effect you'd always wait until he had just clicked the mic on.

Bill just couldn't control himself. Jocks who can't prevent themselves from laughing are usually those just starting out. As time goes on, you find ways to keep it together or stop the laugh before it happens. One newsperson at a station in Philly once pinched his leg as hard as he could after an on-air blooper – the sharp pain keeping him from cracking up.

I owned Bill. I knew just what to do to get him to laugh on-air.

One day, Nick assigned Bill and me to do a fifteen-minute question and answer segment on the benefits of wind power. The sponsor wanted it – and he wanted it yesterday. So there we sat in the studio. The twenty-page script went something like this:

Me: Hi, I'm Frank here to talk with you about the benefits of wind power. I'm here with Bill Scarato who's going to tell us how we can save energy. Bill, how much energy can you save using wind power?

Bill: Well Frank, every year…

It was pretty simple stuff for two professionals. Under perfect conditions we could probably have done it in an hour. But it was a lost cause right from the get-go. Bill and I knew each other so well that the slightest facial expression or favorite Nick phrase set him off. He laughed, I laughed and then both of us couldn't stop laughing.

We'd try again:

Frank: That's amazing, Bill… do you mean that wind power was originally utilized by the ancient pharaohs?

Laughter.

Every day after work we'd try again, Nick getting more and more anxious and annoyed at having to make the client wait.

I'd ask Bill a question – he would attempt to answer. He'd laugh. I'd laugh. Back to square one.

Bill and I finally did it, but it took a lot of editing. I had to sit in a room alone out of sight of Bill, or anything Bill-related and read my lines.

Then, I would leave the station and go back to the St. Cloud Hotel, lock my door and call the station. I'd tell Bill I was home in my room with the door locked and it was safe to go back into the studio and record his segments. I also had to make sure there was nothing of mine in the studio otherwise Bill would lose it. It was a severe case that became more problematic the more we focused on NOT laughing. When it was done the questions and answers were edited together.

Nick spent hours listening to the station. He stressed breaking news. Defining breaking news in a small town of four thousand people, though was tough. Once while on the air in my soundproof booth in the middle of a newscast, I heard Nick upstairs in his office literally jump off his chair. As I continued to read the news, I followed his footsteps toward the top of the stairs. Then there was a rumble and a tumble and a thud!

I stayed focused on what I was reading, but I was sure something terrible had happened. There was some kind of commotion outside the booth and then the door creaked open. From the floor up I saw a hand with one sheet of paper on it. Nick had broken two ribs falling down the stairs and had crawled the fifteen feet or so to the news booth to hand me some earth shattering news. Had there been an assassination? A major plane crash? As I grabbed the sheet of paper almost shaking I imagined my "Walter Cronkite moment", telling WCRV listeners something they would always remember. I could see it in my mind's eye. "Remember when such and such tragedy occurred? I remember I was listening to WCRV and that newsman Frank broke into his regular newscast…" I snatched the paper out of Nick's hand and read it cold. *"Mrs. Darymple reports her prized cow is missing... the cow goes by the name of Molly and was last seen strolling down Route 31 behind the bowling alley."*

That painful moment in the annals of small time radio was made worse by Nick's injuries. In addition to broken ribs, Nick had twisted his arm during the fall. For a couple of weeks, he was unable to dress himself properly. Since he lived alone at the station he'd often ask Wayne or me to tighten his belt or zip up his fly. We refused. He finally got one of the interns to do it. I think he enjoyed it more than Nick would have liked.

●●●

This small remodeled house – turned radio station had last been decorated during the Nixon Administration. It was drab and mismatched. Near the bathroom was a framed charcoal sketch of an Indian squaw and her infant child on her back wrapped in a papoose. She was tiptoeing through a dewy meadow. It was not a bad sketch and to this day I remember it. We all passed it dozens of times a day.

One night, Wayne and I decided we would have some fun with it. I cut out the head of somebody in the newspaper that day, removed the glass that covered the sketch, placed the cut-out head over the infant's face in the papoose, replaced the glass and hung it back up.

Wayne and I giggled for days. Here was this Indian squaw, looking back lovingly at some local car dealer or bingo winner. Nick didn't notice.

We would change the face every week or so hoping he'd catch on. When this no longer amused us adequately, we kicked it up a notch, replacing the face of the infant with local recognizable politicians. One by one, all the local pols took a turn in the papoose: the mayor of a nearby town, County Freeholder Chuck Haytain, then-New Jersey Governor Brendan Bryne. When that didn't get a notice we moved onto the world of entertainment: Madonna, Tom Cruise and so on.

Doing it was funny enough. Nick *not noticing* made it even funnier. We were sure he'd catch on eventually, but if it wasn't something he could throw into the toaster oven and snack on, he really didn't bother.

There was only one thing to do. Make it *so obvious* that he couldn't miss it. We had to make it a face Nick saw enough that it would stand out. Wayne and I decided to use a shot of our Saturday disc jockey Lynette Simpkins. We cut her face out of a promotional brochure and it fit perfectly. We then watched Nick over the next few days to see if he noticed.

Thankfully for us, he did notice while we were both within a few feet of him and the painting. He was speaking with us in the newsroom and headed for the bathroom when he stopped. He looked at the papoose and laughed. This time there was no way he *couldn't* have spotted it.

Lynette Simpkins is black.

Doing a local newscast and "hitting" the network news took some doing and wasn't for the faint of heart. Ten seconds before every hour, a tone would come over the NBC Radio Network. At five seconds to the top of the hour it would stop. And when the second hand hit twelve, the NBC radio network sounder would sound and the anchor would introduce himself. He'd say, "NBC news; this is Gary Nunn…" and then plow into the first story.

My job was to continue to read the news while listening to all of this in my earphones. The tone, the sounder, and then the network anchor intro. I would be saying simultaneously and on the air, "I'm Frank Cipolla, WCRV news. Now, world and national news: here's Gary Nunn." I'd then click the network button, turn off my mic, and Gary would start his newscast.

The hand-off had to be seamless, as if Gary were sitting right next to me. In reality, he was eighty miles away in a Manhattan studio and – until we switched the network button – only in my earphones.

I got very good at "hitting" the network. I never really knew what the lead story would be and ultimately that led to a very funny incident. NBC Radio News had been following the pending execution of a St. Louis mobster named Frank Copolla. His execution had been delayed for months.

One morning I wrote the news, jumped into the booth and did my newscast. As usual, at the end I said, "I'm Frank Cipolla, WCRV news. Now world and national news: here's Gary Nunn."

I hit the network switch and the first words out of Gary Nunn's mouth were, "Frank Copolla is dead." I laughed out loud and I'm sure the listeners did as well.

Today there are countless radio bloopers on the Internet. Some of the radio classics we in the business know by name. The 'Ponderous Blooper' from Casey Kasem, the 'Ice House Blooper'... and more. My favorite is the one involving the flustered news anchor who reported the death of circus fat lady Dolly Dimples. There he sat dutifully, reporting and trying to end the network newscast in time, but got his words mixed up and reported she "had died of a fatal fart attack."

It was not beyond us to force a fellow on-air personality to mess up. We would even roll tape in the back room in anticipation of the blooper so we would have it for posterity. This was always made easier when it involved a "breaking news" bulletin.

You'd be on the air and someone would open up the door with a concerned face on and hand you a piece of paper. You'd read it "cold", just as I did with the lost cow story that sent Nick tumbling down the stairs. Although in this case the story was fake; the announcer realizing it only after it was too late.

One time during an on-air contest we were awaiting the twenty-fifth phone caller. The prize was announced; the jock happily hit the song and waited for the calls. I moved into action. I had pre-written the winner's name on a sheet of paper and after waiting two minutes, frantically ran in while he was on the air and handed him the paper.

The jock – anxious to deliver the good news – announced the lucky winner.
"And our winner of our trip to the Paper Mill Playhouse is Doctor Hugo Kutyourcockoff." The jock's face turned red. We laughed for about an hour. And of course it was caught on tape!

Nick was the king of the blooper. After I had been at WCRV for about a year, I was taken by Heidi to a seldom-used office. It had all the trappings of a special and secret ceremony, as she unlocked a small file cabinet. Inside the cabinet were twenty to thirty recordings of Nick bloopers. Each and every one was a gem. Heidi made the mistake of letting me listen to a few just before I went on the air. I barely made it through the newscast. I read the news while thinking of some of the classic Nick bloopers. They included takes of various commercials, Nick's distinctive voice flubbing through all sorts of stories and his interaction with callers on his daily radio show.

Every weekday at eleven A.M., Nick hosted a talk show called "Comment". The calls included the same cast of characters just about every day: elderly shut-ins, woodsmen, farmers and all around goofballs who did not work or drive.

The "Comment" studio was not insulated properly, so periodically you would hear an eighteen-wheeler rumble down County Route 31 right outside the station. It was a nice touch that added a little ambiance during a detailed discussion of the state budget or the avocado crop.

"Comment" was a relic of the past, a time when FCC rules required some part of a station's weekly airtime to be devoted to public affairs. After a while, "Comment" ran on automatic pilot. Nick would read from the local paper, comment on it and then take phone calls - the same shut-ins and goof balls calling again and again. Once we had a temp fill in to screen our calls and her wires got crossed.

Nick: "Comment – this is Nick. You're on the air."

Caller: (pause) "Ahhhhhh…"

Nick: "Yes?"

Caller: "Nick, this is Pam from Rosenfeld... I need to talk to you about some spots we have to run."

Nick: "Awwwww, shoot!"

In short order, Wayne had *his* Nick impression down to a T. And just like Bill, all he had to do was look in the news booth window while I was on the air and do the "Nick face", and it was all over. In that regard, he owned *me*. It usually took everything for me to keep my composure. As he got bolder and bolder and better at it, he'd take more and more chances. He'd often stand right behind Nick and imitate him while Nick was talking with me.

One day, Nick was chatting with me. Wayne was right over his shoulder doing his Nick impression – distinctive twitch and all. I was looking at two Nicks at once. I used every cell in my body not to burst out laughing. Nick sensed something was wrong and made a quick turn. He caught Wayne mid-twitch. I'll never forget the look on Nick's face. Wayne never forgot either. Nick was genuinely hurt.

I taunt Wayne with that guilt till this day.

Our off-air play time also including mixing wacky audio with various reports from the NBC Radio Network. One reporter based in New Delhi, India was a favorite of ours. With his old pre-WWII British accent, he would report on the tragedies that regularly befall that great nation. Floods, cyclones… anytime anything happened in India, Ron Jon Gupta was there. NBC, looking to save money in a remote part of the world, was happy to have him.

Ron Jon's overly dramatic reports and our trusty sound effects record made the perfect combination.

As Ron Jon Gupta stood in the New Delhi Parliament, we'd imagine he was at a circus or a house party and mix the sound effect in. It was hilarious! One report, on the early 1980's Soviet occupation of Afghanistan, caught our attention. From Ron Jon's voice you could tell he was tense; maybe in danger even though he was probably in his pajamas reporting from his living room. His voice dripped with drama. Wayne and I knocked our heads together and came up with something that would add further drama to Ron Jon's fearless report. We located the sound effect of an artillery explosion and did some back timing.

One third into his report, as Ron Jon spoke in hurried tones about the Soviet onslaught, we mixed the sound of a bomb in the far away distance. As Ron Jon went on about the danger of the war spilling over into Pakistan, we mixed in another bomb. This one a little louder – and to the ear, a little closer. And then came his wrap up.

"Ron Jon Gupta for NBC news…New Delhi."

KA-BOOM!

It became one of our favorite bloopers.

Chapter 6
LEARNING ENOUGH

For all his foibles, Nick was a stickler for news. News truly excited Nick. When there was a breaking story, Nick wanted to be in the middle of it. It was simple for Nick. Get to the story. Get the facts. Report it accurately.

Sometimes, sticking to that credo meant taking on powerful politicians in northwest New Jersey. Many of whom thought the station's news department was there to exploit only during the election cycle and to feed their egos. Other times, they would mock our twangy country music format. One county official called me one morning on the breaking news line to tell me he had a scoop he wanted only me to have.

His "scoop" was that he had gotten a hole in one at the Warren Hills Country Club the previous afternoon. "Could you slip it into that morning newscast?" I declined.

When bad things happened, the local politicians wouldn't brook you reporting it. Good news was fine, but something that reflected badly upon them was expected to be off limits. As a city kid – a bit brash and full of myself – I was unaware of these special rules of engagement. Nor did I care. I'm a journalist and Nick's lesson was always: *"If it's news, do it."*

That's what happened the morning word came that the son of the most popular politician in our part of the state had been arrested in some incident. It was our lead.

I read the story right down the middle and moved on. This street fighter local politician would have none of it.

Right after the story aired, the phone started ringing.

"Hello?"

"You son of a bitch… you got the story wrong… I will not allow you to slander my son."

"Freeholder," I said, "these are the facts as we know them. If you want to speak with us on the record, I'll roll tape."

He hung up with a slam.

Bottom of the hour – I ran the story again. Phone rings again. More of the same. Slam!

I was looking at Wayne who was hosting the morning show saying, "Is this guy nuts?"

Phone rings again. This time, the irate politician threatened to come over and beat the crap out of me. It was one of the very few times, day or night, that we locked the front door of the station.

This same politician who later rose through the ranks and actually ran for governor went down in flames when it was revealed he allegedly had a romantic relationship with a campaign aide. Typical of New Jersey's back room political wheeling and dealing, his considerable legal fees and civil damages were paid for by the Republican state committee.

Nick especially loved the big story and if it happened any time day or night and I wasn't there, he was. Many times, I'd show up for work at four-thirty in the morning to find Nick in the newsroom banging away at his typewriter. He had learned someone of significance had passed away during the night or that a truck had flipped over along Route 78.

Nick also instilled in me that a newsman should look the part. He put up with my college frat style clothing but he didn't like it. One day, he said we needed to talk.

"You look terrible. When you're here and especially when you go out on a story, you must dress like a serious newsman," he said.

Nick was serious – and in that day and age – that meant a suit and tie. By coincidence, later that week we were both set to cover the inauguration of newly elected governor Thomas Kean, who years later would head up the 9/11 commission. I would use this event to show Nick I had changed my ways.

With Nick's words ringing in my ears, I sprung for an expensive black suit. Coupled with a snazzy tie I was ready to go. You can imagine my shock when Nick walked down the stairs in a Kelly green suit. Not just green – *Kelly* green!

All the way down to Trenton (a trip that took about an hour and a half), I was shaking my head. *He tells me to dress up for an event where every mover and shaker in the state will be; meanwhile he's dressed like a green M&M?*

I must have been distracted by Kermit the Frog in the passenger seat, because we got lost and arrived late. We had our press passes and nothing else. Didn't matter. In the strangest twist of fate we drove down a side street and found an open spot at the corner. We took ten steps and looked right and we were at the head of the parade coming right at us. We looked at each other and grinned, not believing our luck. Leading the parade, and with no other reporters in sight, were outgoing Governor Brendan Bryne and incoming Governor Thomas Kean.

Nick and I pressed 'record' on our tape recorders and got to work. I spoke with the soon-to-be inaugurated governor. Nick rolled on the outgoing governor. The other reporters were a block and more away and kept at bay by New Jersey State Troopers. Somehow, we had breached security and no one was going to stop us.

We got great tape. Terrific stuff no one else had!

Governor-Elect Kean was slated to be sworn in at the War Memorial Building in Trenton, an ancient structure dripping in history. Its large stage and seating area were ringed with a balcony. That's where the press was ensconced. Others in the news media – namely Nick and me – had our own plans.

We followed the flow of the parade and the governors right back stage. Every politician from every corner of the state was back there. I spoke with Senator Harrison Williams, who would later resign after getting snagged in the F.B.I. Abscam sting operation of the early Eighties. I also interviewed Ray Donovan, the former Reagan Labor Secretary who was later investigated by Congress based on accusations he was mobbed up.

Nick and I worked the room like pros, rolling on one exclusive interview after another. As the ceremony was about to begin, a State Trooper finally figured out I didn't belong. I was ordered up to the balcony with the rest of the news media. I made a quick pass to see where Nick was, but didn't see him. I just assumed they had hustled Mr. Kelly Green suit up to the balcony.

When I got to the balcony press area I searched for him. I knew I had done him proud. Dressed like a professional, I had gotten more tape that I knew what to do with and had conducted myself in the most professional manner. The Star Spangled Banner followed the presentation of the colors. I glanced down at the stage now and again and continued to search for Nick.

As I looked over the balcony yet another time something caught my eye. It wasn't subtle – it was more like a starburst in sea of black. There, about six rows behind the podium (which would be used to swear in the new governor), sat Nick, his green suit glowing. I had to laugh. People must have been saying, "Doesn't this guy know how to dress?"

It reminded me of a special suit jacket Nick had. It was right out of the clown closet at Barnum and Bailey, with a bright plaid pattern that featured every color under the sun. It was Nick's equivalent of the kind of lucky jacket compulsive gamblers wear to the track. Nick wore it while working in his brother's band. On weekends, he would occasionally join his brother's band playing a wedding or anniversary. Nick played the mandolin and made some extra pocket cash.

One night while leaning in to deliver a tableside love song – mandolin in hand – the arm of Nick's jacket caught on fire. A guest quickly doused the flames with a vodka and club. Nick wasn't hurt, but the elbow portion of his plaid jacket was singed to the lining.

The next day, after the obligatory questions and the inevitable "smoking jacket" jokes, Wayne and I asked Nick what became of his now liquor soaked rainbow warrior of a jacket. Did he finally give it a proper burial alongside Joseph's Amazing Technicolor Dreamcoat?

No, instead Nick found a local tailor who said he could replicate the funky plaid pattern.

The tailor tried, but it never really was the same. The one bad plaid pattern at the elbow of Nick's jacket sort of whirled into another.

●●●

I'm sometimes amazed at the chutzpah I had when I was a cub reporter. Two instances come to mind. One in a cornfield in northwest New Jersey, the other in the very epicenter of world power.

Soon after taking office in 1980, President Ronald Reagan began inviting reporters from local markets to the White House. His plan was to pitch his policy proposals directly to news people in each market, thereby, avoiding the filter of network news. I thought, why not me?

Why should just the big guys in New York City get invited?

After my shift one day, I popped a sheet of paper into my typewriter and punched out a letter to the White House.

Mr. President – my name is Frank Cipolla. I work as News Director at WCRV in Washington, New Jersey; about eighty miles from midtown Manhattan.

Often you have reporters and anchors visit the White House for lunch, but sadly, you ignore those reporters and anchors – especially in radio – who work in and around those large markets.

Might I respectfully ask that the next time you entertain the news media from the New York metropolitan area, you include me?

I addressed the envelope to 1600 Pennsylvania Avenue, pressed a stamp on it and threw it in the mailbox in front of the Saint Cloud Hotel.

A week later a call came. By coincidence, the President would be having lunch with the news media from the nation's largest markets and would I like to come.

Next thing I knew I was jetting to Washington, DC.

It's a pretty powerful feeling when you walk out of the airport in DC, hop into a cab and say, "The White House please…"

I rolled up to the gate and was examined by security and escorted to a large room that resembled a Congressional hearing room. A couple of presidential aides briefed the crowd of reporters on what the president would be saying at lunch. We then filed into the presidential dining room.

A woman played the harp. Uniformed waiters whisked back and forth. Flowers decorated every table. Finger bowls sat quietly on the table waiting for smudged digits.

Since I was part of the New York City delegation – and since New York is the largest market in the country – our table was right next to the Presidents'. I sat there with Roger Grimsby from WABC–TV and other New York news biggies. Mostly though, I just stared at the President. *"There he is,'* I thought, *'Just ten feet away!'*

Sometime after the main dish and just before dessert I said to myself, "The hell with it." I stood up, walked around the President's table, and caught him mid-sentence.

"Hello Mr. President, I'm Frank Cipolla from WCRV in Washington, New Jersey. Thanks for inviting me." The president, clearly startled, mumbled something about being pleased as well. I put out my hand

and he shook it. Every one in the room took a gulp and stared at this twenty-one-year old kid who had foolishly breached the president's security net.

I must have caught the Secret Service napping – but not for long. I turned around and into the chests of two gargantuan Secret Service agents. They gave me a cautious smile and watched me slowly walk back to my table. They must have read my body language and knew I meant the President no harm. But, they had every reason to worry. It was just five months after John Hinkley had shot him outside a hotel in Washington. The President almost died that day and here I was – less than a half a year later – sneaking up on him in the bosom of the White House. I'm lucky I didn't end up on the floor with a knee jammed in my back.

When I got back to the table I was beaming. I had actually shaken the president's hand!

A minute after I returned to my table another reporter stood up and tried to make his way around the president's table. No go. One of the burly Secret Service agents who had greeted me stopped him in his tracks. "Please let the President eat his lunch," he said.

To be a reporter you have to be pushy. You have to do things no one in his or her right mind would do. That's part of the job and quite frankly part of the fun.

I got to test those qualities again on a steamy August morning about a month before I left WCRV. Like so many big stories, it came out of nowhere.

Wayne and I were doing the morning show when the phone rang. "Something's wrong." said the elderly voice on the other end of the phone. "It sounds like a jet."

We got a lot of calls on a regular basis. One woman actually spent fifteen minutes on the phone one day telling Wayne and me she saw God while she was on the toilet. This was a new voice, but Wayne and I concluded it was just another wacko.

The phone rang a minute later. Another person saying, "It sounds like a jet is nearby."

"A jet?" I said. "What the heck is going on?"

At that moment, I looked over to Wayne who was on the other line fielding a similar call. He threw me a puzzled look through the studio window.

It was about seven-fifteen. We had been on the air for two hours. When we both hung up we talked briefly. Just then another call came in about a "whirring" sound several miles from town. We made a decision. Wayne would spin records *and* do the newscasts. I would go out to the location given to us by our first caller and take a look.

We weren't supposed to leave the studio during our shift, but Wayne and I had a hunch.

I drove through the mist of the early August morning. I turned onto Route 57, breezed through Washington and toward the outer reaches of the town. After three or four blocks, Washington just sort of melted away to farms, horses, cows and expansive fields of corn.

Then I saw it: It was odd to see in this rural landscape – something that looked like a skyscraper. It was a huge pipe, fifty to sixty feet tall. Shooting out of it was a natural gas flame reaching up another 200 feet. I stuck my head our my car window and mumbled, "What the hell…?"

Using its flaming finger as a guide, I found what I thought was the road leading to it. My '69 Dodge Dart rumbled into a gravel parking lot of a closed farm stand. Next to it was a long road blocked by a low chain link fence. In the distance I heard sirens. I had to make a decision. With police and fire crews on the way, I knew in moments my passage down that road to whatever it was would be blocked.

I didn't think twice. Reporters don't. I grabbed my tape recorder, flipped my press ID onto the dashboard, bolted out of my car, hopped the small chain link fence and sprinted down the road as fast as I could. I was running straight toward the flame.

About two hundred feet down the road, I heard several cop cars in the distance pulling up behind me. I made a sharp left and into row upon row of corn stalks, each of them two or three feet taller than me. I could have stopped, but you earn your stripes by getting as close as you can to whatever the story is, not watching from a distance.

Once, I darted off the road into the cornfield. I took a moment to get my bearings. The closer I got – the hotter the air became. To my right, I heard cop cars racing down the road.

As I ran in the summer heat, sweat now beading up on my forehead, I saw movement on the other side of the road about twenty feet in. It was a reporter from the local newspaper, camera in hand, running in the corn stalks and heading in the same direction. I smiled. He would get the photos, but you can't beat the immediacy of radio.

The cops circled through and assessed the situation, then headed back out to get help. When they drove off, I popped out of the cornfield and back onto the tiny main road leading to the flame. As I did, I stopped dead in my tracks. There, about a football field away and straight up, was the steel pipe. Out of it spewed a blowtorch of flame. The flames were coming from a natural gas substation in the small town of Stewartsville. The substation abutted a large farm and at the end of the road right near the substation was a modest wood frame house. I assumed it belonged to the farm's owner. If I could get inside, I could call the station with the story.

Looking closer, I could see four cylindrical gas tanks surrounded this angry ribbon of flame. All within about thirty feet of the pipe. They were slowly heating up. I had never seen anything like it. Ten seconds went by before I was able to jolt my brain into action.

I ran down the road some more, the temperature rising even more as I got closer. When I got to the small farmhouse, I ran up the steps and banged on the door. No answer. I jiggled the doorknob. Locked. I ran around the back of the house and did the same thing, cupping my hand against the kitchen window and peering inside. No one was there. Decision time. Do I break in to get to a phone? I thought about what I had read several weeks before in Dan Rather's autobiography, *The Camera Never Blinks*: "*It's not a story unless you can get it on the air.*" Bottom line: I had to find a phone, and pronto.

As I was gathering my thoughts I saw another structure. I stared at it with dread. The main office of this natural gas facility stood within fifty feet of the flaming torch. I had come this far; run a mile or more, and I wasn't going to turn back now. I walked slowly down the two or three wooden steps at the back door of the house and made a run for it.

The air got even hotter as I sprinted across the gravel road and into the gas tank nerve center through an open garage door. It was cold and dark inside. My eyes took a while to adjust. I yelled out for anyone who might still be there. No one answered. In the corner of the building there was what looked like a supervisor's office. I pushed the door open and again got my bearings.

In the corner of the office, up against the window, was a desk. On it, a half-cup of coffee, steam still coming out of it. Whoever was here left in a hurry.

Next to the coffee cup was a phone. Pay dirt! I picked it up and heard a dial tone. That's when I knew I was in business. How long I would be in business was another story. Just outside the window the propane pipe hissed and belched. The police cars were back by now. They could only get so close to the facility until the fire fighters got there. They were being cautious. I wasn't. I was young and not really thinking. The story was just too big to worry about my personal safety. I immediately called the station.

"Wayne – it's a fire. I'm looking at it. It's some kind of gas flame shooting – maybe two, three hundred feet in the air and yes, it sounds exactly like a jet propeller."

By this time, Nick was up and working the phones. The raw tape of Nick grilling police and fire officials is classic stuff. Wayne and I chuckled when among all the usual who, what, when, where and how questions there were serious inquires by Nick about what exactly the evacuees in the area were being fed.

"So… everyone who's been evacuated is comfortable and you've got plenty of food. What kind of food? Bacon and Eggs? What kinds of sides? Hash browns?"

Meanwhile, the road leading to the facility was now closed. For the first half hour or so, I was on the air continuously. I didn't have much information, but I answered questions from Wayne as best I could. I used some paperwork left on the desk to fill in the blanks - company name, location and so on.

It was great radio and all of northwest New Jersey was listening in along with the police. Every ten minutes or so they'd drive down the road searching for me. At one point, addressing me by my name on their car speaker:

"FRANK – THIS IS DANGEROUS. PLEASE COME OUT. IT'S NOT SAFE."

They knew I was in there somewhere. They had an idea, but they were not going to take a chance of getting killed by stepping out of their cruiser to track me down.

By this time, the New York and Philadelphia TV and radio stations had caught wind of the fire. WNBC-TV in New York called Nick to get details on the fire and how they might get to WCRV.

About an hour later those at the station heard the WNBC helicopter overhead. The pilot seemed like he wanted to land.

Nick was wound up like a cub reporter on his first story. He blew through the station's front door and into the field next to the station. There, as the chopper hovered about a thousand feet above, Nick started waving his arms. He then yanked off his jacket and started waving that.

He wanted them to land and get a chance to hang – even for a little bit – with the big guys in New York. The pilot instead interpreted this sign as Nick waving him off and just flew away. Nick stood there for a moment and uttered his now familiar refrain, "Ahhh, SHIT." Meanwhile, I started calling other stations from my corner office over looking the flames. I spent the rest of the morning doing reports for WCRV, our sister station WFMV and at one point WCBS in New York. I was sweaty, exhausted and exhilarated.

The first of the fire trucks arrived and immediately began dousing the tanks just below the pipe to cool them off. When the situation seemed under control and I had touched all the bases, I snuck out of the side of the building and melted away into the throng of emergency workers. I was holding my tape recorder and was otherwise easy to spot, but the emergency crews were so busy they didn't notice. Neither did the police who just stood staring at this angry flame – which by now I had gotten used to.

I left the same way I entered, using the giant corn stalks to hide my escape. I came back to the station a hero. Slaps on the back and a big day for WCRV news. Nick gave me a big grin. He knew on that day *we owned the story.*

These were the stories Nick would brag about at the yearly New Jersey Broadcasters Association meeting in Atlantic City. Wayne and I used to marvel at this annual get-together.

All year long the men who owned radio stations in New Jersey fought each other tooth and nail to prove they had the best signal, the best news department, the best station.

It was a good-hearted competition that sometimes got ugly. Our main competition about ten miles north was WRNJ in Hackettstown. They had a news department too and Nick didn't so much like the owners. He impressed upon us that we were to be better than WRNJ at all costs, so when the yearly convention in Atlantic City came rolling around he could show off.

The morning news guy at WRNJ was Jeff Grant, the son of radio legend Bob Grant. I recorded Jeff's newscast every morning and I'm sure WRNJ recorded mine. We first wanted to make sure we had all the stories they had and – in line with the dark humor that lives in the belly of every radio newsperson – we waited for the inevitable screw up.

One of my favorites is the audio of a fill-in news guy. The blooper starts with the top of the hour WRNJ news ID. A voice of God announcer:

"This is WRNJ, Hackettstown. News fast, first and reliable…"

But, instead of a news sounder (the music introducing the newsman), there's silence. Dead silence – every broadcaster's nightmare.

Then you hear the door to the news booth open. Even better, it's a squeaky news booth door. Next, you hear the news guy sit in his chair. It's a squeaky news booth chair. Then comes the sound of the news guy jamming the audio cart into the machine in the news booth and pressing the button to trigger the news sounder.

The news sounder trumpets the arrival of the newscast, but instead of talking at the top of the news sounder, it just goes on and on – the news guy clearly fumbling to put his pages in order. About ten seconds later the sounder begins to fade and then, just then, the news guy starts to talk.

"This is WRNJ News… Lee… Lee… Douglas reporting…"

It's brutal to listen to the stuff that radio nightmares are made of. A new classic has been making the rounds recently and has been added to my collection. A fairly well known and experienced radio news anchor starts his network newscast and doesn't have his script in front of him. He ran into the booth without it.

This network news guy – with hundreds of stations listening coast to coast – realizes what the situation is and begins apologizing profusely. Thirty or so seconds later, his news copy is located and run into the studio, but not before some very uncomfortable stammering – it always sends a shiver up my spine.

Years ago, radio broadcast on-air flubs were lost forever or heard by a precious few who worked at the station. Now, they're up on YouTube before you end your newscast.

Although, one of my favorites comes from the same station mentioned a moment ago – WRNJ. This time, it's a different news guy throwing to a report by WRNJ reporter Steve Schmidt.

"A report by the Warren County Fisheries Department shows the Pequest River Hatchery may be overstocked. WRNJ's Steve Shit has more…"

There are all sorts of words to avoid for a newscaster. In the world of business news, you always avoid the name of the restaurant chain *Fuddruckers*, the tool manufacturer *Federal Screw* and most importantly, Amsterdam-based international food retailer *Ahold*.

You also want to avoid all words that rhyme with "fuck" and if you can, be careful with the word "peanuts" which, if you're in a hurry, can easily come out as "penis."

I recently heard a radio commercial for a place called Hunts Country Furniture. You can bet it was pre-recorded because that has disaster written all over it.

One sound or consonant out of order on the air and you're done. One of my all time favorite news anchors and dear friend Brian McFadden had one early on in his career that's a classic.

While anchoring for the United Press Audio Network he did a story about the discovery of a "deadly organism". Only, in his rush to wrap up the newscast, it came out as a "deadly orgasm". The network received a letter a week later from a man who said his elderly father had heard the newscast and had his son write to find out if there was anyway he could get more info on this deadly orgasm.

Beating out our competition on these big stories was the stuff to brag about when the owners of stations attended the New Jersey Broadcasters Association meeting in Atlantic City every year. Nick used to drive down to Atlantic City and come back exhausted. Between the food, booze and bragging it was a weekend not to be missed.

Nick, who so loved radio, was eventually squeezed out of WCRV and its sister station WFMV. Strapped for cash, he started selling pieces of the station he loved so much until he no longer had a controlling interest. He trusted one investor to let him stay on even though he was no longer in control and the businessman went back on his promise. He was forced out in January of 1982. It was not the same without him. Nick was the soul of WCRV.

Food seemed the next logical stop for Nick. He knocked around the food industry for a while; inventing and marketing for a time – the "Walk Away Italian Dinner." Nick thought it was the next big thing. It was ravioli, meatball, a piece of sausage, a wedge of pizza and a piece of bread covered with sauce… on a stick. You had to see it!

On the fiftieth anniversary of Nick's radio career, Wayne picked him up at his apartment in downtown Washington and drove him to a radio station in Flemington, New Jersey. There, we did a retrospective of his career that aired both on radio and the local public access TV channel in the area. Nick was suffering from chronic health problems and was a bit disoriented, but loved every minute of it.

It ended for Nick as it has for so many of the men who I admired. One day the call came that Nick was ill. I monitored his situation until word came that he didn't have much longer. My only concern then was to make the trip to his bedside at the Warren Hills Nursing Home as soon as possible. I found him sleeping. He sensed someone was in the room and woke with a start and a smile. I had made a long journey to see him and he probably figured my visit along with Wayne's and others meant he didn't have much longer.

I spoke quietly with him. We laughed about good times and bad. On August 17, 1997, I received the news Nick had passed on. It was exactly seventeen years to the day I started at WCRV.

At the time, I was anchoring a morning TV show at News 12 New Jersey. I insisted we do a story on Nick's passing. I dug out one of my favorite photos of Nick and wrote a brief obituary. I think he would have liked it.

His wake was the most unusual I have ever attended. Photos of him chasing stories surrounded his casket. My favorite was of a young Nick interviewing Robert F. Kennedy during a New Jersey campaign for his brother JFK in 1960. You could see from the photos that Nick was in heaven.

But, what struck me at his wake were the frequent bursts of laughter from every corner of the room – people reliving stories of Nick and doubling over as they did. Years later, while freelancing in radio, I was informed by my news editor that I could not use the same name while doing reports on two stations in New York City. In this case I was a traffic anchor one day at one station and a business anchor at another station the next. When the news director at the business network asked me to pick another name for my reports I told him, "I want to be called Nick Dirienzo."

"Who?"

"Nick Dirienzo."

Nick had to be with me. As fate would have it, the station was WCBS-AM in New York and the news anchor during my shift was our old buddy, Wayne Cabot. Wayne and I were in on the secret name I was using during those two days and laughing off air, reminiscing just before I went on. He sometimes threw to my report with a "Nickism" connected to some story at WCRV that only Wayne and I would know. We still do it every time I fill in and Wayne's the anchor.

The rest of the week I got calls from old friends and former employees of Nick who wondered who that was using Nick's name. I think Nick would have loved it. He always loved WCBS. He may not have made it to his favorite New York City radio station – but on those two days he did. I'd say he *would* have loved it – but I know he did.

Several days after I was Nick on the air at WCBS, a woman approached me randomly, as I sipped a cup of coffee outside a local Starbucks.

"You're with the news media, aren't you?" she said.

"Yes."

"I saw your press plates. I'm a medium," she went on, "I connect with those who have passed."

"Really?" I said. I've never been a true believer in those who get messages from the great beyond, but I tried to be as gracious as I could.

"May I do a quick reading?" she asked.

"Knock yourself out…" I answered between sips.

She then went into this kind of trance grasping her head with her hand and then, just as suddenly stopped, looked me straight in the eye and said, "Who's Nick?"

Thanks, Nick. Message received.

I spent two years, a month and a day at WCRV. I was a kid in a hurry and even though I was having the time of my life, I knew it was time to move on. In this business, the longer you stay in one place, the worse it looks on your resume. You have to appear as though you're too good for the station you're currently working for – and good enough to hop to the next one.

I would look back later at those years at WCRV as the most carefree of my life. Till this day, I have a recurring dream in which I am walking though the hallways of WCRV – or on the air. I can see everything vividly. The dreams become more frequent during stressful periods in my life. I guess I'll always long for the simplicity of that special time. I made the transition to my next station by getting advice and counsel from those further along in their careers. I called Frank Settipani. Frank was, and still is, the morning anchor at the CBS Radio Network. When I grew up in Queens he lived right around the block.

"I feel like I need to move on." I told Frank over the phone.

"What about WJDM in Elizabeth?"

I had heard of WJDM and what I had heard about it was not good. It had the reputation of being a dump. A 500-watt day-time station with a hodgepodge of a format and a signal that could hardly be heard in the station's parking lot.

Settipani, however, had worked at WJDM early in his career and had fond memories of the place. I sent out a tape and resume to news director Claudia Coates. She called and asked me to come in for an interview.

As fate would have it, WJDM was on the verge of a renaissance. Weeks before the absentee owner had hired a new general manager who was one of the most savvy radio guys I have ever met.

The interview was set for a Saturday. I had no idea what to expect as I drove into downtown Elizabeth, New Jersey. The city, just south of Newark, is a mostly Hispanic lower-to-middle class enclave in the upscale county of Union, New Jersey.

On my way in I listened to the station. It was bizarre. Commanding the airwaves was a man named "Freddie the German Cowboy". He was the owner of a local country music dance club who apparently paid the station to do an hour or so of country music every Saturday morning. It also gave him an opportunity to feed his oversized ego. He was joined – like Batman to Robin – to Stuart Weiss, who billed himself as the "Professor of Country Music." Odd I thought: a German guy with a Jewish side kick, spinning country music records in the middle of downtown Hispanic Elizabeth, New Jersey.

The station sat on the second floor of a two-story building next to the Union County courthouse. It was right above a five and dime store. Spanish music blasted from the front it as I walked around the corner looking for the entrance. Toward the side there was a small glass door with the WJDM logo on it.

When I pulled on the handle and peeked in I was hit with a wave of body odor. Apparently, a homeless man had been using the dark, tiny first floor landing as his studio apartment. As my eyes adjusted to the darkness I saw, directly in front of me, a long stairway. The tile on the steps was chipped and worn.

At the top of the second floor landing you made a right and walked down a long marbled hallway. It was cold and dark like a mausoleum. Then it was a left turn down another hallway to double wooden doors and the station.

When I entered, I could hear Freddy the German Cowboy in full throat. He was screaming his tag line, "I hear you, I hear you und I gonna love you," in a thick German accent.

Since it was a Saturday, no one was around. I poked my head into the newsroom and then looked into the studio. Freddy was standing up, holding his mic and staring out into the distance; entertaining an imaginary audience. Stuart Weiss was sitting quietly next to him shuffling though his extensive library of country music singles.

There wasn't much to the station: just a few dimly lit offices, a main studio, a talk show studio – which also served as the offices for the sales staff – and a production studio way in the back. The owner's office was in the corner of the building. All of it above the C.H. Martin five and dime store.

Claudia finally popped up behind me and I introduced myself. We went through the standard interview. Then it was off to a meeting with the new general manager, Rich Rapiti.

Rapiti was a blur, zipping around like a bumblebee, pollinating as many flowers as he could before moving on. His right-on management style was to tell you what he wanted and then let you do it. We respected him for that. His "go do it" mantra sounds so simple, but many managers get too involved in things they really don't know how to do.

I sensed right away that Rich was determined to make this station work. He was like George Steinbrenner just after he bought the Yankees: He knew he had something to work with – all he needed were the players. He had already made some changes, but needed to beef up his news department. He was impressed with me and I with him.

I left the station with a good feeling. It was now up to me. Was I going to take a shot on a guy with a dream, or wait a few months to find something better? The decision wasn't even close. I had no intention of staying any longer than I had to at WCRV. It had served its purpose. It was time to move on.

I gave my notice at WCRV a few days later. Nick had been forced out about six months before and Wayne was actively looking to move on. Even my girlfriend Heidi has skipped town after she found out I was dating someone else. On September 18, 1982, I started at WJDM in Elizabeth. Since I worked there, I'm occasionally asked how do you get into Elizabeth. I usually say you start with dinner, maybe some wine… (Badda BING!).

Chapter 7
ELIZABETHTOWN

Going from a rural setting to the heart of New Jersey's fourth largest
city was rejuvenating. I no longer had to lead the news with missing
cow stories. Elizabeth is a lot like Queens. It's diverse and rich in
history. President-elect Washington spent the night in Elizabeth before
taking the first oath of office in downtown Manhattan. Aaron Burr's
father founded the church across the street from the station. The
famous haunted Ritz Theater was a few blocks away. Elizabeth was
abuzz with excitement and energy. Sometimes after my shift, I would
walk the streets of downtown Elizabeth, soaking in the sights and
sounds.

Like any city, it had its own cast of characters. I'll never forget the
small deli down the block. It was owned by a couple who had little or
no personality. They were successful in spite of – not because of –
themselves.

One morning, I ran out between newscasts to get a quick snack and
was surprised to find the deli closed. When I looked closer, I saw a
sign on the door. Scrawled in chalky black ink on a torn piece of paper
were the words (and this is verbatim and with the exact spelling):

"Closed because of Jew Holliday. Won't be open. Cabeesh?"

Classic.

WJDM also had a regular bum who slept in the downstairs stairwell,
the one whose odor attacked me on my first visit. You just never knew
if he was going to be there when you arrived at four-thirty in the
morning. Often, I didn't know whether to shoo him away, or tuck him
in.

During the 1985 gubernatorial campaign, incumbent governor Tom
Kean showed up for a live interview. He passed the bum on his way up
the stairs. We wondered what would happen if the bum asked him to

take a photo with him. Would the shot be standing up or would the good governor lie down next to him?

By far, the weirdest character was the woman who shared the offices with us on the second floor. This decrepit two-story building had many offices, but only two were occupied. Ours, and one used by the owners of the Drake School of Business. Drake was a trade school where you could learn to type or take shorthand run by a crotchety old lady and her nerdy son.

She was always complaining about something, mostly the laughter in the hallways from young people enjoying their jobs and having fun with their colleagues at WJDM. Odd that someone actually enjoying their work made this woman crazy. Wasn't it her mission to get her students into jobs they liked?

Her complaints about the noise fueled our desire to make the old bag miserable. We'd slam the nearby bathroom door, pound our feet up the stairs, even jam something into the elevator door near her office and then run off. The thump-thump-thump of the elevator door trying to close drove her nuts. Sometimes, we would wander in during her classes pretending to be lost.

It was your usual adolescent, borderline-harassment and funny as hell.

I was given the afternoon shift and quickly got into a groove. Instead of soundproofing, I did my newscasts in a shag-carpeted closet of a news booth during the Glen Turnbull show. He was a creative type who sat at the console, puffing away on his smokes and creating characters to join him in studio.

There was the old guy "Stubby Scatz", who used to "call" complaining about one thing or another. But mostly, you didn't need to make up characters. There were plenty out there ringing our phones every day. Stanley was one of them. We'd hear his raspy voice on the other end of the line several times a day…

RING…. RING…

"… (breath), this is Stannnnnley… "

As if we didn't know.

We also had a mid day call-in show, hosted Angela Baddolato. She was a friend of the owner's. The show, called "Viewpoint," was a catch-as-catch-can of topics ranging from the new county prison to how to wrap salmon in tin foil to get the best results on the barbeque. We had a field day with her name. During her time there, a very popular local TV host had his own show. His name was Steve Addabato. We often wondered if Angela Battalato married Steve Addabato, would that make her Angela Battalato Addabato?

Angela lucked out. Her friendship with the absentee owner, John Quinn, allowed her to continue her talk show long after it was relevant. She lucked out again when she married a very nice man whose last name was Evans. This, we thought, was a golden opportunity for her to change her nine-letter last name to something every tongue could handle! Sadly, it was not to be. After getting back from her honeymoon, she opened her show with:

"Welcome to Viewpoint, this is your host Angela Battalato-Evans."

Angela also had her share of screwball callers. One regular had a high-pitched, squeaky voice that sounded like a rake over a chalkboard. No matter what Angela was talking about, or whom she was with, she was not the least bit interested. Her free association calls always came at the worst times. On the rare occasions, when Angela would score a premier "get" – like a U.S. Senator or Hollywood C-lister – her wacky friend would strike.

"We're here with Mindy Cohn who played Natalie Green on the hit TV show *Facts of Life*. We're so happy you're here. We'll start with our first phone call for Mindy."

Caller: "Angela! I'm calling from Rahway. I would like to talk about those damn dogs next door who keep crappin' on my lawn. It's terrible what they do… is there any way I can legally keep those dogs from crappin' up my lawn?"

Angela: "Well, that's interesting. Do you not see them when they're doing it? Maybe because you're watching Mindy on *Facts of Life* at the time?"

Caller: "Who?"

Click.

Sunday on WJDM was a train wreck. It was where old radio shows went to die. A radio hospice that included everything from untrained radio hosts playing Portuguese music, to an Irish music hour hosted by the city's bigger-than-life mayor Tom Dunn.

Dunn was my first introduction to a big time New Jersey politician.

He ruled with an iron fist and made no bones about pushing everyone around including the press. He was feared. When I got to WJDM, he had already been in office eighteen years. No city employee headed for the john without first checking with Tom Dunn. And if you crossed him he'd let you know.

One day he "summoned" me to City Hall, about three blocks away from the station. He set up the appointment as late in the day as he could. I was doing mornings, so I think he wanted to see how late I'd stick around after getting up at four A.M. just to have an audience with him.

When I got to the office his secretary hinted he might have a news exclusive for me.

I was ushered in and he took a look at me. I sat down and we talked about nothing for ten minutes before he sent me on my way. It was about control and he wanted to make sure I knew he was the sheriff in this town.

A couple of years later, I got a call from WWOR-TV/Channel 9 in New York. They asked me if I would be a guest panelist on their Sunday morning TV show '*Meet the Mayors*'. It was one of those public service shows and mostly fluff. The questions included things like:

"Mr. Mayor, what's it like to be mayor of a city of fifty-thousand…"

"Mr. Mayor, are you thinking about re-election yet?" That kind of stuff.

But, I was laying in wait. I had done my homework and was ready to see if the mayor would jump *for me*.

One of the hot issues of the day was the mayor's tacit refusal – or so some said – to appoint a significant number of Hispanics to the school board. Of the school boards' nine members, there was only one Hispanic. This is a city that was nearly fifty-percent Hispanic!

Out on stories, Hispanic leaders in the community often complained to me, and rightfully so. The mayor, like all big time mayors, packed the school board with friends and political allies. Nothing wrong in that, but still, one Hispanic on the board? That was not exactly a way to appease the majority of your constituents, but he seemed not to care.

I sat on the panel as we taped the show for Sunday's broadcast. It was the first time I had ever been in a TV studio. The show went pretty much as planned until the host said, "Frank Cipolla of WJDM in Elizabeth joins us. Frank do you have a question for the mayor?"

Mayor Dunn turned his head toward me waiting for the softball to knock out of the park. I was instead thinking about him "summoning" me to his office a couple years before.

The softball question never came. Instead, I dropped the controversial question of his not appointing more Hispanics to the school board. He bristled. You could see he wasn't ready for it and surely didn't like it. The thirty-minute public affairs show ended on the nose and we all shook hands.

The mayor, though, wasn't done with me. The next day I got a call from Channel 9. The mayor was not happy having to touch the third rail of questions about Hispanics on the school board. He wasn't happy I asked the question. He wasn't happy, period.

I stated my case to the show's host. Tried to reason with her. I also reminded her of the news media's duty to ask the fair and tough questions, but it was not to be. My first appearance on *Meet The Mayors* never happened. Mayor Dunn used his iron fist to kill the show and he never cooperated with me again. It was my first lesson in raw political power.

Dunn had so much clout that when President Reagan was running for re-election in 1984 and New Jersey was in play, he picked the heavily Democratic stronghold to show he could persuade voters of all stripes to support a populist presidency. So, on a cool September afternoon in 1984, the president showed up in Elizabeth.

It was an easier time then. There were metal detectors for sure, but the news media for the most part was not really scrutinized. They would wand us, ask us to run our tape recorders – or for TV guys, their cameras to make sure they weren't bombs, and wave us in.

I was on the air and after the last newscast, ran over to cover the president's speech at Elizabeth City hall. In my rush, I accidentally wandered into a restricted area. I was about a hundred feet from the president's limo, which had pulled up next to a school building, before a Secret Service agent noticed me. The president was just about to step out of the limo when the agent waved for the president to stay put and another agent stepped toward me and with his hand on his holster and shouted, "Who are you?"

"I'm Frank Cipolla from WJDM, I must be lost."

"It's that way." He pointed. I walked away.

I guess he didn't remember me from my lunch with the president two years earlier. If he did, I probably would have been on the ground with a knee in my back.

I tell this story because it now seems so innocent. There was never any panic. The agent sized me up immediately, realized I was lost and not a threat, and calmly directed me to the area secured for the news media.

Up on the platform, overlooking this campaign style event, I could see Mayor Dunn. He was in heaven. He smeared himself all over the president that day before endorsing him in front of several thousand cheering people.

Covering the presidential campaign as it rolled in and out of New Jersey in 1984, I witnessed the power of the White House press corps up-close. One afternoon I was sent to cover a press conference at a landfill in New Jersey. Senator Gary Hart was vying for the Democratic nomination and was still in the running before he conceded to former Vice-President Walter Mondale.

I showed up at the landfill early. The advance team had cordoned off a small area with yellow tape. At the time there were just two of us, as I was joined by a diminutive Asian female reporter from another station. She had to be all of five feet and ninety pounds.

As we waited, a giant bus pulled up and Gary Hart jumped out. He was followed by a small coterie of supporters and aides. This was odd, because the press corps usually shows up first and *then* the candidate.

Minutes later an even bigger bus rolled in kicking up dust as it came to a sudden stop. The throng of reporters and cameramen barreling out of the bus to catch what they could of Hart's appearance was a blur.

The burly cameramen and anxious reporters came into the cordoned off area like a wave. The tiny Asian reporter was knocked to the ground and I almost fell, as well. She was slightly injured and her dress and hair were mussed up. The local and network TV cameramen didn't seem to care. For them the video came first.

●●●

In February of 1983, an unusually talented disc jockey arrived. Jim Bosh was funny, engaging and quick on his feet. I remember first hearing Jim as he did a WJDM promotion one afternoon for a local bank. It wasn't long before Rich Rapiti realized what I did: Jim was too good to be wasted on afternoon drive. Rich realized he might have something if he put us both together on the morning show. Rapiti, like a great coach, knew his player's strengths and weaknesses and how to take advantage of them. In this case, he was right. He shuffled the on-air deck and Jim and I became the morning team.

We hit it off right away. About the same age, we were both steeped in the same kind of New York area pop culture that led us to all sorts of jokes on-air and off. Jim was the master impressionist. He brought the famous and not so famous made up characters to the airwaves. There was the Spanish receptionist, "Susie Coochi-Choochi". Rich became the "General Mangler". The owner of the station, John Quinn, became "Mr. Dim".

In a few weeks, Jim had workable impressions of all the jocks and newsmen – including yours truly.

Every morning the show started with a countdown. Being a space exploration buff, I had dug up the countdown to the first orbital flight by American astronaut, John Glenn, in February of 1962.

At the start of the show you'd hear, "Ten… nine… eight… seven…" At about four, a long-forgotten NASA geek is heard saying "Godspeed John Glenn." And then, "LIFT OFF… we have lift-off and the clock is running."

Jim loved to screw with the listeners. Stanley was the first to get his comeuppance. Stanley would call as usual and say, "This is Staaaanley."

Jim would answer him right back imitating Stanley's voice. Stanley apparently couldn't process it all and the first few times hung up, believing he was hearing his echo. This went on for days.

One morning, a woman called just before the show, as Jim and I were talking in the newsroom. It had been snowing all night and many school districts were deciding whether to call off school for the day.

"I'd like to know, please, if the Linden school district will be closed today," she said.

Jim, without missing a beat, said, "Hold on a moment." He lifted the lid to the chattering Associated Press machine next to us, shoved the receiver into it, closed the lid and left the receiver in there for about ten seconds as it noisily clicked away. He then reached in, pulled it out and said, "Nope, nothing on the wires" and hung up.

It wasn't long before Jim and I got into the bad habit of carousing after the show. Many a day we'd wrap up at 10 A.M., have a quick meeting or something, and then walk across the street to the local pub. The restaurant we selected was an unusual place, paneled in oak both inside and out. It featured American fare served by tall, skinny, big-busted women who spoke with thick German accents. Often, they were difficult to understand, which made it even funnier to Jim and me as we peeked down their blouses. We would sit at the bar and talk about the business. Strangely, it was following these free wheeling, out of office lunches that we were most creative. We'd jot down an idea and the next day either try it out on the air or in the production studio.

That's where we came up with bits that those in and around Elizabeth still talk about including "The Strange Ranger".

The character "The Strange Ranger" was an outwardly effeminate western lawman. He was joined by his sidekick Tonto. "The Strange Ranger" was always complaining about getting his chaps dirty, or having to dive into dirt during a gun battle with the local banditos. He also was always trying to get Tonto to take a bath with him.

As Tonto, I would say in a deep stunted delivery, "Me no want to put towel round you, Kemosabe…"

Jim played the role of "The Strange Ranger" in a Richard Simmons voice. It was hilarious!

We also did a takeoff on the popular show at the time, *Fantasy Island*, starring Ricardo Montalban and his assistant "Tattoo."

I did a great imitation of Montalban, whose character's name was Mr. Roarke. Jim had Tattoo down to a tee as well.

Jim would ring a bell – just like the opening shot of the show – and say in his Tattoo voice, "Da Plane… Da Plane…" At which point, Mr. Roarke would try to quiet him down before taking a shotgun and squeezing off a few shots at the tower.

The biggest names in the news at the time would show up on Fantasy Island. And after trading one-liners we'd, as usual, end in confusion. Often, with Mr. Roarke arguing with Tattoo to stop ringing the bell. It was funny stuff.

There was also a bit we called "At the White House", which featured me as President Ronald Reagan and Jim, as his loyal assistant Bob. Bob was always bailing out Reagan. To make it funny, I portrayed the president as a dimwit who had to be told what to do.

The bit went along with me, as Reagan, insulting White House guests, saying inappropriate things and generally getting tongue-tied. Occasionally, there would be a female visitor to the White House and in those cases we pressed WJDM's traffic coordinator into service. Janice Lyons was quick with a joke and expertly played any female characters we needed.

In one "At the White House" bit, she was the voice of disgraced 1984 Miss America Vanessa Williams. She and her agent had arrived at the Oval Office to take some semi-nude photos on the president's desk and of course the president had no idea what was going on. Bob ended up saving the day.

There was only one unbroken rule for our "At the White House" skits. They, like the other bits, *had* to end in confusion.

Reagan: "Bob… you see… now I've gotten this jar stuck on my head…"

Janice: "Sir, may I present to you the Israeli Ambassador."

Reagan: "What? Bob?" (shouting with echo)

Israeli Ambassador: "Mr. President it is a pleasure."

Reagan: "Huh?"

Bob: "Mr. President, please…!"

Reagan: "I can't get this thing off my head. Bob?"

Bob: "Sir, maybe if I hit it with this…"

At that point Bob would hit the jar. The "Hail to the Chief" music would start and the entire bit would end with everyone talking over each other.

Jim and I didn't know how many people enjoyed "At the White House" until we did a live broadcast outside a supermarket collecting cans for some local food pantry. We were trying to get shoppers to stop and talk in the middle of February, when one guy approached us out of nowhere.

"You guys are the dudes that do the White House thing on the radio, right?"

Jim and I looked at each other and smiled. It was nice to know someone had noticed.

"Yeah," Jim said.

"That shit's hilarious… and the president… thank God he's got Bob, because Bob bails him out all the time. The president can't get a word in edgewise." This guy actually identified with the characters – which is the highest compliment we could get.

We also paired up the most unlikely characters in parodies of late night infomercials. Jim in his announcer voice: "Order now and get Julio Iglesias and Mr. T. singing love songs."

I also started goofing on Jim and the other jocks. I especially enjoyed one prank. In radio, going to the bathroom during the show is an art. Timing is most important. A good jock will hold it in until he's ready to bust. Then, especially if the visit is going to be a long one, he'll put on the longest song he has something like *"American Pie" by Don Mclean* which runs about eight minutes. Once he hits that tune, and if he's disciplined enough – a jock should have just enough time to sit, defecate, wipe and get back to the studio just in time.

At WJDM, the bathroom was all the way down the hallway. It was a trek, which added to the stress of taking care of business and getting back in time. I would watch as Jim – or the other very talented morning jock, Lauren Pressley – hit the crap song and then waddled down the hallway as quickly as they could. While they were in the bathroom I would lower all the speakers in the station and studio, so it appeared as though the song had run out. Dead air is the curse of any disc jockey. It keeps them up at night.

When the trap was set, I'd peer down the hallway from my comfortable chair in the newsroom and enjoy the fun. First, they would turn the corner and head for the station with an incredible look of relief. My friend Lauren Pressley once said it so well: "Sex is the most overrated human activity. A good dump, the most underrated."

Anyway, there they would be this sense of peace and accomplishment on their faces for a job well done and timed perfectly. But as they got closer and didn't hear the music the look would change to sheer terror!

They'd race at warp speed down the hallway frantically trying to get into the studio to press the button – any button – that would fill the silence.

After they realized the song was playing and they had plenty of time the terror would turn to anger and then amusement.

120

I used the prank sparingly and always got a chuckle. It was just another reinforcement of the kind of macabre humor radio people are known for.

As far as all the bits we did, I'm glad we saved a lot of them. Going to work every day, doing the news then writing and performing funny bits was like not working at all.

The credit again goes to Rich Rapiti. He had heard from the listeners and sponsors that they loved "Bosh and Cipolla" in the morning and he let us be as creative as we could; until we crossed the line.

As Jim and I got to know each other better, the silliness got out of hand. Rich loved us on the air – making mischief in the middle of the business day was another story.

Often, it ended with him throwing us out but not before the damage was done. We'd come back and flirt with the sexy new receptionist. One day, we opened the convertible couch in the lobby and started dancing on top of it to the theme song of *Fame*.

Another time, Jim and I snuck back into the station and hid in the newsroom. It was the mid-1980's and one of the most popular shows on TV was *Bleeps, Bloops and Blunders* hosted by Dick Clark and Ed McMahon.

Bleeps, Bloops and Blunders was a weekly montage of TV outtakes from shows old and new. Entertainers also played tricks on each other. It seems old hat now with reality TV and YouTube but back then it was cutting edge TV.

You'd watch old actors screwing up lines, tripping over things and occasionally you'd get a glimpse of a racy overseas TV commercial.

On this day, Rich was especially busy putting together the most important remote broadcast of the year. We were going to broadcast live from "Septemberfest" at Dunn Park in Elizabeth (yes, named after Mayor Dunn). Rich cashed in all his chips for a prime spot right at the entrance of the fair where no one could miss the WJDM van, and see the live broadcast. All seemed in place and then the call came.

Rich thought it was from one of the event organizers. Instead, Jim and I had solicited the services of one of the salesmen to call from the newsroom twenty feet away and tell Rich "there was a problem," all the while rolling tape on the phone call.

The set up went like this: There had supposedly been a mix-up with the permits and Rich did not get the prime location for the Septemberfest broadcast. Instead, he had to take what was left and that was a booth all the way in the back near a busy highway, where no one could possibly see the WJDM van or hear the live broadcast.

Rich's response was classic: First, shock. Then, anger. Then, confusion. Halfway into the five phases of grief, he screams out for one of the salesmen helping with setting it all up to find out what the hell was going on. He needs help. He's panicking. All of his best laid plans are going down the tube and just when it seems like his head will explode, I grab the phone from the salesman and say, "Rich – you've just been a victim of *Bleeps, Bloops and Blunders*!"

I looked back for Jim, but he was already out the door running down the hallway. I immediately hit rewind on the tape machine; knowing if I didn't secure the tape we wouldn't be able to enjoy this prank call for years to come. I could hear Rich going office-to-office looking for the culprits. I'm standing in front of the reel-to-reel machine talking to it.

"Come on… come on!"

The reel rewound to the end and the tape is flapping when Rich locates me. It's too late. In an instant, I run past him laughing my ass off all the way down the hallway and out of the building.

As our popularity grew, Jim and I became bolder. We started making fun of our neighbors down the hallway. The old broad who owned the Drake School of Business and her son. They were easy targets.

At first, we didn't mention them by name but eventually it was too hard not to. One morning, Jim started talking about the lady's nerdy son, how he was always flitting around the building looking busy but actually doing nothing. We talked about how his mom looked after him and what a geek he was. We laughed on-air and off until I heard a knock on the door. Apparently, mom and nerdy son had begun to monitor the program on the advice of friends who listened periodically and heard us taking pot shots at them.

The door was always kept locked because we arrived early in the morning. While Jim was on the air, I unlocked the door and peeked out. The nerdy son tried to push his way in but he was a skinny guy and I was able to slam the door shut and lock it again.

Next the phone rang. It was the old broad. She was going to speak with the owner Mr. Dim, because enough was enough. This time they were going to sue. Like a mother hen she was coming to the defense of her chick.

Based on what we said, she could have sued. We had clearly defamed the poor bastard.

The Drake mom knew, after speaking with her attorney, that every station was required to record the day's broadcast and keep it for several months. The tapes were saved should there ever be a situation in which someone was defamed or an attorney needed it to use a news broadcast in a court case.

I guess we all learned something from growing up in the Watergate days, because as soon management found the offending banter on the giant reel-to-reel machine called a Metrotech it was replaced with another and the original was destroyed.

Later in the day, Mr. Dim was called. The lawyers had contacted the station. The old broad even made a visit while we were at the German pub across the street but lo and behold "Exhibit A" – the master tape of the show and the insult to her son – was never found. The lawyers were kept at bay.

We had one last round to fire at the antique of a lady down the hallway before a truce was declared. One day, after a mid-morning creative session, Jim and I returned to the station. We bounded up the stairs and started making noise just to piss off the drake-o-doodle marm. She excused herself from her class and briskly walked toward us as we were doubled over laughing about something.

"It's a travesty that young men your age act like this," she screamed in that high-pitched scratchy voice. "Making noise while I'm trying to conduct a class. You know what you're doing and you should be ashamed. You will pay!"

Jim calmly straightened up and quietly said, "Listen, if you keep this up we're not going to buy any more of your cakes and pies." I fell on the floor laughing. She walked away never to hassle us again.

Rich quietly put up with our nonsense as long as we kept the sponsors happy. We were on a very long leash, but a leash nonetheless. The last straw came on one of the most important days for WJDM. As word spread that the station and its disc jockeys were not to be missed, and as the ratings climbed, Rich decided it was time to make a play for some of the giant sponsors – the New York City sponsors who wouldn't give WJDM a second look had it not been for the wonderful combination of talent, including midday jocks Jan Ochs and Ziggy (who is now the voice of WCBS-FM and others).

On this afternoon, Rich was pitching a giant car dealership. One of the owners had inquired about WJDM since he had never heard it.

Rich was in full pitch mode. There he sat in the office of the man he had been trying to see for months. This was the client that was going to bring in some monster ad bucks and Rich was on his game. Talking about Bosh and Cipolla, the funny bits, the hard-hitting local news, the playlist of songs – everything that made WJDM stand out. Sure, it was a small "day time" radio station, but it was ready for prime time.

Back at the station, it was another day of having fun and harassing the staff. Jim and I were walking around after our show like peacocks, supremely confident in our ability to make the pretty receptionist laugh while at the same time talking dirty to the sales chicks.

Enter the mid-day news guy.

His most distinguishing feature was his hair, or lack of it. News guy had one strand of hair left on his head. Every morning he expertly weaved that one seven-foot strand into a full hair helmet. It was a work of art. You knew there was a baldpate underneath, but by the time he worked his magic the naked dome was safely disguised under a hair hat. The hair stayed in place as long as the winds did not exceed 50 mph, or some migrating birds did not need a place to spend the night.

In the 1980's, all music and news sound was played on carts. When the news sound was no longer needed, the material on the carts was "bulked" using a giant bulk eraser. It was a weird contraption. The bulk eraser was essentially a giant tabletop magnet. You'd click a switch and it would buzz like that old rattling football board game from the 60's. The magnetism generated from this one-foot-by-one-foot giant magnet pulled the electrons that were imbedded on the tape off so when you were done it was clean and ready to be used again.

You always had to take your wristwatch off when bulking a cart. One swipe of your watch would mess up its magnetic field.

There was a technique to properly bulking a cart: You'd place it on top, hit the "on" switch and then with your hand on the cart make a few circles. The trick was to pull the cart off with a slow snap of your arm. Pull slowly back and up. We were all taught that. By pulling the cart slowly back and up you erased the tape.

When racing to make the newscast, the newsperson looked like Tony Manero from *Saturday Night Fever*, throwing his arm up after a disco spin.

One day, the combination of me rushing to bulk a cart and "news guy" met perfectly. He was passing through the newsroom and I was minutes from a cast. There I was jerking my arm back again and again to get the cart clean. Just as news guy walked by, the cart slipped out of my hand and spun in the direction of his expertly coiffed hair.

He wasn't hurt, but his carefully sculptured middle-aged 'do' was finished. For the rest of the day he walked around looking like a Pablo Picasso painting; his weirdly misshapen hair helmet not exactly lining up with the rest of his body.

News guy was a bizarre man. He was great at the gathering, disseminating, and writing of news. He kept extensive files, following up and often breaking news stories. He possessed all the skills of a great *newspaper* reporter. On the air, though – not so good.

His delivery was stunted and it seemed to any listener that he was just a flubbed word or a tickle in his throat from panic. Jim and I avoided him but there were times when razzing him was just too irresistible.

One day, newsman was just beginning his one P.M. newscast. It was the usual stuff. Some knucklehead had tried to rob a bank in town and ended up being blasted by a red paint canister placed inside his bag of loot. The Elizabeth city council had voted to buy a new dump truck. And there was a serial "fondler" on the loose – the usual combination of madness and mayhem that make up any local newscast.

Our diligent news guy sat in the booth. In front of him was a small soundproofed window used to signal the disc jockey in the other room if need be.

About a minute into the newscast, Jim and I made our move. At that very moment across town, Rich was making his final move to nail the owner of the giant car dealership. He was now coming in for the kill, visions of mucho advertising sales dollars dancing in his head.

As our news guy's tinny voice relayed the events affecting Elizabeth and its environs, Jim and I pressed our faces against the news booth window. Newsman didn't look up, but he could feel our presence and it set him to stammering.

Now Jim pulled out the big gun: his impression of Rich.

As Jim impersonated Rich through the window, news guy glanced up and then labored mightily to keep from laughing. Jim's giant head was on the other side of the glass – a mere twelve inches or so from news guy. The giggles became cackles and guffaws on our side of the window and, as other employees walked through the hallways and heard the laughter, they popped into the main studio to see what was going on.

The main studio was filled with people laughing at Jim as he tried to get newsman to look up again. News guy's face was red now. He was the center of attention and, like a good build-up to a sneeze, there was shortly going to be a point of no return.

Back at the car dealership, Rich was down to getting the final yes – the "okay, let's do it" that every good salesperson lives for. You've starched your shirt, you've done your homework, expertly worked the room and now – as they say just before a big launch at NASA – it was "go" or "no go"– the moment of truth.

The owner of the dealership wanted one last reassurance that he was doing the right thing. After all, this was a lot of money to be spending on a small daytimer radio station. Would it translate into sales or was he just throwing his money away?

That's when Rich said those fateful words. "Look, forget the ratings and what you've heard about WJDM in the past. Give us one more listen. Let's turn the station on right here – right now and once you hear again what we're doing, I'm sure your decision will be easy."

Rich reached over to a radio on the owner's desk and clicked it on. He did so the exact moment news guy looked up at Jim again.

News guy giggled first, then choked on his own phlegm, pulled it back for a moment – read a half sentence or two and started laughing again. Then he read a bit more and giggled.

Our work was done. Newsman's newscast had been foiled because he had not been trained in "holding it all together" as I had when Wayne blatantly imitated Nick at WCRV, not more than six inches from the back of Nick's head.

The car dealership deal was dead. All of Rich's work and time down the drain because Jim and I decided on this day, at this time, we would play.

For the second time in my short career, I almost got canned. Rich spoke with a few people at the station and then called Jim and me into his office. We sat there and took the heat. All I remember is Rapiti yelling, then asking if we had anything to say for ourselves.

I thought for a moment. I was thinking maybe he could at least find the humor in what we had done. Forgive us. Remember, we were doing it to keep the morning show interesting for our listeners.

"Well....", I said

The sentence ended there. Rapiti glared at us and said, "Get out."

•••

Right down the block from our station was a small record shop. In those days, we'd buy records and transfer them onto carts.

Once the song was on tape, the front of the cart would be labeled, numbered and placed in a tall rack. During the show, you'd pull the carts off the rack, pop them into a cart machine and play the song. Or, in my case, a particular piece of news sound – something called an "actuality."

In short, it was like cueing up a record, but on a tape format so it worked better. No pulling the record out, placing it on the turntable and finding the right spot. And, it came without the usual scratches that showed up on an album after repeated plays.

The tape in the carts would often tangle, or the screw that kept the cart together would rattle loose. The song would play over the air just fine, but in the studio the cart would whir and whistle. It was then that you –

as the disc jockey or newsman would have to pause for a moment – sit down and take a screwdriver to it, tightening it there, rethreading the tape here. It was a delicate procedure, one we referred to as "open cart surgery".

Badda bing! Had to get that one in.

Doing a fairly popular radio show in a smallish market was very rewarding. But, after a couple of years, Jim and I both wanted more. I needed to know if I was good enough to work on-air in New York. Jim longed for that too, but he also wanted act in TV commercials. Doing a TV commercial, depending on how many times it runs, can be quite a racket. While you're at home in your pajamas your local or national spot runs on TV and every thirteen weeks – presto – you get a check. Residual money is what commercial actors live for. And, if you do one good commercial and it runs for years, it's a check in the mailbox again and again and again.

Jim approached this project with laser-like focus. He first took a course on being an actor in TV commercials. He got some head shots. He worked hard.

My goal was to get noticed by some radio news folks in New York: news directors looking for a hardworking, funny morning news guy. With these two goals in mind, Jim and I joined forces to make it happen.

Our day usually began about five A.M. Jim and I were on the air until ten A.M. and then we'd begin the second part of our day. Skipping lunch across the street, we'd head directly to the Elizabeth train station down the street and hop on the North Jersey shoreline train into Manhattan. It was about a forty-five-minute ride that dumped us out at Penn Station.

Then, like little bees buzzing in the streets of the Big Apple, we'd hit a series of pre-determined stops. There were maybe four or five radio stations I could pop in, say hello, schmooze and drop off an updated tape. Then, we were off to the offices of a few casting directors. Jim would drop off an 8x10, do some schmoozing himself and we'd call it a day.

Although, it wasn't always as easy as that. Like zillions of would-be actors have discovered, getting through the doors of these casting agents was a job in itself. That's where I came in.

I'd go in first and engage the secretary in conversation. I'd flirt with her – tell her that her hair looked great, or she had on a wonderful necklace – whatever. Then Jim, head down, would breeze by us and get to the back offices. He'd have some kind of contact name for the agency that he got from his acting class and once in the back he'd go looking for that person.

When he was done he'd signal me – or just walk by headed for the door. I'd wrap up my conversation and follow him out. It worked about seventy-five percent of the time. The other twenty-five, we'd get thrown out on our ears.

I had my own little scam going, as well, as I left off my tapes at radio stations in New York. It was based on the premise that a security guard – fearing whom he might possibly offend – would never stop a well-dressed man from entering any building in Manhattan.

It was a trick I learned from my mom. Walk confidently.

Perception is everything, and pre-9/11 the security in most Manhattan buildings was lax. In addition to walking confidently, you had to dress the part. Your best suit and tie and shined shoes got you into any building.

I'd get in to see a radio or TV news director by making it appear as if I knew exactly where I was going. No one will stop you if you appear as though you belong.

I'd walk into the building like I owned the place. Confidently, I'd stroll right past the security guard. The clincher was the greeting. I'd look the guard right in the eye and say, "Hey – good to see you again. How's the family?"

Not knowing – or not wanting to offend me – he'd say something like, "Great, great, just got a new grandson."

"Super," I'd say, all the time heading back toward the elevators.

I'd hit any old button and get out on that floor. I'd then say to the first person I saw, "You know what, I'm lost. I'm looking for the WCBS news director, John Smith."

"Oh yeah – he's on the seventh floor."

While this was going on, the rent-a-cop downstairs was still trying to figure out in his head who I was. But, by that time he had convinced himself, he knew. Bottom line: Since he did not challenge me coming in, he surely didn't want to get himself in trouble by asking a supervisor, or sending someone to search for me – because the first question to him would be, "How in the world did you let someone in without checking his ID?"

I'd always wave and say goodbye to him on the way out. That made sneaking in next time that much easier.

Jim and I made these stops sometimes twice a week. He'd hit five or six casting agencies and I'd do the same number of radio or TV stations. We'd also pump each other up, talking about how important it was that we persevere, how it was going to happen any time now. Jim would get the commercial on national TV and I would get the news anchor gig at a station that my family members in and around New York could actually hear.

●●●

Some of the major radio stations were heard in New York but were not located there. One was WAPP. It was situated along side an expressway in Queens. It was new and hot and perfect for Jim or me. Once on that station, we assured ourselves, we were going to be big stars!

Jim cooked up an idea. To stand out from all the other would-be jocks and news people trying to get jobs there we would go a different route.

Jim would dress up as a clown. We'd drive there, Jim would get out, march into the lobby of the station and say something like, "If you want some really fun stuff on your station – Bosh and Cipolla are available," and then hand the program director our tape.

The pitch would be so unusual and we were so confident that it would work that we were already writing our resignation letters to WJDM.

On the appointed day, Jim and I wrapped up our shift at WJDM. Jim got into his clown costume. We hopped into my car and off we went.

Me, in my circa 1970's mustache and polyester suit and Jim, sitting next to me dressed as a clown. You should have seen the looks we got as we cruised along. We pulled up at the station and Jim, with all the enthusiasm he could muster after getting up at five A.M., bounded into the lobby of the station.

I stood toward the back and near the door eyeballing the situation to see if I was needed as a decoy or a diversion to get Jim into the back offices.

We never got that far. The secretary nervously giggled; Jim in a wacky voice pitched us. The program director came out to see what was going on and then encouraged us to leave.

The ride back to Elizabeth was a somber one. Forty-five minutes of me staring aimlessly at the road sitting next to Jim, now the Pagliacci of the Long Island Expressway. The Emmet Kelly of Queens.

Talk about seeing a clown cry. It gets me every time.

Jim finally got his commercial. A national TV spot!

We all gathered at Jim's house to watch the commercial when it finally aired. It was for a computer company and Jim played the role of the office nerd. Great casting. Great commercial. It ran one cycle. Jim made some nice money and we were all very proud.

It also got me to thinking again. When was my call going to come? It would, but I would need help from a very tall woman with some water front property off lower Manhattan.

Chapter 8
"WHAT A FRIGGIN' BUSINESS"

The second and third years at WJDM brought more talented people. Others moved on and to the consternation of everyone, the formerly-absentee owner suddenly became more involved in the day-to-day operations of the station. I also got married, swearing off the nice smelling radio sales women and agreeable female jocks.

The new people added new life to the station. It was also an affirmation that the format, thanks to Jim, was tight and attracting attention. Like a baseball team that suddenly starts winning, we saw that quality talent in and around New Jersey wanted in.

Two new jocks were added – Ziggy and Lauren Pressley. Ziggy had a long German name, so we called him Ziggy. In Lauren's case, her real name Pletzner became Pressley and for years after that I used to introduce her as the illegitimate daughter of Elvis. I seemed to be the only one who got a kick out of that and I kept saying it long after I should have stopped. Including now.

Ziggy had excellent pipes, a deep baritone voice that shook the room. He liked the name Ziggy, but on a tight budget we couldn't afford a personalized jingle – what we call in the business a 'shout' – for him. A "shout" is quick musical version of your name that's professionally sung and is played between songs or right after a commercial during your show.

Have no fear. The ever-industrious Jim figured something out. The company that originally did our 'shouts' messed up a few names. They sent us the entire jingle package and when the mistake was pointed out, they fixed it immediately. What was left over was a "Dave" and a "Delore." Instead of having them go to waste, Jim mixed the "Dave" and the "Delore" and Ziggy became – ready for this? *Dave Delore.* You probably saw *that* one coming a mile away.

Laure Pressley was, and is, a doll. Although, our first meeting wasn't the love fest it should have been.

As the "veterans of the station", and because Jim and I were now our biggest attractions, General Manager Rich Rapiti finally gave us our own office. It was big stuff. In our cramped quarters an office was gold.

I had been wandering around the station while Jim interviewed Lauren. They were in our office chatting away. I listened as I passed by. She sounded pleasant and enthusiastic. When Jim called out to introduce me to her she was sitting in my chair. In my chair, behind MY desk!

I know this sounds petty but my ego wouldn't allow it. Who was this interloper?

I sneered at her and told her to get up. She looked at me like I was crazy and then quickly and graciously complied. I didn't realize how traumatic this little incident was to her. She had listened to Jim and me on the radio and genuinely liked us, and here I was telling her to get the hell out of my seat.

She never forgot it. She still talks about it almost every time I see her, as if only intense therapy will help her work it all out.

John Quinn – the station owner we referred to as "Mr. Dim" – had the corner office which overlooked Broad Street in Elizabeth. When he called you into his office you had to strain to listen to him over the sound of shoppers haggling in several different languages in front of the five and dime one floor below.

His new secretary, Janice Lyons, was a blast! A Jersey City girl with attitude. Mr. Dim wasn't ready for how very blunt she could be. It was clearly an adjustment for both of them and lots of fun to watch, sort of like *The Nanny* starring Fran Drescher. Mr. Dim would set the boundaries. Janice would set new ones.

Instead of using the buzzer on his phone when he needed assistance, Mr. Dim bought a small bell, which he shook to get Janice to come into his office. I don't know if he thought she was a waitress, a house servant, or had some Pavlov's dog-type experiment going on, but

Janice cringed every time she heard it. It was stupid. He was within earshot of her. All he had to do was call her name or buzz her phone.

Anyway, about the fourth or fifth time Mr. Dim rang the bell, Janice marched into his office and said, "Why the hell don't you just call my name or buzz my friggin' phone?" Mr. Dim stammered a bit as Janice snatched the bell out of his hand.

"You see this bell? You see this bell?" she said.

At that, she walked over to one of the decrepit, half-opened windows in his office and tossed the bell out onto Broad Street… slamming the window behind it.

Mr. Dim never crossed the line again with Janice. The bell? It jingled and jangled as it hit the concrete below and most likely found its way into one of the sidewalk sales bins in front of the five and dime where it was probably sold.

For someone so enamored with something as low tech as a bell, it's hard to believe Mr. Dim was also into some very cutting edge technology. For a while, he used to work in his office wearing a headset that was plugged into his phone. He thought this much more convenient and attractive then just picking up his phone, about ten inches from his left hand. You'd see him in his office walking around tethered to his phone. Once in a while, he'd walk too far and from several offices away you could hear the phone crash against the floor. And then, there was his large illuminated board, on which he used funky colored markers to make presentations to the staff. You'd plug in this four-by-six-foot backlit board and with the special markers it came with everything you wrote on it glowed. It was like sitting next to an exploding star. When clicked on, it buzzed with an eerie glow. It was annoying to be near or look at directly. We half wished Janice would find a way to toss *it* out the window!

With the reemergence of Mr. Dim came the arrival of his in-office harem. Sassy middle-aged MILFs whom he brought on board to help out.

Fran was one of them. She arrived halfway through my stay at WJDM. With Mr. Dim's blessing she also secured one of the very few offices. Before long, she was holding meetings, making suggestions and generally getting on everyone's nerves. She had to be neutralized.

One scheming employee – who's name remains a secret till this day – decided that it was time to let her know she was not welcomed. One night, after we clicked off the air, he snuck back into the station and dragged everything in Fran's office into another empty office on the other side of the building. Everything. Desk, file cabinets, chairs. When he was done, Fran's office was bare. As a bonus he also removed the hinges on her door. But that wasn't enough. He thought we needed an historical record to capture the moment when Fran turned the key the next morning to find her office empty.

The call came very early. I was in the newsroom writing one of my reports. The deed had been done and now this employee wanted me to help out. It all seemed kind of sinister.

Fran's office was right next to the production studio where every day Jim and I would record our "Strange Ranger" and "At the White House" bits.

Between newscasts – and before everyone came in for the morning – I connected a wire to the production studio console. Then, I pulled a microphone stand out into the hallway and popped a mic on it. The stand and microphone stood within three feet of Fran's office door. I put a long-playing blank reel-to-reel tape on the recording machine in the production studio and pressed "record."

There the quiet sentinel stood, waiting for the moment when Fran would come in and open her office door.

As the morning show rolled along, we waited for the familiar sound of Fran's footsteps. She was running late and now my concern was whether she would come in before the production studio tape ran out.

With about two minutes left on the giant reel-to-reel recording tape, we heard Fran.

First, we heard the click, click, click of her heels. The jingling of keys, the door slamming against the floor and then a horrified gasp!

Back in the studio – even through soundproof earphones – we heard the cursing. We knew this was bad. In the midst of the commotion I quietly snuck back to the production studio, dragged the mic stand back in and secured the reel-to-reel tape. Thankfully it was, as they say, "caught on tape."

Everyone at the station endured a couple of days of interrogation before things quieted down. But, this act of insurrection triggered an internal war that simmered from that moment on. Fran never found out who was behind the prank and we never told. But, I'm sure she suspected we were involved or knew who was.

We weren't exactly sure why Mr. Quinn had decided to return to the station on a more regular basis. He told us he had health problems and now felt better. We just tried to stay clear of him.

He didn't stay clear of us though. Quinn had a plan. For whatever reason he was going fix up the station. Throw some money into it and see what happens.

The first order of business was to get our antenna out of the Shop Rite Supermarket parking lot.

An explanation: The antenna that pumped out the great sound, talented jocks and news people from WJDM was constructed in a small empty lot in a town right next door to Elizabeth. It must have been more suburban back then but it surely wasn't now. As the area grew, land was purchased to the left and right of the antenna site and before you knew it our "stick," as it's called in the business, sat in the parking lot of a Shop Rite along a very busy county road.

The antenna looked out of place. It was so close to the supermarket that every time someone yanked a can off the shelf in Aisle 12, the movement of metal would throw off our signal. On the rare occasions that we would join the engineer to check out the antenna, we would stand there mouths open. Cars were parked right next to it. Supermarket carts bumped up against the small fence that surrounded it.

To be taken seriously by an even wider listening audience and the small community of radio professionals in New Jersey, Quinn decided we had to upgrade and relocate the antenna.

After much deliberation and endless FCC and local approvals, a new antenna site was selected. A platform and antenna would be erected in the same small township but in a county owned park.

Quinn conferred with our new engineer, Jerry Turro, and shortly after that work on the wooden platform that would surround and support the antenna began. It was impressive. A small wooden staircase led to a wooden platform about twenty-five feet up. From there, an engineer could climb the antenna to do whatever maintenance was needed.

The remote site for the antenna provided plenty of room and unfortunately plenty of cover for the kids from nearby local high school. They began to vandalize it. Periodically, Quinn would get a call that someone had set the wooden platform that surrounded it on fire, or that the lock had been tampered with.

Quinn took action. He called the principal of the high school and asked if he could talk to all the students at the next assembly about the antenna and the dangers of tampering with it. So, there was Quinn, in front of all these kids telling him not only where the antenna was – in case they hadn't seen it – but also why it was dangerous.

The kids loved it. Now intrigued, the incidents of vandalism increased.

There were other problems. One evening after a violent and sudden rainstorm, Jim and I came in to find we couldn't turn the station on. The roads were flooded throughout our listening area and the floods had short-circuited the antenna. Just when our listeners needed us most to get the local traffic, weather, news and other information, WJDM was silent.

We called station engineer Jerry Turro and played around with the buttons. Nothing. The morning drive was more than half over and our listeners had not heard a peep from us. WJDM was off the air without explanation.

I was in the newsroom reading a newspaper, not knowing what to do when Jerry – who had arrived a short time earlier – popped his head in. He needed me to go with him to the antenna site so that he could turn it on manually.

"What do you need me for?" I said.

"There's been some flooding at the antenna site."

"So?" I said.

"I'll explain. Just come with me."

Most of the time AM antennas and water go together well. Under every AM antenna is a series of in-ground cables buried in a radius around the antenna right near the surface. The signal from the top of the antenna is yanked down by magnetic forces, which push out giant radio waves. On these waves ride the music and banter of the station.

In fact, owners of AM stations love it when they can plant their antennas in a small lake or pond. The water works like a super conductor and makes the radio waves that find their way to the ground even stronger. The WJDM antenna in the county park was placed in an area that occasionally flooded.

I figured we'd drive up to the antenna and Jerry would get out and click some switch and we'd drive back to the station in time for me to do a quick newscast, wrap up my shift and head off to lunch. In my mind, I was already enjoying a scrumptious burger and visualizing the buxom German waitresses across the street.

So there we were rumbling down some county roads on our way to the antenna site.

"We have to stop at the County Parks Department equipment yard first."

"Huh?" I said, half listening.

"Gotta get the canoe," Jerry said, almost nonchalantly.

"Un huh… what!?"

"The canoe."

"What the hell are you talking about?'

That's when I found out the antenna's wooden platform was under six feet of water. To even get to the antenna we needed two people. Both of us had to row out to the antenna site. I would keep the canoe docked to the wooden platform while Jerry did his thing. Then we'd row back to the car. Jerry knew this. I, sitting there in my dress clothes, had no idea.

The head of the Parks Department was waiting for us when we pulled up. He and some sweaty well-worn parks employees – with a minor assist from Jerry and me – hoisted the canoe on top of Jerry's car and secured it with rope. They gave us a half-hearted wave good-bye and returned to their Egg McMuffins.

All the way out to the antenna site I was thinking, *What the hell did I agree to?'*

There it loomed. WJDM was a small station, but the antenna stood high and proud scraping the clouds. We got within a quarter mile of it before we had to stop. It was canoe time.

In the muck of that damp, misty spring morning Jerry and I yanked what felt like a two-ton canoe off the top of his roof and plopped to the ground. Since I was dressed up I got in, and Jerry with a shove sent it into the drink, hopping in at the last minute.

The closer we got, the taller the antenna looked – and the deeper the water. Once in a while, I'd push the oar in and see how deep. I wasn't happy. The water looked like motor oil and smelled like crap.

"Oh, one other thing…" Jerry said as the water splashed about the canoe. "I've never done an emergency on-site start up. But, from what I know, there's an outside chance that one – or both of us could be electrocuted."

"Come on Jerry, stop."

"No," he said, "I'm serious. From what I know – sometimes in an emergency on-site start up the pent-up current shoots out supercharged and the electricity can find its way into the surrounding area."

It was not unheard of. Many of us in New Jersey radio had heard the story of WXMC in Morris County. WXMC's antenna was right next to the station and sat in a small lake. One Sunday night, the station's antenna was shut down completely so an engineer could climb up in the middle of the night and do some routine maintenance. He was expected to be done by morning but things got a little complicated and there he was still working on the antenna when the just-out-of-college cub reporter showed up for the morning show.

He hadn't gotten the memo. When the kid clicked on the antenna the engineer was blasted off the top of the tower like a Roman candle and fell flat on his back into the lake below. Thankfully, he was not seriously hurt.

Meanwhile, with each row of my oar I was thinking, '*How does this end? Are we electrocuted in what would soon be renamed 'The Jerry Turro/Frank Cipolla Memorial County Park?'*'

"I'm not comfortable about where this is going, Jerry."

"Don't worry," he said with an impish smile. The canoe bumped into the wooden platform right near the steps. For two guys who had never served in the Navy we hit our target right on.

"Okay," Jerry said, "I'm going up and I'll be right back. Just stay here."

"Will do," I replied. Meanwhile, I'm thinking, "See ya!"

With every step Jerry took in climbing up to the top of the antenna, I paddled twice. I wasn't going to be around when the poor bastard was toasted, and secondly, I had to make sure I wasn't hit by the hurtling body.

I got to about two feet of water, took my shoes off, rolled up my pants and jumped in. I ran the last few feet to the relatively safety of mud.

No bolt of electricity ever came. No hurtling Jerry – just a click of a switch and WJDM, four hours late, was back on the air. Just in time for the mid day jock to review all the weather and traffic details that every damn station in the New York Metropolitan area had on while Jerry and I were playing *McHale's Navy*.

On the way back to the station I sat in Jerry's car staring out the window. Here I was a communications major from a great college, an experienced newsman. My judgment on how to handle a story and in what way to present it was something I was proud of. I had to laugh. What lesson had I learned in college that could have possibly prepared me for this?

"Okay class – today in Radio and TV Broadcast News advanced training we are going to learn about technical emergencies. Did everyone bring their oars?"

●●●

Even though WJDM had a very limited signal, Jim always conveyed to the talent that we were bigger than our signal. He even had a giant sign over the door of the main studio that said, "THINK BIG."

Thinking big and having the bucks to be big was a different story. Jim slowly but surely placed things in the budget that could make the station sound better. He added the kind of electronics that would make our voices sound fuller, the songs clearer. As engineer, Jerry also complied by tweaking the signal again and again. Our tinny five-hundred-watt signal was boosted and boosted again, no doubt in violation of FCC regulations. But, it was Jerry's contention – and ours – that, who the hell was going to know? Were there Radio Police with blue uniforms and hats along with official and very important looking patches that had microphones on them cruising the streets of every city? Of course, not – so, away we went.

Jerry was constantly telling Quinn and Rapiti that they needed this and that, that they had to upgrade this machine, or buy another one of these. Both, Quinn and Rapiti, gently tried to tell Jerry that even though they were making more money than they ever had, upgrades of the equipment had to be done gradually.

At the time, my small news booth had a microphone you would find in a toy store. Jim's mic was state of the art. Mine was Playskool. The average listener probably couldn't tell the difference but we could, and that was enough. Jim and I badgered Rich about the upgrading my mic but to no avail.

Rich wrote up his wish list of equipment for the quarter, crunching the numbers again and again, then crunching them some more to keep within budget and satisfy Mr. Dim. It was painstaking for Rich. He spent hours and hours making decisions on what was absolutely, positively needed. It was a procedure that Jim, Jerry and I totally ignored.

Before the equipment order was out, Jerry was asked to take a look. He squabbled with Rich over pennies and then eventually gave in. Rich was sticking to his guns. This, again, is where as young men our total disregard for authority reared its head.

With a quick couple of words here and a check of the box there Jerry, with the blessing of Jim and me, added a new and expensive microphone to the order list and then sent it on its way. We waited for delivery, all the time scouting out places we could hide once Rapiti put two and two together.

We didn't have to wait long.

About a week and a half later the box arrived containing everything Rapiti ordered. Before he could sort it out, I distracted him as Jim slipped into his office and pulled this beautiful Electrovoice RE 20 microphone from among the items. Jim wasn't able to snag the invoice or alter it, so we just installed the mic in the news booth and quietly gathered our things. We could sense the trouble, but we figured if we got out of there he would snap, think it over, and then just chalk it up to the two crazy morning guys.

We didn't make it.

Rapiti – so excited to get the new stuff – rifled through the box crosschecking the items ordered.

It started as a low rumble. He was talking to himself first. "What the hell? Where did this come from?"

Our strategy was to deny and distract. We agreed beforehand that Jim, Jerry and I would just deny we knew about it, say we had no idea who ordered it, and then refer all questions to the each other until Rapiti gave up.

As I got out of the news booth after the eight-thirty update, he was on me. "Who the hell ordered this microphone?"

"What microphone?" I said.

"The one on this invoice." He then poked his head into the news booth and saw it.

"I don't know Rich. I was asking myself that question as well. I just sat down and there it was."

Ten minutes later, it was Jim's turn.

"Do you know how this mic got here?"

"What are you talking about?"

"This microphone that was ordered… I didn't order it!"

"I have no idea," Bosh said.

Next, it was Jerry's turn. He referred Rich back to me and so it went. This Merry-Go-Round of denial lasted several hours before some call came in and Rich was needed to speak to a client. He had to admit my mic sounded much better on the air, so after a while he saw the logic behind it.

Every year, the New Jersey Congressional delegation sets off on a train trip to Washington. It's a giant rolling schmoozatorium. Every mover and shaker, every would-be mover and shaker, every candidate, every person thinking about being a candidate, various lobbyists and a bunch of sexy looking ladies take this interminable train ride down to the nation's capital. There, they attend a New Jersey Congressional delegation dinner, sleep over in Washington and head back the next day.

A train trip from Elizabeth to Washington takes about three hours. This ride takes about seven. The engineer takes his time so that there's more time for handshaking, policy making, drinking and making plans later to play 'power politician and naughty constituent'. In addition to all the politicking going on, the train ride is hot, stuffy and pointless. One politician told me not too long ago that he gets on the train in Newark, walks through shaking everyone's hand, and then gets off in Philadelphia where his driver, who's waiting, takes him back home.

If you're not into it, it's a very unpleasant journey. I've done it once and will never go again. Rapiti assigned one of our salesmen Chuck and me to make the trip in February of 1985. We got on in Elizabeth. Chuck was all smiles. I had a low-grade fever. In retrospect I never should have gone. With each hour my temperature rose. Now, I was trapped in a crowded train that was rocking back and forth. I was on the verge of vomiting; not exactly conducive to schmoozing.

Chuck was in heaven. The sexy lobbyist ladies on the prowl were checking out everyone so Chuck was sure to score. Somewhere between Philadelphia and Baltimore I lost track of him. The train was about twenty cars long and I was getting sicker by the minute, so I wasn't about to walk through all of them trying to find Chuck. When we pulled into Washington I used whatever strength I had left in me to yank my luggage off the floor, sure I'd see Chuck at the check-in desk. He had all the check-in information and as soon as he showed up I could get to our room and lie down.

Minutes passed – and then hours. No sign of Chuck. I had one of those flus where your whole body aches. I was uncomfortable standing up, sitting down. Even breathing hurt. I stood in the lobby of the hotel for four hours on the verge of falling over from the virus. Finally, Chuck swung by. Apparently, he had met up with one of those sexy lobbyists and wasn't thinking so much about me. When we got to our room I gave it to him. He left me stranded for some nookie knowing I was sick and couldn't check in without him. We didn't speak for the rest of the trip.

The next day the train sped toward Elizabeth with the same cast of characters who were now suffering from hangovers, fat stomachs and whatever else. It was snowing hard but the capper came when Chuck and I silently got off the train in Elizabeth and walked separately to the parking lot across from the station.

As Chuck hopped into his car and drove away, I, my fever now about 104, reached into my pocket only to find I had locked my keys in the car.

●●●

One day, I came up with an idea that seemed so logical, I couldn't figure out why no one at the station hadn't thought of it before. Why not connect with a popular local TV weather guy and have him do some weather for us in the morning? The popular weather guy would make some extra cash. His TV station would get some free publicity and best of all, we would get some prestige in the market by having a big time weather personality heard on our station.

For me, there was only one person who could fit the bill. Lloyd Lindsay Young.

Lloyd is an anomaly, a relic of local TV news that sadly no longer exists. Nowadays news personalities are cast. The agent, station consultant and news director sit down. The consultant who knows everything about anything even though he or she has never worked a day in local TV news will say, "Okay we have the young African American, the cute Asian American and the blonde. We need the handsome soap opera type weather guy."

It's true. I once had a talent agent say to me that he'd love to take me on as a client, but first he had to "move some redheads." Apparently, he was top heavy with redheads and couldn't get them placed at various TV stations around the country. I fit into the 'ethnic looking Northeast market anchor category'. In other words – big cities, with lots of Italian-Americans.

Lloyd is a goofball and deliberately so. I love the guy but upon first meeting or seeing him you would swear he had some kind of a developmental problem. He's odd looking and his weather presentation is off the wall. He's famous for highlighting a town in his weathercast and screaming its name with a giant "Hello!"

As in: "HELLLLLLLOOOOOOOOOO HOBOKEN!"

His arms flail during his weather forecast. His fingers point in different directions. His delivery is disjointed and checkered with silly puns. While explaining how a front is moving in or out, he'll stop and scream, "IT'S SCIENCE!" There's a very subdued version of him doing the weather at WWOR-TV in New York currently on YouTube. It's the Lloyd after the consultants came in and told him to tone it down. Makes sense right? The one thing that made Lloyd stand out for viewers is the thing the consultants told him not to do.

Lloyd's back story is a thing of legend. He worked every shit hole station throughout the west and southwest. He absolutely loves weather, but doesn't possess the polish that usually comes with working in a major market nor the soap opera star good looks. As a result he never got a chance to work in a major city. One day after twenty years of working on-air he gave up. He decided he'd never work in a major market so he put down roots wherever he could to do what he loved to do for as long as he wanted too.

He told me he was absolutely resigned to the fact that he would end his career in some tiny market doing weather for the local yokels. Then lightning struck (no pun intended).

It was a night just like any other night. He was doing his regular evening weather forecast on some small station in Ogden, Utah, at that time an up-and-coming ski area for California's rich and famous. Then, the phone rang. It was a TV news director out of San Francisco who loved his act and wanted Lloyd to do weekends at KIFI-TV. Lloyd, figuring he was being played, hung up.

The guy called again. Lloyd laughed him off and hung up again. The third time he didn't. The big time news director was on a skiing vacation with his wife and family and caught his weather forecast. Next thing you knew, Lloyd was doing weekend weather forecasts at KIFI in San Francisco and human interest pieces three days a week. He was a bona fide hit in the City by the Bay.

Soon after, the call came from the Big Apple. The brother of Tom Leone, the news director at WWOR-TV in New York City, lived in the bay area. He heard his brother was looking for a new weather guy and said he had to check out this guy Lloyd. Lloyd was hired and spent a dozen years beguiling viewers in and around New York. I spotted him early on and thought his also doing weather at WJDM in Elizabeth, New Jersey might be a good idea.

After a brief conversation with him Rapiti took over. He offered Lloyd a leased car from a local dealership and a small monthly stipend of about a hundred dollars. Lloyd was on board.

Every morning we'd record his weather forecast and play it on the morning show. Lloyd was famous for giving a wacky mic test. I'd ask him to talk so we could set the levels before we recorded – only to have him blow out the mic as soon as he started recording.

"Ready Lloyd? Give me a test," I'd say.

"This is double L Lloyd Lindsay Young… test, test, test," he'd respond.

"Okay Lloyd, go ahead."

"HEEEELLLLLLLLLLOOOOOOOOO LINDEN!"

Lloyd was dynamite showman. A meteorologist? Not so good. Often, his forecasts were way off. And since he recorded them early in the morning and then went on his way, I usually took the hit.

One day in the newsroom after a freak snowstorm blanketed the New York metropolitan area, the phone rang.

"WJDM news. Can I help you?"

"Yes you can," the angry voice said, "TELL LLOYD I JUST SHOVELED FOUR AND A HALF INCHES OF PARTLY CLOUDY OUT OF MY DRIVEWAY!!"

SLAM!

Always connecting the dots, Rapiti decided to maximize Lloyd's celebrity. That led all of us at WJDM to come into contact with another one of those radio station-connected characters that stay with you the rest of your life.

"Caz" – we never found out his last name – owned a bar and grill not too far from the station called "Stan and Ollie's." The bar was named in honor of the famous comedy duo. At either side of the front door stood statues of Stan Laurel and Oliver Hardy. Inside there was a huge rectangular bar, dozens of tables and a small stage near the back wall.

Caz had been around the block a few times. He was round and messy and told it like it was. He always treated us to lunch, so naturally, Jim and I loved him. We'd pop into the restaurant after the show and Caz would set us up. A giant burger, a couple of vodka and tonics and some unhealthy French fries later, and we were good. I'd drive home to Staten Island from Stan and Ollie's eyes half open, loaded up with carbs, and exhausted from being up since four A.M., then I'd nap the rest of the afternoon.

Jim lived a mile away from Stan and Ollie's, so he was often snoring within ten minutes of leaving the restaurant.

Rapiti figured one way to get some free publicity was to have Lloyd do the weather forecast for Channel 9 with Jim and me live from Stan and Ollie's. We'd be seen by our listeners and other New York radio bigwigs during Channel 9's noon newscast, Stan and Ollie's Restaurant would get a plug, and Lloyd would be forever be connected to WJDM. It was a win-win-win.

As with everything else, Rapiti approached the task as if he were planning the invasion of Normandy. It wasn't enough that Jim and I would be on TV with Lloyd – we had to look great. He worked out a trade with a tuxedo rental place. We were fitted for tuxes, drilled about what was required of us that day, and sat through several meetings with Quinn's blinding illuminated board going over it again and again.

Lloyd would do his noon weather forecast from the small stage at Stan and Ollie's. Jim and I would be by his side in our tuxedoes, say a few words about the station and plug Lloyd all in front of an audience of clients numbering about fifty and thousands of viewers throughout the tri-state area. Jim and I were very excited.

When the day came and the light went on Lloyd went right into his shtick. A big HEELLLLOOOOOOOOOO to WJDM, and short chat with Jim and me and then his weather forecast. It was pretty heady stuff and if you count my appearance on WNBC during my high school strike, it was the first time I was on New York television in more than a decade.

●●●

During this time, my mother kept abreast of my progress at WJDM. She saw the appearance on Channel 9 with Lloyd and was proud of course but was hoping to see and hear more of her son. I worked at a station too far away for her to hear me, but you'd never know it by the way she spoke.

By this time, my Mom had remarried and owned a small Italian restaurant in Queens with my stepfather. Everyone that came in got an earful. Her son was working at a big station in Jersey. He was the news director with a big staff of reporters. When I came to the restaurant she'd embarrass me.

"Here's my son. He's a newsman. A news *director* at a big station in New Jersey… "

One day it backfired. I was off duty one summer weekday walking around in my shorts and a polo shirt and stopped in to see my Mom at the restaurant. She went into her usually spiel. This time though she wasn't very specific.

She kissed me and then told a gentleman and his date at the table, "This is my son. He's delivers the news."

The guy took one look at me, my shorts and shirt, figured I slung newspapers off the back of a truck and without missing a beat said, "Yeah, what route?"

She was always pushing me to take the next step. Being on the radio in New Jersey was fine, but she wanted her friends to hear me. One day, she pulled me aside to sort of get an idea of how I was doing. Was I networking? How was I networking? Who was I talking too? Could she help? How about the direct route?

I said, "What do you mean the direct route?"

"Show them you have some moxie. Take a chance."

"What do you mean?" I said.

"Well, she said, "You interned at WNBC. Why don't you just get on the phone and call Mr. Amos."

"Who?"

"You know, "Amos in the Morning.""

Apparently, she got her decades wrong. I had to explain to her that Amos and Andy were big in radio in the 40's, and long dead. She meant Imus – _Imus_ in the Morning.

My mom knew all about networking and getting into places simply by virtue of her will.

I was in a local play with her many years earlier and marveled at her poise. I learned a lot from that play and from my mom. No matter how nervous you might be – don't show it. Often, even now, when I am called upon to speak before a group of people, I remember how she was able to remain perfectly calm. To be able to speak or perform before so many people without a worry is a gift.

The restaurant that my Mom and stepfather owned was also a great place to show off. Before I got married, I would take my new girlfriends out to dinner to my Mom's restaurant and give my Mom a chance to be an actress again.

The girls had no idea my Mom owned the place, or even who she was. But, the act was always the same. I'd arrive and she'd hurry to the door.

"Oh, Mr. Cipolla – so great to see you again. Your usual table?"

"Yes." I'd say, pretending to be annoyed at the attention she was showering upon me. Didn't she know the last thing that someone of my celebrity wanted was to have attention drawn to him?

"Right this way," she'd say.

"Thank you."

"Are you having your usual?"

"Yes, the ginger ale with a splash of water."

Then I'd pause and add, "And Mary: this time, just a splash, okay?"

By this time, my date was intrigued. How did she know me? I must be very important; they are fawning all over us. This went on throughout the dinner. Even the busboys and waiters played along. By the time, dinner was over you would have thought I was the mayor of New York. The best was saved for last. When I asked for the check my Mom would hustle over and say, "Please no – we couldn't possible charge you. It's our pleasure to serve you and your beautiful date."

At this time my date was so impressed.

When they found out it was my Mom they loved her even more. She was friendly and obviously a jokester like her son.

Her talk about being more aggressive in my career gave me an idea. I had been working in New Jersey for several years. I knew the issues and the players. Maybe I could make some extra cash "stringing." In radio a "stringer" is the reporter who contributes stories to a bigger station in areas that the station has neither the time nor manpower to cover.

I had heard from my contacts that one of the biggest radio stations in the country, New York City's all news 1010 WINS – might be looking for someone to help cover a New Jersey story now and again. I put together a demo reel of my stuff and then, during one of my usual trips to Manhattan with Jim, stopped by the see the WNBC news director at the time, Meredith Hollaus. The same Meredith Hollaus, whose bed I had slept in – alone – as an intern.

I wanted to ask her if she wouldn't mind me using her as a reference, or even calling over to 1010 WINS to put in the good word for me. And then she just blurted it out.

"Why not string for us?"

I was momentarily stunned by the question. Why hadn't I come to her in the first place to ask if WNBC needed a stringer? Nonetheless, if I heard correctly – and I think I did – she was offering me an opportunity to be a stringer for WNBC. For all intents and purposes, a freelance job as a reporter for WNBC.

I grinned. Of course I said yes. No one worked harder for WNBC and Meredith for the next couple of years. Every day after my show, I would call up with a couple of story ideas. My friend and one of the great radio anchors, Judy D'Angelis, would pick one. I would put together a thirty-five second report for WNBC and feed it to her over the phone.

Later in the day, I would hear myself on the great WNBC-AM! I would pop up in newscasts around the clock. I'd be driving home from my shift and she'd throw to me. I'd crank up the volume and hope the person in the next car would somehow make the connection that the voice on the radio was mine. One day I stopped at a hot dog stand on the way home and the guy had WNBC on. Sure enough, as he was slathering my frank with mustard and sauerkraut, I came on.

I couldn't resist. I looked at the guy and said, "That's me." He looked up with a half smile and then returned to slathering on the mustard.

The best was waking up one day at four-thirty to my clock radio to hear myself say, "In New Jersey I'm Frank Cipolla, WNBC News." That morning, Frank woke up Frank. I received ten dollars for every story I fed. Not a lot of money, granted, but when you do five to seven reports a week it adds up, especially based on what I was making at WJDM. The taste of the big city made me yearn for the big time even more. I wanted to be on the air full time in NYC and by stringing I was getting close. I resolved to make sure I worked as hard as I could and stood out until the call came.

●●●

In July of 1986, New York City was abuzz with activity. I mean, more than usual. The world was coming to the Big Apple to celebrate the 100th anniversary of the Statue of Liberty. In the harbor there was an armada of ships from every nation. July 4, 1986 would be jam-packed with activities. The president would speak; there would be fireworks and the harbor loaded with ships.

I was interested but when you've live in New York for a long time one exciting event seems really no more special than any other. In New York they come with regularity. The highlight of the year for medium sized cities like Louisville and Cincinnati is just another day in the Big Apple.

Jim and I had just come back from one of our visits to New York City. We had done our usual rounds checking in with news directors and agents and headed home. When we arrived in Elizabeth, Jim and I said goodbye and he hopped into his car. I went back into the station to get my briefcase and found a note from WNBC that they were looking for me. It seemed kind of odd since I had already fed them a story for the day and thought I was done, but it was not unheard of for WNBC to call me later in the day if there was a breaking news story they needed covered. At that moment, aside from the disc jockey on the air, I was the only person in the station. Everyone else was either on vacation or gone for the day. For a radio station it seemed oddly quiet.

While the Big Apple was preparing for this once of a lifetime event WNBC had a problem. The anchor person who was supposed to do the weekend newscasts the Fourth of July weekend had to take off. Any other employee who could fill in for her was on vacation or had enough seniority to say no. The only thing that seemed out of place was that the message was from the news director, Doug O'Brien. It was unusual for him to call. But again, I thought it no big deal.

He told me what the problem was and asked whether I could anchor on WNBC the Fourth of July weekend. Again, I was stunned for a moment. It was the kind of call you wait for, the one I had imagined again and again and again in my head. The call that comes down to the minor leagues that says, "We're ready to give you a shot." After I said, "Sure," I got some details, thanked him, and hung up.

I sat at my desk for a minute. I was thrilled of course, but nervous, as well. Years of preparation and hard work had led me to exactly where

I always thought I would be. On my favorite station, anchoring the news. Was I up to the task? The doubt occupied only a small portion of my brain. In my mind I was *more* than ready.

I'd like to think it was pure talent that got me my chance. Maybe it was the "universe" working in my favor. Maybe Mom – who had passed away four months before – had negotiated a deal with the "Big Guy." Maybe, it was just luck. I don't know. They say, "Luck is the residue of design." This business is odd. Some people are on the air and they shouldn't be – others, infinitely more talented, are not and you're left scratching your head. It reminded me of those afternoons with Jim sitting at the bar at Stan and Ollie's and knocking back a drink or two after a morning shift. Occasionally, Caz would sidle up to us and order one for himself. He had his own mug full of problems. Purchasing enough food, paying the bills, dealing with incompetent employees and rowdy customers. That's when this man of very few words would lay on us the only words of wisdom he could muster, words that applied to his situation and ours. He'd take a swig, glance and Jim and me and say, "What a fuckin' business."

Chapter 9
BECAUSE I'M SOUPY...

On July 4, 1986, I plugged my $6.95 Radio Shack earpiece into the console at WNBC. It was the same earpiece I had jammed into the console at WJDM in Elizabeth the day before. WJDM'S signal reached about fifteen miles in every direction. Later today my voice was going to be sailing along the eastern seaboard from Maine to Cape Canaveral.

The radio business began with WNBC. Just going through security to get to the elevator bank was a charge for me. As people waited on line for the NBC tour I whizzed by. It was time for me to step up to the plate.

As the long Independence Day holiday weekend glided past my window, I sat inside the local radio newsroom on the second floor of 30 Rockefeller Plaza with a smile that extended from the Hudson River to the East River.

WNBC was an exciting place. During the week it was home to morning show icon Don Imus. He was followed by one of my childhood TV idols, Soupy Sales, he of the famous "pie in the face" routine. And in the afternoons a cutting edge jock named Howard Stern was tearing the city up and piling up the ratings. Later Joey Reynolds would join the line-up.

I arrived three hours before the first newscast. It was an afternoon of five-minute hourly newscasts but instinctively I knew that I was going to get one chance to get this right. I needed to make an impression, or otherwise, it was back to the minor leagues for God knows how long. There wasn't anyone in the newsroom that weekend so I just sidled up to the one and only manual typewriter and started banging away. Today, I was technically in charge of the same newsroom where years before as a college intern I had nervously learned my craft. I don't remember looking around to take it all in. I should have, since it really was a career-changing event, but right now I was more concerned with getting my one o'clock newscast written.

The news booth was a far cry from the shag rug carpeted studio at WJDM. It was clean and properly soundproofed, and when I sat down for the first newscast I spent a few seconds marveling at the equipment. At one o'clock on the nose the disc jockey hit the sounder and away I went; nervous for sure – but focused. In addition to all the listeners who were enjoying WNBC that holiday weekend and preparing for the all-day Statue of Liberty Bicentennial events, I knew my colleagues from other stations and, more importantly, my family would be listening. I have always found it most hard to do my job knowing loved ones are listening. You know them so well that even if you do badly they are going to say you did well.

I thought I had a good shift: solid writing, hit all the sound on time and was very proud of myself. No matter what happens, I thought, I did my best. Now I had to wait and hear how I did from the powers that be WNBC. I also needed some more luck if I was going to make this permanent.

It didn't take long. Within a week the newswoman who usually did the shift told News Director Doug O'Brien that she was leaving to work in Washington. Unbeknownst to me, O'Brien was actually testing out two people for the job, a very talented newswoman named Debbie Gross and myself. I would do the first weekend, she would do the second and then he'd decide. The following weekend I listened to Debbie fill in. She was good. My ego assured me I was better. What I had going for me was an ongoing relationship with everyone at WNBC and what I thought was a solid fill-in shift on a day when they had really needed help.

I also had Judy D'Angelis. This radio legend in New York, who now works at the most listened to station in the nation 1010 WINS, was pulling for me. She worked the back channels and talked me up. The call came a few days later.

"Can you do weekends on a steady basis here?" said Doug O'Brien.

"You bet," I said, stepping on the last few words of his sentence before he even had a chance to spit them out.

I hanged up the phone and leaped in the air.

Debbie Gross would go on to become a great TV and radio newswoman in the city for many years to come working on TV at News 12 New Jersey, on radio at CBS-FM and WCBS-AM and elsewhere. More importantly she's a friend. But in this competition at least, the job was mine.

There are very few times in a person's life that a goal is set and then met exactly as he imagined, whatever that goal might be. I had received the call I had imagined since I started my career. It had happened in seven short years, three years ahead of the schedule I had set for myself. A lot of hard work and the willingness and power of the universe paid off. I would be leaving my friends and going to one of the most popular stations in the history of radio. Jim Bosh, Raptiti, Wayne and everyone else who knew how much I wanted it were as happy as me. The Knights of the News Table would welcome the kid from Queens. I gave my notice at WJDM and stepped up to the majors.

Just after I started at WNBC, a beautiful homeless woman started appearing inside 30 Rockefeller Plaza at the door I used every day to enter and leave the building. She appeared out of nowhere. To my surprise, she was the spitting image – possessing the exact face – of my deceased mother Mary who had passed away just months before.

This stunned me. I'd come in and she'd look me right in the eye as I passed. I'd leave and she'd look me in the eye as I left the building. I didn't know what to do or say. What were the chances that a woman who looked exactly like my mother would be just inside the building at the door I used every day?

I wanted to talk with her, but I was scared. It seemed as though she could look right into my soul.

Thirty Rockefeller Plaza is not only a busy building – it's a tourist attraction. Seldom are the halls and corridors empty. My homeless woman sightings went on for about two weeks. Each time I passed her, she'd stare right at me.

One day while leaving the building, I turned the corner headed for the door and she was the only one there. Odd, I thought, with all the hustle and bustle of the building that she and I would be there by ourselves. She was again staring straight into my eyes.

As I approached the exit – and as if on cue – a Rockefeller Center security guard stepped out of nowhere and said, "Okay Mary, you can't stay here all day. You're going to have to leave."

Just as the guard said the name "Mary", my mother's name, she smiled at me. The look conveyed a sense of immense pride and a 'knowing' that now the two of us understood why she was there. It was as if the entire scene had been staged for me.

After that I never saw her again.

●●●

In radio and TV, you hope to be heard or seen as much as possible. I always preferred the shift that got me the most airtime. Sure, there are investigative reporters out there who work weeks and weeks on breaking the giant story. They come on the air for two or three nights and make a solid impact. I admire them tremendously. They are the unsung heroes of this business. Sadly, as stations cut back, their ilk is becoming scarce.

My weekend shift at WNBC was Saturday and Sunday from eleven in the morning until seven in the evening. I made more in two days then I made in five working at WJDM. I worked those two days and used the rest of the week to take care of other business. But, I knew that I needed to be heard more. During the week I took care of errands, checked in with the station and kept busy.

In June of 1988, the news writers union struck. The writers' strike meant everyone – including management – had to do more with less.

That's when WNBC News Director Doug O'Brien called me in.

"We're going to change some things. We need you to work Monday through Friday."

I was being bumped up again. Working during the week meant I would be heard by a lot more people and would be working with the bigger names at the station. Imus, Soupy Sales, and Howard Stern. I was assigned to do the news on the Soupy Sales Show.

Soupy! The funny, irreverent kiddie show host I worshipped as a boy. I couldn't wait. Everyday Charles McCord, wrapping up his shift on the Imus program, would hand me whatever he was working on and there I sat, suit and tie and all business.

Guests who appeared on the Imus and Soupy shows often passed the main studio door and wandered into the newsroom. I'd look up to see Stevie Wonder, Senator Barry Goldwater, Bill Maher, Frankie Avalon and Annette Funicello, sportscaster Bob Costas and so many more.

Soupy had long ago established himself as a pioneer of local TV. Imus's status as the top disc jockey in America was undisputed, and Howard Stern justifiably believed himself to be the heir apparent to Imus and the voice of his generation. All three had a legitimate claim to their place in radio and TV history. There was plenty for them to feed on, but like three lions roaming the Serengeti, only one could be the alpha male.

I liked Soupy and he liked me. His studio was an extension of his old TV show; he was surrounded by a wacky cast of characters including his sidekick and friend Ray D'Ariano. Ray was a radio novice, but the two were close friends and when Soupy needed a #2, Ray was it. Ray was there to generally set up Soupy's punch lines and keep Soupy on time. Rodney Belazaire was Soupy's producer, but his real job was stroking Soupy 24/7 despite how funny or unfunny Soupy's puns were. One day, not knowing, I asked Rodney what exactly do you do for Soupy. He said, "I'm his official laugher. I laugh at everything he says."

I wondered what Rodney put on his tax return under "Occupation."

I chuckled now and again just to keep Soupy happy. I wasn't sure, but I suspected he was taking notes on who chuckled the most and the loudest.

Then there was Paul. Paul supplied the music on a small stand-up piano that Soupy had placed in the corner of the studio. Soupy would come in – tell a joke, Rodney and Ray would laugh, Paul would wiggle his fingers over the ivories and all was well. Soupy would sing a song now and again with Paul busting out the tune.

Soupy would also occasionally knock on the console – like someone would knock on the door and say, "Who's at the door?"

That's when a pre-produced bit would begin. The guest at the "door" would be any one of Soupy's old TV show characters like: Onions Oregano, his trusted dog friends, White Fang and Black Tooth, or maybe his buddy "Pookie." It was all very hokey and childish – but, that was Soupy.

Some guests, though, would not come on the show no matter how hard Soupy tried. At the time I was working at WNBC. There was, in the same building, the dean of New York news anchors, Chuck Scarborough. Chuck has been the local news anchor at WNBC for years. He was universally respected and is to this day. Once in a while we'd bump into Chuck in the elevator and the conversation was always the same: Soupy would compliment Chuck and then ask him politely to come down one day and be on his show. Chuck would graciously decline. He was either going to be out of town, busy or just couldn't make it. It became clear to everyone but Soupy that Chuck had heard the show and the wackiness made him uncomfortable. He continued to duck Soupy at every turn.

What made us uncomfortable was Soupy asking Chuck again and again even though Chuck continued to say no. Soupy would not have it. He began to wonder aloud why Chuck was not coming on the show.

We'd giggle while Soupy ranted in his raspy North Carolina drawl. "I don't know why Chuck won't come on the *shooooow*. He's in the same building… ". Bill Grundfest, one of the weekend jocks, was filling in for Soupy one week and lo and behold, as we got into the elevator there was Chuck. Bill, not really knowing the history of Soupy's attempts to get Chuck on his show, made small talk with New York's most popular local news anchor finally blurted out, "So Chuck maybe you can come on the show one day. How about tomorrow?"

Chuck without missing a beat said, "Okay."

I cringed, because I knew that there would be hell to pay once Soupy returned from vacation. The second Soupy found out that this fill-in weekend jock had been able to nail the one guest that had eluded Soupy for months it would be all over for Bill.

When he did return we tried to keep the secret but to no avail. Soupy found out and promptly iced Bill out.

On Soupy's show everyone except Soupy played second fiddle. I've never been able to adequately play the role of second fiddle. I mean, I can joke and fully understanding that the jock is the star, but I need to know that I am at least equal in the eyes of those around me. For Soupy there was no equal. He – was – *Soupy*! All the energy of your day had to be directed toward making him look good.

One day early on, he told all of us that he would be appearing on a local cable show hosted by comedian Robert Klein. He implored us to watch indicating that there might be a pop quiz the following day on what happened.

Wanting to ingratiate myself with the Soupman, I dutifully watched. Soupy appeared on the show second. Before he came on, Robert Klein brought out a couple of hand puppets. He started interacting with the puppets and, being a sucker for that kind of stuff, I found it hilarious. It was top-notch improvisation by a very funny comedian. Soupy was next and he was mildly amusing. When the show ended I was still chuckling over the puppet segment and had committed to memory everything that Soupy had done and said.

Fast forward to the next day: I finish the ten A.M. news throw it to a commercial. It's test time.

"So, who saw the show last night?", Soupy says.

All of us joined in singing Soupy's praises. He looked great. Had lots of terrific punch lines. Wonderful stuff.

I kept on talking when I should have stopped.

"You know Soupy, you were really, really good, but did you happen to see those puppets before you came on? That bit was funny, too… really funny."

Rodney, Paul and the other guys in the studio winced. I could see the gathering storm. Soupy squinted his eyes and look across the console at me.

"Puppets?! Puppets?!" he screeched, "I was *much* funnier than the puppets."

It reminded me now of that now-classic scene in the movie *Goodfellas* when the Joe Pesci character quizzes Henry Hill. You know the scene: "Waddaya mean I'm funny… How the fuck am I funny? Funny like a clown? I amuse you?"

At first I thought Soupy was kidding, but then quickly understood my transgression and began to furiously backpedal.

"Well, of course you were hilarious Soup… I just meant the puppets were funny too."

Soupy looked at the others in the room. "He thinks the puppets were funnier than me. The puppets! I'm Soupy!! I'm funnier than the puppets. You know what?" He glared at me, "You're an asshole."

I was shocked. This man of the pie-in-face, funny man Soupy Sales, the guy I had watched as a kid in my pajamas while sucking on a Popsicle, had just called me an asshole. I tried to process it all.

After that incident things weren't quite the same.

Meanwhile, that same monstrous ego was also starting to wear on the other jocks. The difference was they had the clout to push back. And they did. As Soupy began to suck all the air out of the room, people like Imus and Stern began to work to make sure his oxygen supply was cut off.

Imus was first. The first newscast of the Soupy Sales show came at the end of the Imus show and the start of Soupy's. My five-minute newscast gave the crews of both shows a chance to clear out and set up. One day, I popped in at the end of the Imus show and at the sounder began reading the news. As I read about President Reagan and other world and national news, the Imus crew quickly made way for Soupy. Imus often ate breakfast at his console. In between playing tunes and running bits, he'd chomp away on some cereal. His favorite was corn flakes. This day, in his haste to get out of the studio, Imus and his team missed one. *One* milk stained corn flake. It had slid off the side of the bowl onto the console and sat there like a lonely sentinel just waiting to be brushed away.

With everyone cleared out and me chattering away about some shooting in the Bronx, Soupy breezed in. There just below his elbow was the cornflake. A culinary insult if ever there was one. How could someone, anyone, leave a part of his breakfast at the station where Soupy would perform. This was Soupy!

As I continued, I could see out of the corner of my eye that Soupy was agitated, angry at Imus for this clear insult. He had left a dirty table for Soupy to work. As far as Soupy was concerned, this was an outrage!

One of Soupy's underlings quickly wiped the flake off and tried to make light of it but the fuse was lit. Soupy would spend the next hour railing about Imus during the commercials.

"Who the hell does he think he is? How can someone be so careless?" And my favorite, the phrase I would hear again and again in the years I spent with Soupy.

"Doesn't he know who I am? I'm *Soupy*!"

I tried to stay out of it but Soupy rallied the troops. "Am I right? Who doesn't clean up after himself? For crying out loud, I'm *Soupy*!"

Word about Soupy's temper tantrum got back to Imus. He wasn't pleased and he surely wasn't going to take any crap from some ancient kiddie show host. The next day I returned to the studio. The ten A.M. sounder played and I began my newscast.

"This is WNBC News, I'm Frank Cipolla, A house fire in Brooklyn…" Out of the corner of my eye, I could see the Imus crew gathering up their stuff. But this time, something was out of place. First of all, Imus was still in the studio. By the time I came in he was usually gone. Also, out of place, was a box. A really big box!

As I hit the sound bites, I glanced over the console at this box trying to process what exactly was inside. It looked like a cereal box but it was huge, one of those industrial sized, big box store cereal boxes with enough inside to feed a family of eight for a year. I didn't know where this was going but it couldn't be good.

I continued my cast "The latest economic numbers show the housing market… "

Just before the last of the Imus crew left some unspoken signal went out. A nod, some kind of move that I caught as I picked up my eyes from my copy. At that point, Imus ripped the top off of this giant cereal box full of corn flakes and waved it around the studio. In the middle of a story about the capture of some fugitive, the corn flakes began raining down. It was a corn flake squall with flakes going every which direction and landing everywhere. Each one that headed in my direction somehow stuck to my carefully coiffed, sprayed down hair.

Then Imus walked out flinging the box on the floor as he went.

I wrapped up my newscast and sat there for a moment taking this all in. I knew my next move was to get the hell out of the studio before Soupy came in. I didn't make it.

"What the hell… this is unacceptable," Soupy said when he came in. "I'm gonna kill him. Who does he think he is… doesn't he realize that I'm *Soupy*!"

Imus's salvo triggered a war on several fronts. I heard buzz in the building that Imus, Soupy and Stern had each at some time insulted the other two, sometimes deliberately, other times by not properly "kissing the ring" of the one believed to be superior. They each had their own claim to stardom – but these three egos would not allow the other to get the upper hand.

Next, it was Stern's turn to take his shot at Soupy. Since he came on *after* Soupy, Stern had plenty of time to execute his plan. The only remnant of Soupy that was left in the studio was his stand-up piano. Stern first began making fun of the piano on the air. Then he would razz Soupy for his 1960's songs like "The Mouse." Then it was on to the sabotage.

Stern would roll up wet napkins and wrap them around the piano hammers. When Paul would come in the next day and start to play it seemed one or two notes were off key. At first he couldn't figure it out, but when he look under the hood he saw the napkins. Soupy steamed. He'd go on the air and make a joke about this or that, and when the mic when off again he'd rail. Ending each sentence with the now familiar punctuation: "I'm *Soupy*!"

I quietly watched and tried to stay out of the way. As the piano continued to fall victim to Stern's vandalism, Soupy complained to the program director. Sizing up this schoolyard brawl right away, he stayed as far away as possible. He would be there to hold their jackets but he was in no way going to get in the middle of this.

Then Stern kicked it up a notch.

I came in to do my newscast one day and I was hit with an electrical charge that seem to shoot out of Soupy's head. Everything seemed in its place except for Paul. He was just sitting in the corner on a piano stool with no piano to play. Soupy was apoplectic.

Soupy's piano was missing! Without the piano, there would be no musical "stingers" when Soupy made one of his corny jokes and no music for Soupy to sing one of his crusty old kiddie tunes. It altered his show.

I was already on Soupy's shit list for telling him the puppets were funny, so aside from a few "that's awful"s, I stayed clear. I would not speculate, take sides and get crushed among the monster Imus, Stern and Soupy egos.

After a long afternoon of Soupy complaining, I stepped out of the studio following a late newscast and headed for the men's room.

The General Electric building takes up an entire Manhattan city block. The hallways run parallel to the street. As I pushed the door to the men's room open, something caught my attention. It seemed tiny, so far away, but at the same time familiar. I poked my head into the men's room, then stopped and poked my head out again.

At the end of the hall, more than a football field away, was Soupy's piano. Someone had pushed it to the other side of the building. It was up against the wall, out of place and kind of sad-looking. I could have gone back into the studio to say something, but I didn't. The very idea that I had seen it could somehow smear me with guilt.

Back in the studio, Soupy ranted and raved, arms flailing. There was a commercial break and he was heading into the men's room just as I was exiting. We passed in the hallway and I smiled, then immediately tried to put some distance between me and the Soupman before he saw what I had seen. I rocketed out of there like the Millennium Falcon in *Star Wars* trying to pull out of the galaxy before the Death Star blew up. It didn't take long: when Soupy saw the speck of a piano in the distance, he started yelling and cursing. He called out to Ray and Rodney, and directed Paul to go get the piano and roll it back into the studio. I ducked into a small, seldom-used studio to wait out the storm.

With Soupy on the run, guessing where the next attack would come from, Stern again turned up the heat. He began talking about the piano-napping on the air. About how Soupy had snapped.

The Cold War suddenly flared up into an all-out offensive. While Soupy battled Stern on the Russian front, he was taking hits launched from the European theater. Imus was getting bolder and bolder in his on- and off-air attacks. This psychological warfare was intended to play with Soupy's head – and it was working.

At one point, if communication between the feuding jocks was necessary, it had to be done through WNBC Program Director Dale Parsons. Soupy would direct his assistant Rodney to tell Dale to tell Imus such and such. It was a long, giant-ego-driven game of Telephone.

Soupy felt compelled to reestablish his celebrity status. That meant making more demands and playing weekend club dates in Atlantic City.

Soupy would return from Atlantic City and prance around the studio all aglow. Just to be nice I'd say, "So Soup, how'd the Atlantic City show go?"

The answer would always be the same: "SRO. SRO." Short for "Standing Room Only." No matter what time of year, no matter what the weather, even if there was a blizzard that weekend, Soupy would tell us it had been "SRO. SRO."

I cornered Soupy's producer Rodney in the hallway one day after a weekend of Soupy's "SRO, SRO" performances. "Hey, Rodney," I said, "it must have been a great show. You were there. Packed house, right? SRO?"

"The place was about half full."

Soupy was bullshitting.

In the fall of 1988, Howard Stern chucked it all to head over to 92.3 K-Rock, an FM station in New York that recognized his full potential and paid him tons of money. It was at K-Rock that Stern really blossomed. Out from under the thumb of the corporate NBC suits he excelled. His departure made way for another talented disc jockey, Joey Reynolds, to move into his slot.

WNBC also was blessed with having a really extraordinary traffic woman. Jane Dornacker, an actress from San Francisco who had appeared in a couple of movies including *The Right Stuff*. She played the stiff Nurse Munch who peers through the window of the pressure chamber to check on the astronauts' progress. In real life she was bubbly and perpetually happy, even after the WNBC traffic helicopter, "The N" Copter, had touched down hard in the Hackensack River soon after taking off in New Jersey. Thankfully, the chopper came down in shallow water and both the pilot and Jane were able to escape before it tipped over. Federal Aviation Administration inspectors moved in and fined WNBC. They said the chopper couldn't fly again until pontoons were attached to its struts. NBC complied and within a few days the chopper was back in the air with Jane in the co-pilot's seat.

I had been in the "N" Copter once about a year before. The whole experience was nerve-wracking. First I drove out to a small airport near East Rutherford, New Jersey. Then I ducked my head to get into the Volkswagen Beetle-sized helicopter with a Plexiglas floor. I stand about 5-foot 7-inches so you can imagine how small it was if I had to duck. The day I showed up, I popped my head into the hangar where I saw a skinny, pimple faced kid about eighteen years old working on one of the backup choppers. He didn't exactly seem qualified to be doing repairs.

The views from the "N" chopper though were fantastic. We flew along the Hudson River and around the World Trade Center.

After the chopper hit the Hackensack River with Jane on board, she appeared on the Soupy show. I heard some trepidation in her voice, maybe the same kinds of concerns I had from my one flight in the "N" Copter.

The next time I saw her was on October 22, 1986. I was in the newsroom getting my stuff together for a cast and she was ready to head out to the airport. I really didn't know her well but I did what I usually do. I said, "Jane – what's going on? Come on, come here and give me a hug."

I said in my best Sammy Davis Jr. voice, now familiar to everyone in the newsroom, "I love ya babe, and you know that." She laughed, we hugged and she headed out to the airport and another jaunt in the "N" chopper.

Later that afternoon – in the middle of her five-thirty report over the west side of Manhattan her voice suddenly tensed up. Then we heard pure raw fear, and finally she screamed, "Hit the water, hit the water!"

Then silence. The afternoon jock Joey Reynolds did what he could to cover.

Jane Dornacker's chopper had tilted and gone down from a height of several hundred feet. In a strange twist of fate the pontoons that had been installed several months before were sheared off by a fence along the west side of Manhattan as the helicopter slammed into the river, capsized and sunk.

The woman I hugged hours before was dead.

Police scuba divers were able to get to the pilot of the chopper but not before he suffered severe brain damage. It was the last time the "N" chopper flew. To add to the tragedy Jane's husband had died of cancer about a year earlier, and her death left their two young children without parents.

●●●

Back in Soupy-World things were getting interesting. Soupy's contract was up for renewal. It seemed clear in Soupy's mind that the only discussion was how much more money he would get paid – and how much longer he would continue to grace the airwaves at WNBC.

When the appropriate time came Soupy sauntered into the program director's office to offer his continued services if the price was right. "Well, Soup," Program Director Dale Parsons said. "We were kind of hoping the ratings would be a little better by now. I mean you've been here almost three years and the ratings are about the same from when you took over. You can stay for sure – but I don't think I can wrangle a raise for you or your team."

Soupy exploded. How dare he and his team not get a raise? How dare he not get a new contract? In Soupy's mind they had all done a super job in putting WNBC back on the map. He also made it clear that if he and his crew did not get a raise and a new deal they would walk. It was the kind of ultimatum the 1960's kiddie show Soupy might have gotten away with. This Soupy and with his mediocre ratings didn't stand a chance.

And this is where it should have ended. But there was one last twist in the Saga of the Soupman. With the decision by Soupy on behalf of his crew – the countdown was on. If WNBC wanted to blink it could. Soupy was insulted and wouldn't compromise.

The folks at WNBC had once last trick up their sleeves.

Dale Parsons met privately with Soupy's friend and sidekick Ray D'Ariano. As the story was told to me, the conversation went something like this: "Soupy's leaving – if you take over the show with the same crew, we'll up your salary to what Soupy is making and sign you to a new three-year deal." D'Ariano thought about it for about minute and then threw Soupy under the bus. Who wouldn't?

The transition had to be done very delicately. First and foremost, Ray and everyone else had to swear not to say anything. Soupy had fulfilled his contract and on the last day the Soupy crew would leave the building. Hug. Wave good-bye and Soupy would get into the cab and promise to stay in touch. The next Monday Ray would be back on the air with the whole crew minus Soupy. It all seemed so easy. Then the shit hit the fan.

Several weeks before Soupy and his team were scheduled to leave he started the show as he always did. A big hello from Soupy, then some piano and a joke from the Milton Berle collection, followed up by some rapid-fire puns. But as the show went on it seemed Soupy had a secret. The first thing that tipped us off is that he started taking lots of phone calls. They were very fatalistic sounding.

"Soupy we love you and what they're doing is wrong."

In the newsroom down the hallway my ears perked up. "Doing? Doing wrong? What the hell are they talking about?"

Next caller: "Soupy respect is something you've earn and deserve. After all, you're Soupy."

At that moment, I jingled up Oliver Tyler, the chief engineer at WNBC and whispered into phone, "You rolling on this?" He was.

The buzz around the station started to build: curious looks in the hallway, executives huddled and whispering. What was Soupy up to? And in the back office there seem to be some kind of a mobilization going on among the executives. Calls were being made. Back in the studio the calls kept coming in.

"Soupy – I love you. It's a shame that in this day and age there aren't enough people who will stick to their convictions. I hope to see you real soon."

The second hour of the show Soupy's on-air persona turned from his usually 'happy go lucky' to dark. It was as if the anger inside of him was starting to build.

Another caller: "Soupy, when will we hear or see you again?"

"I don't know. I just want to leave here and not come back," Soupy said.

The hastily organized meetings in the Program Director's office now had an even more intense urgency. Everyone sensed this could get ugly. I remained in the newsroom, eyes on my news copy, ears on the small on-air monitor at my desk.

At about eleven forty-five, Soupy started to hijack the show. The small brush fire became a raging inferno. He took no more calls and played no more songs. He began to rant. "It's a shame that after all these years I am treated like this. Stabbed in the back by those around me."

Outside the studio a commando team was being organized. They would have to storm the studio and take control before Soupy snapped. Soupy had found out that his friend Ray D'Ariano would be taking over and when Soupy went to a commercial about ten minutes to noon Parsons entered and said, "You have to go Soupy, NOW!"

I tried to keep my head down but as I headed to the studio for my noon newscast Soupy and Ray starting pushing each other and swinging out in the hallway. No pies this time for the Soup-man, just fists back and forth before one of the producers jumped in to break it up. I stood there with my mouth open. For Soupy it was over. My childhood TV hero would never return to radio again.

Oh – and one footnote. Ray stayed on the air in Soupy's slot for about a year before he was canned. And Imus? He had a field day, bashing Soupy unmercifully for weeks after. I even joined in. While filling in for Charles McCord now and again I would share some banter then pause and knock on the desk waiting for someone to inevitably say, "Who's at the door?".

Chapter 10
WNNNNNNNNNNNNNNNNBC

With Soupy gone and Stern having left before him, WNBC took on the aura of a lumbering giant on its last legs. The fact that Soupy had even been on the station was an indication of the listeners WNBC was attracting – and in this business if it's an older listener or viewer, advertisers aren't very interested.

Stern sensed that and bailed out, although he may have been pushed. The story went that he had been hustled out of the door after he had pissed off the wife of the NBC chairman with some snide remark on the air about her and her husband. She pressured the exec and he pulled the plug on Stern.

Meanwhile other shows were being cut. There were more commercial-free hours. Old familiar faces suddenly were gone with new jocks popping up, talented guys like Gary Bridges and the great Dan Taylor.

I was enjoying what I was doing and still thrilled to be at WNBC, but I knew the end was near. I asked to see News Director Doug O'Brien to find out what was happening.

As I walked into his office the door closed behind me. The click of the door is the most feared sound there is in radio. It's usually followed by the infamous, "We're going in another direction," or "we really hate to have to let you go; you're truly one of the most valuable people at the station" speeches.

My friend Dave Barker, whom I worked with in TV, got that speech once. His comeback was classic. "If I'm so damn valuable why are you getting rid of me?"

Of course there's never an answer to that. The suits already know the reason for your departure. They've been told to cut back on the budget, get younger sounding voices or faces, or dump you because you make too much money.

Luckily for me, this time it was not that kind of speech. O'Brien did say however that the WNBC frequency was being sold because NBC was getting out of the radio business.

With the end near, I reverted to my old cut-up self. My Sammy Davis Jr. impression was a big hit, as well as another I cooked up of New York Mayor Ed Koch. It was flawless. Alan Colmes, who had taken over for Ray D'Ariano, would call me into the studio between casts to do my impression of Sammy.

One day I was called in and came face to face with Alan's guest that day singer Mel Torme. The "Velvet Fog" had actually known Sammy. He was a big fan of the Candy Man.

I went all out. Put on the sunglasses, grabbed a cigarette and a nearby glass of water and said in my best Sammy impression, "You know Mel, I love you babe, and you know that… Aha… Aha… Aha…"

I looked at Mel to receive my obligatory guffaw. There was nothing. No facial expression whatsoever. I nodded to Alan and slunk out of the studio. I never figured he'd be offended.

It's funny because another time Alan called me in to whip up my Sammy for Monty Python member Michael Palin. He cracked up. Here's a guy who's around funny dudes 24/7 and I made him laugh. Go figure.

Some Wall Street honcho called me one day with a proposition after hearing my Ed Koch impression. "Hey, one of our guys is retiring and we'd love you to do a taped farewell from the Mayor as a tribute." Two days later he was in the lobby.

"Okay here's the script," he said.

It was all of six sentences. I read it in two takes and the engineer gave him the cassette.

"What do I owe ya?"

I sized him up. Checked out his suit and shoes and said, "You know give me a couple of hundred and we'll call it even."

"Ahhhhh," he said, " I can do better than that" With that he peeled off five one hundred dollar bills and gave me a nod of thanks, a handshake and walked out the door.

I should have gone into the financial world.

Alan Colmes was super to work with and I was thrilled to be able to connect with him. He would go on to fame and fortune as one half of Fox News' *Hannity and Colmes*. For now he was this irreverent disc jockey doing all sorts of bizarre things on the air.

His on-air personality attracted a quirky kind of guest, the creepy crawly of New York's underbelly. Elmo was one of them. He'd call up every day – sometimes twice a day – and start all his questions by saying Alan's name.

"Alllllllllaaaaannnnnnnnn."

It sounded like a cross between the Rain Man and a whiny witch.

Alan would say, "You're on the air…"

There would be a long pause and then, "Alllllllaaaaaaaaaaaaannnnnn."

To this day whenever I speak with Alan the first thing I say is "Alllllllllllllaaaaaaaaaaaannnnn."

Unlike Soupy, Alan actively invited me to be part of the show. He'd have me hang around after each newscast and join in on the fun. We'd have a guy who would call up every week or so. He was the ultimate Eddie Albert fan. Eddie Albert was a talented actor and certainly had a place in the annals of TV comedy as the star of *Green Acres*, but to have an obsessive Eddie Albert fan? Alan and I didn't know what to make of him.

He knew all of Albert's movies. Obscure Eddie Albert trivia. His likes and dislikes. It was spooky. It became so obsessive that Alan reached out to Eddie Albert's people so the fan and actor could talk on the air. The exchange was weird. At the end of the interview even Eddie Albert was creeped out.

As part of Alan's crew I was also invited in the summer of 1987 to play in a charity softball event at the "Hole in the Wall Gang" camp in Westport, Connecticut. The camp was owned and operated by actor Paul Newman and his wife Joanne Woodward. Newman bankrolled the camp for underprivileged kids and later famously donated all the proceeds after taxes from his many food products to support the camp.

After wrapping up the show one August evening Alan and I got into our WNBC softball uniforms and hopped into a waiting limo outside 30 Rock.

The game was terrific. I got to meet singer Meat Loaf and some other celebrities and banged out a single with nobody on. Imus was there. He pitched a few innings before Alan took over. I took in as much as I could.

On the way home we gave Lisa Sliwa a ride. She at the time was the wife of Curtis Sliwa, the man who founded the Guardian Angels, a civilian security force that prowled the streets of New York City protecting the masses. Sliwa now hosts a popular radio show in New York. Lisa works as a TV reporter at the Fox affiliate in NYC.

At one point as we cruised along Connecticut's Merritt Parkway on our way back to the city Lisa stood up, opened the moon roof and screamed out the window. It was the end of quite a day. I had rubbed elbows with celebs, taken my first real limo ride since my prom and was treated like a special guest by everyone. I had to pinch myself.

Back in the studio Alan was still cooking up all sorts of wacky interviews. One day he convinced a few exotic dancers to hang out with him. I came in to find the shades in the studio closed so the tours that regularly came around could not look right into the studio and all of his guests naked. I did the four o'clock news that day on the flagship station of the NBC Radio Network with some sweaty, skanky stripper giving me a lap dance. Try to say, "WNBC News time four-oh-six," with breasts in your face. My cast sounded muffled now and again and for good reason.

The voice of basketball's New York Knicks, Mike Breen, was also part of the fun at the station. At that time he was the host of our evening sports show called the "WNBC Sports Magazine." It was a look at the day in sports and a preview of tomorrow's games. One afternoon while reading my script Breen leaned into the news booth and set it on fire.

It's an old radio prank and if you're not prepared, it can spell disaster. The key is to keep composed and get to the end of your script before it goes up in smoke. I calmly picked up my pace, hit the commercial, shook off the flames, and while transitioning to the weather forecast stamped it all out with my foot. All during this episode Breen was smushing his face again the studio window trying to get me to laugh. No dice. Wayne's impression of Nick years before had given me nerves of steel.

I laughed with Mike when I got out of the studio and immediately began planning my revenge.

NBC at the time was airing a popular TV medical drama called *St. Elsewhere*. One *St. Elsewhere* episode had been promo-ed for weeks. The NBC affiliates along the line were warned because it involved what was for then a racy scene in which one of the lead characters drops his pants and says to a hospital administrator, "You can kiss my ass pal."

I saw an opening.

I made sure to videotape that episode and put the offensive sound bite on tape. I then covertly secured Breen's show sounder ID. It was a singing sounder that went, "MIKE BREEN! 66WNBC."

I was in my car on the way home when Breen – about fifteen minutes into his nightly show – hit his personal show ID sounder. This night, thanks to some nifty editing on my part, his sounder was different. "MIKE BREEN – you can kiss my ass pal – WNBC."

I almost drove off the road.

Sometimes – in addition to my anchoring duties – I was given a special assignment. In the last days of WNBC News Director Doug O'Brien assigned me to cover the trial involving Baby M.

The story involved a fortyish couple, Bob and Elizabeth Stern, who had contracted with a woman, Elizabeth Whitehead, to be their surrogate mother. In 1987, the whole concept of surrogate motherhood was new. The twist in this battle was that after giving birth to the Sterns' baby girl, Baby M, the surrogate mom changed her mind. She wanted the baby. The Sterns, who thought the deal was done, now had to fight for the right to get their infant.

I would travel to the Bergen County Courthouse in Hackensack, New Jersey every day and listen to testimony in the case. Some of it was compelling, lots of it technical and boring.

At the end of the day we'd run outside, set up and wait for the obligatory press conference from both legal teams. Then I'd run back into the courthouse, grab a pay phone and report back to the station. This was before cell phones, so locating and laying claim to a public phone was of the utmost importance. It was the difference between being beaten on the story or being first.

For those of us on the outside looking in the case was pretty clear-cut. The Sterns had a contract. They had paid the surrogate mom. Now she was reneging. They tried to make an accommodation allowing Whitehead to see the child but Whitehead wanted custody. She felt she had carried the baby and it was hers.

It was gut wrenching to watch. Elizabeth Stern was a skinny, frail-looking woman. Every time I saw her I saw the heartache eating away at her. The media coverage, some of it from as far away as Russia, just added to it the circus atmosphere of the trial.

On the other hand Elizabeth Whitehead clearly had a connection to the child which could not be explained away by words on a piece of paper. Day after day we'd watch these two women battle it out. It was like watching two fighters exchange punches in the late rounds.

The judge had ordered the media to stay away from the child and her nanny until his verdict was rendered. He threatened to toss us in jail if we came within twenty-five feet of her. Up until that point none of us had really seen what Baby M looked like. One afternoon I got a tip that Baby M was being watched by a nanny not too far away.

I found the house nearby and stood on the curb concealing my tape recorder. As the infant was taken out of the car in front of the house I stood a good forty feet away and described for my listeners what I was seeing.

"The nanny is now getting out of the car, opening the back door and reaching in to get the infant we have come to know as Baby M. The child's cheeks are red, her eyes half-closed, as she cradled by the nanny from the icy cold January weather. She's bundled in a blue blanket…" and so on.

I was the only radio or TV reporter there. It wasn't earth shattering or game changing but it was good radio, a reporter getting for the first time a glimpse – albeit from far away – of this precious baby whose birth had opened up dozens of nagging questions about surrogacy.

The judge wasn't happy but he let me slide. I had kept a safe distance and as far as he could determine I did not have any impact on what was being argued in the courtroom.

The judge also had other strict rules about how many reporters were to be allowed in the courtroom. If you showed up late, he'd make sure you were kept outside the courtroom until there was a break in the testimony. So when the verdict came down, I was stunned to see hundreds of reporters jammed into a small auditorium instead of in the courtroom where the case had been heard.

I had alerted WNBC that as soon as the verdict came down I would be on the phone reading it for our listeners. The reporters who had parachuted in at the last minute were at a distinct disadvantage. Those who had been there almost every day knew the lay of the land. More importantly we knew where the phones were.

There I sat looking around at the royalty of radio and TV News. I was thrilled that after months of testimony and chatting with the usual cast of characters I was among some big time broadcasters. I had the great thrill of sitting next to NBC Reporter Richard Valeriani. As an Italian-American Valeriani had been an inspiration to me as I was starting out.

Sitting there waiting for the final verdict I again remembered what Dan Rather had written in his great book *The Camera Never Blinks*. It's not news unless it gets on the air. I was determined after months of following this trial to make sure it would get on WNBC first. It was going to be a challenge but I wanted to show my fellow more experienced reporters that I was the one to beat.

I didn't wait for the full verdict. When the initial decision in favor of the Sterns was read I shot out of my chair and galloped down two flights of stairs to a phone bank I had long since staked out. Within seconds other reporters barreled into the phones booths next to me. Doug O'Brien put me right on the air. I read what I knew and hopped upstairs to get the rest.

When the judge was finished and headed off to chambers, the press – about a hundred and fifty of us – were herded into another giant courtroom. We set up, sat down and awaited the arrival of the Sterns.

When they arrived there was an awkward moment of silence. There was no one "handling" the press conference so for a moment or so they looked at us and we looked at them. Finally I yelled out, "So how do you feel?"

Me calling out the question was heard later that night on the NBC Nightly News.

It was the last story I covered for WNBC radio. A new concept in radio was about to be launched and WNBC and its frequency, 660AM – would be sacrificed. The new format was all-sports radio and the new call letters were WFAN. WNBC wanted to get out of the local radio business and sold our frequency. For the first time since the dawn of the medium there would be no WNBC radio.

One by one as our contracts expired we were gently shown the door. For those whose contracts did not expire, a check was cut, and it was over. All that was left for all of us was to gather up our memories and go.

There were some things that I needed to do. I needed proof of my two short years at WNBC. I took the obligatory pictures of the newsroom and had others take photos of me at my desk. When I first started at WNBC I brought along my manual typewriter from WJDM. Man, I loved that thing! Typing news on an old typewriter was a blast. You'd pound down on the keys and get a real feeling that you were making something. Like a craftsman you were creating something for all to see and hear. That didn't last long.

One day Doug came to me and gently tapped me on the shoulder and told me the days of the typewriter were over. My colleagues were complaining that it made too much noise.

It took some time to get my head around a computer. Now of course you can't take five steps without seeing one, or a handheld version of one. I tell people I never saw a computer in college and they look at me like I'm Ben Franklin.

Anyway as the slow fall of WNBC became painfully obvious, I did want to retrieve my old typewriter, which had been put in a small storage closet right across from the main on-air studio.

The storage room was for engineers only. Once in a while when the door was open I would peek in. It was a treasure trove of equipment and WNBC memorabilia. I made a mental note of what was in it should I need something. I had also made friends with the engineers so I could be sure they wouldn't mind if I grabbed a thing or two.

When I next saw the door open I was shocked. Apparently the engineers had begun to walk off with stuff. It was more than half empty. I quietly stepped in to see if my typewriter and a small cassette recorder I had given the engineers to fix had survived. The tape recorder had been given to me by my mom so it had sentimental value. Both the typewriter and the tape recorder had apparently been tossed, the typewriter because it was now ancient and the tape recorder probably because it couldn't be fixed. I suspect that the typewriter is actually on display somewhere at the Smithsonian.

I figured while I was in there I'd grab at least something that said, "I was here." I didn't know when I would have another opportunity. I wanted to make sure years later I could tell my kids that yes indeed, your old man did worked on WNBC radio.

Then I saw it. It was a promotional hardback poster for WNBC. It featured a photo of Imus, Soupy Sales and Joey Reynolds. Above it appeared the words "There's Only One Place for People Like Us." I love it and as I write this it sits above me, framed, on my den wall.

I can't recall the exact time or place when I was told it was over but in December of 1987, an eventful and exciting two years after I arrived at my dream job, my time at WNBC was up.

•••

I followed some of my colleagues over to WFAN, which had purchased the WNBC frequency. WFAN is unique in that it's in a residential neighborhood in Queens at the Kaufman Astoria Studios. Next to this block-long three-story structure were homes fronted by small patches of grass and separated by narrow driveways. Kaufman Astoria Studios was where countless movies from the Thirties and Forties were filmed including several Marx Brothers movies. A block away was a small church, "Our Mary of the Bloody Wounds" or "Our Lady of Perpetual Homework," or something like that.

Kaufman Astoria Studios is home to all sorts of entertainment related businesses including recording studios, movie equipment suppliers, and more. Some of its sound stages were also being used to film TV commercials. The big excitement for me at least was it also home to *Sesame Street* and the then very popular *Cosby Show*.

The studios for WFAN were affectionately called "The Bunker." You'd come in through the main entrance, walk down a small hallway and take an elevator straight down. Then you'd meander through some small hallways peeking into the *Sesame Street* set as you went, walk down another hallway and find WFAN's front door. "The Bunker" was right!

It was small and cramped but also home to budding radio and TV stars and superstars like NFL Broadcaster Ian Eagle and ESPN anchor Steve Levy, who like Ian was just a kid at the time. One of the interns, Eric Spitz, went on to become the station's general manager.

Since the format was all sports, news didn't exactly play a big part. I was first told to keep the newscasts down to thirty seconds. And when that seemed like too much I was told to keep them down to fifteen seconds.

"I'm Frank Cipolla with WFAN news headlines. President Reagan is overseas, the markets are down again today, and it will be high in the eighties today, cooler tonight, same tomorrow. I'm Frank Cipolla, WFAN News."

I'd come in at three in the afternoon, sit in a small room, type a fifteen-second newscast, go on the air and spend the next hour writing another fifteen-second newscast. I was done at about six and left for the day. It was easy but not very rewarding. News people are action junkies, and if there's no action, there's no fun.

I was assigned to do these very compelling newscasts during the Pete Franklin Show. Pete was a character. A hard-edged, old school, in-your-face sports nut. He was about sixty then with his pants up near his belly button and a sports encyclopedia for a noggin. When one of the know-it-all Mets fans would call - Pete would unload on him.

"What the hell you're talking about… that's idiotic. You don't know anything about baseball… hang up, ya scum bag!"

The first time it happened as I prepared to deliver the news in Pete's studio I was stunned. Then I couldn't stop laughing. "Scum bag" became his signature phrase. Sometimes as I wrapped up the news and threw it back to Pete he's still be ranting where he left off.

"I can't believe someone would think… THINK… of trading Richard Todd to the Rams. What a moron."

Sometimes he'd drag me into the rant. "Can you believe that Frank?"

I'd egg him on, "You know what that guy is Pete?"

"He's a scum bag!" he'd yell.

Pete wasn't around long. As I remember it was some kind of a contract dispute. I next did news for Greg Gumbel, brother of Bryant. He was a delight but it was obvious the suits at WFAN weren't in love with him. They had their eyes on a bigger prize.

The shake-up in the line-up first meant the news had to go. The cushiest radio news job I ever had – and the least exciting – was coming to an end. I thought I would be able to find my way into the morning show or scare up a gig in some kind of serious news department but it was not to be.

WFAN signed a big contract with Imus, brought the whole crew over, and let me and some other guys go. For the first time since I began my career I was out of work.

Chapter 11
GOING IN A DIFFERENT DIRECTION

Being a radio or TV broadcaster comes with its own set of hazards. It's not like being an accountant or a lawyer. Over the years I have been asked how I got my cool job. The short answer is I studied hard, worked harder and endured many years of crappy pay.

What looks easy to the viewer or the listener though is actually the culmination of years of hard work. So when someone says, "So you talk for a living," they don't know anything about the behind-the-scenes maneuvering or the years of training and experience that allows a broadcaster *to make it look easy.*

They also don't see the down times. News is entertainment. You're on the top of the world one day and before you know it the phone's not ringing. My friend Dan Taylor – one of the great disc jockeys in New York – once told me from the point of view of those who hire broadcasters a career in radio or TV goes like this:

#1) Who's Frank Cipolla?
#2) Sound like Frank Cipolla
#3) Get me Frank Cipolla
#4) Sound like a young Frank Cipolla
#5) Who's Frank Cipolla?

I spent my first few months of idle time after WNBC doing the best to scare up some work. I had been on WNBC with Imus and Soupy. I thought it wouldn't be too long before I could rustle up a new full time job.

I also threw myself into a minor remodeling of my kitchen at my home in Staten Island where I was now living with my wife. The genes my dad possessed – that inherent ability to fix anything – never found their way to the Frankster. I ripped up some paneling in my kitchen, got out a paintbrush, and when the room was done it looked worse then when I started.

I was able to get some part time work as an overnight editor at Mutual News. I also nabbed a part time job at Shadow Traffic but neither one lasted. A funny thing happens when you're out of work in this business: As in combat, people in your business first feel bad that you took the bullet, then are relieved it wasn't them. Finally – as if to ward off the bad spirits – they avoid you. They stop poking their nose in the door to view the patient for fear they'll catch whatever you've got.

A friend of a friend finally called to say some help was needed at the NBC Radio Network. It wasn't an on-air gig, and it wasn't full time, but after several months of no work I needed something, so I took it.

The NBC Radio Network was a proud collection of some of the finest news anchors, reporters and stations around the country. It wasn't at 30 Rock but instead on the ninth floor of a building across from the Ed Sullivan Theater in Manhattan, where today they videotape the *Late Show with David Letterman.* As a college kid I used to go to that same theater with my friends to watch the taping of *The 20-Thousand Dollar Pyramid* with host Bill Cullen. One time Captain Kirk himself, William Shatner was one of the celebrity guests. Coincidentally, so was Soupy.

While I worked at the NBC Radio Network the theater was being used as a soundstage to videotape the sitcom *Kate and Allie* with Jane Curtin and Susan Saint James.

The NBC Radio Network anchors were known especially as the home of the "thunder voices" of radio. They roamed the halls like the great dinosaurs. Every time they passed I stopped and watched in awe. The biggest lion on the NBC Network Serengeti was Alan Walden. He was a throwback from another age. Just before his afternoon network newscasts he'd walk the newsroom like a captain inspecting a mighty ship just before it whirled into battle.

He walked with a finely crafted cane, puffing away on a pipe, and often seemed agitated about something or other. He stopped for a moment, looked into one of the edit bays and to no one in particular say, "Dammit!" puffed his pipe and walked on.

We never really found out why he was annoyed. Walden was joined by anchors Don Blair, Mike Moss, Gary Nunn and many others who made the NBC Radio Network sound so good.

I was assigned one of the seven-by-six-foot edit bays where sound, interviews and reports from far-flung reporters came in every day. I'd sit in the edit bay watching TV or reading until a disembodied voice blasted through a small intercom speaker jolting me out of my trance. The voice came from the giant assignment desk in the center of the newsroom.

"Jay Barbree from Cape Canaveral on line four. Cut it up please; we need it for the next newscast."

After two months of this I was bored stiff. And for me that is the most dangerous state to be in. It wasn't long before I was flirting with the assorted twentyish blondes, regaling the future news Twinkies with impressions I had whipped up of all the NBC radio anchors. I'd walked to an edit bay next door and in my best Alan Walden voice say, "Dammit" and walk on – leaving my colleague in stitches.

The more I did it, the worse it became for Alan Walden *and* my fellow workers. As Walden took his usual walk stopping to make his now familiar pronouncement the faces of my co-workers would distort as they tried to hold back their laughter. That made Walden angrier at which time his "Dammits" became even more pointed and louder which made them funnier. Which made it harder to hold back the laughter, which made Walden do it more frequently and with more authority, which made it funnier… you get the picture.

I also cooked up an imitation of anchor Don Blair. When I overheard that a call had come in for him, I'd grab the phone before he did and answer for him.

This kind of low-level mischief went pretty much unnoticed – but *not* being noticed is not what I wanted. As I've said before, news is an ego-driven business. So the gears started to turn and I started to get bolder.

The Mayor of New York at the time was Ed Koch. In the summer of 1978 Koch had risen from his congressional district in lower Manhattan and in a loaded field of more recognizable names, he won the mayoral primary and then cruised to an easy mayoral victory in heavily Democratic New York City. Koch is the quintessential New Yorker, accent and all. And my imitation of him was flawless.

One day while sitting in my edit bay watching the Geraldo Rivera talk show with the sound off and trying to guess the topic, I heard the editor yell across the newsroom that he had made a call to the Mayor's office to comment on some racial incident gripping Gotham. I sprung into action. I yanked the sliding door of my edit bay closed and read what the story was all about on my computer. I then waited about ten minutes and called the assignment desk.

"Hello, ahhhhh… this is the Mayor of New York. How am I doing?"

The editor – who wasn't much older than me – bought the impression hook line and sinker. Not once did he stop and think why the mayor would make the call himself. Wouldn't his secretary call and then put him on the line?

"I am ahhhhhhh in between meetings and was told you were looking for me. How can I ahhhhhhhh help you?"

The editor – so excited that the mayor himself had called back – jammed the intercom button on his control panel and told my colleague next door to take the call. I had gotten past the gatekeeper and from here on in it was gravy. My editor friend – a young blonde – picked up the phone in the edit bay next door.

"Mr. Mayor – thank you so much for calling back. We are going to roll tape and talk with you about this terrible incident in Harlem," she said.

I continued, "I… ahhhh… just want to say that I BEE - lieve the City of aaahhhh New York… will survive this latest incident… "

My colleague was thrilled to be speaking with the mayor and pleased that this important interview had been entrusted to her.

She went on, "Mr. Mayor, this shooting is the third one this year. Why have this and the earlier shootings, not been dealt with more aggressively by your administration?"

Now she was challenging me. I mean the mayor. This is where I began to test her.

"This situation *has* been dealt with…by… myself and the … ahhh city of New York … and that question shows you know nothing… it's an idiotic question!!"

At this point my future cable news bimbo seemed a little put off. She was wondering if the mayor of New York just insulted her.

She tried to change gears, "Well, the Reverend Al Sharpton has called your position on this shooting inflammatory. What do you say to that?"

This is where I went for broke.

"Aaahhhhhhh all I can say is that Reverend Sharpton is ahhhhhhh… a jerk!"

There was a long pause. My blonde anchor wannabe was clearly trying to process this. Did the Mayor of New York just call a prominent African American leader a jerk? On tape?!

She came back but it was too late. The pause got to me and I cracked up. Next thing I knew she was in my edit bay screaming at me. I couldn't keep it together and headed to the men's room to try and control a laughing fit.

The blonde took her revenge. Shortly after her interview with the "mayor" my lunch disappeared from the refrigerator in the NBC Network kitchen. No clues, no witnesses.

This epic struggle and her assault on my lunch would not go unpunished. I had started this feud. Now I would kick it up a notch and see how far she was willing to take it. Compared to sitting in a small room for nine hours every day editing tape, this was actually exciting.

Where would I strike next? Where would *she* strike next?

It took a few days but I finally hatched a plan. The doors to the edit bay slid open and closed. I eyeballed one for a long time one day and figured it was time to make my move. I still had some wood left over from my kitchen renovation. I slipped in a tape measure one day and clandestinely measured the exact length and width in the bottom groove of her sliding edit bay door.

That night like an expert carpenter I cut a piece to those exact specifications. I jammed it into my shoulder bag and the next day headed off to work. To pull off the stunt I had in mind it was essential that it be planned to a tee. There were times in the NBC Radio Network newsroom when there were fewer people than usual, right after the top of the hour newscast when folks would head to the rest room, wander away, or take a break. I left right after the six o'clock newscast, which was when most people cleared out.

To get back at my colleague I had to first cut her off from any form of communication with the newsroom. I wandered up to the assignment desk just before the six o'clock network newscast. I said I had to get something but when the editor was busy I turned down the volume button to her room, the one that allowed her to converse with the assignment desk through the intercom. Phase one was complete.

I then waited for the end of the newscast and watched from my edit bay as the shift changed. People left one by one until there were only three or four on the other side of the room, all of them busy settling in or getting set to go. In one fluid motion I yanked the perfectly measured two-by-four out of my shoulder bag, threw the bag over my shoulder, quietly closed her edit bay door while she was inside and not paying attention, laid the wood in the groove of the edit bay door and headed for the elevator.

She was locked in with virtually no one to help. Five minutes later as she was ready to head to the ladies room she realized the door would not open. She tried the intercom but no go. It was too late anyway. By that time my car was aimed toward the FDR Drive and I was headed home. I'm told she ended up banging on the door to get out and when no one heard her had to call the newsroom from her edit bay phone to get someone to remove the wood and slide the door open.

There was a discussion the following day with the news director about what was funny and what wasn't. He eventually stepped in to enforce an uneasy peace. I thought the prank was brilliant and imaginative.

She was pissed!

With no one to play with and the boredom pulling me in like quicksand, I started wandering off during my breaks to examine what else and who else might be on my floor. I found out that some other shows were produced on the other side of the building and utilizing my old "I belong here" bit that Mom taught me – I walked past guards and nodded to various rent-a-cops. That's when I bumped into Steve Allen. THE Steve Allen. Steverino was on the back end of a long career. He had a daily talk show on the NBC Radio Network that was listened to by "ones" of people. He was old, feisty and a consummate professional. The *old* part though killed him. Radio listeners of the Eighties weren't so much interested in Steve Allen anymore. Being a historian of radio though I was thrilled to meet him. Doctor Ruth Westheimer also did her show from that floor.

I wandered into the bathroom one day and the man at the sink seemed familiar. It took about a minute to realize it was Don Pardo, the long time NBC announcer and the voice of *Saturday Night Live*. Pardo was sixty-nine at the time but his voice was as crisp, clean and low. We talked about his voiceover introduction for the local WNBC news station. I even imitated him. He smiled and then went off on a rant about how he had to sue someone who was imitating him. He wiped his hands, bid me adieu and walked out. As he spoke his voice – thanks to the perfect bathroom acoustics – echoed as if he were God.

One time Larry King was being interviewed next door and came to take a look at the network. King was doing his overnight syndicated radio show at the time. He was a big deal even then, but not as big as he would get years later when given his own TV talk show on CNN.

King popped his head into the newsroom and when I saw him I went over to introduce myself. He shook my hand and then began to talk to the guy next to him about how important he was. As a fellow New Yorker I knew his act. I had seen it many times before. A mixture of bravado and insecurity; but you could not take away the fact that he could do a great talk show.

Another of the not-so-famous but beloved broadcasters I encountered was Stan Martyn. Stan did sports on the NBC Radio Network, but his real forte was telling a great radio or TV story. He had hundreds. My favorite involved the time he spent at the ABC Radio Network: In the main radio newsroom there was a giant map of the world, and on the map was every ABC news bureau around the globe.

It's hard to believe now, but back then there were reporters and producers stationed all around the world and not just in the major cities. There were about forty news bureaus. On this giant map the location of each bureau was designated by a specially designed pushpin. When plugged in the electrical current in the map illuminated each pin to show visitors in searing lights that ABC covered the world. It was pretty impressive. It was also very, very bright.

For those radio anchors working in the newsroom the map became more and more annoying. The light off the pushpins would ping pong around the room and the board itself would heat up the immediate area where many worked. Finally – without regular visitors to impress – someone yanked the plug out and it stayed like that for weeks. Radio people are kids in adult bodies who like to play. It wasn't long before a couple of radio pranksters began experimenting with the pushpins, making shapes of animals, playing tic-tac-toe with them and so on.

Fast-forward to a couple of months later. Miss America stops into ABC to be interviewed by Howard Cosell and to meet and greet ABC management including the illustrious network president Roone Arledge.

During their tour of the building – including the radio network newsroom – Roone decided he'd like to get a shot with Miss America and Howard in front of the giant map showing all the ABC news bureaus around the world.

One of the anchors respectfully tried to discourage it saying it might not be the best of times but Roone was adamant and you don't say 'no' to the most influential man in the history of ABC. Then, just before the official cameramen from ABC and Miss America were ready for the shot, Roone says, "Doesn't this map light up?" Somebody mumbles yes and a secretary traveling with the entourage starts looking for the plug behind the map. By then many of the anchors and reporters had melted away. Later they were told the shot was priceless. The lovely Miss America, the great Roone Arledge and broadcasting legend Howard Cosell all standing in front of the giant map illuminated from behind with pushpins spelling out the words FUCK YOU.

•••

On rare occasions – and knowing I had a reporter's background – the network used to send me out on stories. I covered the Fourth of July fireworks in the East River in 1988 and then one night was pressed into duty to cover a midtown Manhattan press conference at the offices of oil giant Exxon.

It was March 1989. The Exxon Valdez, under the command of Captain Joseph Hazelwood, had just crashed and sprung a leak in Alaska's pristine Prince William Sound. Eleven million gallons of crude were leaking into the Sound. The photos of wildlife struggling to rid their feathers, beaks and fur of crude oil were damning and Exxon had to do what it could to stop the bleeding.

I ran with my recorder to the Sixth Avenue building that was the New York home of Exxon. Other reporters were waiting outside and they were angry.

They had covered countless stories of mayhem and murder, but shots of fuzzy little animals dying under a blanket of oil was just too much. I heard the mumbles.

"This is not right – these oil company bastards have control of every goddamn thing and they use their money to get what they want."

"Have you seen the shots of this spill? I wish I could I take the CEO and cut his balls off."

"You'd think they would have made precautions for this. And the captain wasn't even on the bridge at the time!"

It went on for about a half hour. I really had never seen regular reporters – regular New Yorkers – so angry about one particular story.

As we shuffled in place to keep warm, Exxon sent down a young woman to take us upstairs to the executive offices and our press conference with the CEO of Exxon. My colleagues were still angry and now even more annoyed that corporate handlers had left us standing outside in the cold for a half hour.

We traveled up a few floors to a small conference room and when we got out of the elevator we were met by a PR executive who apologized for the wait and said the CEO would be with us as soon as possible. In the meantime we could warm up and have a snack. There were some more grumbles and general displeasure on behalf of my colleagues, but we had no choice.

It was at that moment that a set of double doors swung opened to reveal a huge exquisitely appointed dining room. There was a buffet laid out for us the likes of which I had not seen before or since: Tables of delicious food, carving stations, all sorts of desserts, a full bar, flowers, pleasant, relaxing music and to assist us, four uniformed servers.

The look on the faces of these battle-worn news reporters was priceless. To press people, who grab a bagel when we can, this kind of offering was unheard of. Burly TV photographers put down their equipment and surged forward. The radio reporters followed. It was as though we had found a fountain of water after days in the desert.

There was jostling to get as close as possible to the feast. Grown men grabbing and chewing. Stuffing down our mouths and into our pockets what we could – and as much as we could. Some of my colleagues headed straight to the bar and quickly began knocking back a few.

Meanwhile two of the servers did their part to entice. They were beautiful young ladies dressed in what looked like teddies with cleavage spilling out of their tight tops. For those who were so inclined the food would wait. Those reporters and producers chatted with the young ladies and peeked down their blouses as the girls served exquisite cuts of meat and sashayed about with their trays held high. They'd lean in once in a while like Playboy bunnies and give the middle-aged reporters and cameramen a peep show.

It the perfect combination of seduction and salad. A high-end version of the American male's ultimate dream. Sort of like beautiful blondes serving ice-cold beer while you watch your favorite football game.

The PR assault went on for about an hour. The battlefield preparation now over; the call came for us to head into an adjacent room for the press conference. Some guys grabbed extra sandwiches and furtively stuffed them into their satchels. Others ordered one more drink "for the road" and for those who were living in the world of their youth they tried unsuccessfully one more time to get info on the knockout servers who had teased them with their cleavage.

The once angry mob of self-righteous reporters was now a stuffed, buzzed and titillated rabble of wrinkled clothes and crumb-faced apathy. Don't get me wrong, we were still on the story and eager to get the facts, but what seemed so important an hour or so ago now seem not so vital. The anger had dissipated like the cloud of steam coming off the delectable tray of shrimp scampi we had finished off moments before.

As the CEO droned on about how Exxon was saddened by this mess and that it was Exxon's responsibility to address it as quickly and as environmentally safely as possible, I looked around the room.

I saw my colleagues in all stages of digestion and inebriation. The combination of food, booze, scantily clad servers and a dull CEO had done the trick. One extra large cameraman had actually fallen asleep. Several reporters struggled to keep their eyes open.

The story got out that night as it always does, but the edge had been taken off by some genius of a PR guy who made sure we were fed and liquored up before we were served the final course.

The NBC Radio Network was eventually sold to Emmis Broadcasting. One day one of the key executives came up to check out the operation. Earlier in his tenure he had ordered the anchors to do their newscasts from the newsroom, which seemed strange. Doing *TV* news from the newsroom was all the rage at the time and it made great sense. Viewers got a chance to look behind the curtain. To be "part" of the TV newsroom. But doing a radio newscast from the newsroom? You can't see anything anyway so it just made for a newscast with a lot of extraneous chatter. The new owner – a young turk full of himself and maybe full of some booze as well – rolled in one day just as the newsroom newscast was kicking off and yelled, "Hey I'm fucking here." Some cringed, others laughed while part the word "fucking" made it on the air.

He couldn't fire himself so he covered his mouth when he realized what he'd done and stumbled out. Shortly thereafter we went back to doing the newscasts in our soundproof studios – *where they are supposed to be done!*

While at the NBC Radio Network I also got another jolt of what it's like to be in big time radio. Every old movie set in an office includes at least one scene when the gruff manager calls a subordinate into his office and screams, "You're fired!".

But in the past thirty years, and especially now, employee termination comes wrapped in a brightly colored package with a bow on top. If management is nice about it they'll let you spin your own story about why you're leaving. The "we're going in a different direction" speech is often followed by the press release saying the on-air talent is either leaving to "pursue other interests" or "to spend more time with his/her family."

The other day I saw one of these bullshit press releases concerning a beautiful early forties TV anchor in a medium market who said that "after careful consideration and lots of soul searching"– another term that is often used – "she'd decided to leave to spend more time with her young children." Yeah lady – you're leaving a six-figure job in TV so you can get up every morning, change a diaper and pour bowls of Froot Loops for your kids. Give me a break!

It seems odd that in a business where the truth is most cherished, when the ax falls we just can't tell it like it is. My favorite is what's happening now in the struggling car industry. One press release I recently saw said – *"Congratulations! You're just been selected for the home relocation program."*

Thanks a lot.

If you're lucky you have a long-range, no-cut contract, so when the fresh pimple-faced geek of a news director comes in to "shake things up" and tells you that the station is "going in another direction," you can stay home taking a break now and again from the family to head down to the mailbox and collect your gigantic weekly check for doing nothing. And that happens more often than you think.

One New York local news anchor friend was wooed to the competing station several years ago and given a multi-million dollar three-year contract. No sooner did she warm up her anchor seat than the news director who hired her was blown out the door. Excuse me, "He left to pursue other interests." The new news director canned her soon after.

Anyway, last I heard she's home, except for the times she's shopping or heading to her mailbox, collecting millions.

Another friend of mine hit the jackpot. He was canned from WCBS-TV with a couple of years left on his contract. The station had to pay him more than $700,000. Soon after that he moved over to a new financial station launched by Pax TV. Several months in, Pax pulled the plug, and started paying him for the rest of his multi-year contract. Now he was receiving checks from two contracts! I heard he went to Italy for a year and now is occasionally heard on a local radio station.

The "we're going in a different direction" speech usually ends with a handshake, a frown and silence from management and your colleagues until you finally walk out the door. It many cases it's planned like a mob hit. I've been on the receiving end and close enough a couple of times to get splattered by the blood.

If you're on the bubble the worst thing you can do is plan a vacation. I don't know the exact statistics but I'm sure at least half of these "hits' come on the Friday before your vacation.

One time I was wrapping up a TV morning show and chatting after the cameras went off with my last guest. He was a fascinating man who had taken photos from the tops of every major bridge in and around New York. To my left the weather guy was adjusting his morning weathercasts and updating them for the noon show.

Out of nowhere the news director walks into the studio. He strolls up to me and says, "Could I ask you and your guest to continue your discussion outside the studio?"

My hackles went up. I quickly hustled my guest off the set and took the conversation out to the lobby. He left a few minutes later. I then took my usual walk to the Post Office across the street to mail some letters. When I came out the weather guy was stepping out of his car in front of the post office. I was puzzled.

Before I could say anything he said, "I've been fired."

I glanced over to his car and everything he had accumulated in his four years there was in his back seat. Just like that he was history. That's how it happens. You often don't know when you're going to get "whacked" and when you do it's usually an inside job.

Another time news broke that a popular radio news anchor at WCBS had gone home and committed suicide. All of us in the industry were pretty shaken up.

Well, not all of us.

The phone call to the news director at WCBS-AM the *following day* is stuff of legend.

"Hey, Harvey I just heard. Awful! He was so young. What compels someone to do that? I feel terrible," the caller said.

At this point the news director grunted something as both lamented a life lost.

"I guess you're going to have to shuffle around the schedule until you find a permanent replacement," the caller continued. Then there was a pause. "Can I come to drop off my tape and resume later today?"

Classic.

One storied network radio sports anchor inadvertently did himself in. He was a giant in the business with whom I worked at the NBC Radio Network. This soft-spoken guy was beloved by all. That wonderful sense of giving back shone itself when he brought in a young kid he thought had tremendous promise. He spent years showing the kid the ropes. Confiding in him. Helping him make contacts and network.

That good will was paid back to him when security showed up at his office door one day and told him he had to leave. He thought it was a joke. It wasn't. The news director popped in to confirm the veteran sports anchor's twenty-three-year career at NBC Radio was over. He was to pack up and get out. Humiliated, he put his stuff into some boxes and then was paraded through the newsroom followed by security.

Oh, and the guy who took over for this legend? The same kid he had brought in as an intern. Seems the kid was scheming behind the scenes to dump his mentor. Nice.

Another anchor who had been at the NBC Radio network for about ten years came in one day to tell everyone his wife was going to have their second child. He was very excited. There was lots of back slapping especially from management. In this sometimes jaded business it was a very nice tableau. The anchor, his new baby on the way, smiles all around. They even threw him a big party when the blessed day came. He handed out cigars. Two days later he was fired. The suits figured they'd wait until after the baby was born to show him the door.

My job at the NBC Radio Network was the first I had in which I wasn't regularly on the air. I missed it terribly. I knew I had to move on. But I had no idea where.

I finally got some on-air work at a new and short-lived venture called "News Phone." It was in a small office on the twenty-third floor of a building along Third Avenue. It seems incomprehensible now with the proliferation of smartphones, laptops, netbooks and more but back in the late 1980's News Phone was cutting edge. Here's how it worked:

People who wanted to know what was going on in the world and did not have access to a radio – silly, I know – would call a phone number and get the latest news in thirty seconds from yours truly and other out of work news people. The news would be updated every fifteen minutes. I'd write a thirty-second newscast, go into a small studio, record it on the phone, save it, and then fifteen minutes later do it all over again, adding any additional breaking news. Customers called a 900 number and the owners of the company made money by taking a piece of the $2.95-a-minute charge. The announcers would also tack on a short commercial like – 'This News Phone report brought to you by the Rainbow Room. Where fine dining…etc'.

News Phone was an offshoot of Sports Phone. Right next to us our sports friends were doing the same thing. Doing sports reports and updating game scores every fifteen minutes for the sports junkies and gamblers who needed to know what was going on.

One day after doing my report I walked out of the studio to see all of my colleagues jammed against one of the building windows, pointing and craning their necks. I thought, what happened, an accident? A fire?

On the roof of the smaller building next to us – about fifteen floors up – were a naked man and woman.

The woman was bent over and partially hanging over the side of the building, her breasts pointing straight down at the pavement.

The man was entering her from the back and both were having a ball. Between slow thrusts the man looked up to everyone in our building and waved. The woman glanced up every minute or so and smiled and then went back to enjoying herself. It was raw exhibitionism and something that could only happen in New York. Every guy at the window in our building was with the guy on the roof; we were loving it as much as the woman was.

When they finished up both waved again, took a bow, and skipped across the roof and into the stairwell, their private parts swinging to and fro.

For a bunch of horny young guys this was outstanding! When I came in several days later I turned the corner to start my shift there they were. Binoculars lined up against the windowsill. If it happened again some of my colleagues wanted to make sure they were ready!

As interesting as News Phone was I had to get a full time job. Things were happening at home. My wife was pregnant and as she expanded it was a very strong reminder that I was an underemployed dad who needed to find steady, reliable work.

I considered everything and anything. Through some contacts I was able to get an interview at the Staten Island borough president's office. He was looking for an assistant press secretary. His chief of staff seemed impressed by my contacts in the media and how he could use them to get his boss some press.

I was still living in Staten Island at the time, so it seemed a no-brainer. I could get to work in about twenty minutes, use the press plates on my car to park near Borough Hall, schmooze some movers and shakers and be home by five-thirty. I mourned for a few days about leaving radio but I was desperate. My then-wife was a month or so from giving birth and it was crunch time.

I thought it might be good to see how things worked on the other side of the news machine. Instead of digging for stories I would be spinning them.

I was "headed in a different direction".

Chapter 12
SPINNING FOR A LIVING

I often tell friends and business associates looking to get some publicity that I have been in the kitchen where the sausage is made. I have seen how stories, good and bad are developed and, if need be, spun any which way you want them. The first lesson in the art of spinning came in the crown jewel of buildings along the north shore of Staten Island. Staten Island Borough Hall, a grand hundred-year-old brick and marble building overlooking Manhattan and a few hundred yards from where the famous Staten Island Ferry docks.

Staten Island is a unique place. It's tightly knit and more like a small town than part of the biggest city in the country. People there fall into two categories: city workers like police, firefighters and sanitation employees who make up the lion's share of the residents, and business owners. The business owners consist of about ten percent of the population. And they all know each other. That's both good and bad. If you're a legitimate and honest businessman your reputation becomes known throughout the island. If you screw up or get yourself involved in some nefarious activity everyone—and I mean everyone— knows about it inside of twenty-four hours.

Sometimes I'd hear something about someone that had just happened. Later in the day – on the other side of the island – a friend would say, "Did you hear about so-and-so?" On Staten Island gossip travels at the speed of light!

I rolled into Borough Hall in September of 1988 to begin my job of Assistant Press Secretary to the Staten Island borough president.

The borough president – for lack of a better description – is the mayor of the borough. In New York City there are five boroughs. Manhattan, Brooklyn, Queens, the Bronx and Staten Island. Staten Island is the smallest in population but the way the government was set up at the time it had an equal vote on important matters.

My boss was borough president Ralph Lamberti. He was an old-fashioned politician, a street fighter who had risen up from the tough neighborhood of Castleton Corners, clawing his way with moxie and determination to the highest position in the Democrat party on Staten Island. He was both feared and admired.

I was a cabinet member. I served at the pleasure of the borough president but my most immediate supervisor, the man I reported to, was Mike Azzara. Mike had come from the borough's premier daily newspaper the *Staten Island Advance* and had been snatched from the newspaper by Lamberti to become his chief of staff.

Coming from the go-go environment of hourly newscasts and breaking stories to the laid-back environment of the backwater Staten Island politics was a transition. Everything moved at a snail's pace.

On my first day I was shuffled into a giant office and shown my desk. I had a sinking feeling. I was never a "desk" kind of guy. I preferred to be on the move, out and about seeing new things. My eyes wandered to the gentleman's desk next to me. It had all the signs of a "lifer." Photos of his family, a wilting plant. And it stank of a life long since given up on.

I would have walked out then but I had few options. My child was due and no one in New York radio or TV was interested in taking me on. I sat down, looked around and vowed to make the best of it.

My phone rang. It was Mike. He wanted to see me.

Mike was an unusual man, calm on the surface with a face that had seen it all or most of it. He was an old-time newspaper guy. His office was small, and because he was a chain smoker, it stank of cigarette smoke. He rambled on in a low monotone sometimes for hours. I could have handled that, but he also insisted on having his office air conditioner on three hundred sixty-five days a year. This posed two problems:

First, even in the dead of winter with flakes clinging to the windows, his office was always twenty degrees colder. Sitting inside was like being stationed at Ice Station Zebra. The second and more pressing problem was the whir of the air conditioner. Between Mike's low wandering voice and the air conditioner, I could hear only about twenty percent of what he was saying. Unsure how to proceed, and not wanting to look like an idiot, I just nodded.

He would say something profound or make a joke and either one solicited the same response – a knowing nod. Once in a while I'd get a troubled look or a grin not knowing if I had just endorsed pedophilia, or if he was talking about his grandson's soccer game. Worse yet, he'd usually end this marathon meeting with what I thought was some kind of assignment. Then he'd send me on my way. I'd sit at my desk next door and try to recreate the conversation, to decipher what the hell he had said, and what exactly he wanted me to do.

An hour later he'd come into my office and ask me if I was done. With what?

I'd tap dance around and finally figure it out, screwing it up because I was in a rush or still wasn't totally sure.

It reminded me of the *Seinfeld* episode in which George is given and assignment by his boss at the New York Yankees and hasn't heard what he's said. He spends the rest of the episode trying to figure it out.

Many of the employees at Borough Hall had been there for years, crossing the days off the calendar and trying to stay out of trouble so they could put in their years, retire with a pension, and spend the second half of their lives doing what they really wanted to do.

They protected their turf and God forbid you got in the way.

After about two weeks of muddling along, I got bolder. As Mike droned on behind a cloud of cigarette smoke I stopped him in his tracks, asking him to repeat, at a volume above a buzzing bee, what the hell he was saying.

He said he was determined to shake things up. To show the borough president and those entrenched in their jobs, especially those in charge of the BP's image, that there was a new sheriff in town. And he had found just the man to do it. Wow, I thought, this should be interesting. Who's the schmuck he's selected to transform decades of local Borough Hall politics? To get the old timers moving in another direction and put the younger political operatives on notice? You know where this is going: He thought *I* was just the guy to throw into the gaping jaw of the monster. And you know, my ego was just big enough to agree with him.

The media department, which recorded, videotaped and photographed every big event the borough president was involved in, consisted of a bully and his pleasant but frazzled assistant, a very nice woman in her twenties who always seemed to be late for something.

I guess I should have asked some questions about how I was going to "change" the Media Department, but I didn't and it wasn't long before I was back in Mike's office surrounded by a swirl of Marlboro smoke nursing my bruises. Next up I was assigned to work under Press Secretary Bob Huber. Not to change anything but just to observe. Bob was a brain box. His vocabulary was extensive and his grasp of every complex issue made me dizzy. I suspected he didn't need me to help him explain policy in tightly written impressive memos and speeches. He was doing a great job of it all by himself.

So soon I was back where I started, rolling in at nine and trying to look as busy as I could for eight hours. I did find one friend and his office was right next to mine: Deputy Borough President Nick LaPorte.

Nick was chosen not so much for his ability, but for what he could do to get his boss elected. In this case, to bring Ralph Lamberti much-needed votes in an area of Staten Island he regularly had problems winning.

In a lot of ways Nick was the high end version of everyone else at Borough Hall. His political connections got him where he was and in a few more years he would retire himself. The difference was Nick had a borough car and a personal driver to take him anywhere he wanted to go.

I loved Nick and our talks became a daily ritual. I'd sit in his office, not to discuss policy but to listen to him tell me where the best food was on Staten Island. Several times on my way home I'd spot his car in front of his favorite place for ravioli or Italian pastry.

In early 1989, less than a year after I arrived, it was time to gear up for the re-election campaign. After sixteen years on the political scene Lamberti looked like a shoo-in for reelection. He knew everyone who mattered on Staten Island and was the second most popular politician in the borough. The only person more popular was the immensely beloved former borough president and now Congressman Guy Molinari. The Molinari name was gold on Staten Island, like the Kennedys in Massachusetts.

In anticipation of his reelection campaign Lamberti started raising his visibility. He couldn't be everywhere so the deputy borough president was asked to make more and more appearances. As Nick Laporte's self-appointed press secretary, I'd sit next to him in the back of the chauffeured car and he would regale me with stories of political shenanigans on Staten Island and in New York government. He'd talk about the people to ignore in Staten Island politics and the ones to fear. Then we'd have a long discussion on how to make the best pasta sauce.

Nick was the consummate professional politician. He taught me many tricks of the trade: the sincere smile, the engaging handshake, and some other things I'll never forget. Nick always told me that before you head to a big political dinner where you are to speak or be the guest of honor always have a big meal. He'd say, "Eat at home. Eat what you like so you're not grabbing for food, scarfing it down or chewing when you should be going table-to-table shaking hands."

He also taught me how to manage a crowd. I'd seen it done before but no one knew how to do it better than Nick. He understood the "schmooze" and honed my skills. He even knew how to do the "switch" which is when you expertly break off a conversation with someone important to speak with someone even more important like a city official whose support you really need.

Turns out it's in the handshake.

The politician's handshake is about control. It includes the obligatory firm grip with your right hand and a gentle squeeze of the person's right shoulder with your left.

It's that body language that signals the politician is in control of this conversation. Watch politicians whom you admire, from the President on down. They all do it.

Now, once you have control of the conversation you dictate when it ends. When you spot the city commissioner with whom you must speak before he leaves, you look the mother of three who has a problem with a barking dog next door in her eyes, tap her left shoulder. Shake her hand again, let go and move on.

Nick had an easy smile. It was displayed many times for me. At the end of a long day Nick would step out of his car – me tagging along – and bound up the stairs of Borough Hall. Along the way he'd wave to whomever happen to be sitting on the steps of Borough Hall enjoying the sun, or just passing by.

Except for Mookie.

We never found where Mookie came from, who he knew, or why he was always so angry. He was a dirty, mussed up, crotchety old man who spent hours – rain or shine – on the steps of Borough Hall. Mookie got to know all the movers and shakers on Staten Island and even those important people who worked behind the scenes formulating policy. Mookie did not have the social graces to express his displeasure with the way the borough was being run through the proper channels so instead he'd wait until the borough president, deputy borough president or some mucky-muck showed up and loudly curse at them.

He'd sit, sometimes stand, on the steps of Borough Hall and as you walked in or out Mookie would yell, "You motherfuckers are killing us… fuck you… you bastards… you'll get yours," and stuff like that.

His guttural voice made it sound like his curses were coming from the depths of Hell. The other folks sunning themselves on the steps of Borough Hall would recoil. The elected officials had no choice but to smile weakly and take it. They'd shrug their shoulders, look at the other people sitting nearby as if to say, "Well, ya know, he's nuts!"

This went on for months. The deputy borough president and I would come back from some luncheon or another function and in the short time it took to get out of the car and into Borough Hall Mookie would cut us a new asshole. It got to be part of the usual ebb and flow of the day. Go out and get some lunch, bring it back, Mookie curses you out. Go inside and eat. Go to an off-site meeting. Hear some constituent concerns, drive back, Mookie curses you out. Go inside, do some more work.

One day Nick and I were coming back from some late evening function. It was dusk and cold as it could be. The wind was whipping off the harbor and right down the street in front of Borough Hall.

When we arrived at Borough Hall I was shocked to see Mookie. He was bundled up, seated on the steps – and angry that he had to wait for us to launch his last profanity-laced fusillade of the evening. I often wondered if he had a list at home to make sure he harassed all the important people he could that day and how many times.

Anyway – because of the icy weather when we got out this time and headed up the stairs I noticed Mookie was the *only one around*. All the sane people were home getting warm.

As Nick and I bounded up the stairs it began. "You bastards are stealing from us... you'll get yours. When the time comes the people of Staten Island will throw your sorry asses out... fuck you..."

Nick had had enough. Like a good politician he moved his eyes left and right to make sure no one was around, smiling all the time. When he was sure no one was remotely in earshot, Nick stopped, pointed and said, "Fuck you Mookie! Now get the fuck out of here and don't come back."

Mookie was stunned. Nick shot me a grin. I nearly fell over laughing. Traveling with Nick during the campaign was not without its hazards. One night the borough president told Nick to attend an especially contentious meeting on the south shore of Staten Island. It involved some school issue and parents were out in force. The borough president had stirred up a hornet's nest over this issue and Nick and I had to head on down there to essentially get our balls whacked.

Nick took the brunt of it. He sat on stage with some other city officials as one parent after another walked up to the microphone in this large school auditorium to blast him, and indirectly, the borough president. I stood stage right near a set of small steps that led directly to the stage. It was just plain brutal. After an hour of so of this – and with no end in sight—Nick gestured to me.

While one of the other officials was trying to reason with some mother of three, Nick walked over to meet me at the top of the steps. I walked up half way hoping to hear some more pearls of political wisdom on how politicians handle a rowdy crowd. Maybe a life lesson on how every issue is local.

Instead Nick leaned over and whispered, "Find a back entrance and get me the hell out of here!" I got his driver, Nick made his apologies for leaving, and we hustled him out the back door.

●●●

One of the things I absolutely despised about working at Borough Hall was the Board of Estimate. The Board of Estimate, before it was abolished, worked like the U.S. Senate. Five boroughs, five equal votes regardless of the size of the borough or its population. The board met every couple of weeks in a public session at City Hall in downtown Manhattan. All the city's business was decided in those meetings and all votes had to be unanimous. Everything from a vote on a new bridge in Queens to a variance to allow a small street to be extended twenty feet in the Bronx was approved by the Board of Estimate. Since New York City is huge, there were literally dozens of issues that had to be voted on every two weeks. As you might imagine, there was lots of horse-trading. One borough president would let another know through his aides that if he voted in favor of that new museum on Staten Island, he'd give his vote when the time came to approve the other borough president's pet project.

But there was a secret to how everything got done. The board held a private meeting every Wednesday *before* Thursday's public meeting where the borough presidents told each other how they were going to vote. Most of the horse-trading was done there and by the time the meeting was held the following day, ninety-five percent of the votes had already been decided.

The meetings began in the late afternoon and regularly ended at about ten at night. The borough presidents were seldom there. The BP would send an aide to listen to citizens drone on and then have that aide – when the time came – vote they way he wanted them to.

We'd have a staff meeting at Borough Hall the morning of the Board of Estimate meeting. I noticed right away that these particular meetings were sparsely attended.

The borough president would go over each Board of Estimate issue affecting the borough and then let everyone know what he thought and how he would vote. Toward the end of these meetings I also noticed something else. Key members of the borough president's cabinet who did attend were "suddenly called away." Then I found out why. At the end of the meeting the borough president would select the person he wanted to vote on his behalf at the Board of Estimate meeting. In other words, the person whose day would not end at five but instead ten p.m. or later.

I was fresh meat at Borough Hall and for the first four or five Board of Estimate meetings I was "it." I'd sit behind this giant bench in a grand old room at City Hall and, along with the other shlumps who got "picked" by the other borough presidents, listen to my fellow New Yorkers babble on about this or that. They never knew that the fix was in. That no matter what they said and no matter how long they said it, the vote had been decided the day before. I remember one contentious issue that sparked major protests. Busloads of people showed up and jammed into the Board of Estimate meeting room. After twenty-five or so people had testified – some of them really angry – I looked over to my counterpart from the Bronx and whispered, "So what's the vote on this?".

He didn't say a word. He just looked over at me like a great Roman emperor deciding the life and death of a gladiator and out of view of the angry constituents gave me a "thumbs down."

The one thing that I did enjoy about those especially contentious issues was the testimony kept me awake. Most times, as discussions about a new sewer drain in Harlem went on and on, I did all I could just to stay awake. It was torture.

One night every issue on the agenda had been voted on except one. The representative from Manhattan though did not know how his boss, Manhattan Borough President David Dinkins, wanted to vote. Worse yet, Dinkins – who would go on to become mayor of New York – was nowhere to be found and the meeting could not end until this timely issue was addressed. They called his office. His home. His favorite restaurants. Nothing. The Chairman eventually called a recess while they tried to track down Dinkins. Some of those who came to express their views before the board hung around until about midnight before throwing their hands up and shuffling off. Those who were required to stay till the bitter end – like me – tried to find someplace to sleep. One of my colleagues from the Bronx used a couple of books for a pillow and lay down in the pew-like benches. I pushed my chair back and thought, *what an idiotic way to run a city.*

They finally found Dinkins – I forget where – and the vote was taken. I got home at four in the morning. You can bet that from that day on I made myself scarce during our Thursday morning meetings at Borough Hall.

Aside from my periodic outings with Nick the prevailing policy at Borough Hall was to look busy and keep your head down. I did make friends with an office mate named John Vasquez. He was brought on by the borough president to shore up the vote in the growing Hispanic community. John turned out to be an excellent diversion from the tedium. He taught me Spanish and kept me company during lunch. We found a place down the block called the Cargo Café. It had a small bar and a pool table and not much else. John and I would head out at noon, eat a burger, have a cocktail, and over the course of several weeks he taught me the intricacies of billiards. I got really good at it.

We'd come back still talking about the game we shot and before you knew it, it was five o'clock. And five was the witching hour.

Every day, the departure of my colleagues who worked within the drab government-issue offices of Borough Hall took on a feel of a long played-out ballet. At about 4:45 there was the shuffling of the papers. A call out here and there about how busy the day had been (when it had been anything but) and then at about 4:55 everyone sort of imperceptibly made their way to the door. By five on the nose there wasn't a soul to be found. Coming from a news operation – where people hung around after the newscast to work off the adrenaline – it was a comedown. These folks couldn't wait to leave. It represented another day clocked toward their eventual retirements without a memory of what they had done that day or whether they had made a difference.

The upcoming re-election brought some excitement to this otherwise dull existence. Nick and I were called upon more and more often to make appearances. I welcomed getting out to meet new people.

One time the borough president summoned me because there had been a serious fire in a tenement on the north shore of Staten Island. The New York media was there and the BP thought I could get him some airtime. Since we were in reelection mode, he wanted to be seen as much as possible.

Lamberti – the street fighter – was excellent at turning himself on and off. He was the consummate campaigner one moment – glad-handing everyone he could see – and a political calculator the next. As I sat in the BP's chauffeured car with his press secretary Bob Huber, waiting to head to the fire scene, I could see the borough president on the steps of Borough Hall. He was smiling and waving to everyone, even stopping with a sincerest of smiles to talk for several minutes with a potential voter. It was a scene right out of a Norman Rockwell painting. Political Campaigning 101 at its best.

I sat in the middle seat in the back of the borough president's chauffeured city vehicle. Bob next to me behind the driver. As the BP came close to the car his face darkened. He opened the door, sat down, slammed the door shut and in the loudest voice I ever heard him use he screamed, "That motherfucker! You know what that motherfucker is saying about me?" It came out of nowhere. He then went on to blast the popular Congressman Guy Molinari. It was a ten-minute tirade. Bob tried to calm the BP down but he was in no mood. I sat there, head down.

Moments later we pulled up to the apartment complex where the fire had occurred. The BP jumped out. His face – just like that – changed to compassionate concern. Seconds before he was screaming – and *bang* – the next second he was back in politician mode. It was impressive.

There was no reason to believe the borough president would not be reelected. He was leading every potential opponent except Molinari. Meanwhile the Congressman was ensconced in Washington and there was no reason to believe he was going anywhere.

Enter former New York Mayor Edward I. Koch.

New York City's gregarious Mayor Edward I. Koch. Koch was nationally known. He was well liked and immensely popular, although now seeking a fourth-term his "How'm I doing" bit had begun to wear thin. Most New Yorkers eventually get sick of a candidate who overstays his welcome and the sense was Koch could be overstaying his.

Whatever popularity Koch had left, Lamberti was more than happy to sponge. Koch wanted the reliable Lamberti around so Koch, who needed as many Staten Island votes as he could get, would pop up once in a while at an event or at Borough Hall. After the Mayor got the Mookie treatment a couple of times, a cop was assigned to watch the grounds of Borough Hall for security reasons and to keep Mookie at bay.

In a classic political blunder that will go down in the annals of Staten Island history, Ed Koch answered some questions at an event with the BP about the possibility of Congressman Guy Molinari returning to Staten Island to run for borough president. It was preposterous. A trial balloon set off by a local reporter making crap up.

Koch bit. "I don't think Molinari has the guts to come back to Staten Island and run against Ralph Lamberti," he said.

When word of that comment got back to Borough Hall a pall descended. We weren't sure if this was a pre-emptive strike because Molinari was considering running for BP, or a misfire. Either way telling the combative Guy Molinari he couldn't do something was like smacking a beehive with a broomstick. Lamberti needed this like a hole in the head.

To make matters worse Koch wanted to put a state prison in a politically sensitive area of Staten Island. He needed to do it for the sake of the city but the location and timing was horrendous. Lamberti tried to put the best face on the proposal – job creation and so on – but Staten Islanders weren't biting.

For a week or so we waited for the word either way about Molinari. During one of our usual Thursday staff meetings we gathered to go over the Board of Estimate agenda. The meeting was fully attended. Odd, I thought, but this was a fact-finding mission. His staff wanted to check out the BP's body language. Look for clues. Plan their futures, if need be.

In the middle of the meeting as one of my fellow cabinet members droned on about a permit to put a walkway over a small section of wetlands in one of the borough's parks or some such nonsense, Press Secretary Bob Huber was called away.

I – and several others – shifted our eyes to watch him depart. Again we were sniffing for clues. He returned about ten minutes later and walked directly over to the BP and whispered in his ear.

The meeting went on for a few seconds more and then the borough president interrupted, "I guess you're wondering what Bob just told me. Well, you'll be among the first to know. Guy Molinari is leaving Congress to run for borough president."

The silence at that very moment was like none other. The room we were in was transported to the most remote place on earth where no natural or artificial sound is heard. The silence was broken about fifteen seconds later by the sound of a barking dog maybe right outside the window – maybe a block away – who knows. All I knew was that the clock had begun ticking. For me, and every other cabinet member, it was going to be a long campaign.

The borough president placed the meeting in the hands of an underling, got up and walked out. The rest of the day the phone wires grew hot with gossip and calls to contacts. The copier machines glowed red hot as they spit out resumes in unprecedented numbers.

As cabinet members, we had to at least put on the veneer that this was a winnable race. We found out later that Congressman Molinari wanted out of Washington as a way to allow his daughter, New York Councilwoman Sue Molinari, to run for his seat. The BP's job would be an excuse to leave Washington and advance his daughter's career. It also was a way to get back at his archrival Lamberti.

One of the first things I was assigned to was a walking campaign with other staffers to get the word out about Ralph Lamberti. Handing out brochures and such – chatting up the BP and all his accomplishments. I was joined by Marlene Markoe, a young staffer who, like the rest of us, had a vested interest in getting Lamberti reelected.

Marlene and I first walked through the impoverished area of Port Richmond. Driving through this remnant of the Main Street shopping areas of the 50's, 60s, and 70s, it was tough to get a real feel of how urban it was; walking those streets long past their heyday was scary.

We walked into one storefront that said "Bakery." There were no baked goods anywhere. After we called out, a man came out from behind a beaded curtain and eyeballed us up and down. We mumbled something – thanked him for his time and hustled out. We did not want to disturb the pimp while his ladies were working the back room.

The following week Marlene and I walked into a popular garden center in another part of the borough and told them we were from the borough president's office and that he was running for re-election.

The owner said, "Guy Molinari?"

"No," we said, "Ralph Lamberti."

The man without batting an eye said, "Lamberti's running for borough president too?" Obviously name recognition was going to be a problem. This Staten Islander didn't even know Lamberti had been BP for the past six years!

I was also called upon by the media department to hit the road with a camera and get some "warm and fuzzy" shots of the borough which later could be used in a local TV commercial. I took a one-day camera operator's course at Borough Hall and was told first to go to the North Shore where the BP was proposing the renovation and re-electrification of the long defunct Staten Island North Shore train link.

The area was desolate. There were high weeds, trash and crack pipes and God knows what else. The folks in the media department said they needed shots of the urban decay to juxtapose with artist's renderings of what this decaying area would look like if the BP was re-elected.

I drove one of the city cars to this scary landscape and set up right on the long-since-abandoned railroad tracks. First I unloaded the tripod, then the camera, then all the accessories. As I began knocking off some pulls and pans of the area I heard some rustling behind me. With one eye in the lens I used the other to see what the hell was going on behind me.

There he was: a hulking, scraggily homeless man who saw a young guy, a running car, and some expensive camera equipment he could steal and drive off with. I'm not sure when I learned this but if you live in a major city you know when and how to act in these situations. It's what we call "The Subway Face." You put on "The Subway Face" in dangerous situations to warn those who are looking for any opening of vulnerability that you proceed at your own risk. "Who knows," The Face says, "I could be nuts, I could have a gun. If you want to take a chance, go ahead." It's all in the body language.

We stood face-to-face for an instant checking each other out. My "Subway Face" plastered on as soon as I knew this could get ugly. I slowly started to pack the car up, making small talk as I went. I conveniently kept within arm's length of the tripod and made sure to pack it last. I knew this was the heaviest of the items and the one that, swung the right way, would knock him out.

He sensed I was in "abort mode." If he was going to make his move it'd have to be soon. With my hand clenched to the tripod I hustled myself into the driver's seat, threw it in behind me and drove off.

It was the last time I listened to the idiots in the media department.

Election Day was still way off, but seeing what I had seen so far on the campaign trail I hedged my bets and started looking into other part time gigs. I made some calls and within a week or so I was offered a weekend job doing traffic reports on New York radio stations. I told the BP that I needed the extra work to pay my bills and he graciously gave me permission to work some weekends on the air.

I had to be in every Saturday and Sunday morning at six, and got out at about one in the afternoon. I'd work a full week at Borough Hall and then pull myself into Metro Traffic every weekend and do traffic reports for WFAN (the station I used to work at) and some other stations on Long Island. WFAN was really the only station I had to worry about. It had regular updates and once they hit the traffic sounder you had to be there. As you might imagine there wasn't much traffic to talk about on a weekend morning at six. I'd tap dance and fill a minute or so with road closings and chatter about whatever delays there were at the George Washington Bridge. I mostly spent my time between reports trying to keep myself awake.

The Metro Traffic headquarters was in the north tower of the World Trade center on a floor by itself. There were no interior walls, so you could wander throughout the entire floor. I did that many times marveling at the wonder of the construction of the building. The World Trade Center had all of its important components in the center of the building, in a long column that contained the elevators, electrical lines, power and plumbing. It was constructed like that so the floor space was wide open. When standing at one end you could literally see all the way across the other side. It was huge! Being there early in the morning, it seemed eerie. The building would sway slightly in high winds. It was designed to do that, and in the silence of a weekend morning you could actually hear and feel it move.

Before the first attack on the World Trade Center in 1993, getting upstairs was a snap. I look back at those times of innocence and smile. Often I'd show up and flash the guard my World Trade Center ID. Sometimes I didn't have it and he would just wave me in.

Frequently he wouldn't even be at his post. I'd stroll in unchallenged. The ID card was made for me at the security office in the bottom floor of the sub-basement. I stood there in 1989 as they took my picture and handed me my card never knowing that I would be standing in about the same spot as a TV reporter years later – this time without either of the buildings above me.

It wasn't long before one of the other guys whose shift overlapped mine started bringing in a Wiffle ball and bat. I wasn't surprised in the least. I have never worked in a newsroom that didn't have a Wiffle ball and bat or a football. Next time you're watching the news take a good look. It's back there somewhere just over the shoulder of the pretty blond telling you about the latest mayhem in your city.

When we got bored between reports we knocked the ball around. No harm done since both the bat and ball were plastic. When we got bored of that we used the huge open floors of the WTC to map out a baseball diamond. A fruit-stained paper plate was first base, someone's jacket second, and so on.

When that got stale, we stepped it up notch and brought in a softball. Now lining a Wiffle ball came with the knowledge that no real harm could be done to the pitcher or the surroundings. A softball – which is considerably heavier and harder – was a different story. One lazy Saturday I pitched one in and my colleague hit it right on the button. It flew from one end of the empty WTC floor to the other and slammed into the glass partition where a empty office had been partitioned off. The glass broke and a huge chunk slid down like a guillotine.

The powers that be never even asked how it happened. The floor – which made up the Metro Traffic headquarters – was just temporary. The company that would take over the floor – whenever that might be – was going to change the configuration anyway.

I was working non–stop, seven days a week and it began to take its toll. Five days a week at Borough Hall, late nights for the campaign, a Board of Estimate meeting occasionally, and weekends at Metro. Even though I was thirty years old at the time, after a few weeks I was totally exhausted. One morning it all caught up to me. I was there alone (my Wiffle ball buddy came in later) getting ready to do my report on WFAN. I knew I had to step up my game because when you're tired and need to be on the air it's important that you pay attention. To avoid any screw-ups I grabbed a cup of coffee, set up early and waited for my cue from WFAN to bang out my first report. I even turned on my mic in advance. So there I was, eyes half closed, waiting for the sounder and my introduction.

A minute or so before I was to go on I thought, *let me just put my head down for a moment on the desk and as soon as I hear the traffic sounder I'll do my report.*

The next sound I heard was the phone ringing. It took me a spilt second to remember where I was.

"Hello... ahh... Metro Traffic... can I help you?" I said.

"Frank?" the voice said.

"Yes."

"Where were you?"

"Where was I when?"

"We threw it to you and all we heard was someone snoring."

I also sniffed around for some part time work at the nascent cable operation on Staten Island. Staten Island Cable was only about a year or two old so there was plenty of opportunity. I cooked up a plan to do a talk show about baseball card collecting, which was all the rage in the late 1980's, get some sponsors and keep the difference when the half hour was paid for.

I pitched the idea of being a sponsor of the show to one of the more prominent jewelers on Staten Island. He asked his advertising sales manager from Staten Island Cable to sit in on the meeting. That's how I met Fred Fiore.

Fred listened to my pitch to the jeweler and it was pretty good. After the meeting Fred stopped me outside and said, "Why are you wasting your time working for Lamberti and selling a small time public access show? Come sell for us at Staten Island Cable and you'll make three, maybe four times what you're making."

I was a bit shocked and flattered. Apparently I had learned something from watching my Mom sell syrup all those years. I was a bit of a salesman, which is the most useful quality anyone can have. Think of that for a moment – aren't we all salespeople? Don't we spend part of everyday convincing, cajoling, and persuading others to see things our way whether dealing with a spouse, parents, kids or co-workers?

I was intrigued by the offer. I gave it a couple of days and then called Fred back to say no thanks. I wasn't sure I wanted to be a salesman. Back at Borough Hall everyone involved in the campaign began going through Molinari's congressional record with a fine-toothed comb.

One day the BP's campaign manager called me in to help him figure out which way Molinari had voted on a particular bill. He hoped to find one of those buried votes that he could used to bash Molinari with. He cracked open this huge book that contained every Congressional vote Molinari ever made.

"Can you make heads or tails out of this?" he asked. "I'm going to read this to you and you tell me what the hell this means: 'Those voting no on HR352 agree – in the negative – not to support the measure which does not call for the implementation of a home port security detail not exclusively used for the security which involves the use of no police officers...'" You get the picture. After he read the entire bill – which Molinari had voted against – he asked me what it meant. I had no idea what the hell he just said. I pretended someone was looking for me and made a fast getaway.

When I did make a getaway I usually ended up on the other side of the building. I had made a friend who shared my same irreverence. He had gotten a desk job working for the city after a long stint at Mount Loretto on Staten Island. Mount Loretto is a home for wayward kids from some of the toughest, grimiest neighborhoods in the city. These were not the cute "Bowery Boys" mischievous kinds of kids we used to watch on Sunday morning TV. These were the "Don't Screw with Me Or I'll Slit Your Throat" kinds of kids.

My friend taught physical education at Mount Loretto but after he was jumped and beaten senseless for the fourth or fifth time he decided he needed to spend whatever time he had left working for the city somewhere safe. He needed to put in another six years or so in city government before he could retire. The guy was tough and had all the earmarks of a combat veteran. He also didn't take shit from anyone, which was fun to watch.

In one of the worst pairings ever conceived, they put my friend in a private office with one of the most uptight city employees you'd ever come in contact with. His office mate John was self-important, anal, and a control freak. Occasionally when I was asked to reach out to him to ask a question or take a quick meeting he'd respond, "I can't really see you at this moment. Can you come back at about three twenty-three this afternoon?"

Three twenty-three? Really? Your day is planned to the minute? Are you that goddamn busy?

It was annoying and soon he became the focus or my humor. People used to pop in and see me and I'd say, " I really don't have the time now. Can you come back at four-fourteen and seventeen seconds? Or better yet, see if John has an extra twelve seconds to spare and I can tack them on to my meeting with you."

My friend on the other side of the building loved this bit. We used to fall over making fun of John. After lunch and our usual verbal tirade from Mookie on the way up the steps of Borough Hall, I'd say something like, "So have a nice afternoon. If you need to follow-up on what we talked about or should you want to grab a cup of water at the water cooler I have twenty-seven seconds I can spare. I'll call you with the exact Greenwich Mean Time coordinates later."

Meanwhile as Election Day 1989 drew closer, the borough president assigned me to assist in polling voters for the upcoming race. His challenger, the almighty Guy Molinari, spent money on a professional polling company. The BP did it on the cheap using his loyal staff to work evenings making calls to specific election districts from a nondescript building along the north shore of Staten Island. Every weekday evening I supervised a cabal of blue haired ladies and volunteer city servants whose only interest in getting the BP re-elected was to keep their current office and desk assignments. In the city of New York the administrations may change but the daily full time tenured workers remain no matter what.

Some though actually liked the BP as a person and while impartial pollsters were making calls for challenger Molinari, our callers were making friends. I'd listen in as they dial up Democrat voters around the borough. It was a disaster:

"Hello – this is Marge calling on behalf of the borough president. In the upcoming election whom do you prefer on the issue of redevelopment? Borough President Ralph Lamberti or Guy Molinari? Molinari…okay. On the issue of…"

After the voter had told one of the BP's secretaries over and over again that he was voting for challenger Molinari I'd hear the lady say to the woman polling next to her, "But he's such a nice man. I'm going to change this one and say the person I called is going to vote for Ralph. I think he'd like that."

End result: out of loyalty or not to get Ralph mad our pollsters skewed the numbers. I would pass on the numbers to another employee who would present them to Ralph on a daily basis. Poor Ralph, as far as he knew he was leading in all the key areas he had to win.

Even when we couldn't get an adequate number of respondents Ralph got what he wanted. One night of polling produced just three respondents in an election district of about fifteen hundred people. Two said they would vote for the BP, one said he would vote for Guy Molinari.

I handed in the paperwork the next day and about twenty minutes later the phone on my desk buzzed. The man whose job it was to update the BP wanted me to join him to brief the borough president that morning.

He and I sat in the BP's outer office until we were summoned. As we strolled in the BP was surprisingly bubbly. He wanted to know how the polling was going, what the numbers looked like in each election district. When we got to the district where the night before we had only received three solid responses he said, "So how are we doing in Election District 22?"

My colleague, standing next to me and with a straight face said, "We're leading 2-1." "Great," said Ralph and sent us on our way. I wasn't sure how three responses from a district of fifteen hundred potential voters could be representative of the entire district and of course it was not.

Close to Election Day I reached out to my childhood friend Charlie Degliomini. The same guy who helped me with my paper route when I was a kid. Charlie was doing some consulting work for Molinari.

"Charlie," I said, "our polling – albeit a bit skewed – shows us ahead by four percentage points."

"Odd," he said. "Because ours (which was done by a professional polling company) shows us ahead by six percentage points." My heart dropped because I knew he was right and I knew that our blue haired civil servants at Borough Hall were wrong.

Just before Election Day there was some last minute Borough Hall drama. My friend in the office down the hall with the uptight office mate had had enough. There was a commotion in the hallway. Someone was saying, "Quick, get help, please get somebody!" I thought an intruder had gotten into Borough Hall with a gun.

I peeked out of my office and could see a small gathering in front of the office of my friend. I headed across the corridor and joined some other people who were looking into the office. Apparently my Mount Loretto buddy had snapped. After the umpteenth time of asking and receiving from his anal-retentive office mate the exact time to meet, he couldn't take it anymore. My buddy had John jacked up against a wall and was ready to beat him to a pulp.

Working with the rough and tumble kids of the street was one thing; trying to navigate the passive aggressiveness of a long time city employee was too much. No one was hurt and after a few days of gossip it was forgotten. Last I heard he was back at Mount Loretto. Something with which he was more familiar.

•••

Election night was planned like a commando mission. The borough president had secured two locations for the evening. One was a long time meeting place for Democrats called the Columbian Lyceum. It sat in a residential community along one of the first roads ever built on Staten Island. It was an odd combination of bowling alley and catering hall. Often we'd attend party rallies there or hear speakers from around the city talk about the pressing issues of the day while upstairs a bowling ball rumbled down alley five followed by a burst of cheers. The borough president had rented for he and his extended family a huge suite at one of the premier catering facilities a mile or so away called The Staaten. As far as the BP knew, based on what he had heard from our "polling," it was going to be fairly close but he would win. The election results would be tallied at the Columbian Lyceum and then at fifteen-minute intervals a member of his staff would drive over to The Staaten and update the BP on how things were going.

One employee would drive over as soon as the polls closed at nine p.m., another at nine-fifteen, a third at nine-thirty and so on. I got the nine-thirty slot. As soon as the BP was assured of victory he would hop into his city car, family in tow, and stroll into the Columbian Lyceum to accept the adulation of his supporters.

Even before the polls closed the Columbia Lyceum was rocking. Music was blasting, people were smiling, the booze was flowing and everyone was patting each other on the back. It was so loud it drowned out the 'tha-thump, tha-thump' of the big bowling tournament upstairs.

I was huddled in a corner with Tom Lamanna, one of the BP's chief aides, eyeballing the early numbers. We looked out of place. While everyone partied around us we were busy figuring out how this was going to end. The early numbers looked disturbing. To win in Staten Island a Democrat must win the heavily Democratic North Shore, break even in the middle part of the island and expect to lose the heavily Republican South Shore. The North Shore votes – the area with the most Democrats – always come in first.

Tom was on the phone, jotting down numbers, and trying to smile when a drunk voter wandered over to talk with him about the big reelection win. Once in a while I'd interrupt him with a "Well?

The party had begun at about seven-thirty and by nine-fifteen, everyone who wanted to get drunk was drunk. Backers, contributors to the campaign, and city employees were boozing it up at the bar and laughing like crazy. More than two hundred-fifty people. It looked like a giant wedding.

I headed over to the bar and returned to the election results table at about nine twenty-five. "Well?" I said again.

"It doesn't look good", Tom mumbled. "Here, grab these numbers and drive them over to The Staaten….the BP is waiting." I pushed my way through the knots of drunken supporters laughing and groping their dates and headed out to the parking lot and over to The Staaten.

The silence of The Staaten was in utter contrast to the wild party I had just left. I wandered in and asked a worker there, where's the borough president's party?

"Upstairs," he said, and wandered away.

As I climbed the stairs I thought he must be wrong. I didn't hear a sound upstairs. I poked my head into one empty ballroom, then another, and finally I hit on the third. And there was the extended Lamberti family. It was if I had wandered into a wake. There had been a death in the family, a political death, and I was the funeral director coming to tell the family it was time to leave for the cemetery.

The silence of the zombies was broken by a muffled sob. Someone was crying on the other side of the room. The borough president, head held high, walked over to me.

"Whatta ya got?"

"Here," I said letting my eyes wander around to take in this macabre scene.

He ruffled quickly through the papers, hastily folded them in half and looked me in the eyes.

"Frank," he said. "It's over."

He turned, walked a few steps and hugged his wife and family. I turned and walked out. At that moment I was the one and only staff member who knew it was truly over. The political wannabees, big time donors, cabinet members, and happy go lucky party minions at the Columbia Lyceum had no idea. The "polling" had showed the borough president was going to win reelection.

The mile back to the Columbia Lyceum took on the feel of a funeral cortege. I had a secret and it wasn't a good one. All my fears had been realized. For the second time in three years I was going to have to find something to do for a living.

When I got back to the Columbia Lyceum the festivities had really kicked into gear. There was smoke, booze and broads (to use a Rat Pack term) while everyone waited for the triumphant entrance of the newly reelected borough president, Ralph Lamberti.

I shuffled over to the bar again pushing aside kissing couples and leaning lushes.

I ordered a drink. A colleague from Borough Hall saddled up along side me and said, "It's going to be great. When's he coming here – do you know?"

"It's over," I mumbled.

Within twenty minutes the word had gotten around. I could see jaws drop across the room. Some folks hustled to grab their coats and beat the traffic out of the parking lot. Others shuffled out in silence. The place was empty in an hour. I was home in half that time.

The borough president lost by six percentage points.

The day after he got his political head handed to him and as I got ready to go to work the next morning my home phone rang. It was Fred Fiore from Staten Island Cable. The conversation was short.

"You ready now to come work for us at Staten Island Cable?"

Again I was flattered. I told him I'd think about it and let him know.

As the day went on I actually felt like a weight had been taken off my shoulders, the kind of feeling you have when you know you're not right for something and the universe makes a decision to get you the hell out of there.

In the next few weeks I spent more time at the bar down the block extending my lunch hour to play more pool with John Vasquez, my Hispanic liaison friend at Borough Hall.

Fred called again and I finally called back. I was heading to television. The experiment in "spinning for a living" was over.

"IT SHOCKED EVEN US!"

The signal sometimes didn't even reach the parking lot, but no one cared.

WSJU-AM, St. John's University 1977

My first radio station.
This converted house along side a small county road was home
to some of the best radio memories of my life.

WCRV Radio station

Nick DiRienzo gave me my first job in radio.
Years later he sent a message to me from the great beyond.

Nick DiRienzo

WCRV's old Associated Press machine.
The closet it was in held a dark smelly secret.

Lloyd Lindsay Young and me celebrating the 15th Anniversary of WJDM in Elizabeth, NJ.

March, 1985

The very talented Jim Bosh and I hop into a tub along Route 22 in Union County, NJ. Just another stunt Jim cooked up to draw attention to WJDM in Elizabeth, NJ.

**My first official head shot.
Tom Brokaw sat in the same chair just before I did.**

FRANK CIPOLLA
WNBC Radio

In the WNBC studio getting ready to do my hourly newscast on the "Soupy Sales Radio Show".

WNBC, 1987

238

The gracious man 'The Bride' and I first met in 1993 turned out later to be reviled by the press. Then 9/11 happened.

Rudolph Giuliani – Staten Island.

We laughed so hard on the set my sides hurt.
If only the News 12 New Jersey viewers could have seen all the fun we were having *during* the commercials.

Mizar Turdiu

I idolized him as a kid and then anchored along side him.

Rolland Smith

When Frank Field called for me from across the newsroom I never thought it would end like this!

Just before show time on the news set at WWOR-TV.
I'm sitting next to a real pro – the very talented Cathleen Trigg.

Alan Colmes – my friend of 30-years.
Both of us a long way from my time as an intern and his disc jockey days at
WPIX-FM.

Chapter 13
STATEN ISLAND.......LIVE!

I've always been comfortable and familiar with radio and figured I'd remain in radio forever but life is a puzzle: Once in a while it hands you an oddly shaped or colored piece and you have no idea where to put it. Only later do you find out it's not only needed but without it you could not finish the section you're working on.

The knowledge I gained working at Borough Hall gave me the insight, and more importantly the political contacts to make my next job a success.

In January of 1990 I met with Fred Fiore and his most immediate supervisor Josh Caplan at Staten Island Cable. We sat in a glass-enclosed office as busy people breezed back and forth. I remember seeing a couple of good-looking women walk by sizing up the new salesman. Inside the office I talked myself up, impressed them with my radio background and did some name-dropping. Fred had spiced up the deal to get me to Staten Island Cable by combining several jobs. I would sell TV advertising on the cable system, do some professional commercial voice-overs for them and also host a local talk show.

On the other side of this sprawling building in an industrial section in the northwest corner of Staten Island was the sales department. Fred took me over. It was a ten-foot-by-ten-foot area that contained four semi private cubicles.

I met some of the staff including a stunning woman named Lauren Vinik. I remember the exact spot where I shook her hand. I was checking out my new surroundings, processing the info Fred had given me, and wondering if I would be able to pull this off. I had no idea at that time that the woman whose hand I shook would change my life forever.

I officially started on February 1, 1990. I had a strategy and I was hell bent on making it work.

I wasn't thrilled about selling but I found – thanks to watching Mom – that I could do it and do it well. Selling is an extension of your ego; you convince someone that they need a legitimate service to grow their business and when they say 'yes' it's a rush.

Staten Island primarily runs on three main businesses: pizza parlors, bagel shops and Chinese restaurants. Now you're probably saying, "Come on – there are other businesses…" Sure there are, but every block along every major roadway in Staten Island had at least one of those. Bagel shop on one block, along with some other businesses, pizzeria on the next along with some other businesses. Chinese restaurant on the next.

Every cop and fireman opened one of those businesses eventually, or went into business with his brother-in-law or father while still on the job. The plan on Staten Island is that you work for the city for twenty years and then retire. About ten years in, you open your side business so when you retire you can work *and* receive a city pension. Some guys just skipped the side business and retired whenever their twenty years were up.

You'd see these guys hanging out watching their sons and daughters play baseball, or walking around the mall wearing a Jets t-shirt. They're as happy as can be. While everyone's working, they're home receiving a paycheck with health insurance for the whole family and nothing to do. I never understood that philosophy but more power to them. Most of these guys die well before their time because when you stop working and start coasting, the clock starts ticking.

Humans are meant to stay active. In the end the joke is on them. Ailments, real or imagined, begin to sap their strength and they spend more time complaining, or in the doctor's office, instead of "enjoying the good life."

One of my former clients is the founder of Staten Island's largest oil company. To this day he loves going to work. He always has a smile on his face. He's nearly ninety and as spry as ever. The key is to keep working, keep discovering and keep active.

To be a sales person you must have that wonderful gift to make small talk and on any subject. John Corso, a colleague and one of my dearest friends, was king at it. John is well versed in many subjects. He speaks some French, is very well read and when it comes to conversation can hold his own with anyone. He is also a superb storyteller. One thing John knows nothing about though is sports, and on Staten Island that was a distinct disadvantage because sports on Staten Island is religion. You needed to know what the Jets, Giants, Mets and Yankees did the night before or the guy who owned the pizzeria would have no respect for you.

I had a pretty good knowledge of sports but John was clueless. Being a smart dude, he devised a simple strategy to combat that. John spoke in sports clichés.

The client would say, "Boy big game this weekend, the Giants and the 49ers."

John would pause and say, "Yeah – these are two teams that really don't like each other."

The client would say, "You got that right…boy, in the last game they really mixed it up."

John: "Well, when you look at it, it really comes down to who wants it more."

Client: "Shit yeah – and the Giants need it this weekend."

John: "They also need to play tight defense."

Client: "You got that right…"

This would go on for several minutes, John talking but not really saying much and never revealing that he had no idea if the Jets were a football team or a baseball team. I knew it worked well because one day I had to fill in for John while he was on vacation. I drove over to a client to collect a check and while I was there the guy started telling me about how much he liked John.

"One other thing," he said. "That guy knows everything about sports!"

Another colleague – Steve Adelman – perfected the fine art of the "negative sell." The negative sell is tricky and not everyone can do it but Steve, with his "get over" demeanor had it down to a science.

We'd watch in amazement.

Steve would call an especially obstinate client, maybe one we had all taken a shot at and had all given up on.

"Hi, this is Steve Adleman at Staten Island Cable. We know we have approached you before about advertising on cable and we don't want to bother you anymore. So we're calling as a courtesy to let you know we're going to take your name permanently off our list. Sorry for the inconvenience – and we… what? No, no sir… really… we want to make sure no one ever calls you again about advertising on Staten Island Cable."

At that point the businessman started to get nervous: What do you mean I can't advertise on Staten Island Cable? Ever?

Steve would then turn it up a notch. "Yeah, but that's okay we'll find someone else in your category to advertise." Now the guy was being told his competitors would be able to advertise but he would never, *ever* have a chance to.

By the time Steve hung up the guy was begging him to come on down and take his money. Steve's philosophy was simple. Tell the client he or she can't have something and they want it more. It was something he learned while selling rugs. He'd tell the customer they were out of the rug they really wanted and then at the last minute say, "If I could find a few hundred square feet somewhere would you purchase it today?"

One of Steve's clients included a strip joint near Exit 13A of the New Jersey Turnpike. Sorry, a nightclub featuring "Exotic Dancers." With Steve on vacation one week I was asked if I could pick up a check for their late hours advertising on one of Staten Island Cable's many networks.

For shits and giggles I took another salesman – a religious sort – to get the money. Not so much for the ride but just to see his reaction.

Off we head over the Goethals Bridge and pull up in front of the place right off the turnpike. It's a typical strip club. No windows, skanks standing on the steps outside dragging on cigarettes before their sets.

I walk into the place with my religious friend and before I could say, "boo" he's at the bar ordering a drink and ogling some 20-year old slithering up a pole.

The owner, I'm told, is in the back office. I walk past a couple of dressing rooms and poke my head into his office. It was about five-feet-by-five-feet with stuff stacked all over the place so it was pretty tight. I sat in one of those cheap plastic chairs and presented an invoice for payment.

As he went rooting around his desk for a checkbook a young woman comes in. Now, whatever personal space I had in this hole of an office was gone. She was four inches from me leaning over his desk.

"I'd like to do some dancing. You have work?" she said.

"Sure, show me your bod," he replied as he tried to get a pen that worked.

Without blinking an eye she started taking off her clothes. Leaving her shirt here, her stretch pants on the floor, her panties draped on the side of my chair. I was getting a personal peep show and this guy was not even paying attention. He finally looked up and said, "Okay." And with that she started putting on her clothes.

I thought, *it must be great to be this guy!*

I got my check went to get my God-fearing colleague in the "Main Room" but he doesn't want to leave. Forget Jesus, he was laser fixed on some skinny blonde with huge chest pillows.

"Hey," I said, "Let's roll."

"Wait, wait," he says "Just watch when she does this upside down pole twist."

•••

With money coming in selling advertising, it was time for Fred Fiore and me to begin planning my TV show which would air on Staten Island Cable's locally-produced channel. The show was to be called *Staten Island Live* and would be a weekly hour-long show with an interview segment and phone calls. It would air several times each week. They built a set for me, a couple of talented editors used some Staten Island landmarks video to cook up a snazzy open and we were off and running.

In the first year we interviewed future mayor and presidential candidate Rudolph Giuliani. He was on the show about eight years before he became "America's Mayor" following 9/11. Unlike my encounters with him later in his career, he was charming. We had met following a visit to Staten Island while he was gearing up for his second and successful run for mayor. After he addressed a huge crowd at New Dorp High School he stepped off the stage and located me. He had been told I was a former reporter and anchor at WNBC and had a live local talk show. The consummate politician, he wanted to make sure he made contact with the person who could get him seen throughout the borough.

Giuliani introduced himself. I introduced my colleague Lauren Vinik who was also there and then he asked if I would like to come backstage. We talked some more and he introduced me to his wife Donna Hanover, who at the time was an anchor at Channel 5 in New York. I knew of her work. Little did I suspect that when I met this engaging politician and his beautiful wife what was to become a train wreck once Giuliani found Christine Nichols and then Judith Nathan and was finally kicked out of Gracie Mansion by Donna.

Other guests on Staten Island Live included "Bob" from *Sesame Street*, comedian Pat Cooper, local talk show legend Joe Franklin. The word had gotten out that a professional broadcaster was hosting an hour call-in talk show and suddenly it became the stop for every politician who wanted to be seen on Staten Island. First the local politicians appeared and then those from other boroughs who harbored mayoral aspirations and needed to be seen by a wide audience on Staten Island. I also was able to book former vice-presidential candidate Geraldine Ferraro.

The congresswoman was about a decade removed from her run for the vice-presidency on the ticket with Walter Mondale in 1984. We are both from Queens so we spoke the same language.

"Congresswoman," I asked her point blank, "when did you realize the race was over for you and Vice-President Mondale?"

She was amazingly frank. Didn't duck the question and to my surprise remembered the exact moment she knew she would not be the first female vice-president.

"At the second debate," she said. "When the question about President Reagan's age came up and whether or not at the age of seventy-four he would be able to handle the rigors of the presidency for another four years. Reagan, she said, responded, "I want you to know that I will not make age an issue of this campaign. I am not going to exploit, for political purposes, my opponent's youth and inexperience."

"That," she told me on the show, "Was when I knew we weren't going to win."

Between working at Borough Hall and now hosting my own TV show I had rubbed shoulders with some influential people. Enough so that I was able to fulfill one of my long time dreams, to attend a national political convention.

In the summer of 1992 I leaned on a lawyer friend who was a delegate to the Democratic Convention in New York. He was able to get me a pass to the first night of the convention. This was well before 9/11 so getting in and moving around the convention floor was no big deal.

There were all sorts of political movers and shakers and lots of celebrities. I bumped into and chatted with actress Mary Steenburgen for a while and then saw comedian Jackie Mason.

I couldn't resist. In his staccato voice I said, "Are you Jackie Mason?"

He said, "Yes, and who are you? Are you a Jew?"

"No," I said, "Are you?"

He then looks at the woman who's standing next to me and says, "Is she with you? Is she a Jew?"

"I don't know." Now again in Jackie's voice I say to her, "Are you a Jew?"

This little give and take goes on for a couple of minutes before we both cracked up.

•••

The men and women working behind the scenes at Staten Island Cable did the best they could but with live TV there are always screw-ups. We did not have a seven-second delay so the phone calls came in as they happened. Once in a while we'd get a Howard Stern inspired nut who would ask a question followed by a "babba booey" but for the most part the questions were pretty good.

Some politicians came on and never returned. They thought it would be a warm and fuzzy interview and it turned out not to be. I have always been a tenacious interviewer. I have analyzed my conduct over the years, and concluded I have a problem with authority. I feel no matter what office you hold – you work for me – or us. Respect, yes. Fawning, absolutely not. I also respect a politician who wants to mix it up. And I think they respect the host, and the show more, if you ask the tough questions.

Many a time a politician who screwed up and was hoping to get some sympathy in the form of softball questions regretted agreeing to be interviewed by me. It has gotten me into trouble over the years but I really don't care. A politician should be held accountable. And if I'm the interviewer I'm going to make sure he or she is. The TV interviewer's desk and the interview are about control. I ask the question. You answer. And nothing is off limits.

The Mayor of New York in 1992 found out that lesson the hard way. We drove to city hall in the spring of 1992 to interview Mayor David Dinkins and waited in the Blue Room for him to come in. I guess he figured some local yokel from Staten Island would toss him a few easy questions and he would knock them out of the park. Not so. I was waiting on the good mayor. I – and other Staten Islanders – had every reason to be angry with him.

Our esteemed mayor, in my estimation, had not shown the respect due one of the New York boroughs. He hadn't visited Staten Island in nearly a year and had not addressed some of the borough's pressing problems he said he would during the campaign. In short he believed he didn't really need the two hundred thousand or so voters in the borough and was ignoring us.

There I sat in the Blue Room of City Hall fully loaded and ready to fire. The Mayor walked in. We shook hands, made some small talk, the cameras rolled and I kicked off the interview.

"Mr. Mayor – there is a perception on Staten Island that the issues you promised to address in the borough when you ran have fallen by the wayside. In fact you have not even visited the borough in almost a year. What do you tell Staten Islanders who feel they have been ignored?"

Mayor Dinkins eyebrows went up and he shifted in his seat. The consummate politician then blurted out some nonsense about having to handle this and that and said he'd make a point of visiting soon. I don't know if he had a little alarm in his pocket or if he told his staff to come get him after five minutes but right after that question the deputy mayor popped his head in and said, "Mr. Mayor are you going to be long? We need your input on something."

Before he could answer I said, "Mr. Mayor, this is a half hour show. Even with the commercials we'll need at least 20 minutes of interview time." He was on the spot with the cameras rolling so he sat and took it for the next fifteen minutes, but he never forgot it – or me. Months later when he came to Staten Island for a luncheon as promised in that interview I approached him and said, "Mr. Mayor if you have a moment maybe we can speak with you after lunch?"

His face locked onto mine and he leered at me saying, "Can I eat my lunch and then I'll decide? Thank you!" He turned away and sat down.

When the luncheon was over he ducked out without looking back or talking to me.

One of our state assemblymen from Staten Island agreed to be on the show. He was a bit of a TV whore who could not resist the spotlight. I guess he had not been briefed or maybe had not seen the show. Like a lot of early guests they expected some retired fireman who was handsome and in awe of the power politicians held. Not a professional broadcaster who was going to ask the questions they did not want answered. This assemblyman had the previous year been involved in a minor scandal. He was able to wiggle his way out but the stink of it was still on him. So with this as a backdrop, I thought I'd do him a favor. Give him airtime to speak directly to the people of Staten Island about what had transpired.

He expected banter about how wonderful it is to represent the people of Staten Island or some crap like that. Again, a costly miscalculation.

When I broached the subject of his recent scandal he glared at me. He was well trained in how to misdirect a question and stall for time so the question was never really answered. I asked again. Again, figuring I'd do him a favor – more tap dancing and a nasty stare.

When we went to break he leaned into me and pointed his finger, "That was a low blow pal!" And stormed off the set. It was the first time a guest ever walked off my show. I learned a valuable lesson that night, one you see all good interviewers employ. Always ask the most uncomfortable question last. That way if you guest leaves in a huff, you already have what you need in the can.

There was also a slip up that got me on CNN. Susan Molinari – daughter of borough president Guy Molinari and the same guy that had beaten my former boss Ralph Lamberti had – as planned – replaced her dad in Congress. She was now Congresswoman Susan Molinari.

I had heard some things from my Borough Hall and police contacts. The word out there was the Congresswoman had done some drugs as a kid. Smoked some pot. A minor and understandable transgression but I felt as though we had to set the record straight. So I did.

On the show I asked, "Has this Congresswoman ever smoked marijuana?"

Her response was quick. "No – I understand why a lot of people did, but you have to understand me, I was born and raised Guy Molinari's daughter. My father was always involved in politics. We were always visible, and growing up I was always reminded. So I grew up trying very hard not to make the mistakes that other kids were allowed to make. Marijuana was not something I was particularly interested in, and in college it was not really available."

Fast forward to the 1996 Republican Presidential Convention. She was among the delegates at the convention. Another reporter asks her the same question and she says, "Yes – I have smoked pot." I remember hearing that and saying, "What the…?"

After some cajoling and pressure on the folks at Staten Island Cable, where I was no longer working, the video from the 1993 interview was released and sent up on the satellite. Suddenly I was receiving phone calls from friends from all around the country who had seen the clip of me interviewing Molinari on CNN.

And there I was, a little younger, hair bushier and confrontational as ever. The funniest line came from the sports guy at the TV station where I was working at the time.

He walked over to my desk. Looked at my head, looked again and said, "Was your hair really that long?" As for Congresswoman Molinari – I heard from friends of hers that she was pissed with me.

Oh well.

One night we had a psychic come on. She was very good so we invited her back. The viewers loved it. I was a bit skeptical. The third time we called her to be on the show she was unavailable. It had already been advertised so we were kind of stuck. I said, "Don't you know of anyone else who can fill in for you?"

She said, "You know there's this psychic on Long Island; Maybe he can come on down."

"Okay," I said and one of the producers called him.

Five minutes to show time our guest was nowhere to be found. He was supposed to be on for the hour, so without him the live show would be pretty weak. What was I going to do: take some calls and make some psychic predictions?

"New Dorp, Staten Island you're on the air. Does the letter 'D' mean anything to you?"

You get the picture.

Anyway *30 seconds* before the show is to begin we heard activity in the hallway. The door opens and the guest is very quickly brought onto the set. I shake his hand, introduce myself, and the intro music begins to play.

"Welcome to *Staten Island Live*, I'm Frank Cipolla. Our guest tonight is psychic medium John Edward. Stick around we'll be right back." We go to a commercial break.

Ten seconds into the commercial John, whom I had never met before and now is internationally known for his books, TV shows and seminars about contacting people who have passed on, says to me, "Who's Mary?"

I'm half listening as the director talks in my earpiece about what's coming up and where I should be looking when we returned from commercial.

"What?" I said as I peeked up from my notes.

"Who's Mary?"

The only Mary I know is my deceased Mother. She'd been gone about seven years by then and I had been thinking about her because it was my birthday in a few days.

"Mary was my mother," I mumbled.

"She's here now," John said, "and she wants to wish you a happy birthday."

I could feel the hair in the back of my neck stand up.

He continues, "She's with Joe."

"Joe?" I thought, as the commercial begins to wind down.

"Yes, Joe's beside her."

As the countdown begins to return to air I wracked my brain. "Ten... nine... eight... " Shouts the director.

Then it hits me. The 'Joe' is my deceased Uncle Joe who is buried in the same cemetery not fifteen feet from my mother.

As you can expect the shock on my face when we return from commercial is classic. I didn't speak about what had happened during the break because the show isn't about me. But I was spooked. I also didn't sleep that night.

We also had Joe Franklin on. Joe – for those who don't know him – is the oldest living TV interviewer in the country. Joe all but invented the TV talk show format. He'd interview Broadway types and New York's movers and shakers. At about the time the first TV set was sold, Joe started doing his quirky talk show on WNEW in New York. It lasted more than forty years. About twenty years into his run it evolved into a "must" interview for every weirdo and wannabe in New York. By sheer volume and length of service, Joe stumbled upon some real talents at the very beginning of their careers, bands like Squeeze and soon-to-be superstars like Madonna. I asked him how he felt about being the first to interview the people who would go on the stardom. He was frank.

"Well I'm proud of that. But once they become famous they never return."

"Why?" I asked.

"I don't think they want to admit that I gave them their first shot."

It was a startling revelation but if you knew anything about Joe's show you'd understand. Joe's show was a relic of a bygone era. Joe, hunched over his desk, would introduce guests who would appear and then stick around for the next guests to arrive. A dominatrix would end up chatting with Tony Bennett, an aspiring comedian would "yuk it up" with a scientist from NASA. And all the while Joe would ask the most bizarre of questions, breaking off one interview suddenly to ask the guest at the end of the couch if he had ever played with a Rubik's Cube. Sometimes a guest who was appearing at the Boom Boom Room on 43rd Street would lip-sync a song and at the end you'd hear about seven people applauding: Joe, his guests and the two or three cameramen working the floor. All of it was parodied years later by Billy Crystal on *Saturday Night Live*. Do yourself a favor. Go to YouTube and check out *The Joe Franklin Show*. There'll never be another one like him.

Joe's empire was run from a small office in midtown Manhattan. It was a fire hazard of books, notes and videotapes piled floor to ceiling. When he appeared on my show he told me a very interesting story: Joe said that he was in a studio at WNEW in early fall of 1960. Next door they were taping the last of the three Kennedy-Nixon debates. By this time Kennedy had gained some momentum but the race was still very close.

As Joe was talking to his guest the man clutched his chest, gurgled a bit and fell face first onto the floor. The taping was stopped and people scrambled to get help. An ambulance was called as Joe did the best he could to help. At one point Joe's leaning over the guy and feels others right behind him looking down. He turns and there is the next president of the United States! Both Kennedy and Nixon heard the commotion, stopped the debate and rushed in to see what was happening. Kennedy of course eked out a win in November. The guest was not so lucky. He suffered a heart attack and died shortly there after.

Joe also taught me one of the best lessons in television. He said, "Frank the most important thing in television is sincerity (pause) and as soon as you learn to fake that you've got it made".

Soon I was being recognized around Staten Island. I enjoyed it. People would point at me, walk up and ask me if I was that guy on Staten Island Cable. One night at a restaurant a guy and his wife at a table near by bought my guests and me drinks. At first I was uncomfortable with people staring and thinking because I was on a show they watched I was their instant friend. I wasn't used to it but I got accustomed to it quickly.

After a while these incidents of being recognized became more frequent so I came up with a nifty response. "Yes, I am Frank Cipolla," I'd say, "thanks for watching the show; that's very nice of you." It was my mantra. Yes I am, thanks, you're nice.

One time at the mall with my son I was in a bit of a rush. A guy approached me and said, "Hey... hey... you're... you're..."

I was really pressed for time and I had experienced this scene before.

He went on, "You're the guy.... that... give me a second... you're... you're..."

Finally to speed things up so I could get going I said, "Yes, I'm the guy on TV. The one who does *Staten Island Live*. Thanks for watching. That's very kind of you."

The guy looked at me puzzled. "No – you're Tony's friend right?"

Being a celebrity on Staten Island also exposed me to things I would otherwise never have experienced. When the Clyde Beatty Circus came to Staten Island they wanted to pump up ticket sales by featuring the most popular Staten Islanders. They located me and asked if I'd be ringmaster for one of the performances.

One catch. You had to enter the circus on the back of an elephant. Then slide off and start the circus.

Elephants, I quickly learned, walk with a wobble. They sway, actually, and with each step you feel like you're going to fall off. It takes some getting used to. All I kept thinking about was I'm going to fall on my ass in front of hundreds of people.

I didn't and for that I thank 'Betsy' the pachyderm.

The notoriety was great but something else was happening on a personal level. My first marriage was falling apart. I got married too young. In a break-up there's always plenty of blame to go around and I certainly needed to mature a bit. I am thrilled to this day though to have my son Charles whom I am very proud of.

In the fall of 1991 I moved out of my house and into a modest apartment not far from Staten Island Cable. It was right down the block from a small neighborhood bar. Between the break-up and the stress of moving and shaking up my life I got into the bad habit of drinking too much, sometimes with funny consequences.

When I had time I would stroll down the block to the bar and have a couple of vodka and tonics. On one of those days my local celebrity status worked against me. A little buzzed I was headed back to my apartment when a man watering his lawn recognized me from TV.

"Hey, you're the guy…" I heard through a vodka buzz.

Of all the times to get recognized!

"Millie!" he yelled, "Millie, it's that guy – the one from the show we watch."

Mille, who was in the backyard working on her begonias, lifted her head and grinned. My brain was firing about thirty percent and at this point I didn't know what would happen next.

"Come on," my neighbor said, "We just got the barbeque going…come have dinner with us. Millie? We have enough for the TV guy, right? Your name's Frank, right?"

My brain was on autopilot, my head spinning as he became more insistent about guiding me toward the backyard with his giant arm around my shoulder. Things started to get blurry. At this point Millie had joined in and was yanking my arm.

As if on command and out of nowhere I belched, "Thanks for watching. I apreeeeeshiate it."

I struggled a bit and told them I was in a rush but he would not take no for an answer. Next thing I knew I was in his backyard. He began introducing me to his grandkids.

Hot dogs were rolled onto the grill. I was able to leave at some point. To this day I'm not sure how. I don't remember what I said or even if I ate. I do know for a while after that I took a different route to the bar and avoided my fan and his wife anyway I could.

Many TV news people have appeared on air drunk – especially some of my older colleagues. If you're shocked, don't be.

One famous New York anchor for a while anchored two newscasts a day. One at noon, the other at seven p.m. Between newscasts he spent every moment he could at a bar right down the block from the station. He knocked back as many as he could and then the assistant news director would call the bar about six and ask the bartender to let the anchor know he should start heading back. His seven o'clock newscast, to his credit, was always perfect. But as for being drunk on the air – he was far from the only one!

Booze is still a big part of the news business. A few drinks with a source from City Hall can help you get a real good story. It loosens lips. In early TV many of the reporters and anchors came from the newspaper business. With its lazy deadlines you had all day to chase down a story and, if need be, ply a low-level city official into oblivion until he gave you the facts you needed.

As word got around that my show was good, the soon-to-be-launched all-news cable station for New York City called 'New York 1 News' came calling. The folks at New York 1 News began asking the movers and shakers on Staten Island who might be a good reporter to cover the borough. I was the clear choice, so they called. I went on the interview. They called back to say I was hired. My heart dropped though when they started talking money. They wanted to pay me $10,000 less than I was making at Staten Island Cable. I told them to meet my current salary and I was theirs. No go. I passed on the offer and after some pangs of regret carried on.

Besides *Staten Island Live* Staten Island Cable was airing a very popular sports show hosted by Joe Nugent. Joe is a well-liked and respected sports writer for Staten Island's premier newspaper the *Staten Island Advance*. His TV show is beloved. Every week he talks with a local or city sports hero, chats about the week's big sports story and then makes predictions for the weekend. Staten Island, being sports obsessed, made his show a must see.

Joe was most proud of his accuracy in predicting games. Every week he'd challenge a special guest or local celebrity to try and beat him. Most didn't even come close. Joe was so good at picking games correctly that he began making it interesting. If the guest beat Joe he'd give the guest a $20 gift certificate to go toward dinner at a local restaurant.

Joe saw me in the hallway at Staten Island Cable one day and said, "Frank, you ought to come on the show."

I am a sports fan but not a fanatic. I love football, can talk baseball; basketball and hockey, not so much. I played organized football as a kid but had second thoughts after a neighborhood bully on another team flattened me as I cut across the middle. I can still feel my body pounding to the ground all these years later.

"What do you want me to do?" I asked Joe.

"Come on next Tuesday," he said, "We'll talk sports and you can make some football predictions. I haven't been beaten in seventeen weeks," he said with a grin.

Joe and I had a friendly rivalry. Joe thought his show was more popular than mine. I made sure to let him know that my show was more popular. We'd smile about it but deep down each one of us thought he was more well known on Staten Island.

He might have been right. One night Lauren and I – whom I was now romantically involved with – attended a high school basketball game that was being broadcast on Staten Island Cable. The cameras panned the crowd and caught Lauren and me in the front row watching the game. It was a quick ten-second shot with Joe and the color guy doing the game talking briefly about us and other people in the stands.

Even though I had a weekly show – that was repeated often – for months after that people were saying, "Hey I saw you on TV at the Tottenville High School Basketball game." Like I said, Staten Island is sports-obsessed.

For Joe, having me on *his* show was more than just mixing it up with a TV rival. I suspect he secretly wanted to make sure he buried me on the air with his encyclopedia-like knowledge of sports.

The day of the show was especially stressful. I spent most of my morning in my apartment dealing with some personal issues and having a drink or two. It was late in the afternoon before I realized I had to appear on Joe's show. By that time I was drunk.

I rubbed my face, which I could no longer feel, combed my hair, picked some clothes off the floor, threw them on, straightened myself out and headed over to the station. The trap had been set. For Joe, my drunkenness was going to make beating me so much easier. Climbing the two steps onto Joe's set was a job in itself. Its sports themed colors gave me a headache. The chairs were high with no back support – so I swayed a bit during the interview.

After we spent fifteen minutes talking football and sports in general we came to the part of the show to make predictions. I had not done my homework and wasn't a hundred percent sure who was even playing that weekend.

Anyway the games came up on the screen and Joe – having analyzed each team based on past performance and things like statistical trends and injury reports – made his usual educated and well-thought-out picks. Each one backed up with the kind of supportive evidence you'd find in a Supreme Court ruling.

I, on the hand, might as well have used a dartboard. I picked the games based on what team my eyes focused on first or how they came up on the screen. It was a shot in the dark and I was sure Joe would be crowing the following week about how he dusted the station's newsman and embarrassed him once and for all.

Sunday night after the games I turned off the TV grinning. Even drunk I picked every game right. Joe got two wrong. His seventeen-week winning streak was over. He grudgingly gave me the $20 gift certificate and never bothered me again.

With my new celebrity I was able to get and see things on Staten Island most other residents could not. A quick flash of recognition from a viewer was enough to get just about anything I needed on Staten Island.

One day while taking the Staten Island Ferry across the harbor I was spotted by a deckhand who loved the show. I figured I'd give this celebrity thing a test. "You know I always wanted to be on the bridge of the ferry when it docked."

"No problem," he said.

We climbed up a few stairs and then up a small outside ladder near the back of the ferry. The next thing I knew I was walking across the top of it as it cruised by the Statue of Liberty. You have to lean forward as you walk across because the head wind is so strong. I glanced back at lower Manhattan, waved to the Statue of Liberty and when I got near the front the deckhand graciously held the door open for me and we walked onto the bridge.

The captain was just as excited to see me and seemed to enjoy that someone was so interested in what was to him the mundane task of docking a huge ferry into a small slip. He showed me the 'steering wheel', which was no bigger than a standard stick shift on a sports car, and the docking pole that jutted off the bow of the ferry which he used to guide her in. It was exciting to be there!

One day while cruising over the Verrazano Bridge I looked up and thought how nice it would be to stand at the very top of that bridge, on one of the 780-foot towers. This was the perch from which the start of the New York City Marathon is broadcast every November.

A couple of days later I got the name of the manager of the bridge and gave him a call. He knew me, watched the show, and said it wouldn't be a problem. That was easy I thought. I was really getting used to this TV celebrity thing.

I invited my Staten Island Cable colleague John Corso to come along. We picked a gorgeous day in May and asked if we could climb up to the top of the tower. By coincidence the upper level of the bridge was closed for maintenance. Everything was going just as planned.

John and I drove to the main office and signed a waiver that freed the Triborough Bridge and Tunnel Authority, the agency that operates the bridge, from any liability should we get hurt. We then hopped into a maintenance truck, which took us to the tower on the Staten Island side. The Verrazano Narrows Bridge – one of the longest suspension bridges in the world – is named after the great Italian explorer Giovanni Verrazano. He and his crew first sailed through the Narrows on their forty-foot ship The Dolphin. The bridge was constructed in the early 1960s and opened in November of 1964. It's so long that its engineers actually had to consider the curve of the earth in its construction.

We drove to the Staten Island side tower and got out. It was kind of strange to be standing in the middle of the roadway with no cars around. The stanchion had a small submarine type door with a circular handle that had to be turned to get inside. We squeezed through it and into a tiny elevator that would take us a third of the way up. It rattled and groaned as it made the trip. The door then opened inside at the point where the stanchion starts to curve inward.

We climbed a few flights of standard stairs with railings and then came to the next landing. This one was at the point where the cables arch up to meet the tower. A small door there allowed us to look right down the curve of the cables. You can look at the bridge from the roadway today and hardly see the door, but it's there. It's the entrance for crews who climb up the small walkway between the cables checking for problems. When they're done they open that door, head down the stairs, into the elevator and down to the roadway. We were headed in the other direction and we weren't done yet.

The last part of the journey came in the form of a steel ladder from that landing right up to the top of the tower. Our guide went first and like the hatch of a submarine turned a small wheel, popped it open and the sun came streaming in. We were one short ladder climb from the top of the Verrazano Bridge.

I looked at John, he looked and me and we grinned. I climbed the rungs and poked my head out to see all of Staten Island and the rest of New York in crystal clear clarity. We marveled at the views.

The top of the tower is the size of a tennis court with a small knee-high railing near the edge. I could see recognizable landmarks on Staten Island. Fort Hamilton, named after Alexander Hamilton, right at the base of the bridge on the Brooklyn side, sat small and silent. Along with Fort Wadsworth right across from it on the Staten Island side, Fort Hamilton protected the entrance to the harbor right up until the nuclear age when Washington realized a sea attack on New York was unlikely. Plans for a bridge linking Staten Island and Brooklyn had been held up for years because the military feared if it were attacked it could fall into the Narrows and close off water access to the nation's largest city.

The grandest view was of lower Manhattan. There in May of 1994 I stood and took the quintessential shot. My arm outstretched as John snapped a photo of me with both towers of the World Trade Center in the palm of my hand. I still cherish that picture.

As high as we went – I was now ready to use this celebrity thing to go even higher. John and I always talked about parachuting from a plane. It was costly and seemed silly unless you could do it for free. Bingo! I did some pre-Internet research and discovered a New Jersey based skydiving business about forty miles from Staten Island. I talked the owner into coming onto the show but only if I could experience the jump first hand – along with my "producer" John.

So off we went to a skydiving company in Warren County, New Jersey (not far from where I started in radio). We sat through a course on skydiving, signed another one of those waivers freeing the firm from any liability should we hit the ground before the chute opened, and then headed outside for some training including how to pull your emergency chute should the primary chute fail. As the lessons continued, I became more and more concerned. The instructor was an expert but I kept thinking – what the hell did I get myself into? My only consolation was that the entire jump, from the moment I jumped out to my landing, would be videotaped for the show.

Should I happen to go splat, I thought, at least I'll know I'll be on every news show in America that night. That seemed to allay my fears. If you're going to check out you might as well do it with pizzazz! Over the years I've often told colleagues that I always wanted to die at the anchor desk, in the middle of a story, and most importantly during the sweeps ratings period. That way I would be assured of being on every station in the country that night.

After about four hours of skydiving training, it was do or die. Let me rephrase that: It was time to get going. This is how it would come down. Um… this is how the jump would happen: John and I would be brought up to about three thousand feet in a small Cessna two-seater. On command we would individually climb out onto the edge of the wing holding on to only a small cable. Then at the count of three we would *voluntarily* jump off the wing backwards. The parachute cord – attached to another cable inside the plane – would then yank the chute open. All we had to do was jump.

Once the chute opened we would receive expert instructions via a radio hooked up to the helmets. The instructor on the ground would tell us what cord to pull to steer the chute and to ensure we landed as close to the drop site as possible. A giant white "X" on the ground marked the optimal spot. There would be a cameraman on board and one at the drop site to get my jump, descent and landing.

There were five of us on the plane: The pilot in one seat and beside him, next to the door where we would take our stroll out to the end of the wing, our cameraman. Behind them – cramped and sitting on the floor – were the instructor, John and me. We were sitting in an odd position. In our position John could not make eye contact with me but he nudged my leg a few times to get my attention. I never responded. I guess I was in a daze. In fact I remember saying – this could end badly.

The pilot and cameraman were needed for obvious reasons. John and I were there to jump. The instructor was there for several small reasons and one very big one. He would first let us know we were over the drop site. Then verbally coax us out the door and to the end of the

wing. He'd then scream out the door counting us down to three and watch us fall. His most important job though was one no one wanted to do: If we froze at the edge of the wing or changed our minds the instructor's job was to walk out onto the wing and push us off.
As the plane bounced around I waited my turn. I remember just staring at the interior of the fuselage, trance-like. Over the din of the engines I heard the instructor call out John's name. He dutifully got into a low crouch, ducked his head and tiptoed to the edge of the wing. I didn't see all of it and quite frankly I didn't want to.

A minute after John stepped out onto the wing and did his Peter Pan thing, I heard some crackling over the pilots headset. He was saying something but I couldn't make it out.

Oh shit, I thought, *something went wrong. I just killed my friend.*

I looked at the instructor who had a look of concern but I couldn't figure out how serious it was. He said to me, "Okay, you're next."

What? I thought. I yelled, "What about John?"

Over the rattle and racket of the engines he said, "Minor problem.... okay Frank, let's go."

What?? How could you have a minor problem when you jump out of a plane?

The instructor made it clear that once you were up in the air with a chute strapped to your back the only way down was out the door. The pilot wasn't going to land with *me on the wing* so I accepted my fate and started to crawl to the door. In a flash I was out there on the wing. The air was whooshing by, the engines screaming, and all of northern New Jersey in my goggles. Several feet away and down below the cameras were rolling.

I jumped. And image of my chute opening in front of me as the plane sped away is still seared into my brain.

The chute opened awkwardly and spun me around a few times before straightening out. My radio instructions blared. I dutifully yanked on this cord and that and opened my eyes long enough to enjoy the three-minute journey to the ground. I landed about thirty feet from the bull's eye of the drop site. I forgot to roll when I hit the ground and hurt my knee. I got up, limped over to the instructor on the ground and the cameraman and forced a smile.

Once my head was clear I looked around for John and began asking where he was and what had happened. He appeared moments later and said he had a little trouble maneuvering his chute. He landed on the other side of the road almost clipping some power lines on the way down.

Back on Staten Island the separation from my wife was getting messy. It involved the usual court battles over material possessions and the custody of our son. It was costly, foolish and went on way too long.

Although one of these court appearances actually saved my life. On February 26, 1993 I appeared at Family Court in Staten Island, a run down building where angry couples gather to grimace at each other and plead their cases before a rotating cast of disinterested judges.

The judge allowed the testimony in our case to drag on all through the morning and then asked us to come back after lunch. The request to return after lunch royally screwed up my plans. I was planning to hop on the Staten Island ferry – which was right down the block – and take the trip over the harbor to lower Manhattan to pick up my paycheck at Metro Traffic where I was still working part time.

I had done this several times before, always taking the ferry, walking the few blocks from the ferry terminal in lower Manhattan to the World Trade Center where Metro was located, up the stairs and in and through the lobby of the Vista Hotel – which was connected to the World Trade Center. I figured if I caught the ferry at 11:30 I'd be walking into the Vista Hotel lobby at about 12:15 or so.

I stepped out of the courthouse during the lunch break and lamented my bad luck: another afternoon wasted with the nonsense of an angry soon-to-be-ex-wife and a legal system that moves as slow as an arthritic snail. Not to mention a paycheck that I could not get because what was supposed to be a short court appearance was now stretched into an afternoon marathon.

As I stood on the steps of Family Court and stared out across the harbor I noticed smoke coming from lower Manhattan. At about 12:17 an explosion rocked the World Trade center – the first terrorist attack on those buildings. The huge bomb inside of a van parked beneath the building exploded in the area below the lobby of the Vista Hotel.

If the morning had gone like it was supposed to, I probably would have been standing in the Vista Hotel lobby when the explosion went off. It was the only time in my struggle to get divorced that the wheels of justice moved just slowly enough to save me from injury or worse.

A funny thing did happened several days after the explosion. When I wasn't selling advertising or planning my next show, I was bothering my colleagues to go out to lunch. Steve Adleman and I headed out to lunch one day and while we were gone Staten Island received some kind of anonymous terrorist threat.

The entire borough and its businesses were alerted. Staten Island Cable went into lock down. To make matters worse the regular guard in front of the building was off that week so here came Steve and I with no idea of what had happened with a guard who didn't know us from Adam.

As I pulled up to Staten Island Cable the guard jumped out of his shack and stopped my car dead in its tracks.

"Please identify yourselves," he shouted.

Steve and I thought he was kidding.

I glanced at Steve and he gave me a smile like, "go for it."

"Yes," I said with all the authority I could muster, "I will most certainly identify myself. I am retired Sergeant Major Frank Cipolla and this is Lieutenant Steve Adleman, U.S. Air Force."

A brief awkward pause was followed by a terse, "Get the fuck out of the car."
We made it past the guard 15-minutes later after convincing him not to call the police. Steve and I still laugh about it to this day.

The sales thing was going well, my TV show was a hit, but by 1994 I was antsy again. I was making more money than I ever had, but occasionally I would catch the local TV news and get pangs of anxiety, a yearning in my gut that even though I was doing well financially something was missing.

Hosting a talk show on Staten Island Cable and the other news events like Election Night coverage and local parades was good but at the age of thirty-five, I knew if I was going to get into "big time" my TV window – albeit slowly – was beginning to close. TV is a business that cherishes youth. I was anxious to move on but not so anxious to walk away from a really good paying job and my local celebrity.

This is where my beautiful soon-to-be-wife Lauren came in. By 1994 we were living together and slowly trying to reconstruct our lives. She and I met when we were both married and had to jettison our pasts in order to move forward. I liken it to a big bucket: Inside is all that you know and have. The physical items, the emotional items, your feelings, your desires, even your personal belongings. You take that bucket, dump it out, and put back only what you want.

I sorted through my important life items one by one and filled up my bucket again. Dutifully leaving out what I didn't want and adding some new items like Lauren's beautiful and talented daughter Taryn. I know one thing – I could not have made the transition from unhappy marriage to the love of my life without my extraordinary Lauren.

Lauren, or as people know her, The Bride, would occasionally look at me and say, "What are you doing here?"

We're both from New York, so we understand each other perfectly. She has this unique ability to get right to the point. In other words she was politely prodding me to reach higher. Not to settle. To find out what was over the next horizon, and the next, and the next.

"I mean, you were on radio and you have this great show on TV but so what? You should be sending out tapes, calling people, getting out of here. You can't stay here your whole life. It's a waste."

I guess she sensed that there was unfinished business. Her gentle prodding – which she would do again and again throughout our marriage – was aimed at refocusing me. And you know what? She was right. I could have stayed at Staten Island Cable in relative obscurity for the next twenty years, but I realized I wasn't finished giving radio and TV a shot. So I began to look around again. Seriously looking at getting back into the big time news game.

I have told kids over the years who want to get into this business that it's not what you do so much as what others don't. It sounds odd, but it's true. People in positions of power – especially those who have the ability to hire and fire – want to be flattered and respected. Simple things like a firm handshake after an interview, a handwritten thank-you note instead of an email or nothing at all, is what they remember. Some kids forget that and those who don't are the ones who get hired.

So when I noticed an article in a TV trade magazine about the launch of a 24-hour cable news station in New Jersey, my eyes widened. First I did my due diligence. I made some calls, found some more articles and established who was behind it and who the news director was going to be.

It was going to be called News 12 New Jersey and it was going to be one of five all news cable stations that now ring New York City. It was owned by Cablevision, so I knew this was a serious endeavor. In my investigation I also discovered the news director of the soon-to-be-launched News 12 New Jersey was going to be a man named Jeff Marks.

I had two things to do in a hurry. Since I had never done a TV news report I had to get one in the can pronto. I read about a new road down the block from the place I shared with Lauren in the Dongan Hills section of Staten Island that had been a hang-out for drug dealers and other undesirables until the city cleared some brush, added more lighting and paved the street.

It was a warm and fuzzy story, which I was going to use as one of my "news reports." I wrote a quick script, called a friend of mine who owed me a favor, had him shoot some stand-ups of me walking and talking about the weeds and the improvements, interviewed some neighbors and then had another friend at Staten Island Cable edit it for me. All in all it didn't look half bad. I tweaked it, threw in an envelope with my resume and sent it over to Jeff Marks.

Next I had to get an interview with him – or at the very least some quality face time. Here's where serendipity comes in. Marks, it turn out, was to speak before the New Jersey Broadcasters Association in nearby Woodbridge, New Jersey. That would be my chance to pitch him face to face.

It's funny what happens when you make up your mind. What seemed easy to me didn't even occur to others who might want to be part of this exciting launch. I was sure ten other guys had the same plan. And I was sure that when Marks spoke before the New Jersey Broadcasters Association I would have to jockey for his attention, maybe with guys a lot more experienced than I was.

On the appointed day I dressed to the nines, headed over to the luncheon in Woodbridge and made idle chitchat with whomever would talk to me while scanning the room for Marks.

He arrived late with the head of all the News 12 Networks. His speech was less about News 12 and more about allaying the fears of the radio and TV station owners who were afraid News 12 would bury them. When he was done he moved to the back of the room and stood to hear the other speakers. I made my move.

"Hey Mr. Marks – I'm Frank Cipolla – News Director at Staten Island Cable."

"Oh yes," he said as if he knew me.

Good sign.

"I heard about this exciting launch and just wanted to meet you, give you my card and ask if you had a chance to look at the demo I sent you?"

"Yes, I did. In fact I'm in a bit of a rush now but give me a call in a few days."

"Will do," I said.

That's all I needed.

When I called a few days later Marks said they were still building the studios, but since he was of a Jewish faith, and if I didn't mind, could we meet Christmas Eve day. It was Christmas Eve 1995 – my 36th birthday.

Lesson two for kids reading this, the answer to a 'Can you?' question from any potential employer is always, "Yes."

Everything was going as planned. I jotted down the directions and got ready for my interview. Owner Cablevision was pouring millions into the launch of News 12 New Jersey. The studios were being built inside a one story building in an industrial area in Edison, New Jersey near the Garden State Exhibition Center.

I pulled up to the building and walked into a construction site. Since it was Christmas Eve, no one was in the place but Jeff Marks. Jeff saw the potential in me. We talked, he understood where I was going and was ready to give me a chance. I drove home more excited about a job then I've ever been.

Just before this transition began Lauren and I made an important decision. We got married on Thursday, April 20, 1995. We decided on Tuesday. Got everything together on Wednesday and went down the Borough Hall on Staten Island Thursday and a Justice of the Peace made us man and wife.

John Corso – my colleague who had climbed one of the world's longest suspension bridges with me and had joined me in jumping out of a speeding plane at three thousand feet was my best man. Lauren – who would from that point on be referred as "The Bride" – selected her friend Ann Rizzo as Maid of Honor. Our friends from Staten Island Cable threw us a small reception at a restaurant on Staten Island later that night.

It seems simplistic to say that she changed my life. All that followed could not have been possible without her. Including this book. She is the love of my life and my best friend, and everything good that followed was because she was and is always there to support, guide and counsel me.

I started as a reporter at News 12 New Jersey on February 1, 1996. Six years to the day that I started at Staten Island Cable. Radioman would become TV newsman and the fun would continue.

Chapter 14
NEWS 12 NEW JERSEY

The News 12 studios are in an industrial area near the Garden State Exhibition Center in Edison, New Jersey. The location is perfect. It's smack dab in the middle of the state with access to every major roadway. It's also the former home of an ESPN venture that fizzled. Its studios were still there but everything needed to be reconfigured. Every day I'd come in to find walls missing or wires hanging as contractors molded the space to Cablevision's exact specifications.

Another reporter started about the same time. A beautiful blonde from Rhode Island who also had aspirations of getting the experience she needed on the outskirts of New York and then moving up to the big time on some New York station. Because of the constant hammering and drilling Donna DiPietro and I were sent to a small, relatively quiet office in the corner of the building. We were told to sift through the newspapers and develop stories that might be of interest to New Jersey viewers. We had no outlet to air these stories so we just came in and did what we could to look busy.

There were lunches at a restaurant near by and while inside the building we'd bundle up to fight off the severe February cold. The heating system was spotty. I even brought in a thermos of hot chocolate. Often Donna and I would sit there, coats on, fumbling with gloves to turn the pages of New Jersey's daily newspapers.

Things happened haphazardly. One day it got so cold Jeff Marks told everyone to go home. He forgot to tell Donna and me. We sat in the back like Eskimos until a walk to the men's room revealed the place was empty. We had been sitting there for a couple of hours without knowing everyone had gone home.

One day I ventured from the back and as I was walking I was pushed back by a small explosion in the hallway. Next thing I knew I was enveloped in smoke and dust. By order of the local fire department an exit door had to be blown out near the back offices. The workmen set some charges and let 'er go. There was no countdown, no warning just, *Boom*!

It was exciting to watch this start-up station take shape. Every week some new employees would join us including the new operations manager and his wife. They were part of a twofer deal worked out by Jeff. Our assistant news director was Allison Gibson. And, one by one, pretty and handsome reporters started to fill the building; some fairly big names too – among them Lee Leonard.

To any New Yorker Lee Leonard is a legend. He was a big part of the first real all sports show on TV. It came on every Sunday Night in the Seventies after the Channel 5 news at ten. *Sports Extra* was a crude version of what we now see on ESPN. It was a recap of the sporting events of the day and week. More importantly *Sports Extra* was amazing and Lee Leonard was its host. In fact Leonard later became the first person on camera when ESPN launched in the 1980's.

I was thrilled one day when Lee Leonard wanted to chat with me about one thing or another. Here was Lee Leonard, and he wanted *my* opinion on something. He was the first real TV personality from my youth with whom I made contact.

Lee loved a good joke. One day he and I were talking about complaints by actor Danny Glover that because he was African American he had trouble hailing a cab in New York City. Glover's contention was that even though he was a big Hollywood star cabbies wouldn't pick him up – especially at night – because he was black.

I said to Lee, "Maybe not. Maybe they just saw some of his movies."

I was really excited about what News 12 was and could become. My job first was to be a reporter. Any quality or prolonged "face time", as we say in the business, would have to be attained through hard work. I was hopeful of being an anchor on News 12 one day. Those hopes were stoked during my interview when Jeff Marks told me he liked my TV work – such as it was – and thought I was a half step or two from being a good anchor. It said to me that he was open to the idea of bumping me up one day to the anchor desk. And with a twenty-four-hour news station that meant many opportunities to plug me in.

Jeff put up two giant sheets of paper on a wall. As he hired people he would jot their names down on the paper. The list grew week by week. One day just before we launched I passed this list and saw the name Mizar Turdiu. I remember saying, "What the hell is a Mizar Turdiu?" I assumed it was a Muslim man Jeff had hired to further diversify the staff, which now was made up of a hundred and thirty-five people from all parts of the country – the vast majority of us in our twenties and thirties.

The launch came March 26, 1996, a significant date. It was the beginning of spring and more importantly to me the tenth anniversary of my mother's passing. I considered it a sign sent to remind me that she was watching. These important dates pop up again and again throughout my career and always give me reason to pause.

The first newscast on News 12 New Jersey was set for six in the evening. That afternoon Jeff gathered all of us in the newsroom. There were people from every part of the country. He told us how proud he was, what high hopes he had, and wished us well.
We smiled like kids in a candy store.

A giant tent had been set up outside to entertain the movers and shakers in the state while inside our first newscast – News 12 New Jersey's *Evening Edition* – was clicking on for the first time. Lee Leonard – our biggest name – was co-anchoring with the same woman I beat out for the news anchor job at WNBC-AM eight years earlier. Debbie Gross was now Debbie Rodriguez, and as good as ever. She lit up the screen and her perky personality worked well with Lee's more staid and traditional anchor delivery.

My colleague Donna DiPietro was the first reporter to appear on the air. I had done a package that night, but oddly – in a bit of trivia – I was the only full-timer not to appear on the premiere broadcast of News 12 New Jersey. It didn't matter. I was thrilled to be there and knew opportunity was everywhere.

What I didn't tell my colleagues – some of whom had years of TV news experience – was that when it came to TV news production and presentation I didn't know what I was doing. Really. I mean essentially I was imitating my boyhood TV news heroes.
I was learning on the job. I'd ask a technical question – one that any TV newsperson would know – and someone would give me an answer. I'd say something like, "Oh yeah. I forgot. Thanks."

Each report I did got a little better. My stand-ups and live shots improved. I stayed later analyzing them, breaking the reports down, seeing what I could do better the next time.

Jeff originally wanted to put me in one of our three bureaus around the state but that's not what I desired. I preferred to at our headquarters in Edison. I knew that by being there he would see me often. I could show off when I had to and be a constant reminder to him. I could also be around should an anchor call in sick and needed someone to anchor in a pinch.

One day in the spring of 1996 I breezed though the newsroom and saw a stunningly beautiful woman. Outwardly she seemed like a lot of fun. I joked with her and because we were all getting to know each other – asked her name.

"Mizar," she said.

"Oh," I thought. "This is Mizar. She's not a man. Maybe not even a Muslim. So what the hell is she?" Mizar was the co-host of News 12 New Jersey's Morning Edition. I had to cover a story so the introduction was brief, but I got a good feeling about her. She seemed to 'get it'

In the summer of 1996 while riding in one of the News 12 SUVs on the way to cover a story, the radio in our car crackled. It was the assignment editor and I could tell immediately that something was up.

"A bus has overturned on the Garden State Parkway southbound between exits 105 and 100. Head there ASAP.

"Got it – will do," I replied.

My photographer Richard O'Brien made some quick turns and before you knew it we were heading southbound on the GSP. About twenty-five minutes later – and before even the police arrived – Richie and I saw it. It took some time to sink in, but a Tour Bus from Chinatown in New York and headed to Atlantic City, had apparently clipped a maintenance truck which was being used to paint traffic lines. It then veered off the Parkway, broke through a railing and ended up on its side in a cement gully between the northbound and southbound lanes.

There was paint all over the road and white tire marks leading to the crash. The bus was low enough that if you were driving north or southbound you would probably miss it. We pulled up onto the left hand shoulder of the road, stepped out and peered down. About forty feet below the bus sat, its occupants, older, mostly Asian Americans wandering around nursing various minor bumps and bruises.

This is where your instincts as a reporter click in. The site was scary but Richie and I knew two things. First, we had to place our emotions aside for the moment. And second we had to get as much done as we could before the police arrived because once they did our view and access to the injured would be restricted. We never spoke, just looked at each other and with eye contact conveyed those two important messages.

I climbed down the cement shoulder with Richie tagging along. We very quickly determined there was not much we could do to ease the suffering of the injured. Most of the injuries, thankfully, were minor and those not injured were helping relatives and friends while waiting for help.

I searched for the driver but could not find him. I then motioned over to Richie, who had already been knocking off all the video he could, and began speaking with one of the uninjured about what happened. We spoke with another victim before a State Police cruiser pulled up and the trooper ran down to see what was happening.

After calling in for backup his next job was to get us the hell out of there. We could only be in the way. Now more unspoken messages were exchanged. As the trooper spoke the two of us moved farther away from each other. This ballet allowed Richie and me to continue our work.

As the state trooper talked with me about giving him some room Richie was walking around the bus getting exclusive video of the wreck. When he went over to Richie to ask that he stop videotaping and move back, I moved in with my pad on the other side of the scene to talk with victims. It was a two-on-one game the trooper was losing.

This went on for about ten minutes before the trooper's backup arrived. That's when the police tape came out and we were pushed back. By the time the other news stations got there our work was done. And it was prime stuff!

We had exclusive video and led the newscast. Now I know what you're thinking: *You guys are vultures! You shoved a camera in the faces of those suffering and played cat and mouse with a state trooper just to get the story.* I've heard this again and again in my career. Let me just say this. *Getting the story is what we do.* Period. It's our job. Certainly if there is a way to help and comfort those who are suffering we will gladly put the camera and notepads down. I don't know any reporter who wouldn't. But being the first on the scene of a big story and getting 'exclusive' interviews and video is a rush. It means you've won the day. It means we're better than those who did not. And that is what we do.

Say what you want about all the silly stories that pervade local newscasts now, but please know when journalism is practiced correctly it levels the playing field. It gives power to the powerless. And when that camera is shoved in the face of a crook, it reveals his or her soul.

The bus crash also led me to a darker story. As I did some investigating on my own time I learned something about the tour bus business in New Jersey. The bus that crashed was taking about sixty passengers for a day trip to Atlantic City. These one-day excursions are very common and immensely popular in the New York metropolitan area. Retirees, mostly, take the bus down to Atlantic City and spend the day gambling at the dozen or so casinos.

Sometimes drivers make two or even three trips a day. Without resting. And that was apparently what led to this crash. The driver, exhausted from his second five hour round trip, fell asleep at the wheel.

As I dug into the growing number of bus crashes on the Parkway one company's record stood out. Legal considerations don't allow me to mention the company by name but it's the biggest of the bunch and a player in New Jersey state politics.

This intrigued me. First of all, why was this company – with such an atrocious safety record – allowed to continue to haul seniors and others to Atlantic City? Why were the drivers – in an alarmingly high number – falling asleep at the wheel? Why wasn't anyone saying anything? Who did they know? How much influence did they have in state government?

A good reporter asks, "why." I did. And it led to more and more whys.

"I think I'm on to something," I told Jeff Marks. I explained what I had found and told him I needed a few days to do some snooping and digging. To his credit – as he would time and time again – he said, "Go for it."

What I found was that this company had a bunch of sweetheart deals with the state. It also lent its buses to the New Jersey Transit Authority under a special arrangement. And it appeared to skirt federal laws when it came to the way it treated its drivers. At the time the Feds mandated bus and truck drivers could only drive 12 hours at a time before they were required by law to take a four-hour break. Drivers kept logs, but even those were suspect. The bus companies also had to provide enough beds or recliners for these drivers to rest at bus yards around the state.

As I would soon find out this was not the case. And it nearly got me killed.

First, I had to check out the bus yards to see what was going on. There were three owned by this company: one in Hoboken, one in Leonardo, New Jersey in the central part of the state, and one just outside Atlantic City. Photographer Dawn Howes and I secured a hidden camera from the station's engineer and headed to Hoboken. We scoped out the facility but it was locked up tight. There was little chance I could get onto the premises to chat with the drivers to see if there were accommodations for them to rest. The bus yard outside of Atlantic City was another story.

It sat on a couple of acres and had little or no security, and no sign that read, "No Trespassing," which is important legally if push comes to shove. Dawn and I went around the facility and then parked our unmarked car far from the trailer they had set up as their headquarters. We watched from a distance for about fifteen minutes. It was clear this was the place where drivers checked in and since it was the only structure on site, it was also theoretically the place where the bus company had to provide cots or beds or recliners so they could rest.

After we established that, we made our move. We parked, and Dawn and me, who was rolling with the help of a small camera in her vest, walked through the front gate.

We climbed the three or four stairs to the door of the trailer and walked in. Pausing inside I looked around. It was a typical common area of any business. A couple of uniformed drivers stood around talking. There was a small TV blasting a mid day talk show, a coffee machine, a couple of padded chairs and one recliner.

At the end of the trailer a man stood behind a Plexiglas partition chatting to a driver. I glanced at my shooter Dawn Howes and nodded. With her eyes she confirmed she was getting all of this.

"Wow," I said to one of the drivers. "Not much room for all of you to get some rest especially with this TV blasting."

"I know," he said. "You can't rest here and there isn't enough room to spread out anyway."

Great, I thought, *he said everything in one sentence.* As if he was reading my mind.

"Do you sleep at all when you get down here?" I asked.

"Ha!" he said. "I can't sleep anyway. I gotta get back up to New York to pick up some more people. Right after I pick up those I'm going back to Atlantic City. Third trip today."

"Third trip, wow!" I replied.

It was perfect stuff. Another driver chimed in before the guy behind the Plexiglas noticed us.

"Hey," he said. "Who are you?"

In TV news it is unethical not to identify yourself once asked. You can skirt the question, change the subject, but if someone asks you point blank you must tell him or her who you are. I evaded the question best I could but finally I walked to the window and said, "I'm Frank Cipolla, News 12 New Jersey."

"You're not supposed to come in here. Did you call the main office?"

"No."

"Well, I going to give them a call now. Just wait here."

Waiting around was one thing we weren't going to do. We had video of the outside; the inside and some pretty compelling sound bites from actual drivers.

"That's okay," I said. "We're leaving anyway."

The report that aired on News 12 New Jersey's *Evening Edition* was edited expertly, approved by Jeff Marks and the assignment editor, and it was pretty powerful stuff. According to my investigation, this giant bus company was working its drivers to the point of exhaustion. And never – as far as we could tell by all the documents and video we obtained – giving drivers a real chance to get some shut eye. No wonder there were drivers falling asleep at the wheel and hurting people. The passengers were unaware that the driver had not slept – in some cases – for more than a day.

Right after the report aired the shit hit the fan. The owner of the bus company called Jeff Marks. He was ready to sue the station, Marks and me. We were sure our facts were solid so that didn't scare us. The viewers loved it. It was the kind of signature story that puts a new station on the map. I had uncovered so much that I was already planning a follow-up piece that would be even more damning.

That's when the mysterious phone calls and visits began.

Often in the morning before I went out on a story I'd stroll across the parking lot to the post office to mail a few letters. Several days after the story aired I stepped out of the station and as I did a man sitting in a car several feet from the front door stepped out of his vehicle at the same time.

My New York City street sensibilities clicked in. I didn't like the timing of it. I tightened up a bit and picked up my pace but before I knew it he had stepped in front of me.

"You want the real story of what's happening with these bus companies? I've got it."

"Who are you?"

"It doesn't matter. I can give you inside information."

"I have to know your name."

"I can get you drivers who have been taken advantage of by this bus company."

"Will they talk on camera?" I asked.

"I don't know. But I'll call you. Give me your card." I did. "I'll get back to you."

I tried one more time, "What is your name and who are you?"

"Doesn't matter. Just call me John." He hopped back into his car and slowly drove off.

I didn't like what had just happened. He knew where to find me, had waited for me and got me alone. I'm a pretty good judge of character and even though I was spooked I sensed he was truly concerned for the drivers and could be a good source of info.

In the days ahead "John" called several times. And true to his word he set us up with several drivers who had taken round trips to Atlantic City without resting. He said the practice was common and pointed me in the right direction.

I interviewed two drivers in silhouette; one at a union hall in Jersey City, the other at his home in Sayreville, NJ. We made sure to confirm that they had worked for the bus company. They did so by showing us pay stubs. The interviews were moving. The facts were airtight. Somehow word got out and the president of the bus company and his legal team demanded a meeting with Jeff Marks and me before the next piece aired. I resisted, thinking it was a stall tactic, but Jeff said we'd hold off until they met with us.

When they arrived we moved to a small office near the lobby and shut the door. Jeff and I sat across from four men: the owner, his legal counsel and a couple of executives from the company. They complained that their side of the story was not being told. I said I had reached out to them but they did not respond.

"You're here right now, let's talk with you on camera." I said.

"I don't want to do that," the owner said.

"Okay, then let's talk off camera."

The first question was the killer. I stared the owner in the eyes and said, "Have you ever allowed your drivers, against federal regulations, to drive more than twelve hours without rest?"

The answer was lame. The owner looked down and said in a low voice, "No, I know of no instance in which that has happened."

The body language said it all. Low voice means I'm ashamed. Looking away means I'm having trouble lying to your face. I jotted down what he said on my reporter's notepad and the meeting went on. Jeff played good cop to a tee as I bored in. It didn't really matter what came after that; I felt I had these guys in a lie and I meant to prove it. We would add the owner's comments to the piece that would air later and I would continue digging.

The owner and his team left after a half hour and I was pleased. Jeff postponed the airing of the report that night – even though it was airtight. His belief was the bus operator did not have adequate time to respond to the first report and said he wanted to look at it again and make sure all the bases were covered so we would not get sued.

Screw them, I thought.

Later that afternoon I got a call at my desk from a friend of a friend. A Queens acquaintance who lived in the shadows.

"What the fuck are you doing?" he said.

"What are you talking about?"

"Don't you know who these guys are associated with?" he said.

"No."

"These guys are mobbed up and associated with a nasty crew in Newark."

I had grown up a mile or so from John Gotti's house in Queens. As a low level mobster Gotti often came in to have dinner at my Mom's restaurant. And even though this was not Gotti-related, nor was the restaurant a hang-out for mobsters, I didn't need to ask what he meant when he said "a crew." They were mobsters and apparently they had found out enough about me to have a friend call and warn me off.

"Frank," he whispered, "these guys won't think twice about fucking you up. Proceed carefully my friend because this is one of the meanest crews there is."

Click.

As Jeff took a few days to weighed whether to air the report I started parking my car farther away from the station and moving the location where I parked everyday so as not to be too predictable. I also began leaving at different times and from different exits. In addition I began peeking under my vehicle before I got in to make sure there wasn't a car bomb underneath. I never told The Bride any of this.

I was spooked but so much more intrigued. There was more to this story and I was just getting started. Call it youthful exuberance or just plain hubris but I had latched onto this story and I wasn't letting go. Maybe the threat of violence was just that – a threat. I don't know. I'll never know. Jeff canceled the airing of the follow-up piece on this shady bus company. I put up a fight but figured if I was going to hang my head out there I needed to know someone would have my back. The cockroaches that skirted the laws and put people in danger scampered away. It's one of the biggest regrets in my broadcasting career; made even worse by news of the most recent of these bus accidents – the crash of a bus coming back from a casino in Connecticut in March of 2011. Fifteen people were killed. The driver suspected of being asleep at the wheel.

In the fall of 1996 – after I'd been working at News 12 for six months, the station launched a weekend compilation of all the best stories of the week. It was a half hour show and it needed an anchor. Again the stars lined up and I all but volunteered. I had to stay later but it was important for me to establish myself as an anchor.

About this time there were some rumblings about Mizar's co-host on the *Morning Edition,* a nice amiable older man who was finding it harder and harder to get up in the middle of the night and be perky on the air. His work suffered as he dealt with what were brutal hours. I looked on from afar and kept my mouth shut. I had done years and years of morning shows and knew how tough it is. I also knew that if they were thinking of making a change that show was right up my alley.

Working the angles in this business includes never revealing to anyone what your plan is. You proceed with caution and if you can, use surrogates to make it happen for you. You never say explicitly what it is you want only that you have done the job, were great at it, and boy it was too bad the morning co-host wasn't as good as he could be.

The other anchors saw my potential and some, without any prodding, started to say how great it would be to have someone like Frank and his engaging personality working with the other great morning talent Mizar Turdiu.

The whispers about the change on the way became louder and louder. I kept my ear to the ground and my mouth shut. I did some schmoozing and politicking behind the scenes and made sure it could never be traced back to me.

"You got a minute?" Assistant News Director Allison Gibson said one day as she passed me in the hallway. She took me into a very small supply closet – which I thought was weird – and closed the door.

"You may want to be prepared to get up earlier in the morning. There are going to be some changes and I just want to give you the heads up."

At that point I knew it was matter of time. Like so many times later in my career, I knew it was important to play dumb and treat the man I would soon be replacing with all the respect he had earned. Gracious in victory and defeat. It's the most important lesson anyone can learn.

In December of 1996, less than a year after I had started, the announcement was made. I would be the new co-host of the *Morning Edition* with Mizar Turdiu and her current co-host would be shifted to a friendlier 9-5 schedule. I was ecstatic! I knew from past experience that the morning show was the only spot where you could let your personality shine. The Morning Edition was akin to Regis and Kelly. First some news, cooking segments, pet segments, and a small block at the end of every hour to chat about events of the day.

You meet people in your life that are the epitome of goodness. They flow with a spirit that comes from above. Mizar is one of them. We share a similar cultural heritage, come from the same area (she was born in New Jersey) and have lived in the same times (we were born six weeks apart). She possesses a sharp wit rooted in an incredible intelligence. She understands all the nuances of all my jokes and I hers. It was a perfect on-air match.

On-air chemistry is extremely rare. It can be faked, sometimes fairly well, but the microphone and camera never lie. When it's discovered, like a chunk of gold, news directors are wise to leave it alone. Rich Rapiti – my former general manager at WJDM understood this concept when Jim Bosh and I entertained our listeners on WJDM, and to his credit so did Jeff Marks with Mizar and me.

Our show was a mix of hard news, entertaining segments, and inside jokes. It was like eating at a restaurant and watching two people at the next table having fun. You so wanted to be part of it and we allowed our viewers to sit at the table every morning.

Mizar and I would come in at about 3:45 a.m., check our copy – which had been written by some of the hardest working producers and assistant producers around – and then write some segments ourselves for an hour or so. We'd then meet up at the makeup area. That was the beginning of a day of laughter that would not end for another five hours. Some of the funniest things happened at the makeup mirror and during the commercial breaks while on the air, most of it rooted in boredom. The news blocks – essentially the first ten minutes at the top and bottom of the show – were repeated four times. The news copy changed little and by the third time we had read the stories on air, we'd seen the video and were just trying to keep ourselves interested. Yes, news anchors do get bored as well. That's when Mizar would start playing. Mizar would adjust my chair. I'd read about some unfortunate accident on Route 78 and when we went to the video and I was off camera she'd hit the lever on the bottom of my chair and send me slumping ten inches. It was my job at that point to keep my eyes on the teleprompter, read the story, reach down and lift myself up and do it all before the camera came back on me.

I would wait my turn and when she read a story and went to video I'd wet my finger and poke it in her ear. Back to me. I read over some video and she'd take her pen and write, 'Doody Head' on my hand. I'd wait for her to go to video… etc. It was the TV equivalent of two bored kids in the back of Mom and Dad's SUV headed to Grandma's house.

Sometimes we'd get caught. Mizar would see an errant hair on my neck and while I was reading over video about some unfortunate soul who was struck by a car in Jersey City she'd be attempting to yank it out. Or she'd be fixing my hair, or shift my collar and the video would end abruptly and you'd see my face framed on your screen with a disembodied hand stroking my eyebrow. It was distracting and broke all the rules of TV news technique, but it was funny as hell. And the viewers loved it.

When we both come back in a two-shot we'd often be giggling and I'd say something like, "What's wrong Mizar?" She couldn't tell the viewing audience that we had just teased each other with childish pranks in the last five minutes, so she'd just smile and we'd go to commercial.

Sometimes we were laughing so much during the commercial break we had to not look at each other for fear we'd come back and start guffawing through the story about the child who fell out a tenement window in Newark. The floor manager would count us down and we had to pull ourselves back from the brink.

Mizar got every nuance of my sarcastic humor. We were essentially making fun of each other – but doing it with love. Some viewers didn't get the nuance however.

After one show I returned to my desk and as I sat down the phone rang. "Is this Frank Cipolla?"

It was an older sounding woman.

"Yes," I said, "Can I help you?"

"I want you to leave Mizar alone. I'm not going to tell you again. She's a nice woman and you should leave her alone."

"But, she and I…"

"And I know what you two are doing too. She's married, you know."

Click.

This woman was sure we were having sex.

Here's a segue for you:

Mizar was especially brutal when I had to pee. She'd grab the pitcher of water just below the set and slowly, very slowly, pour the water into her glass. I also struggled with lactose intolerance problems which she made fun of. Let me correct myself – lactose intolerance is no longer the right term. How do I know? One day I was in Starbucks and ordered my usual coffee with a touch of soymilk. The woman behind the counter was nice enough to bring it to my table and then said, "I'm curious – why the soy milk?"

I said, "I'm lactose intolerant. Milk is terrible on my stomach."

"Oh," she says, "My sister has IBS as well. Irritable Bowel Syndrome."

Funny when I was the kid it was called the "Runs" or the "Hershey Squirts."

Now I'm so proud to say I have a syndrome. Next there'll be a reality show. I can see it now: "IBS Rehab."

A friend at CBS once told me a funny story about Walter Cronkite. He said 'Uncle Walter' was having trouble with constipation so he took a laxative to move things along. He thought he had timed it correctly but half way into a live broadcast of the CBS Evening News the laxative kicked in.

The story goes Cronkite stood his ground and dumped in his pants rather than leave the set.

"…And that's the way shit is…"

Some of the commercial breaks at News 12 were longer than others and sometimes followed by pre-taped interviews. During these ten-to-fifteen minute breaks in the later hours of the show, we did what we could to keep going. In the winter months we'd sit on the news set and play the "Lilly Pad" game. We'd make five or six circles and then working from the top down trace the career of one of our colleagues. It always began innocently. "Works in small time radio," I would write in one circle. Mizar would follow with, "Moves up to Small TV station in Elmira, NY." After that it took a dark, and for us, a funny turn. I would write, "caught in motel room with sixteen-year-old girl." The last circle or Lilly Pad would always say the same thing: "prison."

Then, after having the cartoonist who creates the comic strip "Mutts" on the show, we came up with the harebrained idea that we could do a comic strip too. Mootz, my nickname for Mizar, would be a flea in the comic strip. Fark, her nickname for me, would be a tick. We would infest the dogs of famous people. Mizar did the drawing – and she was good at it. I provided the humor.

During the summer months we'd take advantage of the good weather and run outside to sling a football I kept in my desk. One summer morning we even had one of the producers drive his convertible around the parking lot and had a contest to see who could drop the football into the moving car from a hundred feet away.

We'd also sling the football around the newsroom but that was always a chancy proposition. At News 12 we'd sling the ball around but before you knew it one of the assistant producers was conked on the head. That's when Executive Producer Patrick Mason stepped in and forced all of us to sign a pact never to throw the football in the newsroom again.

In essence we were just having fun with some of the great people who woke up every day in the middle of the night and needed to let off some steam, the people who made us look good every morning. Folks like Scott "Skeeter" Miller, Pete "Stinky" Finer, Eric "Monster" Mundley, Chris O'Donnell, Kendra Wright-O'Conner, Mike Mariano and many, many more. With management snug in their beds and not due in for a few hours we had the place to ourselves.

Sometimes when we were leaving at eleven a.m. or so, one of the salespeople or management types would say, "Leaving so early?"

I'd just say, "Ya know, why don't you give me your phone number. I'll ring your phone when I get up tomorrow at 3:45." That usually shut them up.

Among the characters that worked the morning shift was Gleen, the floor manager. He dutifully pointed to the cameras we were supposed to be looking at as we read the teleprompter. He was supposed to be named Glen but the nurse misunderstood his mom and instead he had to live with the name Gleen for the rest of his life. Gleen had three jobs. He'd spend the middle of the night and early morning with us and then headed off to another day job and one after that. He was a hard worker but often, especially toward the end of the week, he was exhausted.

Mizar and I watched one day as he stood near a camera after getting our attention. As Mizar read the story over video Gleen started to sway. Next thing we heard was "clunk." Gleen had fallen asleep standing up, fell into the camera and conked the side of his head and collapsed to the floor. He bounced back up, but when the video ended and the camera came back on Mizar she had to use every bone in her body and all of her experience to keep herself from laughing out loud. One of our segments, "Cooking on Daytime" featured a chef who would whip up a quick meal for us, all the while telling us about his restaurant. It was a great segment. We had the hot plate going, the smells were terrific and then we had something to eat when we were done. We respected every one of these people but after a while even this became old hat and the giggles started bubbling up again.

I'd play with the food, Mizar would try and pull me back from the edge; the restaurant owner would scratch his head. In essence we were entertaining ourselves – sometimes trying to fight off a lack of sleep – and the guest just happened to be there as our foil. The audience ate it up (Badda BOOM!).

The "K" Block – the last few minutes of every hour when we sat around and chatted about the news of the day – was supposed to be a thoughtful reflection on what was happening in the news. It very quickly however became a short segment to lampoon someone in the news or make fun of some crazy video. Mizar and I would chat about what we were doing lately, how she had a flood in her home, or the fact that while getting dressed in the dark that morning I'd put on two different socks, whatever popped into our heads. It was *Regis and Kelly* and we had it down pat.

Sometimes we'd do a kicker – something funny like the dog with three legs or the woman who drove her car into a convenience store. I'd always add the sound effects. As a crippled Goose limped toward the pond I'd say over the video, "Ah… ah… ow… ow…" as Mizar read the copy.

About the time of the Monica Lewinsky scandal the U-S Mint was also redesigning the nation's money. We had the guys in graphics give Lincoln a buzz cut on the 'five dollar bill' and then on the other side of the bill there was a small sound truck in front of the Treasury Building. A close up showed it had a sign on it: "Interns Wanted."

The viewers loved the fact that they could get their news and get entertained at the same time. The entertainment news format in the morning was still fresh in 1997 and we were pushing the outer limits of the envelope.

It was the most fun I've ever had on TV before or since and it wasn't long before people were telling the reporters that they loved us. And I was starting to get recognized on the street and in stores. It also wasn't long before we started to crush the competition in New Jersey, regularly beating CNN, WABC, WCBS, and Headline News in the number of New Jersey morning viewers.

In TV, executives who know they have something good will never let on. They need to play coy for fear the hosts will get too demanding. But we saw it everywhere. More and more of the people around the station started making sure we were okay, that we had everything we needed. The sales staff made a point of giving us a "Great job!" We were making Cablevision money but if you asked Jeff Marks and others it was all a coincidence.

In the few times we asked for something out of the ordinary Jeff would try and bring us back to earth. He'd say, "The reason you guys are so popular is that New Jersey has never had a morning show of its own." To which I said, "Right. You mean they never had Mizar and Frank before." I won't lie to you: I was cocky and demanding. I knew we had caught lightning in a bottle and as long as I was up at the top I would make sure everyone knew it.

Mizar and I were among the very few personalities on News 12 – and on all the News 12's that ring New York City – who had contracts. During one renegotiation Jeff told me there would be no more contracts for us. He said Cablevision had a new policy. No contracts for talent. One week later my new contract arrived in the mail. I told Jeff and he played coy again, "Really that's surprising." Again, news directors never want to lead on that you're indispensable. We were. And it was a great feeling. And we got confirmation of that very early on.

In the early days the mucky mucks used to drive in from the corporate headquarters of Cablevision in Westbury, Long Island for a mandatory staff meeting. It always concluded with a look at the ratings for each show.

The first time they came the Morning Edition ratings were far superior to any other show we aired – even the much bally-hoed *Evening Edition* - the show they had poured the most money into. The next time they came the *Morning Edition* ratings were through the roof. After that they never returned. It was clear the show they didn't expect to be the moneymaker was a big hit and management no longer wanted to embarrass the anchors and crews of the other shows.

The sales manager later told me a survey they did found I was especially popular with older Italian ladies. They told those who asked that I reminded them of their sons, brothers and in some cases their husbands when they were my age. I was fine with that as long as they didn't feel compelled to pinch me on the cheeks.

People and organizations soon started requesting we make appearances. They were usually at night so the answer was no. Mizar, God bless her, did say yes now and again and the next day she paid for it. I could see she was exhausted but she loved the celebrity as much as I did.

Many famous people who made appearances in New Jersey and New York also suddenly wanted to be on the *Morning Edition*. We were visited by actors Danny Aiello and Dawn Wells, (best known as Mary Ann from *Gilligan's Island*). It was interesting I always thought she looked Italian and when I asked her off air she said she was. Via satellite we interviewed Helen Thomas, Loni Anderson, Julia Sweeney, best known for her androgynous character "Pat" from *Saturday Night Live* and even Dick Clark. I asked him if he was in his nineties yet. I don't think he appreciated that.

Bill Daily from the 60's TV show *I Dream of Jeannie* stopped in one day. During the commercial we got to talking and he told me an interesting story. He said he no longer looked forward to working in TV. He told the story of the time several years before when he had appeared on a sitcom. He learned his lines, was on the set on time and then found out his lines had been changed. Rewritten. When he asked why or by whom he didn't have to go far. Some twenty-one-year-old intern working on the show decided on his own to make changes to Bill's script. Bill felt he was being treated like a bit player and not someone who had forgotten more about comedy then this kid had yet learned.

Cookie Maven 'Famous Amos' also stopped by, as did Mrs. Fields who makes her own line of delicious cookies. I also interviewed Robert Kennedy Jr. and former U.S. Attorney General Nicholas Katzenbach. Katzenbach is best known for challenging Alabama Governor George Wallace, at the front door of the University of Alabama, to allow that school's first African American students to attend classes there.

Gary Burghoff from the TV show *M*A*S*H* also came by one day. I was a big fan of *M*A*S*H*. When I found out he was in the building I went searching for him. He was nowhere to be found. I peeked outside and there he was in front of the building – all five feet of him smoking a cigarette.

All excited I said, "Gary – hey Gary Burghoff! Great to meet you!"

He took a drag on his smoke, looked at me and said, "How ya doing kid."

Burghoff stopped in to talk about *M*A*S*H and* some product he was hawking that masked the smell of dog urine on rugs. It was a long sad road from *M*A*S*H* to the front of the News 12 building in Edison, New Jersey, and I think he knew it.

It wasn't my first or last disappointment as the B-list of stars of my youth and other A-listers popped in to meet Mizar and me, and get as much exposure in the state as they could. One day – to the great delight of Mizar and me, Mallory Lewis, the daughter of Shari Lewis stopped by and brought the famous 1960's puppet "Lambchop."

I can't tell you how thrilled we were! Both of us had watched her mother Shari Lewis as kids. We felt extremely close to Lambchop and her puppet show friends Charlie Horse and Hush Puppy. Even before Mallory arrived we were telling the producers and assistant producers that Lambchop was coming! They looked at us like we were crazy.

Shari Lewis – who entertained millions of kids like Mizar and me over the years – had passed on about a year before. Mallory had taken over her mom's franchise – learning the voices of all the puppets and appearing around the country. Creating a whole new generation of Lambchop lovers.

As we did the day's headlines we saw Mallory come into the studio carrying a small suitcase. Before you knew it the interview segment with Mallory and Lambchop was underway!

Mizar and I dutifully asked questions but were most interested in Lambchop. What had *she* been doing? How did Lambchop feel to be traveling around again? What was Lambchop's favorite show of all time? We were addressing Lambchop head-on like she was a person.

All smiles, we ended the segment and the show was over. We cuddled with Lambchop. Even took pictures with her. Then as we walked across the studio with Lambchop kissing us Mallory reached over with her other hand and opened the case she had come in with.

Inside were two back-up Lambchops. It was at that moment that Mizar and I felt like idiots. We had told everyone Lambchop was coming. We had squealed when we met her. Took pictures kissing her and it never sunk in that day they she was just a puppet. The power of TV in our youth had made us believe Lambchop *was a person*. We slunk out of the building and headed home giggling and embarrassed.

Years later, I had another encounter with Lambchop. I was working at a TV station during the terrible Southern California fires in 2007. One of the damaged homes belonged to Mallory Lewis. A producer was able to get her on the air live via satellite to talk about the damage to her home. I guess she didn't grasp the gravity of the situation and the damage to the community because there she stood on camera with

Lambchop. At times even asking Lambchop if she was afraid. It was surreal!

We found out later that Lambchop was uninjured. Hush Puppy though had run off into the woods behind her house never to be seen again and sadly Charlie Horse was burned beyond recognition. Good thing Mallory had two backup Charlie Horses.

The interview on Father's Day with Meredith Viera was interesting. As far as Mizar and I could tell Meredith took a liking to me. During the interview she totally and completely ignored Mizar. I'd ask a question and she would go on and on. Mizar would ask one and she'd say, "Well Frank…"

At the end of the interview she thanked me and didn't even acknowledge Mizar was there. When we went to the commercial Mizar looked at me and said, "What's up with that?" We never found out.

Mizar used to read the newspaper on the set between the long commercial breaks and cut articles out for the producers to follow up on. When the producers scheduled the guests they were usually right on. When Mizar perused the newspaper coming up with ideas the results were sketchy. Two stand out: One day the Star Ledger featured the "Littlest Preacher," a child prodigy of sorts who busted out sermons at his church in Newark that were classic 'fire and brimstone'. He was all of seven years old but his belief in God and the way he conveyed it to parishioners at the church run by a relative was impressive. There were photos in the article of him worked up into a frenzy. Veins bulging in his head as he talked about God's love. Mizar was intrigued and pressured the producers to get this kid on pronto.

A couple of weeks later this young man, dressed like a miniature version of Al Sharpton, and his Mom and Dad came into the studio. They decided the Littlest Preacher would do the six-minute interview alone.

The camera came on and Mizar introduced the kid.

Mizar: "So – you have been called the Littlest Preacher; that is quite an honor. What made you start preaching?"

At that point the Littlest Preacher froze up.

Mizar: "Oh don't worry about the camera – it's just us talking. So what made you start preaching?"

Littlest Preacher: "I don't know."

In my head I went to yellow alert. There were still about five and a half minutes left to the interview and we had already started off with the standard three-word answer you get from every kid who goes on TV.

Mizar: "What are you thinking about when you speak of God before all of those parishioners every Sunday?"

Littlest Preacher: "Nothing."

I went to Red Alert. Mizar glanced at me for help but I wasn't biting. I was part sadist and part voyeur at this point. I figured we'd see if and how she could pull this out.

Mizar: "You must be thinking about something as you preach."

Littlest Preacher: "Not really."

Mizar glanced over again. I figured, "Let's have fun with this." I asked the littlest preacher some nonsensical question. It got a two-word answer. I threw it back to Mizar. After all this was her guest. She booked him. I was letting her take the lead.

As the dead air became more prevalent the kid got more and more nervous.

Mizar was struggling. At this point she would have taken one sentence. Two would be a gift. For anyone who has done a TV interview this is the no-man's land of every interview: Too early to

wrap it up; too late to turn back. I looked at the clock on the d___
and I would swear the seconds had slowed down. Each second ___
taking two seconds and we still had four minutes to kill. Speaking ___
kill – I was thinking of killing Mizar at this point.

The kid started breathing heavily. He was a bit overweight so it was
more of a wheeze.

Mizar: "Do your parishioners enjoy your sermons?"

Littlest Preacher: "(wheeze) Yes (wheeze)."

Each deep and wheezy breath was drawing attention to the fact the kid
was scared and Mizar was out of questions.

For spits and giggles I jumped in.

Frank: "Boy, you must really be confident in your ability and your
knowledge of the bible to speak before some many people."

Littlest Preacher: (wheeze... wheeze) "Huh?"

I repeated the question.

Littlest Preacher: "I guess…" His voice was trailing off. Now I'm
thinking Mizar is dead when this interview is over.

It was the longest six minutes in television history. It might have been
the longest but not the loudest. That was reserved for another Mizar
booking.

One day Mizar – who is half Albanian – decided it would be a good
idea to feature the music of her homeland. Maybe she was roped into it
by her relatives. I just remember hopping onto the set for an interview
one day to find two musicians dressed in traditional Albanian garb.

Mizar and I conducted the interview sitting on director's chairs and
about two minutes in, it was time for the duo to sing the songs of
Mizar's heritage.

ackboard mean anything to you? That
welcomed sound compared to what these
ut.

t Albanian people but the singer
ng an appendectomy without anesthesia. She
anian lyrics while her fellow Albanian strummed a
ed up chords on what looked like a cross between a
olin and a ukulele. The music sounded like a carnival in the
distance with the faint sound of an animal in some sort of pain. We
were sitting within three feet of this musical onslaught with nowhere
to hide. For the first time I wished I could be a viewer. At least I would
have an opportunity to switch the channel.

In the middle of their performance the camera caught me with the face
of a man suffering from a hemorrhoid attack.

Mizar, who remembered the music of her heritage more nostalgically
that anything else, held her smile a little longer but just before her ears
started to bleed she turned to me and whispered, "How the fuck do we
get off this Merry Go Round?"

Mizar was forbidden from booking guests for months after that.

We also had a guy from Queens on regularly who had started a
website that sold incredibly discounted products. It was innovative at
the time and he was making piles of money. Mizar and I though had
one small problem with him. He'd come in, head to the bathroom take
care of business and never wash his hands. I saw it, the technicians
saw it; we all knew it. Later when the on-air interview began he
always extended his hand. Mizar and had of course to shake it. If
someone out there was reading our body language we were both *more*
than grossed out.

Those who surrounded us on the set and at the station were all
professionals to varying degrees. Our weatherman at the onset was a
unique kind of guy: about forty-five, into weather, single and shall we
say thrifty. He loved the camera and would talk about weather in terms

that not all of us could understand, which is good since you always want to make sure your viewers don't know what the hell you're talking about. He'd use meteorological terms like "verga" and 'indices" and all this 'I'm smart and you're not' nonsense.

Off camera he also reveled in the fact that he could eat for the entire week for $10 and that some of his shirts were older then the interns in the newsroom. He once told me about a suit sale at a nearby mall. Glowing he said that he had gotten three suits for $99. He paused and as if he had won the lottery added, "with alterations."

I happened to be at that mall a week or so later and with my interest piqued, I couldn't pass up stopping into the suit store he had raved about days before. It contained racks and racks of suits in colors even the indigent would not be found dead in. I shivered as I checked out what was essentially a suit hospice.

Weatherman was also always hovering about the vending machine man as he filled up and emptied the lunchroom vending machines. I guess he was waiting for something to fall so he could run off with it. We later found out he had worked a deal with the guy: he would buy all the old sandwiches at bargain basement prices and eat what wouldn't make him sick. The vending machine company was just happy to get what it could for the rancid meat in the sandwiches instead of throwing them in the trash. One day while we were across the parking lot at the Post Office our weatherman spied the vending machine guy leaving. Not wanting to miss out on what he was about to throw away he raced across the parking lot like a kid chasing an ice cream truck. Mizar standing next to me doubled over with laughter. I stood there with my mouth open.

He said he was giving the sandwiches to needy but no one believed him. In this case – he was needy.

His replacement was another character; full of himself and his station in life. Mizar and he often clashed. I tried to make nice but he didn't so much get my humor, and it wasn't long before he was on the outside looking in as Mizar and I made fun of him.

I don't know what it is about weather guys, but the man who headed up the News 12 weather department had his own problems. He – shall I say politely – wasn't always there. And when I say "there" I mean on this planet. A weather live shot one spring evening led to one of the greatest News 12 bloopers of all time.

Our chief weather guy was reporting live from Great Adventure amusement park in Jackson, New Jersey. The folks there were debuting their Dare Devil Dive ride, a sixteen-story free-fall drop in which the rider plummets down at speeds of nearly sixty miles an hour. Going on this ride when you're 'all there' is scary enough. Being a little buzzed is even scarier.

Anyway – the staid and proper fill-in anchor of the *Evening Edition* tossed to our weather guy and there he was at the top of the ride. He talked a bit about the forecast and what to expect in the days ahead and in the middle of it someone pulled the switch and like opening a trap door the car he was in plummeted. As he held on to the harness for dear like he screamed … "Holy Shit! Holy fucking shit!…"

The techs switched back to the studio immediately but it was too late. The look on our news guy's face was priceless.

Our operations director was also afflicted – as best as I could determine – with the same 'malady' our weatherman was suffering from.

He'd stumble around the building ala Cheech and Chong saying things like, "What the fuck man," about this and that. Both he and his wife were hired as a package deal and occasionally would bring their four-year-old son into work. They kid would scamper around the station while everyone worked.

One morning after getting off the set I heard a small commotion in the back of the building. When no one was looking the kid had wandered into a small office and locked himself in. His hands were too small to get around the door handle and he was frightened on top of it.

He was made even more frightened by his father – the Operations Director – who was screaming, "We'll get you out of there, I'm coming to get you!!" This little drama played on for about five minutes. As I watched someone summoned me back to the set.

While I was on the air things in the back of the building began tumbling out of control. Our Operations manager now comes up with the hare-brained idea of climbing to News 12's only second floor office, which was a mini conference room, and somehow walking along the rafters and beams to find his way into the office below. He really didn't think this through so when he stepped out onto one of the beams and put his other foot on the dropped ceiling he came crashing down in a hallway area.

Off the set again and not knowing what had happened in the last few minutes, I turned a corner to see him shaking off some ceiling flakes and trying to get his bearings. They finally found the key and got the kid out but I kept thinking how I would have reported this to my employer Cablevision. "Hello, I'm in the hospital and won't be in for the next few days. I was injured by a falling employee."

His successor several years later was another winner. He came from the tough streets of Detroit and had perfected, and I mean perfected, the art of looking busy. He'd walk around the station with two or three pieces of paper in his right hand and say as loudly as he could, "Whooo! Damn!" and stroll off. It was performance art of the best kind. He made it look like he was always overwhelmed with work and then disappear for a few hours.

He did tell me a great story about his days as a reporter in Detroit. Seems a car blew up one night as a mobster exacted his revenge on a rival. He was called at home to go and check it out. An officer brought him to the smoldering ruins of the car and both peeked in. All that was left was the torso of the body held in by the seat belt.

He starts looking around for the rest of the body. Finally he says, "Where's the rest of him?" The officer says, "Come here." They get into the police cruiser and take a short drive. The rest of the guy's body was two blocks away.

I got my own shock at News 12 one day while waiting to fill in to do the noon news for a vacationing colleague. On January 26, 1998 President Clinton, who was embroiled in the Monica Lewinsky scandal, was set to appear before educators at the White House. Because he might say something about the scandal, which was now bubbling over, Jeff Marks asked if I could do a live break-in from the newsroom. I'd come on, talk about what the president was doing, who he was speaking too, and chat about the scandal while waiting for him to speak.

All went well. In short order the president took the podium and to everyone's surprise droned on about how kids need books and education money. It was so boring it about put me to sleep.

As he got set to wrap up his remarks I was thinking, *Okay, no news here. I'll just say this has been News 12's live coverage of the president, talk about the Lewinisky scandal some more and head back to my desk.*

Then it happened.

Just as he ready to leave podium following this garden-variety rah-rah speech to teachers he says it.

"I have to go back to work on my State of the Union speech. And I worked on it until pretty late last night. But I want to say one thing to the American people. I want you to listen to me. I'm going to say this again: I did not have sexual relations with that woman, Miss Lewinsky. I never told anybody to lie, not a single time; never. These allegations are false. And I need to go back to work for the American people."

After lulling me to sleep for twenty minutes his comments caught me totally off guard. My heart raced as the cameraman threw it back to me and I've got nothing. I sat on the chair in the newsroom, camera on and didn't know what the hell to say. I danced around a bit and threw it back to regular programming.

Talk about a curve ball after a long speech on schools and kids – I didn't see it coming!

Reporters hoping to make it in New York came from all around the country to work at News 12 New Jersey. One day a stunning redhead came in and was shown around the station by Jeff Marks. Guys' tongues are hanging out. You could hear the sound of muffled boners as she sashayed around the station. She wasn't my type but like a beautiful painting she was nice to look at.

Several weeks after she had been hired I got to talking with her at my desk. I found out she was from Texas. Growing up watching shows like *'Friends'* she just couldn't wait to live in the Big Apple. Little did she know that what she saw on TV and what New York is really about are two different things. First of all, every one of these shows about living in New York is filmed during the summer. It's always sunny, filled with hipsters, and in the case of *'Friends'* the apartments are huge and very affordable! Seems rent money is never a problem even as in *'Friends'* where one character works at a museum and the other at a coffee shop. I'd like a nickel for every kid who came to live in New York after seeing *'Friends'* or *'Sex and the City'* and instead of living in a glamorous apartment, ended up with four roommates sardined into a one-bedroom walk-up above a Pakistani deli.

Anyway, this tall lanky redheaded Texan was going on and on about how she just loved this area. How she *loooooovved* New York, and how every day would be filled with sunshine and she'd always have enough money and men to entertain her. I was polite at first letting her create this wonderland of bliss but at some point I had had enough.

"Listen honey," I said. "What you see on TV is not always accurate. Trust me I've lived in and around New York all my life. I grew up here."

"Oh, but it's so vibrant and there are so many things to do. I just want to stroll up and down the street and hop in a cab and go here and there."

"Have you ever seen snow – I mean dirty filthy snow?" I asked.

"Oh no – but I can't wait."

"I wish you the very best; maybe after you experience a nice New York winter we can talk again."

We never did. One New York City winter was enough. She was gone by May.

We'd often be visited by stunning reporters in every shape, size and complexion. One knockout blonde doing freelance work used to stroll around the station showing off her "stuff." She even had at one point been voted by Philadelphia Magazine as one of "The Most Eligible Bachelorettes" in that city.

I guess the pressure to be on TV was too much for her though. I came in one day to find out that after I had left the day before she fainted face-first straight down in the hallway.

I thought for a second after Mizar told me.

"Too bad," I said, "She should have at least given me some time to position myself."

The *Morning Edition* was humming along. Mizar and I began making appearances and for the first time in my life I was being asked for my autograph. There were photos sessions for and eventually giant billboards across the state featuring the whole morning team. It was pretty heady stuff. There were looks and whispers. One day I was walking in my shorts and sunglasses down the main street in Freehold, New Jersey and a car stopped next to me and the guy and his wife said, "Frank – hey Frank – it's you! We love the show!" I smiled and said thanks. It fed my ego and I used it to my advantage.

It wasn't only in New Jersey. One day I went to visit some friends in the city. While there I thought I'd stop and see my mother's best friend from her youth. Nancy owned a florist with her son on 53rd Street and 9TH Avenue.

My mother always bragged about me to her friends. Nancy got most of it because she was the closest of my mother's friends.

Anyway, I walked into Nancy's florist and she was surprised and pleased to see me. We hugged, knocked around some memories and then about ten minutes later, a woman walks in and starts staring at me.

"You're that guy. The guy on TV! News 12 guy! I love you and that woman. I watch you every morning. Wow!"

She's over the top and making a fuss. I smile, thank her and look over at Nancy.
We're both thinking the same thing: Even in death my mother had to send in some woman to make a fuss over me in front of Nancy just so she could brag about her son.

Nancy never forgot and neither did I. It was another instance in which I knew for sure my mother was hanging around watching. What were the chances that it would be just three of us in that florist at that time?

My ego was so huge at this point that when I didn't get recognized I wondered why not.

One day I called the local minor league baseball team and told the PR guy who I was and of course a front row ticket was waiting for me when I arrived.

The usher who sat me was very nonchalant. There was no, "Hey you're the guy from TV" or anything like that. I was a little miffed. About four innings into the game as I sat there right behind home plate I pulled out my cigar and lit it up. It was an extension of my ego. I'm here, I was saying, and I'm going to smoke my giant cigar until someone notices me!

Two puffs into it, the usher who sat me yells down in front of everyone, "Hey TV guy—put that damn thing out! No smoking in the park."

As News 12 added more cable systems Mizar and I were asked to make more and more personal appearances. Our producer, Kendra Wright, figured we could do a two-day tour of northwest New Jersey—in January!

I begged her not to do it. Northwest New Jersey in the dead of winter is an unforgiving place. It's not unusual for the temperature to hit zero.

We hit twenty-four towns in two days talking to the locals about News 12 and did live hits from some of them and full reports when we got back.

It was one big cold blur but I do remember hitting a softball in an empty snow-filled minor league stadium at seven in the morning, eating at the diner where they filmed part of the Freddie Krueger movies and stepping out of a bed and breakfast on Day Two and hearing coyotes howling in the hills near the New Jersey/Pennsylvania border. I checked the thermostat that morning. It was one degree.

Somewhere along the way I thought I could parlay my celebrity to establish a franchise for myself, something that was mine, which I would produce and get on News 12. A funny story I did on Halloween of 1997 got great reviews and gave me an idea. What if I hung out with the many crazy people in New Jersey, the kind who collect toys, or bungee jump, or work in unusual jobs? This led to the creation of "Frank's Friends."

I searched out – for lack of a better word – the "crazies" and there were plenty in New Jersey. I reported on the guy who collected *Star Trek* memorabilia, the woman who dressed up and performed weddings for dogs, and another guy who had a collection of tiny but drivable cars.

The guy who collected *Star Trek* memorabilia had so much stuff he had to get it out of a warehouse for the interview. We checked it all out. Phasers, action figures, communicators, everything! I did my usual stuff. Wandered around with him, making snide comments about what he collected and ended the piece by "beaming up" to the Enterprise. It was very imaginative.

A week later News Director Jeff Marks received a three-page letter, written in pencil, from this wacko Trekkie. He was insulted that I made fun of his stuff and threatened to report me to the United Federation of Planets. If justice was not meted out, he warned, Jeff and I would be subject to Klingon retaliation.

Then there were the Sumo wrestlers.

I headed over to Union County, New Jersey and the only place in the U.S. that trains Sumo wrestlers. Six guys were waiting for me, the smallest of whom weighed 555 pounds.

Before they started one said, "Maybe we should get lunch. Everybody good with McDonald's?" The question was greeted by low, rumbling grunts. The order was two pages long! A half dozen cheeseburgers for one guy, eight orders of fries on top of that, four Big Macs for the other guy. When the order had been taken one of the sumo wrestlers was handed about $60 and then waddled out to his enormous car and drove off.

I made small talk as we waited for him to come back. After twenty-five minutes I couldn't wait any longer. I began interviewing the wrestlers minus the guy who went off to pick up lunch. I'm thinking *how long can that take? I mean the place is three blocks away.*

Five minutes later the guy returns with some crumbled up wrappers smushed into a McDonald's shopping bag. I didn't even know McDonald's *had* shopping bags!

He tosses the bags in the trash. At that point one of the behemoths turns and says, "Hey, where the heck is lunch?"

"I couldn't wait, I stopped and ate it on the way back."

"Everything?"

"Yeah."

Instead of getting mad the other wrestlers just shrugged and continued talking to me. One finally said, "It's okay; we'll get lunch when we're done here."

I didn't know what to be more shocked about, the fact that one man ate a shopping bag full of food or that the other sumo wrestlers were cool with it.

Apparently all of them had done this to each other at one point or another. In the world of Sumo wrestlers having the guy you send out to get lunch eat all of it before he gets back is apparently an occupational hazard.

There were some serious pieces as well. I was fascinated after reading an article about how some Italian-Americans were treated here in America during World War II. Fearing Italian Americans might provide aid and comfort to the enemy since we were at war with Mussolini's Italy, federal agents regularly visited their homes.

Hundreds of Italian-Americans who were not U.S. citizens were sent to internment camps just like the Japanese. The whole story had never been told. Most Americans never knew Italian Americans who had lived here for years – but were not citizens – were treated just as poorly as the Japanese. In some cases – as in San Francisco – Italian American merchants lost everything. Their property was seized and they were restricted from traveling more than five miles from their homes. If their jobs were farther away, they had to quit.

In and around New York alone Italian Americans by the hundreds were followed and in some cases imprisoned. It is a sad chapter in American history and to FDR's credit, when it came to Italian Americans who at the time were the largest voting block in the U.S., it didn't last long. But there were many Italian Americans in New Jersey who remembered how they were treated and wondered why their stories were never told.

Being an Italian American and having a platform, I wanted to tell this story, not just in one quick report but as a three-part series. I visited Ellis Island where many of the Italian American citizens were imprisoned; among them Metropolitan Opera star Ezio Pinza. I also wanted to go to San Francisco, where there was an exhibition at a museum honoring those who lost everything and were never compensated by the government; even though not one incident of domestic terrorism during World War II was perpetrated by Italian Americans. I pitched the story to Jeff Marks.

For News 12 it was a major undertaking but I was able to convince Jeff that this was a story that had to be told. It involved me taking several days off, traveling to San Francisco with a cameraman and to Washington DC with both a cameraman and a field producer. The fact that New Jersey Senator Robert Torricelli was on the verge of convincing the Senate that this so-called "Secret Story" should be taught in schools sealed the deal. In the spring of 2000 we were off.

I have done many stories I have been proud of in my career and have won several awards, but this by far was the most rewarding report I ever did. I told the story just as it was. We flew out to California and interviewed Italian Americans who remembered being whisked away to internment camps in Montana and New Mexico, just as Japanese Americans were. They were locked up simply because of their heritage, and who, for reasons of national pride or simply because they just didn't get around to it, never became US citizens.

There were tears and anger and all of it was caught on camera. With the help of field producer Casey Corrigan, Editor Michelle Carnesi and Photographer Tony Coco, we were able to make a three-part series that sang. After it aired UNICO, New Jersey's Italian-American Civic Organization honored us with the Mille Grazie award. It's one I'm most proud of for myself, my colleagues and those many hard working Italian-Americans who are portrayed, sadly, again and again, in a not so flattering light.

While we were in San Francisco Tony, Michelle and I were strolling along Fisherman's Wharf when I heard, from at least a block away, a gravely voice that sounded vaguely familiar. As the sound got closer I recognized it instantly. There, strolling the street three thousand miles from his usual haunts – was Harlem Congressman Charlie Rangel. He was in San Francisco for some meeting and was taking in the sights. I had actually seen him earlier in the day on some network news program but had no idea the satellite hook-up was from San Francisco.

I introduced myself. We chatted briefly.

Odd, I thought, I have lived in the New York metropolitan area most of my life and it took a trip to San Francisco and a chance meeting on the street to meet one of the Big Apple's most prominent House members.

One other quick story before we leave this: our shooter Tony Coco was by far the quietest of our team. Twice we drove to Washington, DC to check records and speak with government officials about the treatment of Italian Americans during World War II and both times the conversation with Tony on the way down and back was sparse. He was dedicated, conscientious, and since he drove almost the whole way there and back, focused on the road.

I needed to do a stand up in front of the Capitol for our package. The roads around Washington are sometimes confusing.

As Casey and I spoke in the SUV about the next shot and what we had to do Tony pulled up to a school bus full of kids. In the far left lane and waiting at the light he realized he had to make a sharp right to get to where we were going.

Without warning, and as if morphing into a driver at the Indy 500, Tony sped ahead just as the light changed, cut off the bus and make a sharp right, tires screeching and the SUV struggling to keep all four wheels on the ground. He then floored the vehicle up a short street and to a small empty parking lot right across from the White House and came to a screeching halt.

I was startled and Casey was too. For quiet Tony it came out of nowhere. The screeching tires also drew the attention of two DC police officers who – fearing the worst – began running after our SUV. When we stopped all of us stepped out and were confronted by a couple of cops with guns drawn.

"Sir, sir… " one of them was shouting at Tony, "Do you have any idea what you just did?"

Tony looked around puzzled and calmly and said, "What?"

Casey and I cracked up.

In the summer of 2000 we had Thor Solberg on the show. Thor, who was about fifty-five at the time, is an amazing guy. His family owns a small airport in New Jersey and over time he's become its sole owner. Thor – and you've gotta love that name – is also a full time commercial airline pilot. He flies giant 777s to Europe and back. After he was on the show I talked to him off camera about what it was like to fly these huge jets. To my surprise he said it was easier than flying a two-seat Cessna. The technology is so advanced the pilot is often there just to baby-sit the controls. The plane can take off and land itself but Thor is old school and would have none of that.

"Frank," he said, "I turn off all the lights in the cabin, turn off the computer, take full manual control of the jet and fly it like I would fly out of my small airport in central New Jersey."

Wow – I thought. Here's one guy. One giant plane, and in that giant plane he's in total control!

We also had a brief conversation after the interview that was prescient on my part. About eight years before I met Thor I was flying on a small plane from Detroit to Lansing, Michigan.

A reporter is never off duty and as I sat in this twenty-seat plane I was amazed at how little protection the pilot and the co-pilot had from any crazy who might get on that jet. The only thing separating the pilot and co-pilot from the passengers on this small aircraft was a curtain.

I thought – what if I knew how to fly a plane, or had a gun, or was suicidal. All I would have to do is stand up, push aside the curtain and force the pilot or the plane to do what ever it was I wanted.

"Thor," I said, "what stops someone from getting into the cockpit of a plane? Any plane. Even the ones you fly."

"Nothing really," Thor said matter of fact.

We talked some more and he said pilots were only required to lock the cockpit door on international flights. Most didn't lock the door on domestic flights, he said. Some even left the door open to get some air.

I'm thinking – even before 9/11 – that this is a dangerous thing. I was actually ready to pitch an investigative report to Jeff but other things intervened. Had I done the report, who knows? I might have been the most interviewed guy after the 9/11 attacks or in Gitmo for knowing too much.

Shortly after the airing of The Secret Story – I began to get restless. I was in a great spot. I still had a year and a half on my contract, the fans loved Mizar and me, and theoretically I could have stayed at News 12 forever. But I didn't want to go to the grave with an "if" and the 'if' in my life involved the question of whether I was good enough to work at a New York station? The big time! The number one market in the country.

Leaving News 12 wasn't so easy. Cablevision forbade its full time employees from working elsewhere. They pretty much owned your image and protected it as they did with all on air talent.

About this time – the summer of 2000 – I also lost my dad to prostate cancer. He struggled for months but finally succumbed. It was all very sad. My dad was very proud of me but living on Long Island he never got to share in the New Jersey fame I had achieved.

I had long ago reconciled with my dad who separated from my mom when I was 12 years old. From the age of 26 or so I saw him on a fairly regular basis. He spent the last 25 years of his life happily married to a wonderful woman named Louise. He was truly happy for the first time in his life and Louise was, and is a doll. Nonetheless I didn't see much of my dad through my teens and early twenties mainly because he lived way out on Long Island. He loved me till the day he died. I loved him as well and I know he was proud of everything I did.

I remember one night I was featured on a show in NYC. It aired in his area at one in the morning. Not wanting to miss it and not quite sure how to work the VCR he stayed up until one a.m., hit the record button and shuffled off to sleep. As usual he was up at 5:30 the next morning. One of my great regrets is that my Mom – who died in March of 1986 – never got to see my big break when I was hired by WNBC radio. My dad who died in August of 2000 would never get to see me on New York television. They both missed these major milestones by months. I'm sure they would have been very proud. Proud first of their son and even more proud that their name – Cipolla – and the Italian American heritage that came with it was there for everyone to see.

As it turned out fate would intercede in the months following my dad's death. It didn't seem like it at the time but that's how life works.

Mizar and I were on the set joking around and Mizar – who was always pushing the envelope – thought it would be funny if she placed a Post-It note on the back of our weather guy's back. She wrote on it too. "Kick Me," or something like that.

Our weather guy was a stiff and very enamored with himself. He went on the air with it. You hardly saw the Post-It note on his back but he had to make a fuss over it. He complained to Jeff and to the HR director. It wasn't so much the Post-It note; I just believe he was frustrated that personality-wise he couldn't keep up with Mizar and me. Was it nice? No. But as Mizar would say, "it was damn funny."

This minor incident blew up – thanks to the weatherman – into a major affair. There were separate interviews of all of us by the HR Director and days of waiting. Eventually Mizar and I were taken off the air for a week without pay even though I had little to do with it. I didn't write on the Post-It note, didn't put it on his back, and wasn't even in the studio when he went on the air with it.

I just think Jeff had had enough of our shenanigans and wanted to make an example of us. We were the most popular personalities on the station and he had to draw the line, in short, knock us down a notch or two.

I was angry though. Really angry! I took my punishment even after pleading my case about having no real involvement in the incident. I also started planning my next move. In one of my calmer moments when I was considering whether to go or stay the Bride gave me some solid advice.

"They suspended you for that?" she said. "Well – you know what that means. They have already fired you. Now it's just a matter of time." I thought about what she said. If I was going to be suspended for something so small it was just a matter of time before they found something else.

Mizar and I talked by phone during our suspension. The first thing we agreed too was to send an ice storm toward our morning show weatherman. We simply iced him out. During our on-set banter he was not included. We didn't even look his way. It was a week or so of painful TV and clear to anyone watching that he was now *persona non grata*.

Finally Jeff called me into his office and demanded we begin including the weatherman in the show again. Mizar and I followed his orders but my ego would not allow me to take anymore shit from management.

I made some calls to New York's top all-news radio station – WCBS-AM – which promised me some freelance work and then I got an interview for more part time work at Channel 9 TV in New York. Michael Saint Peter – the assistant news director at Channel 9 – was very gracious. He's a gentleman in a business dominated by ornery executives. There should be more like him. The interview went very well and when I offered him my reel he waved it away.

"I've watched you in the morning on News 12. I know your work." He was a fan – a good sign. Between the two freelance jobs I had built a safety net. Now it was just a matter of taking the plunge.

I went on vacation to Florida for a week in the middle of April 2001 and when I returned I was ready. I drove out to Cablevision headquarters in Long Island and met with the head HR person. I told him what had happened. How I had been treated badly and told him I would be gone in two weeks.

By coincidence the following day a new news director started. Jeff was still around for the transition and his departure had nothing to do with mine. The new news director was stunned about my decision to leave. His first week on the job he was told the most popular morning team in New Jersey would be no more.

There was only one thing left to do: Tell my colleagues. On April 15th, 2001, just before we went on the air at 5:30 I asked the director to patch me though to everyone listening on head sets in the control room and outside in the newsroom.

"Folks," I said. "It's been my great pleasure to work with you but now it's time to go. I want to thank you for all your hard work and wish you only the very best going forward."

The statement was short. My voice cracked at the end. I never realized how wedded I was to News 12. Despite the sadness, I was absolutely certain I was making the right decision. I like to think my Dad – who had passed away several months before – was there giving me the strength to roll the dice and make myself available to the universe as I pursued my ultimate dream of anchoring at a New York TV station.

It was clear Jeff Marks and the others had underestimated me. They thought I was just scared enough to stay even after being treated as I had been. Two days before I left I was humming a tune while I walked toward the lunchroom.

"Frank… is that you?" some disembodied voice called out from one of the back offices.

"Hello?" I said "Someone looking for me?"

"Yeah – can you come in here for a moment?"

In the office sat Jeff Marks, the general ad sales manager, and the on–site HR person. Jeff was slumped in his chair.

"So," Jeff said, "you're moving on."

I was confused for a moment as if the message after a week and a half didn't sink in.

"Yes, ready to go."

"Where are you going again?"

"Oh – going to be doing some freelance work at WCBS radio and Channel 9."

"Reporter?" Jeff said.

"Yeah."

"So they're going to be yanking you around all over the place."

I thought that was a really weird expression to use at that moment. I looked at the sales manager and the HR director like – what is he talking about?

"Yes, that's right," I finally said. There was an awkward pause, I said, "Have a good day," and walked out.

I didn't realize until later that this was Jeff's way of saying he was sorry and hoping I would change my mind. It was clear I had called his bluff and would not allow him to control me or punish me for something I did not do. He thought I needed to stay, when I no longer *wanted* to stay. It was that rare, very rare instance in this business, when I had total control of the situation. No one would lay me off or tell me they were going in a "different direction." I would call the shots now and I had decided to move on. Screw them.

The sales manager was in the meeting because she knew what was at stake. I won't take all the credit because I always suspected the viewers liked me – but loved Mizar. And as I mentioned the success of a morning show is always predicated on "chemistry." At any rate, within three months of my departure I bumped into the sales manager at a local mall. She told me the ratings in the three months since my departure had plummeted. To continue to sell commercials they were using ratings figures from six months earlier and telling clients that's where the ratings were now.

I smiled inside. The success of Mizar and me was real.

For all my bravado and anger at the way it ended I still think Jeff Marks is one of the best News Directors in the business. Much like Rich Rapiti from my WJDM days he understands talent should be allowed to do their thing. Like all good managers he steps in only when he thinks it's necessary and his suggestions always came from a teaching standpoint rooted in years of experience. There should be more news directors like him.

My last day the phone on my desk rang – some public relations person was reaching out to me about scheduling a guest for an upcoming show. She had been sent to me erroneously but I was going to try and help. She said she absolutely loved the morning show. She wanted to know if she could book a guest to be interviewed by Mizar and me. But like so many people she couldn't get Mizar's name right. She fumbled a bit and then said, "So I look forward to meeting you and …. is it Bizarre?"

I said – "Yeah…..bizarre," and hung up.

She hit the nail right on the head. It was a bizarre and wonderful five years and soon it would be over. Bizarre – er… Mizar and I remain friends to this day and continues to be one of my favorite people in the world.

"IT SHOCKED EVEN US!"

Chapter 15
9/11

Leaving the comfort of the News 12 studio I was now roaming the streets of New York City as a radio reporter for WCBS. They liked my work and I liked the freedom of cruising the city.

That's the beauty of radio. You're a solo artist. You make your own music. TV news is more like being in a band where you depend on a group of people to get the timing right.

May of 2001 was the start of what would be a glorious summer weather-wise in the city, and a peaceful one. There's that now-famous interview with the French camera crew that shadowed a group of New York firemen for a documentary they were doing. Before the 9/11 attacks the French documentarians were musing about how quiet it had been in the city. No major crime incidents. No news stories dominating the headlines.

Working at WCBS was the next in a line of dream jobs for me. First, it was the news station I had grown up listening to. Second, I would be in the building where Rather and Cronkrite roamed. One day right outside the building I spotted a hunched-over deep-throated news guy dragging on a cigarette. I was probably the only man within ten blocks who knew it was CBS network radio icon Christopher Glenn. I had listened to his deep voice as a kid watching cartoons. In an effort to hook the next generation of news junkies in between the Saturday cartoons CBS ran something called *In the News*.

In the News was a one-minute news report written for kids about the biggest stories of the week. Christopher Glenn was the voiceover guy for *In The News*. I introduced myself and told him I used to listen to his reports when I was a kid.

He smiled, half-impressed that anyone remembered.

Shortly after I saw Christopher Glenn he suddenly retired. I found out later that the cigarettes had claimed another. He died of lung cancer and one of the great voices of my youth was silenced.

I was also almost silenced in front of the CBS building. One lazy summer afternoon I wandered out to get a sandwich. I was heading back when about ten steps from the front door of the CBS Building on West 57th Street three black SUVs screeched to a halt in front of the building. One of the dark tinted window SUVs was blocking both lanes of traffic. In a flash, a half dozen burly guys dressed in black jumped out, semi-automatic pistols in hand.

I, and another employee who happened to be near the door, froze. I dropped my paper bag with my lunch inside and held my hands up. I also said loud enough so everyone could hear, "I'm not moving. I'm staying right here."

They glanced my way and took up positions between one of the SUVs and the front door.

With a nod another door opened and out jumped a huge guy, also holding a semi automatic, along side him was Israeli Prime Minister Ehud Barack. He was to be interviewed by Dan Rather.

The Prime Minister breezed by me with a smirk on his face. The show of force was part security, part theater and he seemed pleased to be the star of the show.

Working at WCBS also meant I would be reunited with my WCRV friend Wayne Cabot, who by this time was among the most tenured anchors on New York's premier all-news radio station. He was older and even more talented than he was when I first met him at WCRV 21 years before. A lot of time had passed but we always kept in touch and secretly knew we'd be sharing the airwaves one day.

It was also the second time I would be working with Frank Raphael. He was the news director at WCBS and based on the way it ended years earlier at the NBC Radio Network and all the silly things I had done while there, I was determined to prove to Frank that I had grown up as a news guy.

I buckled down and became a tenacious reporter. I never said no to an assignment. At one point I was on the street twenty-two days in a row. They liked me, I liked them, and I was eager to make an impression. At the same time Channel 9 (UPN 9 News) in New York began to call. In a contest between both freelance jobs, UPN 9 won. It paid more and I was on TV being seen by a lot more people including a whole new audience in New York that never got a chance to see me while I was working at News 12 New Jersey.

If I was going to get steady work, Channel 9 was going to be a much harder nut to crack. They had a whopping seven freelancers they could call upon and on that list I was now Number Eight. Some of the reporters in front of me had been waiting years for one of the full-timers to move on. It didn't matter. I kept my head down, plowed ahead and did exactly what they told me to do. Every night before I went to sleep I visualized myself on the station as a full-timer.

Before I knew it I was being called in more and more, and at times I was leading the newscast – also a good sign.

Being back in New York was a blast. I was getting to do things and see things I could only dream of as a kid. One story had me on the field at Shea Stadium. Right there near the Mets dugout! I had been to that stadium dozens of times as a kid and now there I was on the field. I saw an old college acquaintance, John Franco, whom our local college radio station covered when he pitched for the Saint John's Redmen. He was now the Mets' ace reliever.

2001 was also an election year. And as the summer wore on, the race for the Democratic nomination for mayor was heating up. In New York anything goes and I learned that first hand as a radio reporter chasing the four major candidates for the democratic nomination. One day I was told to head on down to Greenwich Village to cover a candidates' forum being held by the Gay Lesbian Bisexual and Transgender Caucus. I know – only in New York – but that's exactly what it's called.

I hopped into my car not really knowing what I would find.

It was July and the place wasn't air-conditioned. It was a huge room with some refreshments set up and a gathering of unusual-looking people. Now let me say that I have no problem with anyone living their life exactly the way they want. Whatever floats your boat is fine with me. However, visually at least, this was an odd mix. The gay men and lesbians were easy to spot, but the "transgender in transition" people were harder to identify. They were either deciding between operations what and who they wanted to be. Man? Woman? Both? It was tough to tell.

As I took in this scene a woman stepped into the room. She was mesmerizing!

I had time before the candidates arrived and like the other straight men who were in the room – and I suspect some lesbians – I was drawn to her. She was exquisite and ramping up the sexual energy were her nipples – which seemed to be straining to pop out of her dainty and colorful blouse.

As I got closer the picture came more sharply into focus. She seemed even more beautiful than from afar. We reached the refreshments table at the same time, and I thought this was the last place I would expect to find a raving beauty.

"Hi," I said. "I'm from WCBS radio. We're covering this forum."

"Hi," she said back to me.

At this point something seemed amiss although I couldn't pick it up.

"Are you supporting anyone?" I asked just to make some small talk about the mayoral election.

"Just want to hear what they have to say," she said as she reached down to grab a roll. At that point I froze horrified.

This dainty little body with slope shoulders and rock hard nipples was attached to giant man hands! Construction worker hands! This gender bender was beyond transition and her/his hands told the story. I gulped to suppress a dry heave.

It was a crazy summer. New Yorkers needed a new mayor and to move away from Rudolph Giuliani. Few remember or will talk about it but by the summer of 2001 Rudolph Giuliani was despised. He had systematically pissed off just about every major constituency in the city. His highhanded bullying ways had worn on the toughest of New Yorkers and his closest family members.

By the summer of 2001 it was well known Giuliani had had an extramarital affair with his aide and was canoodling out in the open with his future wife Judith Nathan. In addition he had been thrown out of Gracie Mansion, the mayor's residence, by his wife and was living in the apartment of a big time supporter and that supporter's gay lover.

It was because of this that – years later – I would chuckle when Giuliani talked to the national media about 'family values.' By the summer of 2001 he had already burned through two wives, publicly cheating on the last one, announced his marriage was over on TV even before he informed his wife, which forced her to respond at the spur of the moment about a half hour later outside Gracie Mansion. He had also appeared on *Saturday Night Live* dressed as a woman and lived with a gay couple. He had come a long way from the engaging and seemingly loving family man that Lauren and I had met in a crowded Staten Island school auditorium years before.

On top of that the press hated him. He was angry and dismissive and snapped at reporters with quips like, "That's a stupid question." I was on the receiving end of one of his outbursts and I'll never forget it.

A month before the 9/11 attacks the assignment editor at WCBS Radio asked me to go to the city's Command Center where the mayor was holding a press conference. I drove downtown and parked my car near the World Trade Center where I had worked years before at Metro Traffic.

The day was gorgeous as I strolled across the plaza between those two giant buildings. The Mayor's Command Center was on an upper floor of 5 World Trade Center, the last of the buildings to collapse on 9/11.

We gathered in the pressroom awaiting Giuilani's arrival. The entire floor of this building was dedicated to handling an emergency just like 9/11. It had been constructed right after the 1993 attack on the World Trade Center. Giuliani – with his usual hubris – pulled out all the stops. Spending millions of taxpayer dollars to put in all the Flash Gordon stuff he could find. It was a multi-million-dollar tribute to the resolve of New Yorkers and to Giuliani's mammoth ego.

I wondered then – and have since the 9/11 attacks – why Giuliani had to be so public in his desire for and construction of this nerve center for New York and why in God's name it was placed only few thousand feet from the building that had been attacked eight years earlier. Did he have to let every terrorist in the world know exactly where the emergency center for New York City was located? Wouldn't it have been smarter to place the emergency apparatus for the largest city in the country somewhere on ground level or below ground and for crying out loud couldn't he have done all of this in secret as to not put a bull's eye on it?

But this was and is Giuliani's way – big plans, big show and as we would find out later, a big mess.

When he entered the room to speak to the press he seemed more testy than usual. The press was hammering away – rightfully so – on the contradictions of his personal and public persona. We were all, including most New Yorkers, suffering from a terminal case of Giuliani fatigue.

As he got the podium someone pulled a switch and like magic the retractable wall behind him peeled away to reveal a room behind him filled with busy looking police and fire officials. There were computers flickering and everyone seemed to be on the lookout for danger. This bit of theater was – like so many things – designed to serve The Great and Powerful Rudy. Not to say these men and women weren't working as hard as they could to keep us safe but they also served as an impressive backdrop for Giuliani's press conference.

I can't really remember what the press conference was about but about halfway in, I asked what I thought was a legitimate question. One any reporter would ask and certainly not out of line.

I was hit with His Highness's response.

"Pfftttttt – what kind of a question is that… geesh… stupid."

I snapped back but he talked over me. I glared at him. "What an asshole," I thought. His reaction went beyond mean and violated the common courtesy reporters and politicians grudgingly abide by.

When Giuliani was done the wall behind him quietly headed in the other direction and once again it was just a blank white backdrop. His majesty had left and now we had to leave too.

It may sound like I am ganging up on him but I have come in contact with many politicians over the years. Giuliani was the only one I couldn't bear to be around.

After I had fed two or three versions of the story Giuliani had expertly orchestrated at his emergency bunker, the WCBS desk told me to just hang tight until it had another assignment. I drove a little uptown and parked my car on the west side of Manhattan. I found a bench along the water and took in the sun. I remember looking down toward lower Manhattan and marveling at the World Trade Center.

The Twin Towers were magnificent to observe at any angle or distance. They could be seen for miles and up close they were almost too much to comprehend. It was mid-August 2001 and I just stared at the towers as the breeze off the Hudson River brushed my face. I realized yet again how tall they really were. It was typical New York bravado. One giant tower wasn't enough for this city. There had to be two.

I thought about watching them grow as a kid in high school. From my home in south Queens you could see progress almost every day as the kangaroo cranes yanked them out of the ground. My brother Sal worked in lower Manhattan for a while, and one day I visited him just as the towers were ready to open. We took an elevator to the highest floor and stared out the window into the middle of the night. You could hear the wind crashing into the building and feel it sway. Soon after, when the towers were officially opened, I went up on the roof.

In December 2000 I took my son Charles to the indoor observation deck on the top floor of one of the towers. He was 12 years old at the time. The rooftop observation area was closed that day. We had lunch and I snapped some pictures. In one, he's looking out the window from one building at the other. When I see those pictures now – one of which has him staring at the giant transmission tower that toppled to the ground just before the building pancaked – I get the chills.

By August of 2001 I was getting called more and more by Channel 9.They liked my work and knew they could depend on me to do a good job. I was juggling all the shifts I was getting between WCBS Radio and Channel 9 – while always giving Channel 9 top priority because ultimately that was where I wanted to be.

In late August of that year there was a small press conference near an amusement park at Coney Island. We were coming to an end of an uneventful and beautiful summer in the world's greatest city. The fire commissioner was there and talked about funding for a fire safety program aimed at protecting the elderly.

After feeding my reports I walked the few blocks to the famous Nathan's Hot Dog stand. It was another glorious day weather-wise.

On line behind me was Fire Commissioner Thomas Von Essen and his spokesperson. We said hello and chatted a bit. Von Essen, like Giuliani, was nearing the end of service to the city. Giuliani's term was running out and in all likelihood Von Essen would not be retained by the new mayor.

I have often thought of that day.

It was less than two weeks before 9/11. Von Essen, who wasn't terribly well liked by rank and file firefighters, seemed satisfied with what he had accomplished and eager, based on my discussions with him that day and his body language, to move on.

That lazy late August day we were just two New Yorkers exchanging small talk. He, his spokesman and I of course had no idea what was coming. It was just another in the millions of conversations New Yorkers had that day.

If only we had known. If only *someone* had known. Imagine if I had a time machine and I could have warned him or told him to tell the mayor that in less than two weeks his world and our world would be changed forever.

There would be one more memorable moment for me pre-9/11.

Two days later came word of the unfortunate passing of a rookie on the New York Fire Department. As is tradition, firefighters from around the city and around the country came to pay their respects. The funeral mass was held at Saint Charles Church in Staten Island.

The mass was celebrated by Fire Chaplain Father Michael Judge. He spoke eloquently about the passing of such a young man; not knowing of course that in less than a week and a half he would be dead.

Officially, Father Michael was the first victim of the 9/11 attacks, killed as he ran into the World Trade Center to be by the side of the firefighters battling the high-rise blaze.

After the mass for this young man I wandered down the street. Hundreds of New York firefighters waited to give their comrade a final salute. As is the way of local TV news I looked for anyone who knew him. I needed a friend or colleague to talk about what he was like.

How many of the firefighters I spoke with and shook hands with that day died on 9/11? I'll never know. How many faces did I look into not knowing of the tragedy to come and the lives to be lost? Three

hundred fifty-three firemen died that day. I must have shaken hand
with dozens of them.

<u>September 9, 2001. Sunday</u>.

On Sunday, September 9, I was working for Channel 9. I had given up
my WCBS radio job and had rolled the dice again. I was in all the
way. I was either going to be a full timer at Channel 9 one day or I was
going to have to live with my decision.

That following Tuesday September 11, 2001 was primary Election
Day in New York City. I was assigned to cover a campaign
appearance by Giuliani. He was to endorse a councilman running in
Brooklyn.

It was classic Giuliani. His white SUV, which we used to call the "ice
cream truck," pulled up at a synagogue on Ocean Avenue in Brooklyn.
He brushed me and a couple of other reporters off on the way in and
promised to talk to us on the way out. He was surrounded by several
burly bodyguards and his always-present aide and spokeswoman
Sunny Mindel. The event was not what you would call a giant news
story. Giuliani's popularity was so low that his endorsement wasn't
expected to make much of a difference.

We weren't allowed into the event so we waited outside. I didn't mind.
It was a beautiful late summer day in New York City – the exact
combination of temperature and humidity that comes about ten times a
year in this part of the country.

After about twenty minutes His Honor emerged from the synagogue
and headed toward his SUV chatting with me and another reporter as
he walked to his ride. He was his usual self. He was pleased to endorse
the candidate, happy to be in Brooklyn, the usual chatter you get when
you pull the string of any politician doll.

As my cameraman and I got close to the sliding side door of the van
we were shoved back by one of his burly bodyguards and admonished
by Sunny Mindel.

"That's it – that's as far as you go – good-bye," she said.

I said, "What the hell?"

His motorcade rumbled to life with his white SUV, cars and sirens blaring away. I turned to my cameraman and he said, "Girlfriend."

"What?"

"His girlfriend's in the van. Didn't you see her?"

Guliani's rule was you were never to videotape his girlfriend.

Later that day I ended the package with a stand-up in front of City Hall. Security had been stepped up following the 1993 World Trade Center attack but it was still fairly accessible.

I remember two things as my cameraman and I stood near the steps of City Hall that quiet Sunday in the city. Memories returned from all the days I had visited City Hall while working for the borough president. Then, all I had to do was drive to the bottom of the front steps in my 1984 Ford Escort, step out and into the front door where a lonely looking cop would give me the once over and let me in.

For new visitors there was a cursory check of credentials but I had been there so many times I just got a nod.

Just before we wrapped up at City Hall on September 9 I looked up at the Twin Towers several blocks away.

I don't know what made me look and admire them one more time – I really think it was the universe's way of telling me to make sure I took them in once more because in less then two days they would be gone forever.

My experiences just before, during and after the attack pale in comparison to the stories of the thousands of people who lost loved ones that day. I'll leave that for others to tell – and for history.

"IT SHOCKED EVEN US!"

Chapter 16
FRIENDLY CHARACTERS

New York is a unique city. Its people are a combination of arrogance and insult. This chapter is about some of the unusual people I have bumped up against over the years and who – whether they knew it or not – made an impact on me.

They don't fit comfortably into any chapter but do fit into the narrative of my life and their actions remain with me all these years later.

SPIRO

Just before and during college I worked as a floral designer. All day long I'd carefully arrange flowers in vases or baskets. I didn't start that way. I learned the business at a small florist along Rockaway Boulevard in south Queens right across the street from a giant racetrack. I'd hauled flowers into a big dungeon of a workroom where full-fledged designers made exquisite flower arrangements and sprayed all sorts of crap on them to color them and keep them fresh. There was no ventilation. God knows what the hell ended up in my lungs. Sometimes I'd blow my nose and the hankie looked like the "Amazing Technicolor Dreamcoat."

Later, I knocked around other florists making $3 an hour before landing at a florist along Queens Boulevard near the Queens County Court House.

Its owner Spiro was a Greek-American. He had long since lost his testicles to his wife. He was the embodiment of Thoreau's men who "lead lives of quiet desperation." His wife occasionally would roll into the florist and loudly berate him in front of his employees and customers, screaming and yelling about matters too personal for anyone but them to discuss.

She also had some fire under her dress because she used to ask Spiro's younger workers what it was like to screw young woman and whether they'd be interested in a more mature woman. It was all very odd.

Spiro didn't much care though because his life was his florist business. It was his mistress. He doted over her, caressing ever corner of the store, making it beautiful for his upscale clients who ordered flowers by the hundreds to be shipped to museums, Broadway openings and penthouses in Manhattan.

As much as Spiro cared for his florist his attitude toward his workers was "the cheaper the better." I'd like a nickel for every owner or manager who thinks he can treat his employees like crap and not suffer the consequences.

Slowly but surely an attitude like that comes back to bite an owner on the ass. Some of Spiro's employees would steal. Others would deliberately sabotage his business. I was just a kid who found this all very amusing.

Spiro used to marvel at me. He saw the carefree young man he once was and when he felt compelled, he'd impart on me pearls of wisdom. They came quickly and without notice. He was an Air Force gunner during World War II and his style reflected that. He'd sidle up to you with a 'rat-tat-tat-tat' delivery.

One day his wife came in and blasted him. She was throwing verbal grenades while we ducked for cover. Spiro she said was 'not working hard enough" he was "good for nothing," and so on.

After that especially brutal sneak attack Spiro shuffled over to me as I cut some flowers and placed them in the refrigerator. I pretended not to have heard what happened but we all did. He brushed his mustache once or twice before speaking, as he often did, and said, "You know son. You've got the world," (pause) "and you don't know it."

Before I could even turn around he was gone.

I had no idea what the hell he was talking about. I didn't have the world. I was a college kid making $3 an hour and driving a 1970 Chevy Impala.

What he was saying of course is that his life was mapped out for him years before, with a crazy wife and a business he was locked into until it was time for him to take a nap in the marble mailbox. I, by contrast, had the whole world ahead before me – an empty canvas to paint whatever life I wanted.

His message sank in years later when I was an adult. I've often told my kids what Spiro told me about "having the world." I hope they got the message.

Spiro would always lie back and wait for a chance to make a comment. After being at the florist a few months, I had worked up a pretty good imitation of him. I'd use it on my co-workers who used to fall down laughing. Spiro caught wind of it and at first seemed ambivalent. In reality though I think he was annoyed.

One day he sidled up to me again while I was busy and revealed what he was really thinking. "You know you're a good kid Frank," he said "but you're a little jerked up in the head." I still smile – as I am now – at this odd observation. And I still joke about it with my friend Tony who also worked at Spiro's florist. Oh, I didn't tell you about Tony?

Tony was another Queens guy and a college classmate. He usually had a smirk on his face and didn't much give a crap what people thought. I got Tony a job with Spiro delivering flowers. He'd come in after class. Spiro would give him a list of deliveries and off he went.

As time went on Spiro slowly got on Tony's nerves. Tony didn't care. His attacks on Spiro were of the passive aggressive variety. I remember one vividly.

Tony waited for one of the busiest holidays of the year – Mother's Day – and knowing his digestive system could only handle certain foods, loaded up on the worst of them during the school day. I thought there was something up because when I saw him in school his smirk was tinged with a faint hint of pain. His stomach was struggling to digest these disagreeable foods and Tony was doing all he could to keep them in place.

I rushed to the florist after school and when I got there the place was packed. Well-heeled customers of Spiro's lightly touching all manner of delicate flowers he had shipped from every corner of the world. This holiday was the time for Spiro to shine, to show his customers how classy his florist shop was. How classy *he was* and why they should send more of their wealthy friends to him.

As I frantically worked on one floral design after another Tony came in. Spiro admonished him for being late.

When Tony had his list together and the flowers were packed into the car he made one last stop. He hustled into the small bathroom in the back of the florist and released all the stuff he had been holding in for hours. He walked out of the bathroom, propped the door open and out came this terrible, terrible stench. The smell was overpowering! Before you knew it had traveled the length and breadth of the store forward to the front doors, which were open at the time.

Tony beat the smell out the door and drove off leaving the rest of us – and Spiro's upscale customers – to suffer. Some walked out. Others took shorter breaths as they quickly paid and raced toward the fresh air of Queens Boulevard.

I swear I saw several flowers wilt.

•••

Now a secret about florists – they recycle. That's right. The same arrangement that dazzles mom, or enchants the wife, may have been part of a funeral arrangement hours or days before. Not every florist does it, but many have agreements with local funeral homes that when the funeral is over the florist will pull up in the back and load the funeral flowers into his van. They bring them back to the florist, pick out each flower that's fresh and use them in other arrangements. It sounds macabre but it makes sense.

Spiro had an agreement with a prominent Chinese-owned funeral home two blocks away. The two owners did business but I always sensed they either didn't like or trust each other.

Anyway, the Chinese gentleman would call the florist, and in his heavy accent tell us there were post funeral flowers to pick up. Spiro would reciprocate by giving the funeral home owner a few bucks. After all Spiro was getting free flowers. It was like found money for him.

One day Spiro handed a colleague of mine cash and sent us over to the Chinese funeral home to pick up a load of funeral flowers. We inconspicuously pulled up in the back of the funeral home and walked in.

The room was huge, and apparently hundred of mourners had just been there to pay homage to a prominent member of the Chinese-American community, because every inch of the room, and I mean every inch, was covered with flowers. The arrangements were stacked up, some reaching the ceiling. It was the Comstock Lode of flowers!

As we stood there wondering how many trips it would take to bring back all – or even some – of these flowers, the owner appeared.

He was a stout, bulky Chinese man about forty-five years old. You could tell he had been brought up in a time and place time where respect and hard work mattered. He was impeccably dressed and clearly proud of what he has accomplished. He bowed his head. We weren't sure how to respond.

After an uncomfortable moment or two we told him who we were and why we were there. He grunted.

As we stood amidst this Niagara Falls of flowers in all sizes and colors – my colleague reached into his pocket to hand the owner Spiro's small cash offering.

The Chinese man suddenly tightened up, clenched his fist and started loudly grunting at us in Chinese. It looked like he was ready to charge and we were not going to be around to see if he knew Jujitsu.

Like two schoolgirls we ran toward the door screaming, hopped into the van and raced off.

No wonder Spiro did not get along with the Chinese funeral home owner. His cash offering for the hundreds of arrangements and thousands of flowers to this proud and prominent Chinese businessman was five dollars.

HERMAN

Working with us at the florist was a quintessential New Yorker. Herman was hired as a deliveryman. About sixty at the time, Herman has seen it all and had bought the t-shirt. He lived through World War II, knew the city inside and out and had that innate ability most New Yorkers have of moving in and around any situation.

Herman's skin was wrinkled and worn. He was stoop-shouldered and had a bad habit of suddenly snorting up mucus and swallowing it. He was rough on all the edges and funny when he wanted to be.

He'd often tell us that he and wife had never said a cross word to each other in all their forty-two years of marriage. He'd paused and then say, "We just don't talk."

Delivering to Spiro's high-end clients in Manhattan took on the air of a commando mission. One guy drove, then parked illegally, while the other guy waited in the car to make sure he could move it should the police pull up.

During the slow times I'd often ride shotgun with Herman. As we drove from Queens to Manhattan he would regale me with stories of New York the way it used to be.

Herman did something one day that was so "New York". Coming back from Manhattan Herman and I decided to get some lunch – burgers and a drink.

When Herman was done he tossed the wrapper and the cup out the window. Right there on the street while we were waiting for a light. I was shocked, and a little embarrassed as people looked at Herman and me as if to say, "pigs."

I, on the other hand, had been trained by my Mom never to litter and most certainly never to bring attention to yourself in a bad way. I carefully folded up my wrapper and held it in my hand thinking that as soon as we stopped I would find a trash can and toss it in there.

Herman looked at me incredulously.

"What the fuck are you doing?"

"What?" I said.

"Just throw it out the window; it'll get picked up sooner or later."

Still a bit shocked from his tossing of the wrapper and cup a few blocks before I declined.

"I'll wait until we get somewhere and then throw it away."

"Look," he said. "It's just going to stink up the car. Toss it!" Again I declined. "Okay" he said. "Let me just put it somewhere where it'll be safe until we get back."

"All right." I handed it over to him.

He clawed it with his giant wrinkly hand, made it smaller and said, "Look I'm just going to leave here on the roof of the car," as he reached out the window, "and when we get back we'll make sure it goes into the trash."

At that, the light turned green and he sped off. The wind of course swept the wrapper and the cup off the roof almost immediately and into the intersection where Herman wanted it anyway.

He laughed and snorted and swallowed phlegm all the way back to Queens.

ABE

I only knew the lovely Bride's father Abe Schochet a short seven years before he passed on. He was a typical New Yorker. He and his wife, my terrific mother-in-law Elinore, taught me dozens of Yiddish words. Yiddish – which is a combination of Hebrew and Russian – is a unique language. Some of the words, when pronounced correctly, sound as though you're coughing up phlegm.

Abe also taught me not to stick my nose in other people's business, to avoid situations in which for whatever reason you gain responsibility for something you have no business being involved in.

This lesson came after the now famous "Wheelchair Story."

It started with a visit to my dentist on the north shore of Staten Island. One day while leaving his office I saw a woman in her seventies pushing an even older woman in a wheelchair toward the front door of the dentist's office.

You could tell she was struggling. It got worse as she neared the entrance of the office because there was a concrete step before the front door. At first she was able to get the front two wheels of the wheelchair on the step but was having all sorts of problems lifting the back of grandma's chair up on the landing. She was in a wheelchair no man's land without the muscle to complete the last step of the journey and get wheelchair up on the landing.

FRANK TO THE RESCUE!

"Excuse me madam, can I be of help?"

"Oh, thank you son, that's so very nice of you."

I lifted the back of the wheelchair, and with a bang the chair slammed against the concrete step. I heard a snap. The right back wheel of the wheelchair broke in half.

So there we were. A hundred-and-eight-year-old lady, her seventy-five-year-old daughter and me – a ridiculous, oddball version of the Three Stooges and just as frantic.

I didn't even have a chance to smile at the circumstances because Grandma was going down. Her chair, minus half a wheel, was listing dangerously to port.

Methuselah's daughter started screaming that her mom was headed for the pavement and both of us had to keep the chair from tipping over.

"Oh my God," the daughter was screaming, "She's going to fall!" The older lady looked like she was on the railing of the Titanic and based on her age she may very well have been.

"Oooohhhhhh… ohhhhhhhhh," she moaned.

Now I was thinking, *I'm really screwed. I've made two new friends and inherited a crisis.*

The wheelchair was propped up on the step with three and a half wheels and the slightest wind was going to send Grandma's melon to the pavement.

I was in a rush. I tried to help. I had to go and I couldn't wait for the conclusion of this cliffhanger.

"Ahhh… you know," I said among the cries for help, "I think I might have something in my trunk that can help."

"Please… please." The younger woman was crying, "I can't hold her up…"

Grandma's life meanwhile is flashing before her eyes and based on her age it's going to take a while.

I got the daughter in position to hold the chair up by herself as I slipped away to go to my car. I was able to get help but it took some time.

Later when I recounted the story to The Bride and the great Abe Schochet he just looked at me and laid down some fatherly advice.

This man – who at the age of sixteen had lied about his age so he could volunteer for the Army and later served at Pearl Harbor – looked me in the eye and said:

"Schmuck – don't get involved."

Thanks for being honest Abe.

ROMEO

Yeah. His name is Romeo. Really. The man next door when I was a kid was named Romeo. He became – along with his extended family – a great neighbor and when my Dad's brother married his young sister-in-law, we all became family.

Romeo was also my godfather. He was there at my confirmation. And before you ask, no my middle name is not Romeo. Although that would be great right? "Yeah I'm such a great lover, my middle name is Romeo."

Anyway – as I write this Romeo is eighty-nine years old. Romeo is a great storyteller. Most of his stories revolved around his service in World War II. He was among the bravest of the brave who stormed the beaches of Normandy and on the morning of June 6, 1944.

With bullets flying, Romeo – and thousands of men like him – jumped out of transports in chest high water and marched to an almost certain death; his brother who was with him that day died. Romeo lived and pressed on into France, and then Belgium.

It's tough to convey to anyone the bravery he and all the other soldiers showed that day and all the days before and after. Many men left families, jobs and careers and ended up fighting the Third Reich through Europe or Japanese fanatics on the Pacific islands of Okinawa, Tamara and Iwo Jima. Many never came back. Or came back in pieces, physically and emotionally.

I would talk about D-Day with Romeo and unlike many of his valiant colleagues who could not, Romeo was happy to recount the story of the invasion. In word pictures only those who were there can conjure up he talked about hitting the beach and moving forward, never knowing if his next step would be his last.

After the initial invasion, wave after wave of soldiers fought through the hideous hedgerows further inland. The hedgerows, giant hedges where German soldiers hid and inflicted even more death, also exposed the vulnerable underbellies of the U.S. tanks. Romeo, on the ground and with nothing but a helmet and a rifle, fought on and survived.

He spent three straight days fighting and marching, stopping briefly now and again to get his bearings and push on.

As kids we would look at him transfixed. He told the story with a tinge of sadness about losing his brother who is buried on the cliffs overlooking Omaha Beach. He also spoke with a great deal of pride.

One day after a retelling of the story I said to Romeo, "You marched and fought for three straight days and didn't stop to rest? What happened when things quieted down? What did you do then?"

Romeo looked at me and said, "Frank, we sat down in a small patch of dirt, opened up our K-rations – and ate like men."

Indeed Romeo. Men all of you.

GEE GEE

For some reason Italian-American families love nicknames. I don't know why. Growing up almost every relative either had a nickname or had a relative with a nickname. I had an Uncle Fee Fee who lived in Arizona and an Aunt Cucci. My grandfather who was Sal was called "Sammy," and we even had a relative who was named after her dog. My cousins used to call her "Grandma Mugsy."

And not many people know this but I was named after my uncle. But how would you know? No one called him Frank. He was Uncle Duke.

Among my favorite Aunts was Aunt Gee Gee (pronounced G-G). Her real name was Josephine. Even her mail would arrive at her house with the heading "Gee Gee."

She was not your typical old Italian aunt. She actually looked very much like Angie Dickerson. Thin, fashionable and always with a cigarette dangling from her lips.

Not knowing any better, I figured every family had nicknames. My aunt lived in Queens but eventually moved to northern New Jersey with my uncle, her second husband Sal Dinapoli.

She knew I was on TV but never saw me until one day during a commercial break I got a call on the set at News 12.

"Frank?" the familiar voice came. "It's Aunt Gee Gee. I'm watching you now."

"Wow," I said, "I've been on TV all these years and this is the first time you're seeing me?"

"Yeah, you look great."

"Thanks Aunt Gidge (which was the short version of Gee Gee).

"Okay – Uncle Sal and I are going to continue to watch."

"That's fine because I have to go back on the air."

I came back on camera and was kind of pleased. My aunt has seen me on TV for the first time and she seemed very impressed.

"Okay," I said on the air, "Just want to say hello to my Aunt Gee Gee watching in Westwood, New Jersey today – hello Aunt Gee Gee. Now it's time for the weather and here's Paul Morrill."

We switch to Paul, who grew up in the mid-west, in front of the weather map and his face is frozen in confusion. He looks into the camera and says, "Gee Gee?"

RODNEY

My brother Sal and I love Rodney Dangerfield. The bug-eyed comedian who "gets no respect."

Sal will call and I'll go right into a Rodney bit, "My dog's another one ya know. Why, last night four times he went on the paper… three times I was reading it!"

For us Rodney's tops. First, because as a one-time comedian, I respect his old fashioned style. No long set up, not nuance, just two sentences and BANG – the punch line.

"The bank's another place they won't let you use the bathroom. They say it's for employees only. Last time I had to go so bad I applied for a job."

You get the idea.

My mother remarried when I was about thirteen. My stepdad managed a restaurant in Manhattan. In its day it was a hangout for guys like Sinatra, Dean and Sammy.

One summer night the phone rings at my home. "Someone wants to talk to you," my step dad says.

"Who?"

Before I could get an answer Rodney's on the line and into his act.

"I tell ya… I tell ya… it's rough, it's rough. I thought I'd do something nice for my kid ya know. I bought him a bow and arrow. He bought me a shirt with a bull's-eye on the back."

Rodney stopped at the restaurant for dinner and now was putting on a special three-minute command performance just for me! He'd never met me but he knew he had an audience – even if it was an audience of one.

Years later when I was working as a reporter at Channel 9 word came that Rodney had passed away. As fate would have it I was within a few blocks of the iconic "Dangerfield's Comedy Club" which he owned on the East Side of Manhattan.

I was pulled off my original story, sent there and did a piece on his life and times. It aired in the first ten minutes of the newscast.

Oh, and one more thing. As if Rodney was sending me a message I was dressed, by chance, in *his* classic outfit. A black suit, white shirt and red tie. While on camera I tugged on my tie a few times like Rodney use to in honor of this comedic genius.

KIDS, KITTENS, POLITICANS AND CELEBRITIES

Despite their unpopularity you have to hand to our elected officials. Why do they do it? Is it a need to be seen? To make a difference? One thing I'm sure of, some candidates should have never been elected.

Recently the State Legislature in New York staged an insurrection against a weak governor, shutting down the government and dictating its terms to him. A legally blind Governor who nabbed the state's top position after the man who had chosen him as a running mate was nailed spending part of his impressive fortune on hookers. It'd be funny if it weren't our government.

Politicians are not generally a funny to begin with. They are constantly thinking about what to say, who not to offend, how to pitch a story, defend a decision. It's so rare when a politician goes for the punch line. I think that's why people so loved JFK. He had a sense of humor. Who could forget when in the middle of a press conference an aide handed JFK a note saying NASA had successfully launched a monkey into orbit.

JFK saw the opening and said, "… And the monkey reports all is fine."

Another one of my favorites is a quip by the former senator and presidential candidate Bob Dole.

During Ted Kennedy's infamous playboy days after leaving his wife, he went on a screwing spree. There's one particularly disturbing shot from the 1980's taken from a distance. It's of a pasty white Kennedy in a small boat off shore. He's naked with his ass sticking up and he's clearly on top of a woman.

Senator Dole, upon seeing the photo, hit the ball out of the park by saying, "All I can say is I'm happy to see Senator Kennedy has changed his position on off shore drilling."

My first up close and personal contact with the political animal came in my early days of being a reporter. I was sent to cover the election night festivities for Linden Mayor and State Senator John Gregorio. That's right; in New Jersey you're able to hold two political positions at once while collecting two salaries and later two pensions.

He was everything a small urban New Jersey mayor could be and more. I remember his booming voice and his take-no-prisoners attitude. Mayor Gregorio ruled until, like so many politicians in this state, he was indicted. When I covered the election night celebration in 1982 Mayor Gregorio had just been reelected but was under investigation for all sorts of shenanigans. The Feds were following him and tapping his phone lines.

My job that night was to get reaction on his re-election. Amid the balloons, booze and blasting music one of his hulking assistants escorted me to the back of the ballroom where Mayor Gregorio was holding court with friends and soon-to-be friends. Despite the insinuations that he was somehow conducting business in the shadows he was all smiles.

"Mister Mayor, Congratu… " I couldn't even finish my sentence.

"I own this town, kid. I own this fuckin' town," he screamed, wrapping a sweaty arm around me and squeezing my neck. "You see these numbers?" pointing now to the tally board showing him way ahead, "I own this fuckin' town."

"Great," I replied meekly. "I just wanted to know…"

"You see those police officers there?" He pointed now to the two or three Linden cops on hand for crowd control, "Those are my fuckin' cops. This whole fucking town is mine…"

"Well, that's great Mr. Mayor…" I asked the usual questions about his reelection. How he felt and so on and then like any good reporter I saved the most uncomfortable question for last. "Mr. Mayor, what do you say to those who have whispered that your administration is corrupt?"

"I don't care kid," he said, "I know they're listening to my phone calls. Let them! Shit, that's why when I pick up the phone I always say, 'Hello everybody!'"

You had to laugh.

Even Gregorio could not top Mayor Gerald McCann of Jersey City. McCann fancied himself a mover and shaker, a politician on the rise.

In 1985 McCann ran for re-election. He thought he had everyone he needed to win an easy re-election. He didn't have city council member Anthony Cucci who ran against his fellow Democrat and won the primary. In heavily Democratic Jersey City that was akin to winning the general election, which he did a few months later.

It was hailed in newspapers as the "Cucci Coup."

McCann, my friends in Jersey City tell me, did not handle the defeat well. As a parting gift on his last day in office McCann urinated on Cucci's desk.

I'm not sure how that went over with his cellmates after McCann, who was convicted in 1992 of bank fraud, served thirty-three months in prison.

McCann (who as a I write this book is back in politics as a member of the Jersey City School Board) was recently quoted as saying when he gets into a political fight he – figuratively of course – " shoots bullets."

Probably better than peeing on your opponent's desk.

Newark has always had a history of game-changing mayors who come into office with a flourish and leave in handcuffs.

I was at election headquarters in 1984 when Sharpe James, who was promising a "Sharpe Change" in Newark politics, defeated longtime Mayor Ken Gibson. James was engaging and full of enthusiasm that night talking about how he would change New Jersey's largest city. As time went on the city changed him.

Fast forward to 2005. I'm at a press conference at Newark City Hall as James neared the end of his twenty years in office. Having just had dental surgery he was ornery and short-tempered. Investigators were also looking into some of James's shady land deals in Florida and elsewhere as the walls closed in on him.

James had just refused to meet with a family who felt they had been slighted over one injustice or another.

"Mr. Mayor – the family of Karen Smith claims you're ignoring their problem."

James glared at me. I could see in his head he was asking, "How dare this reporter ask me a question like that?"

"I just got out of a dentist's chair," he told me. "The dentist almost had to send me to the hospital because the infection was so bad."

"I'm sorry about that Mr. Mayor, but how do you respond to the Smith family's claim that you won't meet with them?"

"Did you hear what I just said? I almost ended up in the hospital today."

"I'm glad you didn't Mr. Mayor, but now that you're here what do you say to the Smith family?"

I could now see the mayor was trying to use his dental emergency to change the subject.

We went at it for a while. At one point I thought he might reach over the podium and hit me.

PRESIDENTS

Local politics is one thing – getting a new stop sign in place, helping a constituent deal with his late Medicare check. But being a president? Whew! That must be a thankless gig.

Just take a look at the modern day presidents. Why is it they go into office looking like George Clooney and leave looking like Abe Vigoda?

My first encounter with a U.S. president came at the Flemington Fair in Flemington, New Jersey. A big gathering of 4-H pigs and ponies, food booths, music and tractor pulls.

It was the summer of 1980. Then California Governor Ronald Reagan and Vice-Presidential hopeful George H.W. Bush were crisscrossing the country in a bid to unseat incumbent Jimmy Carter.

Bush was assigned the task of corralling New Jersey's fourteen electoral votes. New Jersey is always a swing state with more independent voters than registered Democrats and Republicans, so it's not only an important bellwether but can make a difference in a tight contest.

Bush showed up at the fair late in the evening and started walking around shaking hands. He was surrounded by a number of Secret Service agents. You could tell they were concerned for his safety, but pre-9/11 this was not the kind of event where you had to worry.

As a cub reporter this was something else! My first encounter with a potential vice president and I wasn't going to be denied. Tape recorder in hand I moved close to Bush and then with a shove invaded the Secret Service circle of protection. I moved the mic up to his mouth and said, "Mr. Bush how's it feel to be ahead in the polls and most likely on the verge of becoming he next Vice-President?"

He was extremely gracious, said he was excited and then moved on.

I've often thought about that night. How easy it was for me to move that close to the vice-presidential candidate. I clearly did not present a threat but no one had checked me out. No one at the fair was frisked or sent through a metal detector.

In 1996 then-President Bill Clinton came to Freehold, New Jersey. Our News 12 live truck was twenty yards from the podium. No one checked my colleagues or me out. I stood in the truck with the door open and watched the president.

Post 9-11 the ease with which you can see and shake hands with the president is gone. It's absolutely necessary in this day and age to protect the president at all costs but it's sad as well. It isolates him from us, and us from him.

In the early 1800s it was not uncommon – if his servants were otherwise engaged – for the President of the United States to answer the White House door himself. Now every waking public moment of the president's life is choreographed.

PIA

I start my story about Pia Lindstrom with Liz Trotta. Liz Trotta is a trailblazer. A correspondent for CBS news in the 1960's, Liz fought for – and received – permission from the then-stodgy network to cover the war in Vietnam and other major stories of that time including the JFK assassination, the Yom Kippur War, Chappaquiddick, the hostage crisis in Iran, the U.S. invasion of Grenada, George McGovern's 1972 presidential bid and many more.

Back then it was unusual for a female reporter to do anything but fluff pieces. Not Liz. She went into the jungles of Vietnam and stood toe to toe with her older male colleagues from CBS and the other major networks.

For me though Liz is one more thing. An Italian-American reporter in a business during my early days that had very few. I bought her autobiography shortly after it came out and tore though it. It's amazing. Not being shy I tracked her down in New York and invited myself to have lunch with her.

She was as engaging and as interesting as I imagined. It's always good to learn what you can from those who have been there. It's a lesson anyone in any business should practice: Pull from the experience of others to make what you do better.

About a year or so after our meeting I got an invitation to her book launch party. Liz had written a book about the life and times of St. Jude.

Liz said the party was going to be at Pia's apartment in Manhattan. There are not many "Pias" in the world and the only one I could think of was Pia Lindstrom, the stunning daughter of the great actress Ingrid Bergman.

At the appointed time and date I traveled to Manhattan for the book party at Pia's place (say that fast three times). I was basically unsure how the world of New York glitterati works.

The building overlooked Central Park. It was old and elegant. I shook hands and made friends. Bill O'Reilly from Fox was there, although he was a couple of years from being the giant of TV he is now. There were also some local TV personalities. I handed out business cards and mingled like crazy.

The funny thing happened though when I showed up for the party. I came right from the news set so I was all dressed up. I checked my cuff links, straightened my tie and walked into the lobby.

"Can I help you sir?" said the doorman.

"Yes," I said proudly. "I'm here for Liz Trotta's book launch party at Pia's apartment."

"Very good sir. Her apartment is on the ninth floor."

The next question was easy.

"Great, which apartment?"

"No sir," the doorman said quietly. "It IS the ninth floor."

What the hell do I know?

Chapter 17
"WATCH OUT FOR THE MONKEY"

By February of 2002 the freelancers on the list at Channel 9 slowly started to thin. From one of eight working freelance reporters the list narrowed to five. Then three.

I had been getting more and more juicy stories and was often leading the broadcast. It was a good sign, but good signs mean nothing in this business. Talent is surely part of it but connections, attitude and professionalism are also factors. You always have to be selling yourself.

On February 13, 2002 I got to do a story in an unusual place: It was about a young boy who had been attacked. But what interested me was that it was literally right down the block from the house where I grew up in Queens. It was in sight of the gas station that my mom and I used to stop in as she took me around as a kid. As we set up for the live shot I glanced back at the gas station and smiled.

The following day, Valentine's Day, I was off. I drove down to Princeton, New Jersey to meet up with an old buddy, a very talented meteorologist named Steve McLaughlin who was working full time as the weatherman at the WB17 in Philadelphia. We chatted about the business and the direction it was going, laughed about our former colleagues at News 12 and generally caught up.

On the way back my cell phone rang. It was the assistant news director at UPN 9 News Michael St. Peter.

"Hey – how's it going?" I said.

"Let me ask you something Frank."

"Yes?"

"How would you like to work for us full-time?"

"I'd love too – great! Thank you and I'm looking forward to doing a great job for you."

The gamble had paid off. I had left a comfortable job at News 12 to roll the dice and they had come up seven

I would also continue to work along side Rolland Smith.

Before the official announcement was made that I was to become the newest full timer one of the long time reporters at Channel 9 approached me in the parking lot.

As any good reporter is – she was sniffing around for information.

"So, I hear tell you're the new full timer."

"Well," I said, "it's not official yet."

"Some of the freelancers who had been here a lot longer than you are kind of upset about that," she said.

I paused to gather my thoughts. "You know, many a time I have been on the receiving end of what they are experiencing. Skipped over for one reason or another. I handled it as graciously as I could and now it's their turn."

She stared for a moment and smiled. I turned and walked away.

My dream of being on New York television was twenty-five years in the making. I had arrived. And no one was going to take that away from me.

My first head-on experience with working in news full time was a revelation. Every TV news show has an editorial meeting hours before the cast. The news director knocks around ideas about what the newscast should look like and who will be covering what.

Ours was held in a small room off the news area at about three in the afternoon. As I sat there the executive producer asked the most important question in the world of major market news.

"What show tonight is our lead-in?"

I thought for a moment. What the hell does that have to do with our newscast? But that is the question in commercial TV news that means everything. It is of utmost importance that you retain your viewers by teasing them in regular programming about what was coming up on the news.

All stations do it: Tie-ins. Grab some issue or angle from a popular prime time show and give it a local tilt whether there is one or not. For us it was difficult. UPN's most popular lead-in was World Wrestling Entertainment. As the meeting went on I could hear Edward R. Murrow spinning in his grave. Or - since he was cremated – rustling his ashes.

"So what's our lead-in?" the executive producer asked.

"WWE Wrestling."

"Okay," he said, without missing a beat. "Let's have Monica head down to the WWE store in Times Square to get reaction on the big WWE Wrestlemania Event. I think Hulk Hogan is going to be making an appearance there today"

Is Hulk Hogan news, I asked myself? Oh well. I wasn't going to make waves.

I looked at the rundown and saw something that said, "Li'l Bow Wow. I'm thinking what's this – a story about dogs? It ended up being some twelve-year old rapper who was in town and was available in case we needed his take on maybe, I don't know, the situation in the Middle East.

The editorial meetings were billed as freewheeling mix-it-ups of story ideas and segments. Everyone was encouraged to submit story ideas,

even the cameramen or as they're called "shooters" or "photogs". One day the EP of the broadcast started the meeting as if he had won the Pick-5 Lottery down at the deli. He was busting out of his shirt.
"It's cold today – really cold and everyone's buzzing about it," he all but screamed. "I mean I'm in the supermarket today and people are saying, 'wow it's cold,' and it is! It's cold; we need to talk about this in the cast, maybe lead with this. Lead with the weather because – it's really cold."

All the reporters sat for what seemed like a minute as he calmed down a bit and searched our faces for support.

Just then from the back of the room one of the shooters Eric Anderson piped in.

"It's December – it's supposed to be cold."

He said what we were all thinking.

After a week or so of this I started to chime in. Maybe the story about the woman who lost her blouse at Macy's and had to walk out in her bra really wasn't a story for the first five minutes of the cast. Or video of two people having sex up in a Central Park tree didn't really have to lead the show.

Michael St. Peter called me into his office following one meeting and set me straight. This was not a democracy and I was not to comment on the story selection unless asked specifically. In other words, the executive producer of the show would decide what stories the reporters covered and you were just to go and cover them.

There was a revolt now and again. It happened a week or so after the infamous "Janet Jackson's Super Bowl Nipple-Gate" incident.

"We need to get reaction to the reaction following the Janet Jackson Super Bowl wardrobe malfunction!" The EP was again jumping out of his shirt. "Everyone's talking about this. "Joanne," The EP said to freelance reporter Joanne Pillegi, "Why don't you track down some psychologist and..." Before he could finish Joanne chimed in.

"No. I think it's stupid and the story is old."

Everyone stopped what they were doing to watch this rare bit of insurrection.

"No, it isn't. Everybody's talking about it."

"Not anymore," Joanne snapped back. "It's stupid and played out – and is it really news? So there was a quarter of a second shot of her nipple. Who cares?"

The EP's face turned sour.

Joanne ended up covering the story and also earned our never-ending admiration. Again she had said what we were all thinking.

A radio news colleague who works for the top all-news radio station in America told me that during the height of the Iraq War she presented a story to her news director. It was the story of a returning veteran who had been injured. He had been shunned by the VA and essentially ignored. It was a heartbreaking story but really told the tale of what this war was doing to some who dropped everything after 9/11 to fight overseas.

The news director's response was telling. As my colleague tells it he said, "No, you don't want to do a story like that. It's depressing. People might change the station."

Ratings are king. Give the people what they want so they keep watching.

•••

There are few people you meet in this world with the charm and calm sensibility of Rolland Smith. He is one of but two people I have met in my life who project a calm that comes from within their core. I sought him out and chatted with Rolland the first month or so I was there. He was amazed by my encyclopedic knowledge of his work. I recounted stories I had seen him do twenty- to twenty-five years ago and even asked him about a long forgotten, except for me, special weekly piece he did on the CBS Radio Network. I discussed one in particular that he slowly but finally remembered. His look at me as if to say – *you remember that?*

He also seemed genuinely flattered. I hadn't intended to flatter him, but only to speak with him about all the great work he had done over the years.

One night after the show Rolland asked if I'd like to have a drink with him at a nearby restaurant. This was big. Rolland respected my work enough to want to get to know me.

As we spoke I made it clear that I wanted to make the best of this opportunity. Halfway through our get-together some of the crewmembers from UPN 9 wandered in to get a late night snack. The timing could not have been better. After that day I was treated differently. The word soon got around. Being seen with Rolland meant I was a player and to be treated with respect.

That's also how this business works. Those who are embraced by the icons of this business are seen as "comers." It helped that Rolland was in my corner.

Another of the TV superstars of my youth was also working at UPN 9. In his day Dr. Frank Field was New York's premiere weatherman. He broke into the business in the early Sixties when WNBC needed someone to do the weather. Frank was not, as some believe, a doctor of meteorology, but rather an optometrist. It didn't matter. His personality shone through on the air. In short order he was doing bits on the *Tonight Show* with Johnny Carson, which was taped right across the hall at 30 Rockefeller Center.

Frank had a long and illustrious career – first at WNBC, then WCBS and now in his eighties as the weekend weatherman at UPN 9. His son Storm was doing the weekday weather forecasts.

Frank and I exchanged pleasantries for several weeks during my freelance days until one day he called out my name from across the newsroom.

"Hey, Cipolla… come over here."

My heart sank. I was thinking – *what the heck did I do to upset Frank Field?*

I strolled over to him and he put his arm around me. "You know," he said, "you're the best damn reporter this station has and if they don't give you a full-time job they're assholes."

"Thanks," I said.

He wandered away and I stood there taking it in. Frank Field – the man I had watched as a kid – had just told me he loved my work. We're friends to this day. He is among the great and classy men in this business and loves broadcasting almost as much as his wonderful family.

•••

I have read over the years that the one of the keys to success is to constantly schmooze upward. Let your most immediate supervisor know that he or she is great and that you support management's decisions.

My policy – and maybe it's because of where I came from – was to always keep the people working directly by my side happy. If they're happy, I look good, and then everyone's happy. And in the case of TV news, that meant the shooters, editors, writers, producers and assistant producers. Those who take my video, edit my report, help back at the station.

There's a classic story about one reporter from WNBC who was despised by the shooters. They considered him difficult and ornery to a fault. One shooter had finally had enough and wanted to make a point.

As the reporter was videotaping his stand-up the shooter kept moving him around, positioning him so that he'd look his best.

When the report aired the reporter was appalled. There he stood on a street telling the story of some New York tragedy and perfectly melded into the left side of his head and coming out the right was a drainage pipe in the distance behind him. This optical illusion made it appear as though the pipe was going into the left side of his head and spewing a torrent of water as it exited the right side. Despite the seriousness of the story the viewer just couldn't help but laugh while watching that stream of water draining out of his noggin.

When the reporter later approached the shooter the shooter simply said, "Don't fuck with us." Message sent. Out in the field the shooter has the ability to make you look really good – or really stupid.

I loved the shooters I worked with. Guys like (in no particular order) Richie McCue, Jim Sabastian, Bobby Hiner, Patrick Horan, Eric Anderson, Scott Pierce, Roy Isen, Paul Tsokus, Jimmy Mitchell, Kenny Sutton, David Rosenfeld, Paul Garret and Fred Senstacke. I could write a whole book just about Fred.

Fred Senstacke came from a very influential Tennessee family. His father owned a chain of newspapers, and was an African American leader with whom President Lyndon Johnson often consulted during the height of the civil rights movement. Fred was college educated and served in intelligence during the Vietnam War. He could have gotten out of serving thanks to his dad's connections but that's not Fred.

Fred is a trained killer. During the Vietnam War he led a small group of men who regularly infiltrated enemy lines and lay in wait for the Vietcong. He'd then report back on their movements. Fred would often lie in a ditch for days. If discovered he was trained to kill quietly – often with a snap to the neck.

Fred was also a news commando. When the story was on the line people like Fred and others had your back. It got rough on the street sometimes and you always wanted to know that those guys were there to protect you.

Fred had a saying: "Watch out for the monkey.' It was based on a long complicated joke that only Fred could tell about a suddenly very lucky guy who is sexually attacked from behind by a circus monkey. The moral was simple. Even when all seems to be going right, something could easily go wrong, so you had to always 'watch out for the monkey."

After Fred told me the story I started bringing in small photos of monkeys I got out of newspapers, *National Geographic*, and other magazines. Fred had about ten shots of large and small monkeys taped to inside of his news vehicle. Reporters used to ask Fred about all the monkey photos and he'd laugh and say, "Go ask Frank."

Fred also had another saying: "It's the same old bullshit."

Often we'd be at one or another press conference about a shady politician, a tragic killing or some other story and Fred would lean in to me and say, "Frank, it's the same old bullshit."

Fred also had a very succinct way of making a point. One night there was a murder in Times Square. With thirty-five minutes to the broadcast the assignment editor looked my way and said, "Fred's in the car outside waiting for you, go... go!"

I raced outside, and found Fred inside an idling news truck. Almost out of breath I said, "Fred, there's a dead body in Times Square and we've got thirty-five minutes to air."

Fred just looked at me calmly through his sunglasses and said, "Frank, the body's not going anywhere." In other words, *we'll get this done. Relax.*

Fred loved his sunglasses. No matter what time of day or night they were on. One time we did a live shot from the base of the George Washington Bridge with no lights on me. I was a shadow. Fred was supposed to turn my spotlight on but the glare from the bridge on his sunglasses confused him. He thought the lights *were* on.

Another night the newscast producer came up with the idea of sending Fred and me up to Hartford, Connecticut to cover the arrest of a priest in a sex scandal that had a vague connection to New York. We could have easily done it in studio or somewhere in and around New York.

The story at best was borderline interesting and certainly did not warrant an almost three-hour ride to Hartford. The newscast producer that night assured us it was a significant story and that we could use the facilities of his old station WFSB in Hartford to edit, write and feed the story live back to our station. In fact, he said, they use the same format as us for their video so we could shoot as much as we wanted and edit at their station.

Time rules when you're a reporter, and it was already five in the afternoon. Our newscast began at ten. The story was from the early morning and even if we were lucky, didn't hit the usual New York City traffic on our way up there, and let's say got there at eight, that left just an hour or so to find the principles involved, drive to their location, shoot the video, go back to WFSB (a station of which Fred and I had no knowledge) edit it in unfamiliar surroundings, set up and go live from Hartford.

Oh, and there was a wicked winter ice storm on the way. This had disaster written all over it.

Fred lives in Pennsylvania, so no matter what time we got back from Hartford he was looking at another two-hour ride home from Channel 9. As a favor he asked me to drive to Hartford and he'd drive back.

As I drove up to Hartford in our black Ford Explorer the skies turned nasty. First a cold rain started and then rain mixed with ice.

It took me two hours and forty-five minutes.

Fred and I pulled up at the station in downtown Hartford about eight-fifteen. We're still in the dark. Not sure where the priest's parish is located or how to get in touch with the family of the victim. The anchors and reporters at WFSB were helpful but they had their own newscast to put together so they couldn't baby-sit us. Fred and I were essentially on our own in a strange city, with no direction, little info and only the video we grabbed on the way out of Channel 9 that included all the New York elements of the story. Oh, and the video format that the producer at Channel 9 assured us would be compatible with what WFSB had - was not. They had changed their format several years before so nothing they had shot, nor anything we could shoot, could be used.

Ten o'clock came – I did some tap dancing with a live shot outside the station – the story got out on the air, and now Fred and I had to head back to Channel 9. By this time the weather was worse; there was ice and sleet, the roads were treacherous and before I could say anything Fred was in the driver's seat, sunglasses on, tired from a long day, and wanting to get back to Channel 9 ASAP. He jams the driver's side seat into a semi-reclined position and screeches off.

There is no one on the road as we pull onto Route 84 West heading out of Hartford. Everyone is hunkered down at home.

Within minutes Fred's eyes are half closed. The car fishtails now and again. I check the speedometer and Fred's going about eighty miles an hour.

"You all right Fred?" I ask. "Looks like you're going a little fast." My voice seems to startle him as if I just woke him up. Fred mumbles something.

Now I start slowly reviewing my life. I was positive that with no one on the highway, a raging ice storm, Fred trying to catch some Zs and speeding at the same time, it was just a matter of time before we ended up in a ditch along side the road. With everyone concentrating on sanding and salting and all our fellow employees already home snug in their beds, it would be days before they found our bruised, battered and frozen bodies upside down in the Channel 9 SUV.

I was saying to myself, 'Okay, I've had a pretty good run here. I've achieved most of my goals. I have a wife who loves me and children that can carry my name."

A giant eighteen-wheeler rumbles by on our left. This jolts Fred, who seems to take this as a sign that he should wake up a little. Five minutes later I hear what sounds like faint snoring.

"Hey, Fred… you okay? I can drive, you know," I said loudly.

Fred mumbles something about 'watching out for the monkey' and then says almost semiconsciously "It's like the Indy 500 Frank…" Whatever that means.

He chuckles. I'm terrified.

I grabbed my seat as another eighteen-wheeler whizzes by on our left. Fred seems oblivious. Fred fishtails into the parking lot at the station, hops into his car and speeds off. I kiss the ground.

I didn't see Fred for three days. He took off to recuperate.

Oh, and Fred drove the same distance I did earlier in two hours and forty-five minutes in exactly two hours and *fourteen minutes*. And in much worse weather!

It was the most terrifying ride in my life.

Falling asleep on the job is sometimes unavoidable. Another shooter told me of the time he and a reporter arrived at a location an hour before they were supposed to do an interview.

It was raining and as they sat killing time the "whoosh, whoosh" of the windshield wipers slowly lulled them asleep. To make matters worse the reporter nodded off with a lit pipe in his mouth.

They were both jolted awake with a rap on the window about an hour and a half later. It was the interview subject outside holding an umbrella and wondering if they were the two guys from the TV station who were supposed to meet up with him.

As they got their bearings the shooter looked around and was startled to see that the lit pipe in the reporter's mouth had fallen out of his mouth while he was asleep and had burned a coaster-sized hole in the reporter's suit jacket.

●●●

Times Square is genuinely the Crossroads of the World. If you want a to speak with anyone about any topic here or abroad all you have to do is walk two blocks through Times Square. Unrest in Albania? You'll find a couple of Albanian tourists. Brazil's economy teetering on the brink of collapse? You'll find a family of Brazilians in Times Square.

But an Angry Clown?

One of the freelance shooters Brian Grob and I were sent to Times Square to cover a lighthearted story about a new flavor from Starbucks; a fluff piece to wrap up the news.

As Brian and I are walking around Times Square we see a friendly looking 30-ish guy dressed in a full clown outfit, makeup and all.

"Hey, Clown… nice day isn't it?"

"Get the fuck out of here," he snaps.

"What?"

If I see a clown, I think happy. But this guy just told me to get the fuck out of here.

I suppressed a giggle.

"Did you hear me motherfucker, get the fuck out here."

I looked over at Brian and now he's giggling. Then out of the Angry Clown's mouth, surrounded by a colorfully painted smile, comes a stream of obscenities.

"Come on," I said, "we just want to talk to you about the new Starbucks coffee flavor."

"How about I shove that flavor up your ass?"

He was not kidding and for us it's getting funnier by the minute. The more the Angry Clown curses the funnier it is.

"I'm gonna fuck you up ya motherfuckers, get that fucking camera out of my face."

I was looking around because I couldn't believe we were the only ones who found this hilarious. He pushes Brian. Brian bursts out in laughter. I laugh out loud too, and this just makes Angry Clown angrier. Which makes it even funnier. Which made him angrier.

At this point he starts swinging.

Brian and I stepped back but find it hard to move away because at this point our sides are splitting from this spectacle. Now we were falling over with laughter.

"I'm going to kick your fucking asses…."

I said something like, "What, with your big clown shoes?" And we both cracked up.

Now Brian and I made a break for it. We start running and the Angry Clown follows, cursing sailor-like vulgarities as he chases us.

Here we were – me in a suit and tie, Brian hauling 25 pounds of equipment, being chased and cursed through Times Square by a guy in full clown makeup. It was something out of a Woody Allen movie.

We never found out why he was so angry but that's one clown you don't want to book for a kid's party.

When you hit the streets of New York City you have to be ready for anything. The shooters always were. They had been thrust into just about every situation, so they knew the score and could turn on a dime.

Some shooters get frustrated and angry. Others seem to have a Zen-like aura about them.

When bad weather hits, that becomes the lead story. The consultants tell news stations again and again that weather is what people want to see. Flooded cars, downed power lines, that sort of thing.

When a storm hit, the word went out to all the shooters far and wide: Stop what you're doing and take some video of the weather. If you were interviewing the mayor you were expected to wrap it up and go take some video of the raindrops.

We've all seen it: The close up nighttime shot of the street light with the rain whizzing by, or the snowflakes lashing the camera lens. It has gotten to be such a commonplace tool of lazy assignment editors that one enterprising shooter decided he had had enough.

And his solution was ingenious.

Whenever the call went out for nasty weather shots he'd just step into the back of the live truck, open up a small drawer and pull out the weather video the assignment editor was clamoring for. It had all been taken a dozen times before and saved on carefully marked videotapes.

The video tapes were lined up and marked:

HEAVY RAIN
HEAVY RAIN / AUTUMN
HEAVY RAIN / SPRING
DOWNED TREES
STRONG WINDS
LIGHT RAIN /NIGHT
HEAVY RAIN / NIGHT
FLOODING
SEVERE FLOODING

Rain doesn't change; snapped trees look the same, so why should he bother taking the video again? He'd wait a half hour or so and then just feed it in. The desk loved the video, never realizing it was months, maybe even years old.

I on the other hand had to go where the wicked weather was. Many a night I stood in knee-high water, or next to an old maple tree cracked in half, or freezing my ass in the middle of a blizzard.

I'm not a fan of it. I mean we all know what that looks like. For news directors, though, it's easy to do and get on the air. My executive producer at Channel 9 found out early that I despised snowstorms and then went out of his way to send me out into the teeth of every storm he could find.

I was whipped around by Tropical Storm Isabella down in Cape May, NJ, and pushed and pulled during another wicked storm on the boardwalk in Atlantic City. And then there was the Snowplow Challenge.

For a time I was handed a Channel 9 franchise. You know how some local news stations have special reporters to help those wronged by something? Every city has a "7 on Your Side" reporter, or "Harry Helps You" franchise. Channel 9 had the 'Snowplow Challenge'.

When the giant snowstorm hit, the EP, knowing how much I *love* the snow and cold weather, sent shooter Jim Sabastian and me out to an area on the outskirts of the city to rank the town's snow clean-up.

Getting to a location, getting all the elements and getting it on the air at ten o'clock was hard enough. Doing all of that while slipping and sliding on the roads made matters worse. In fact, the Snowplow Challenge required us to hit four to six towns, assess the snow clean up, and then rank them with our trademarked on-screen animated snowplows.

It would go something like this: "In Hackensack the roads were caked with snow but the snow itself was not as high as towns nearby. We gave Hackensack two and a half snowplows."

At that point two and a half snowplows would appear on the screen one at a time and when they did there was a loud "Ding!"

"We gave Rutherford three snow plows." DING, DING, DING!

This is what we were doing during the storm to help our viewers. Using cartoon on-screen snowplows to tell them what condition their roads were in.

Believe or not, though – thanks to shooter Jim Sabastian and me – we were able to make a difference. If we found one town really lacking we'd track down the mayor. Then I'd give him or her the speech.

"Mr. Mayor, in three hours we're going to go on the air and say your town had the worst snow and no plows in sight. We're going to interview a homeowner who's going to say he's always the last to get plowed and is stuck in his house for days unable to go to work because his block is forgotten."

You'd be surprised how fast the plows, and then moments later the mayor, would show up. One time we got the mayor at a local restaurant. He dropped his antipasto and raced over.

If he was a good politician he'd make a show of it. Shaking the homeowner's hand, promising to let that never happen again, and pledging to have the streets of his city plowed ASAP.

In that regard we really made a difference. During one especially severe storm Jim and I were able to pull this feat off three nights in a row. I thought it was great TV and told the EP as much. I even had an idea that I thought would make it better.

"Hey," I said as I popped my head into his office toward the end of the week, "I have an idea. Instead of wasting our time driving around checking out the roads of all the towns in one area and ranking them with on screen snowplows, why don't we just called the franchise 'Snowplow Rescue? We could find someone who has been consistently ignored by the town when it snows and save his day and week. Pretty much like we did this week."

You would have thought had I suggested we head down the street and torch a church.

No," he snapped back. "This is the way we do it. You go out and rank the towns based on how much snow they have on their streets."

I was taken aback but his insistence on keeping the "Snowplow Challenge." The animated on screen snowplows would stay.

When you look at it the snow story package you see on your local TV station hasn't much changed in the last thirty years. I'll describe it and you tell me if I'm wrong:

You start with a car's tires spinning. Then the driver on camera says, "I've never seen it this bad."

You have some obligatory shots of drifting and blowing snow then someone heading into a grocery store loading up on the staples his family needs. If you're lucky he's not picking up a six pack but milk for a young child at home that way you can tug on the heartstrings of all the moms and dads out there. Man protecting family!

You get the Sanitation Commissioner talking about how much salt will be spread during the storm. Then you do your stand-up in front of the giant salt mound with some additional nifty fun facts about how much salt is needed to melt every inch of snow.

You finish with a sound bite of some poor woman slogging home and trying to get warm.

You wrap up the package on camera in front of some salt trucks pulling out of the Sanitation Department parking lot and that's it. Runs one minute, fifteen seconds.

I'm not saying it's easy to do. The really good reporters make it look easy. It takes years of experience and nerves of steel to pull it off, but the format is pretty much the same. Just watch your local news reporter next time the "Blizzard of the Century" hits your town.

Shooters have come up with imaginative ideas to keep warm and dry during nasty weather. One day a wicked rainstorm pelted our truck as shooter Rich McCue and I worked a story in northern New Jersey. We needed one last interview. Just as we were ready to move on, a prime subject came walking toward the truck. I established over the whooshing raindrops that we needed to interview this woman. As she talked to me through the passenger side window of the live truck, Rich fired up his camera. I kicked open the door, stuck the microphone out, Richie framed the shot, and I began asking questions. That poor woman stood there, her hand clutching a dancing umbrella while we stayed dry; Richie shooting it all from the driver's seat – me sitting in the passenger seat next to him.

On TV it looked like we were standing with her on the street.

Showing up after a giant storm was always an easy story: Lots of video, people upset, things smashed to bits. Trying to find weather is a different story and a lesson Fred taught me well.

During one of our editorial meetings the fill-in weatherman came rushing into the newsroom yelling, "Hurricane! Twister!" Not really sure if he was kidding I ducked under the first desk I saw as a joke. It got laughs but the weatherman was deadly serious.

The radar back in the weather center was showing a band of roiling storm clouds which – according to the weatherman – would produce golf ball sized hail within a couple of hours. In fact, he was so sure of it and just animated enough that the assignment editor bought it. He looked at me and said, "Go!"

The weatherman gave us a "sure thing; no question about it" location in the center of the state where he was sure golf sized hail would soon be pounding the hell out of anything in their way.

I raced outside to one of the Channel 9 SUVs, hopped in, looked over and said to Fred, "Let's go Fred, Larry says there's some nasty weather on its way to South Brunswick, New Jersey. He's talking about golf ball-sized hail!"

Fred arched an eyebrow over his sunglasses, sighed and jammed the SUV into drive. It took about forty-five minutes to go from northern New Jersey to the soon-to-be shattered and pelted South Brunswick. We pulled into a shopping center parking lot anchored by a giant clothing store and sat.

I imagined the horror to come. These poor people going about their business with no idea, according to Larry, that their entire community would soon be destroyed by speeding, crashing golf ball-sized hail! I imagine myself a later day Hank Morrison watching the crash of the Hindenburg. "Oh, the humanity…"

As the skies darkened a bit, Fred unbuckled his seat belt and stepped out of the SUV.

"I'm going to look for a suit," he said.

"What?" I said, "Our weather guy says this is going to be a giant. It's on its way."

Fred did another one of those arched eyebrow things and said, "Frank, when it comes to damaging weather no one can predict precisely *where* it's going to happen. You need to show up AFTER it happens."

As he walked away I thought about what he said. I got out and joined him in the clothing store.

An hour later we headed back to the SUV. The clouds looked less ominous. There was a break of sunshine here and there. Back in the SUV I was still contemplating Fred's words when a raindrop, *one single raindrop,* hit the front windshield on the passenger side.

Fred waited a beat and then looked over at me. "I guess that's the golf ball-sized hail."
I cracked up.

So much for predicting the exact location of a storm – Mother Nature and our weather guy had wasted our time.

Most shooters are like that. Having covered everything ten times over, they are able to encapsulate an entire evolving situation in one word or a phrase.

One day while working the daytime shift shooter Roy Isen and I were sent to Long Island to cover a protest led by a Long Island politician with his eyes on a higher office. In this case he and his neighbors were protesting a motel that had become the home of prostitutes turning tricks. They're often referred to as 'Hot Sheet Motels."

In that kind of a story you need the politician, neighbors, maybe someone from the hotel and access to the property. The motel was alongside a busy thoroughfare and as we neared the motel and surveyed the scene, we realized every element we needed was there. We could see the politician in the distance leading the protest. Around him were angry neighbors with signs. Also accessible was the motel driveway and a clerk was visible behind the counter, which also faced the curb.

As we turned left to swing around in front of the motel Isen summed up our good luck in one sentence.

"Wow", he said, "A chimp could shoot this story."

Speaking of animals, all reporters have their stories. Look on YouTube and you'll see what happens when reporters and animals meet. The snake goes up the anchor's pants during a morning show, the reporter gets licked on the head while standing next to a horse; you've seen it a million times.

Shooter Frank Deom and I were sent one day to a small New Jersey town where the neighbors were complaining of a terrible smell. When we knocked on the door of the home where the smell was coming from we were met by a middle aged woman and several of her two-hundred-and-thirty-four cats!

She invited us in. Wanting to get the story, we began shooting video and I asked questions. It's tough to describe the stench but I'll take a shot at it. Imagine lying in a bathtub for a few hours covered up by used cat litter.

When we got back to the station I suggested we both strip down to our shorts and have one of the technicians hose us down. There were no takers.

The little cats we could handle. The larger ones were a different story. In an "Only in New York" story I was dispatched with my shooter to an apartment building in Harlem.

Police got a call from one of the tenants a week earlier who said he'd been bitten by a pit bull. He met paramedics in the lobby of his building on 141st Street, was treated at a local hospital, and then fled to Philadelphia.

It turned out not to be a pit bull at all. It seemed a very small, very cute feline he had brought home one day from an exotic animals retailer had now turned into a full-grown Bengal tiger!

The guy was keeping the 350-pound Bengal tiger caged in a couple of rooms in his tiny apartment. The tiger had apparently attacked him. The tenant was able to escape but was now confused about what he did and why it was wrong. Just for kicks this Marlin Perkins wannabe also had a full-grown caiman – a small alligator – living in the apartment as well. The caiman lived in a Plexiglas enclosure to prevent the tiger from eating him. Talk about an odd couple.

A couple of days after the owner fled to Philly the tenant next door was awakened by the sound of a growling, hungry tiger.

Police were called but when they tried to open the door, the tiger pushed it closed. I guess he wasn't expecting company. They sent a small flexible camera from an outside window one floor up to peek into the guy's apartment. In the meantime, neighbors in the building were evacuated while back at Channel 9 we got wind of the situation – along with every other local news station.

The New York Police Department has to be ready for anything. Apparently they have a team of officers who specialized in corralling giant exotic animals. Who knew? Anyway, we watched several floors below as a police sniper rappelled off the side of this seven-story apartment building, made a very small hole in the fifth story apartment window of Mr. Animal Lover and waited. Five minutes later as the tiger headed for the kitchen to see if anything was in the fridge, the sniper fired.

There was a large low growl. Everyone down below gasped and then chuckled at a noise you don't usually hear on a city street. Tigger had been hit and he wasn't happy.

A police spokesman came over to the group of reporters and said, "It will be an hour or so but please, please when we bring this tiger out, and then the alligator, no crowding. Even though they'll both be sedated, we don't know how they'll respond." He gave the same speech to the tenants watching in amazement like us.

Forty-five minutes later the doors to the apartment building opened and right there, in the middle of the largest city in the world, on an urban street out came – on a stretcher – a sleepy seven-foot Bengal tiger with an oxygen mask over his face.

It was just too much. Reporters, tenants, even the police outside surged to see what this tiger looked like. Cameras flashed and whirred, there were gasps and giggles and into an open ambulance went the tiger headed to be examined at the Bronx Zoo.

No sooner had we digested that scene then out came the alligator. Another crush of reporters, tenants and police. More giggles and then another trip to the zoo.

Like I said, only in New York.

LIZA WITH A "Z" AND LORD HOLLIDAY

New York is loaded with celebrities in all stages of their careers. The hottest of the hot like Lady Gaga, one-time superstars – people like

Michelle Pfeiffer and Sigourney Weaver, and the has-beens – people like Phyllis Diller and Joe Bologna.

I've had my sightings and they're always a thrill. In New York stars just walk the streets. One time stepping out of my live truck I literally backed into actress Adriana La Cerva, who played Adriana on the hit show "The Sopranos". Apparently a fan of Channel 9 News she recognized me first. Most times though there are so many people on the street it's difficult to process who just walked by.

Was that Alan Alda? Diane Sawyer? That's the beauty of New York. Even if you are a star, your fans are either too busy or too unimpressed to stop and talk. That's why I think many stars like to live in New York – they enjoy the anonymity.

Then there are the big events – the film festivals, premieres and weddings. Shortly after starting at Channel 9, I was sent to cover the Tribeca Film festival in Lower Manhattan. The festival was the brainchild of actor Robert DeNiro – his way of bringing back some pizzazz to lower Manhattan following the 9/11 attacks.

DeNiro was able to call on his Hollywood friends to flood New York's neighborhood of Tribeca to attend one of the dozens of premieres, one of which was *Insomnia*, starring Al Pacino and Robin Williams.

As a reporter when you arrive at an event like the Tribeca Film Festival, or any such event, you are assigned a spot along a roped-off line. On the ground there are usually small stickers or sometimes a sign hanging from the rope that will have your station's name. That's where you stand. Sometimes you're next to *Entertainment Tonight*, sometimes TMZ, sometimes your competitor. Doesn't matter – you don't get to pick – the organizers do.

In my years at UPN 9, I was able along a roped line to interview people like Tom Cruise, Mary Tyler Moore, Bernadette Peters and other stars of my youth.

So there I am at the Tribeca Film Festival. I'm standing in my spot interviewing minor characters from *Insomnia* when up comes a perceptible buzz from the front of the line. Out from a limo come Pacino and Williams. This is fantastic! I'm thinking, with any luck at all, I'm going to interview one or both. Position is key: If you're near the end of the line and they're late, chances are you won't get a shot at speaking with them. If you're near the front of the roped off line and they're early, or their handlers deem your station important enough, you'll get a minute or two to chat.

My position on the line that day was iffy. I would have to be forceful with their advance guy who was screening potential interviews for them. And I'd have to be lucky.

Williams was first down the line, Pacino right behind.

I looked at my watch to see if they were late or early and was making nice by interviewing some of the minor characters in the movie. Williams, chatting, inched closer to my position.

After watching him for years, beginning with the old TV show *Mork and Mindy*, it was strange to see Robin Williams up close, but there he was. I momentarily looked beyond him to glance at Pacino, who upon inspection was shorter than I imagined and more serious.

Moments later Robin Williams was standing right in front of me; it was time to turn on the Frankster Charm. I pulled out some of my favorite lines out, asked him a few goofy questions and before you knew it we were both laughing. Pacino starts wrapping up his interview with the person right next to me and Williams and I actually ended ours with a hug. But now it was "game-face" time because in front of me was Pacino and he was deadly serious.

I took a moment to take in the face of Michael Corleone but all I could think of was a rather obscure movie he was in so I figured I'd give that a shot.

"Mr. Pacino," I said, "It's really a pleasure to meet you. Before I start I just want to say my wife and I loved you in the movie *Glengarry Glen Ross*. I especially loved the line in which you say (imitating him exactly now), "Not to my knowledge… no!"

The impression was perfect; the pitch of my voice, the pauses, everything. I was him!

It was at that exact moment that actor Al Pacino *became* Michael Corleone. You could see in his sunken staring eyes that he was neither impressed nor pleased. I obviously had not gotten the memo about not imitating the great Al Pacino while interviewing him. He remained cemented in place in front of me only out of obligation. I'm certain that if he could have walked away he would have.

His stare was unnerving and strangely frightening.

I half-expected Clemenza to come up behind me with a steel garrote like that murder scene in *The Godfather* and say, "Hello Carlo…"

I recovered as best I could, fumbling through some nonsensical questions and he moved on. It was clear organized crime would not be a good fit for me.

Sometimes the character – in that case Michael Corleone – is so burned in your brain that you forget the actor who plays him is NOT him.

Another great shooter, Dave Rosenfeld, and I were sent to lower Manhattan in fall 2005 to cover a charity event. The family of a young man who had a bizarre ailment that forced him to shy away from any kind of bright lights and not be exposed to germs invited all of the New York press corps to the event. *Odd* I thought, *invite dozens of people with God knows what kind of germs, and the press with even more germs not to mention all those cameras and high power lights, to talk with a kid who must stay away from both?* At the event was James Gandolfini, better known as Tony Soprano from *The Sopranos*.

He was the celebrity lending his support to this kid in the hopes his family would raise as much money as possible to pay for the kid's medical bills. To further complicate matters Gandolfini had the flu. He was talking to the kid, who was wincing from the bright lights and trying not to breathe Gandolfini's germs at the same time.

Dave and I watched this crazy spectacle as the kid's mother tried to keep him away from the photographers and shooters whose job it was to get video so that we could tell the story and maybe generate some more donations.

Dave and I were waiting for the money shot. The moment James Gandolfini and the kid stood up and Gandolfini, shook the kid's hand and talked about how important this effort was.

When it happened we were in perfect position. Dave had his camera on low light and I had my mic in the kid's mug. Next to him was Gandolfini.

I was within four feet of Gandolfini. He's huge! I'm not thinking about the story now; I'm convinced in my mind that I'm standing next to Tony Soprano. So ingrained in my head is his image on TV. I didn't want to piss off Tony Soprano for fear Paulie Walnuts would find me and "crack my friggin' head open."

Talk about the power of television!

●●●

One of the terrific shooters at UPN 9 was Marco Mastroilli. Marco gets it. And coming from a very traditional Italian American background we both understood and made fun of all of our relatives. We'd cruise New York on a Saturday afternoon laughing at all sorts of things. Marco, who's from the Bronx, taught me the wonders of that borough, starting with Arthur Avenue.

Arthur Avenue is the last and largest enclave of Italian Americans in the Bronx. It's from another time when Italian Americans dominated large areas of this city, when we were among the largest ethnic groups in New York.

Its four or five blocks are filled with small Italian specialty food shops. It seemed that whatever story we were doing, and wherever we might be doing that story, it somehow ended on Arthur Avenue.

The United Nations would have a special weekend vote to authorize the invasion of Iraq. We'd get everything we'd need and then I'd say, "Let's do a stand-up of me in front of the United Nations."

"No," Marco would say, "Let's head to Arthur Avenue."

"What?"

"There's a building right there that sort of looks like the UN – besides, I want to pick up some salami and cheese."

Now I'm exaggerating – but not by much.

One day we had some extra time and Marco said, "I need to swing by Arthur Avenue to get some mortadella." For the uninitiated that's a large Italian sausage – sometimes a cold cut – that is made of finely hashed ground heat-cured pork.

"Okay," I said. "We've got plenty of time. Where we picking it up?"

"Teitelbaum's."

"Huh?"

"Teitelbaum's," he said. "The deli. It's been on Arthur Avenue for more than a hundred years." Who the hell knew the most popular deli in the Bronx's Italian World is owned by a Jewish family?

One Saturday Marco and I got a strange assignment. A Brooklyn man had been attacked by some kids. He was seriously beaten and was in the hospital. That part was not so odd since, sadly, this happens all too often in New York. Just based on the sheer number of people living in the city, there are going to be incidents that end in violence.

We hop into an SUV and off we go. The address we'd been given sounds kind of odd, and neither Marco nor I could pinpoint it off the top of our heads.

As we drive we realized it's close, really close, to the famous Coney Island Amusement Park in Brooklyn. We're puzzled though because the addresses we're following on the way down seem to end right at the park. We call the desk to get some clarification but the assignment editor is also a bit confused about exactly where it is.

We pulled up alongside the park to ask someone if he knows the victim. The guy's getting his amusement park booth ready for the crush of visitors to come.

"Hey, do you know a Robert Holliday?", I say, "He was attacked by some kids last night and is in the hospital."

"You mean Lord Holliday?"

"Who?"

"Lord Holliday."

"I guess,"

"Yeah," the man said. "He lives right across the street there."

This is confusing because right across the street is the park with giant rides and no entrance on that side and no sign of anything that looks like a house.

I'm thinking, *What's this guy Holliday – sorry LORD Holliday—have, a tent next to the Tilt-A-Wheel?*

I'm close. Our friend, Lord Holliday lives *underneath* one of the small roller coasters on the park grounds in a tiny black shack. He even has a stand-up mailbox just inside the gate and the cyclone wire is cut just wide enough for the mail carrier to open the mailbox door and slide in any correspondence.

Is he getting letters from other amusement park royalty around the world? "Hey Lord Holliday! We've got a package for you from Prince

Anthony at Hershey Park. You want me to leave it in there along with the letter from the Duke of Chuckles from Six Flags?

We find out Lord Holliday had been telling his co-workers that he was a lord of the British Empire who came here to live a simple life and get away from the trappings befitting a man of his stature, which included, I guess, living in a shack. We also found out Holliday's job was to patrol the park after dark to make sure no one broke in.

I keep thinking about the Woody Allen movie *Annie Hall* where Allen's character talks about his childhood growing up in a home under the Cyclone rollercoaster at Coney Island.

Marco and I get one of the ride operators to let us in and we peek into Lord Holliday's castle. Aside from a small bed and a hot plate there was not much to it. If he's a lord you could *not* imagine him leaving his abode in stirrups to lead a foxhunt.

We get some of it on video, talk with a couple of his co-workers and called the desk.

"Okay," I say to assignment editor Adam Cousins, "I think we got all we could."

"What about the victim?"

"You mean his Lordship?" I say half kidding.

"Yeah."

"He's in intensive care at Coney Island Hospital. How the hell am I going to get to him?"

"I don't know," Adam says, "But you have to at least give it a shot."

So now Marco and I were head over to Coney Island Hospital. An interview with him or one of his doctors is the only thing keeping us from wrapping up this crazy story. I get into my "important person" mode. I stroll into the hospital with a clipboard under my arm, much like I used to do years before when I snuck into all the networks to drop off air checks, and walked right past the reception desk.

"Good morning, Doctor," a passerby said.

"Good morning," I answered.

I'm thinking *my mom would be so proud. She always wanted a doctor in the family.*

I walk into the ICU and ask where Robert Holliday is. I almost say Lord Holliday. One of the physician assistants points to ICU Bay 7. I poke my head around the curtain and there is His Lordship. Fucked up. Bruises about the head, black eye, bandages wrapped around his noggin and out like a light.

As I left, all I kept thinking was –*this lord really got crowned.*

Assignment editors often send reporters out to cover a story long after everyone is there, set up and ready to go. One time we showed up for a perp walk and were told to stand by for directions. While we were waiting on the other side of the courthouse parking lot I thought I saw what looked like a perp walk. It was. We were supposed to be there in position but the desk had no idea where or when.

Another time the Reverend Billy Graham came to Fresh Meadows Park in Queens for a special day of fellowship. Based solely on his following and his impact on the faithful every station was there early with a live truck and working on a package for their evening and nightly newscasts.
Every station but us.

We were only reminded after folks from the New York Police Department's media relations department called us to say they had reserved a spot for our truck but noticed we were not there. "Are you coming?" they asked.

One time we got a frantic call from the desk that comedienne and talk show host Rosie O'Donnell was on the steps of the courthouse in lower Manhattan to hold a press conference. She was dealing with a legal problem and making a statement. We were woefully out of position and running late.

We screeched up to the courthouse as the press conference was nearing its end. My shooter quickly clicked on the camera. No sooner had the camera started rolling Rosie wrapped up the press conference and walked toward a waiting car. I followed her and jammed my mic in her face, "Rosie... Rosie! Do you think you were vindicated?"

She glared at me. If her eyes could kill I was dead where I stood. I was sure she was going to reach back and smack me in front of everyone. She pushed me aside and got into her limo.

It was only later that I found out that she had started the press conference by warning everyone in a stern voice that she was going to make a statement, answer some questions but when the press conference ended she didn't want anyone following her to the car or asking any more questions. ABSOLUTELY NO QUESTIONS!

I was not on hand for that part and almost got my block knocked off.

And then there's Liza Minnelli.

If you want to make a splash you do it in New York City. Hollywood is glitz with wanna-be actors and actresses everywhere. Speaking of actors and actresses I think one of the best lines I ever heard about actresses comes from my friend, and one of the great radio people in this industry, Brian McFadden. Quoting one of the writers for the Marx Brothers Brian once told me – paraphrasing now – "A starlet is the name for any woman in Hollywood under thirty who is *not* working as a full time prostitute".

I digress. Back to Liza.

I rolled into UPN 9 one day and was told we were going to cover Liza Minnelli's wedding to producer David Gest. It was the wedding of the year with a giant church ceremony in midtown Manhattan – followed by a lavish reception. The daughter of the great Judy Garland, and a star in her own right, was holding one of those only-in-New York weddings.

And guess what? We were late.

"Get going," the assignment editor said, "Patrick is waiting for you."

Patrick is Patrick Horan, my shooter. Patrick is an Irish émigré with a wry sense of humor. He's also a terrific impressionist. His impressions of our colleagues made me roll with laughter. I'm told he also does a spot-on impression of me but the gentleman that he is he never did it to my face.

We hop into the UPN 9 live truck and head for the giant wedding of 'Liza with a Z'. Or as Patrick calls it – "a pig fuck".

We've been here before. A "pig fuck" involves cajoling, negotiating, pushing and eventually squeezing your way into a news conference or a giant interview situation in which you're woefully and totally out of position.

We park a couple of blocks away from the Marble Collegiate Church on Fifth Avenue and run with all the equipment to get whatever we can. When we get there it's craziness. Outside a gaggle of reporters are squeezed into a small roped-off section near the front steps of the church while inside sit luminaries such as Elton John, Diane Sawyer, Barbara Walters, Elizabeth Taylor, Robert Goulet, Robert Wagner, Gina Lollobrigida, Janet Leigh and Carol Channing – all waiting for the service to begin.

Patrick and I are left to pick up sound bites from the has-beens of stage and screen.

While other reporters have already spoken with people like Lauren Bacall and Kirk Douglas, I'm trying to scrounge up sound with the likes of singer Paul Williams and B-actors Joe Bologna and Renee Taylor. I also chat with Phyllis Diller. But based on the constellation of stars we may have had access to ours was pretty sad.

The wedding starts and since no media's allowed inside we stand outside with the rest of the reporters from every media outlet imaginable.

Being a good reporter means being a good observer. You always have to be assessing your situation and wondering how to get the better shot or the better interview.

At this point I looked across the street and see a ten-or eleven-story building. The wedding is going to take at least an hour and a half and with nothing to lose I say to Patrick, "Follow me."

I'm thinking the building – if we can get in – will afford us a clear, unobstructed view of Liza and her husband when they exit the church. That one shot might make up for my riveting interview with David Hasselhoff.

We walk into the lobby. There's a man at the front desk. I make up some crazy story and he let's us go up. The building is a mix of residential apartments and business offices. Since it's a Sunday most of the businesses are closed. That means the elevator will only stop on certain floors. We hit all the buttons and take our chances.

The first stop is the ninth floor. A large woman is standing there and she's not happy. Before I can go into my spiel Broom Hilda starts yelling at us in German like we've just been caught outside the gates of Stalag 17.

Patrick and I smile, press the "door close" button and try to say, "We're sorry." Before it closes I do a quick impression of General Buchalter from *Hogan's Heroes.* She's not amused.

We later find out that major media organizations from all around the world have paid big bucks in advance to rent offices across the street from the wedding to get the kind of sight lines and video we're now trying to get free.

The next stop is the roof. Patrick and I step out and look over the side of the building. We're up much too high. Even with a zoom lens the shot will look terrible.

So now we head back down the elevator deliberately avoiding Hitler's Wolf's Lair on the ninth floor.

Back on the street I take a good look at the building next door. It's not as high but it has potential. The front door is locked and on it is a note.

Scribbled, clearly in a foreign hand, are the words, "Press the bell once and only ONCE!". It's signed "Sheemo."

Now I don't know who the hell this Sheemo character is but obviously he has a problem with doorbells. Or maybe it's some kind of Obsessive Compulsive Disorder involving the number one.

I dutifully followed directions. I ring once and wait. And wait. I'm already planning my next move, my back leaning up against the front door of the building, when Sheemo yanks it open.

He's a combination of Emperor Hirohito and Professor Irwin Corey: short, disheveled, and in a strange way menacing. He also has different-colored paint stains on his clothing. He's the kind of New York City character that if you didn't come from New York you'd likely run from.

"Hey, Sheemo – I'm Frank Cipolla from UPN 9 News." He seems to process some of what I'm saying but not all of it.

I explained that we want to quietly – as to not tip off our colleagues across the street – go up a few floors to get a better shot of what is going on across the street.

He looks at us funny. Patrick jumps in to make a pitch on our behalf but his Irish brogue seems to confuse Sheemo even more. I explain what we want to do again and the third time's the charm.

Sheemo grunts.

With all the heavy equipment Patrick is hauling Sheemo invites him to take the elevator. But since only the two of them can fit Sheemo instructs me to take the stairs. As the door closes on Patrick and Sheemo they start talking. I can only imagine what the hell they're talking about for six floors when neither one can understand the other.

The stairs to Sheemo's penthouse apartment are small, dark and scary – something out of one of those Leonardo DiCaprio flicks that make no damn sense. On one of the landings I hear the faint sound of some girls giggling as if they're having a tickle fight.

I beat both Patrick and Sheemo to the top landing and wait for them to arrive. As I peek from the landing into Sheemo's apartment I feel uneasy. Through a beaded curtain near the entrance I see pots with what appeared to be boiling, smoking, colored plastic ooze. There are also different kinds of plastic sculptures in all sizes. I guessed he's an artist but who the hell knows? He could just as well be a serial killer who preys on anyone daring to ring his friggin' door bell more than once. Then murders them and encases their bodies or body parts in plastic.

Maybe it's a game: ring his doorbell once you live. Twice, you end up looking like a Christmas Nativity lawn ornament.

Bing, the elevator door chimes.

Patrick must have seen the alarmed look on my face because his natural smile turns into a puzzled glance. With my eyes I try to direct his attention to Sheemo's lair. He doesn't get the message coded in my body language.

We're hoping to get on the roof so the next question for Sheemo is how do we get there?

Sheemo – in halting English – directs me to a steel ladder leading up to a hatch that heads out onto the roof. I asked if there's an easier way up but Sheemo just stares at me.

By this time Patrick has peeked through the beaded curtain into Sheemo's apartment and feels the same sense of dread. We both also hear voices inside so we know Sheemo's not alone.

After a couple of uncomfortable moments I jumped onto the first rung of the ladder and head up. When I get to the top I push the hatch open and take a quick look around. It's reminiscent of my journey to the top of the Verrazano Bridge – minus of course the Mad Professor's cauldron of plastic goo boiling below.

Once up there, I wander to the edge of the building and look across at the church. The shot's perfect.

I go back to the hatch, get on all fours and call down to Patrick to tell him the shot is good. My heart sinks. There's no sign of him or Sheemo. For all I know Patrick is already being cut up or being dunked whole into a vat of blistering liquid plastic.

"Patrick," I say, my voice now weak and childlike. I'm legitimately scared.

In a flash I assess the situation. Patrick and I are isolated from everyone with a nut job downstairs who works with molten plastic. And now Patrick, who was there seconds ago, is gone.

Who the hell knows what happened to him? We know Sheemo is accommodating but maybe it's a ploy to get us upstairs. Maybe steal our equipment? And what were those other voices we heard?

I stand straight up and looked around. The only way off the top of this building is a six-story plunge to the curb. Then I see the fire escape. I head straight for it but it's too late. Someone's coming up. With Patrick taken care of is Sheemo coming to get me?

You can't imagine the relief when I saw both Sheemo *and* Patrick coming up the metal stairs. Apparently Patrick had convinced Sheemo to find another way up to make it easier to get the equipment on the roof. Patrick eyes though are bulging out.

Once up Sheemo waves to us, bows his head slightly, and heads back down the fire escape. That's when Patrick tells me about Sheemo's kitchen where Sheemo's wife and another women are busy stirring large vats of boiling plastic. Patrick also tells me about some different shaped plastic sculptures hanging on hooks. It's quite the image.

Putting that aside Patrick and I peek over the side of the building. The shot is doable. It's a beautiful day so we take in the weather and talk about what we need to do.

After about ten minutes a door swings open onto the roof. I hadn't seen it before, but apparently there was another staircase to the roof that did not wind through Sheemo's territory.

Our eyes light up. Out come three nubile young giggly girls. They say hello and skip by us. They want to see Liza's wedding too and figured – just as we did – that the best vantage point is from the roof.

The three lay on their stomachs flat down and peered off the edge of the building. From behind, the sight is glorious. Their asses sticking up just enough to trigger all sorts of naughty thoughts.

I looked over to Patrick with a smile. He's getting married in about three weeks but the view is just too much for either one of us to keep focused.

The attention span of these beauties is short and before we know it they bounce up, giggled past us again and head downstairs.
Patrick and I stay another twenty minutes but realized, as we observe what's happening, that it looks like Liza and her new husband will be exiting on the other side of the church. Well out of our camera range. Now it's a race back down to the street. This time though we use the same door the girls did.

I grabbed some of the equipment, Patrick grabs the rest and we make a hasty escape down the stairwell.

Near the third floor a door swings open and one of the girls we saw on the roof sticks her thin, white, firm-fleshy leg across our path putting up a roadblock that extends from her front door to the banister.

"You're not leaving this building until you help us with the keg", she says.

"What are you talking about?" I say in my best newsman voice.

"I need you strong guys to help us move the keg from the kitchen to the living room. We're having a big party tonight." Patrick and I put down our equipment and go into the apartment. It smells of perfume and panties. We move the keg into the living room.

"Have one on us," one says, pointing to the keg.

"We gotta go," I said, half convincing myself, *"Liza's getting married".*

"Okay, but we expect both of you to come back later when the story's over."

"Yeah," I said, "You can watch us tonight on Channel 9."

Time's ticking away now. Without the "money shot" of Liza leaving the church we're screwed. You never want to go back to the station without the money shot. The young girl crying, the car mangled at the body shop...etc.

When we get to the street Patrick says "Just watch the rest of this equipment. I gotta run right now and get the shot."

Patrick is the best. He used his Irish accent and natural likeability to somehow get to the very front row of shooters jammed in front of the church and got the best video of Liza and David's exit in all of New York. It was an impossibility based on when we showed up and how out of position we were but Patrick made it happen.

As soon as Liza and her new husband hop into the limo it's over. The crowd quickly melts away.

Next stop: the reception hall, but as we drive off we're not sure where the wedding reception is to be held.

We call the desk and find out it's going to be downtown. Not far from Ground Zero. When Patrick hears this he's not happy.

Live shots use powerful microwave beams that go from the top of the live truck's forty-foot high antenna to the highest buildings in your city. For years in New York that was the World Trade Center. With that gone, pulling a live shot off from lower Manhattan became problematic for everyone. The only way to do it was to hit the top of the Empire State Building, where most of the New York City stations are now or, in an emergency, the Gulf and Western Building near Lincoln Center.

With time ticking away and the live shot connection weighing on Patrick's head we pull up as close as possible to the hotel where the reception is to be held. I stepped out to eyeball the situation while Patrick finds a place to relieve himself. When we both get back to the truck we have a new problem.

Patrick, for the first – and probably only time – had locked the keys inside the live truck. It's now 8:45 p.m. and we had to go live at ten. I haven't even seen a second of video.

It was a train wreck waiting to happen and I could see the oncoming lights.
Patrick sprinted off to look for help. I stood there helpless. The desk was calling trying to find out how we were doing, asking if we'd be ready to go and when we were expected to feed our video.

I made up a story to protect Patrick but I knew we had to get into the truck in the next fifteen minutes or things would get ugly. The question was where was he going to find somebody on a Sunday night to pick a lock?

The gods were with us because within ten minutes miracle worker Patrick was back with a police officer who helped get the truck open. I jumped in without thanking anyone and started screening the video. Patrick fired up the power and started putting up the antenna for the live feed.

At 9:20 – another problem.

After trying for a half hour Patrick couldn't get a microwave signal from his location to the Empire State Building. Because we were both professionals no one panicked, but I got a sinking feeling in my gut. Time was our enemy and it looked like tonight the clock would run out on us.

At this point Patrick says he has another idea and starts pulling down the antenna. Meanwhile I'm zipping though whatever video I can and trying to write a script.

At 9:35, Patrick is ready to roll. He bounces into the driver's seat and we screeched away.

I had no idea what the hell this report was going to look like but I was sure going to give it my all. I scribbled something down, made note of a few time codes on the tape and where the live truck had to go to reach its next destination - which turned out to be exactly where we started the day - in front of the church where Liza got married!

Patrick got the antenna up and established a signal and at 9:55, five minutes before the start of the newscast. I fed my voice track and video to be edited to the folks back at the station.
I put on some makeup and jumped out of the truck, thinking, '*This is nuts!*'

Ten minutes into the show they throw to us. I've got nothing written down for my intro. I don't even know what the hell I'm going to say when the light goes on but when they throw to me I reach back on all my years of radio and TV ad-libbing experience and put together three informative sentences. It's flawless. At that, they fire up the pre-recorded package.

They come back to me and I'm equally super.

The light goes off and Patrick and I let out giant sighs of relief. We're looking at each other like, "How the hell did we do that?"

Just then we glance up to the third floor of the building and one of the girls we saw earlier is leaning out of the window in a flimsy top.

"Now you can come up!, she says, " Come on… "

We were exhausted and didn't want to get into trouble, so we just packed up and left.

I rested very well that night. The pressure of the entire day weighed on me and I snored for seven hours straight.

The next day the executive producer saw me.

"Come talk to me," he said. "Great, great report on Liza's wedding! You really spent a lot of time putting it together and it showed."

He walked out oblivious to all the drama behind the scenes with: Liza, Sheemo, the locked live truck…

I laughed out loud.

That's what it's like when you watch the news. It's the behind the scenes stuff that the viewer never sees where you earn your money. For a while I worked on weekends and that is when the thinner staff and looser rules led to some crazy stuff.

There were stories of shooters – now gone – who played with the live shots. One shooter in particular liked to be *in* the live shot. During the live shot he'd be well in the background. Sometimes crossing the street where only those who knew he was going to be on camera would see him. Once in a while he made it more obvious like the time he took a small trash basket out of the live truck and walked well behind the reporter on a busy street with it over his head.

Patrick also had a strange sense of humor. He saw the oddity in things. One weekend he, another shooter Kenny Sutton, and I were sent to do a live shot in Crown Heights, Brooklyn. Crown Heights is an enclave for members of a unique Jewish sect called the Hasidim. The Hasidim look similar to the Amish – right down to the heavy black coats, wide brimmed hats and beards.

Some of them had never seen a live truck so when we pulled up to do our report we worked inside while outside literally hundreds of Hasidic Jews converged on us. I'll never forget the looks as they stared three and four deep into the live truck at how amazing it all was. I felt like an animal in a zoo.

Anyway, Kenny had the unfortunate task of setting up the camera for the live shot and watching it while Patrick and I worked inside to meet deadline.

On top of every live truck antenna is a camera just in case you need to get a shot from a higher vantage point. Once Patrick had the live truck antenna up he motioned me over to his monitor. There he had framed – thanks to the antenna camera – Kenny standing next to his camera surrounded by hundreds of Hasidic Jews. They were crowding him and Kenny was being as polite as he could. We could hear him over the built in camera mic saying, "Excuse me could you just back off a bit? Excuse me I need some more room…"

They'd back off a bit and then ten minutes later Kenny would be asking for some room again. It was hilarious.
Kenny was also on hand with me on a special night when my judgment was not what it should have been: Cinco De Mayo 2005. Kenny and I were sent to a Mexican Restaurant across from Lincoln Center to do a fluff piece about the festivities and fun surrounding that greatest of Mexican holidays.

I did some man on the street stuff about the holiday and then we headed to this rocking Mexican restaurant for our live shot. Kenny and I got all we needed by eight o'clock and settled in to prepare our report for the ten o'clock live shot.

Then the call came: Kenny needed to take a union-required one-hour lunch break. That meant he and I could do nothing for the next hour. The truck had to be shut down. I couldn't screen video. We were essentially directed to cool our heels until the clock clicked nine.

I looked at Kenny. We both looked around the bar, which by now was packed with pretty girls.

Then it happened, at first very innocently. "Want to try a Mango Margarita?" the perky blonde bartender asked me. "Why not?" I said. I couldn't do anything for an hour anyway, so I might as well take a sip.

I looked over to show Kenny my free drink but by now he was on the other side of the bar.

The Mango Margarita was so good I tried another. I wasn't worried. I knew my limit and was smart enough to know that appearing on TV drunk was not a good idea.

That was the last coherent thought I had that night. One hour and six mango margaritas later I was smashed! Wiped out. Silly drunk. Some out of town divorcees were hugging me when Kenny caught up with me at nine.

"We gotta get ready," he said.

"For what?" I answered.
One of the girls said, "You've got to go on TV to do your report. Remember you told us that a little while ago?"

I was glad someone remembered, because I had totally forgotten. Head spinning, I tried to pull myself together. The only blessing was that I would be doing the live shot from the field. I wouldn't be exposed to my colleagues back at the station who could probably tell I was drunk just by the stink coming from me.

I was slapping myself in the truck and trying to get myself ready to go live.

Then the phone rang. "Frank, change of plans, we need you to come back and do the report from the set. Break down and get here ASAP."

My heart sank. Well, it tried to sink but there was enough booze in my belly to keep it afloat. Before we left the restaurant I did a quick tease that aired in regular programming about a half hour before the newscast. Back home the Bride was watching Channel 9 and realized in a second as I shouted above the revelers at the bar that I was over the top drunk.

At 9:15 we headed back to the station. I reeked and there was no way to get me to keep my head upright for any prolonged period of time. I was drinking water and trying to will myself back to sobriety.

I don't remember much else, only that I was able to write and read something in time and when I got onto the set was able to stand erect for as long as it took to read my intro off the teleprompter.

I went home thanking my lucky stars that I didn't vomit on the air.

Part of covering the news nowadays is using the newscast to promote other shows. Once in a while I'd get the call and quite frankly it was a welcome departure from weeks of knocking on doors and talking to parents who had just lost a loved one to random gunfire or a horrific accident.

One day the executive producer wanted me to do a story that tied into a show we were airing on the UPN Network called *Elimidate*. The concept was simple: Three guys went out with one girl, or vice versa, and at the end of the show the girl or guy would pick which one she wanted to see again.

My story was about the *Elimidate* auditions at a bar in midtown Manhattan. I knew about the show but the executive producer wanted my questions to be edgier, so the person in charge of that night's newscast gave me a video of something called the "Lost Minutes of *Elimidate*."

It was the over the top stuff: girls meeting their dates at the door naked, hugging, kissing and nudity in the back of the limo on the way to their first date. All the stuff that had to be cut out to get by the censors on broadcast TV.

So there I sat in an edit bay ordered to watch porn. I remember thinking, *this is the first time I have ever been asked to sit down in a newsroom and watch porn for an hour.*

It didn't end there. To highlight how porn has infiltrated the Internet, UPN 9 News planned a special report during the ratings period on the "Upskirt" epidemic. For the uninitiated, "Upskirt" websites consist of photos taken by guys up the skirts of unwitting women on trains and buses. The shots came from all manner of devices. Lipstick cameras painstakingly mounted on shoes, briefcases with small cameras that are positioned in just the right spot so when the briefcase is placed on the floor it could snap away at the exposed undies of women – or if they were lucky enough – no undies.

I've always thought if these idiots spent one-eighth of their time designing something that could really help humankind they'd be millionaires!

Anyway – the station wanted a hard-hitting piece on why the "Upskirt" phenomenon was so big. So to get to the bottom of it (no pun intended) he sent one of our oldest and most respected reporters out with a shooter to get video showing how easy it *was* to get upskirt video!
In other words we were doing the same stuff these sleaze balls did to show how easy it was to videotape up a girl's skirt. But why should I be surprised? Local news is obsessed with the naughty.

"What Men Really Want," "The Right Bra For You" or the obligatory sweeps month piece on breast exams, which always seem to show lots of breasts.

One of the great radio anchors at WCBS-AM, Gary Mora, who has since retired, used to spoof this kind of news all the time. At least once a shift when Gary went to the traffic report he'd say, "Now it's time to check traffic so let's go down my street and up yours." He got away with it for years and always got a chuckle from his listeners.

Once my shooter and I were sent to do a story on the West Nile Virus outbreaks across the city in 2004.

Several communities saw a spike in the West Nile Virus and the city was taking action. Trucks were sent out spewing insecticide. They'd slowly roll down blocks of the city late in the evening spewing white clouds of gas that were supposed to kill the mosquitoes that carry the virus.

The night we covered the story we were sent to Hunts Point in the Bronx.

"This should be interesting," my shooter said as we headed over the George Washington Bridge and into the Bronx.

"Why?" I asked.

"Oh, you don't know do you?"

"No."

"Hunts Point is THE place in the city for skanky hookers who take care of their 'johns' in parked cars."

"I wonder if the insecticide will have any affect on their boners.", I said.

The streets in that part of the city are dark. Not many streetlights work and that's part of the attraction for the hookers and their cheap sex. Anyway, we set up along a nondescript block and waited for the insecticide trucks to swing by as the sexual activity picked up nearby. It was a humid summer night and we could see men driving slowly down the street and young ladies with skirts up to their "cha-chas" jump in.

It was all sort of a sideshow for us as we got the West Nile video we needed and I started crafting a script.

There was also a vaguely familiar noise once in a while and initially I couldn't put my finger on it. Then it hit me: It was from my youth. Right next to the busiest spot for these Hunts Point curbside in-car encounters was a giant garage where the ice cream trucks that cruised the city parked for the night.

While the cars nearby bounced and squeaked, the ice cream trucks with speakers still on and their familiar musical jingles blaring, headed into the garage.

As the trucks approached the jingles got louder before their pleasant distinctive song echoed against the buildings in the area.

"Ding, Ding, Ding, Dah, Ding, Dah, Ding Ding Ding…"

I noticed it was the same song again and again.

And I remembered what song it was. It was an ice cream truck song for a particular kind of ice cream in New York. I poked my head out of the live truck and thought – *this is ironic*.

Right next to the place where guys pay skanky chicks to get hard was the parking garage for the dozens of trucks that drive though the neighborhoods of New York selling Mr. Softee.

Some of the stories I covered found me. Including one of the biggest of the decade.

In February 2003 the Bride and I were vacationing in Florida. On the morning we were supposed to fly home we were watching TV and packing when we heard that the Space Shuttle *Columbia* – which was due at Cape Canaveral that morning – had not yet landed.

NASA didn't say it at first but knowing how things run like clockwork at the space agency and how telemetry tells them exactly where the shuttle is at all times it was clear to everyone that something had happened to Columbia on its way through the atmosphere.

Amateur video started popping up showing the Columbia breaking up into pieces over Texas and Louisiana on its descent to Florida.

I called the desk. "Hey, I'm here – in West Palm Beach, Florida – I could be at the Cape in an hour or so."

"We'll call you back," said Adam Cousins.

As I organized my thoughts in my head and prepared to drive to the Cape, Adam called back.

"Okay, we have a crew from Miami who will meet you at Cape Canaveral. Start heading up there now." I kissed the Bride who went back to New Jersey while I got on the Florida Turnpike and headed north.

I had only been to Cape Canaveral once as a tourist. I'm a space buff so it was a big thrill for me. This time around though it would be all business. Reporters and TV crews from all around the world were descending on the east coast of Florida. I had to find a New York connection to make this work and I would be relying on the UPN 9 desk to help me.

I arrived at about five-thirty p.m. on February 1, 2003. I headed to the Press Center to get an ID and started looking for my Miami crew. With the help of the desk I found them, one shooter and an audio guy. I was also told that when I was ready to go live I would be doing it out of the CNN Satellite Truck. It, along with the rest of the trucks, was in the shadow of the giant Vehicle Assembly Building. I had seen the building a zillion times in various space documentaries and now I was looking at it with my own eyes. A short walk and I was at the small grandstand about three miles from the launch pad where many of the Apollo moon shots, Skylab and shuttle journeys began.

It was all fascinating stuff for this space geek, but again my main job was to get something together and on the air for the ten o'clock broadcast.

I got acquainted with my Miami crew and we headed out. On site at the Cape is a tall granite memorial to those astronauts who were killed while reaching for the stars. Soon the names of seven more astronauts would be added. It seemed like a fitting place to talk with people. Luckily I found a few New Yorkers who had come to pay their respects on their way back to New York. That, along with the official press conference and a stand-up in front a shuttle mock-up, and I had what I needed.

In this kind of a setting deference is often given to TV stations in the larger markets. A PR guy will often go out of his way to assist reporters in the New York, LA and Chicago markets and hand off those reporters in smaller markets to subordinates. That's just the way it is. There's a pecking order; the bigger the market, the more access, with the major networks getting the most.

I was told an hour before I was to go live that I would have to be at the CNN live truck at a specific time and that I was number four on the runway. Reporters from around the country would be using the live truck and we all had to stand up on a small box with the giant Vehicle Assembly Building behind us, do our live intros and outros, then get out of the way for the next reporter from some other market.

Twenty minutes or so before I was to go on I put on some makeup in my car, straightened my tie, and walked over to the CNN truck. Lou Dobbs was standing outside of it puffing away on a cigarette. He seemed agitated.
"Hey Lou, Frank Cipolla UPN 9 News in New York."

He grunted something but I didn't understand what he said. When we finally got to talking I realized why he was so annoyed. CNN had called him while he was on a golf vacation. He wasn't pleased.

My cue came; I jumped up on the small wooden box, did my two- or three-sentence lead in and out and handed my microphone to some reporter from Philadelphia.

UPN 9 called and said it looked good and told me to stay another night and have an update for the ten o'clock news tomorrow.

The next morning, a NASA press badge clipped onto my lapel, I drove up the main road into the Space Center with the confidence of now knowing the terrain and having done a good job.

Ego check.

"Hold it sir," said some big-shouldered NASA security guard at one of the checkpoints and I tried to move through.

"No," I said, "You don't understand, I'm from UPN 9 in New York City… NEW YORK CITY." (I was making sure I emphasized that so he'd wave me through).

He just smirked at me and in a stern voice said, "Pull over there with the rest of those cars and wait. You can't be cruising in here like you own the place. You have to be escorted by an official NASA representative."

"Oh," was the only response I could muster.

I pulled over and stepped out of my car and chatted with some other reporters who had been stopped like me and stepped out to wait as well.

One was from Des Moines, another from Wichita, Kansas, a third from Columbus, Ohio. So much for the clout of being from a station in the country's largest market. That morning I was just another press slug.

The second day was not as frenetic but just as tiring. Fifteen minutes before the appointed time for my live shot slot, I headed back over to the CNN truck and waited.

That's when I noticed a former colleague of mine from News 12 New Jersey. She had been on vacation as well and was called to cover the story. She was a stunner, beautiful in every way. When I caught her eye she gave me a little wink. Did she want to flirt?

We hugged and she said she was down in Florida about a week with her husband when she got the call. I told her about Bride and me on vacation as well.

My pretty former News 12 colleague was now getting a bit friendlier than she'd ever been. Looking deep into my eyes, giggling at whatever lame joke I came up with. I tried to move on not wanting to read too much into it, but she wouldn't let me go. She followed me around as I wrapped things up. She clearly found me handsome and maybe wanted to hang with me.

She grabbed my arm and asked me a bunch of questions about the business and how things are going at UPN 9.

When I thought things were getting a bit too cozy I said something like, "Well, I have to get going; it's been a long day."

She was just staring now, thinking about what her next move would be. I stared back hoping things wouldn't get too uncomfortable for both of us before I got out of here. That's when she made her move.

"Before you go, can I ask you something," she said. A red light was blinking in my head now but come on: who wouldn't enjoy this unusual attention from a ravishing knockout reporter fifteen years younger than me?

"Yeah, I guess..."

At this point she looked down as if what she had to say could open up a door she might not have want to go through.

"Is there anyway you could get me an interview at Channel 9? I gotta get out of News 12."

Wow, all that sexual tension and all she was really looking for was a new gig.

News interns know this as well and the smart ones use their good looks to break the ice. In 2004 an intern from Kentucky started at Channel 9. She consistently came in with low cut blouses. I didn't know if she was smart enough to use her ample breasts to get attention or wasn't smart enough to know that dressing like that in a business setting was inappropriate. As time went on though she referenced her breasts more and more – and they were huge.

I stayed out of it and tried not ogle her but it was difficult. I got definitive proof about what she thought of her ample cushions after another intern approached me following a live shot along the busy Garden State Parkway.

"Mr. Cipolla", he said.

"Yeah"

"I think the guys are right about her. She's definitely using those things to get attention".

"Really", I said, "How so?"

He said he was standing with her waiting for me to finish up my report when she starting playing a game with him. As he tells it she said, 'If both of us were stranded here along side of the road which one of us with get a ride first?' He said, 'I don't know'. She said, 'That's easy…I would'. 'Why', he says. She then cupped her breasts with her hands and said, 'Because I've got these'.

Nowadays pretty women in the newsroom or on the air are a given. But it wasn't so long ago female reporters were complaining of not getting enough airtime. Just look at the news networks now. The female anchor throws to the pretty blonde reporter in the field, who throws back to the female anchor, who then throws to the perky weather girl, then back to the pouty lipped female anchor, over to the big breasted reporter somewhere in Europe.

I think it's safe to say the "problem" of not enough female talent on the air has been resolved.

I saw it coming. In the late 1980's the grumpy old men began slowly being replaced by talented but stunningly beautiful twenties-ish reporters and with women in the newsroom, things can always get interesting. Remember the radio and TV guy is essentially a kid who never grew up. Especially radio guys who are little boys who like to play.

Many times I have seen grown men fawn over a new female reporter. Some have even left their wives for the new energetic and athletic Brenda Starr. And it's not above the older guys – especially back then – to take advantage of the situation or show more interest than they should with the promise of advancing their playmates' careers.

It most certainly doesn't apply to every female reporter who got there simply by hard work and persistence – but I have seen it happen.

And the flirting continues.

Two people I worked with sat near each other. George and Carol enjoyed each other's company and the usual banter of the newsroom. George was especially outgoing and Carol more reserved.

George used to bring in peanuts. Since he was watching his waistline he'd ask Carol to hide them in her desk so he wouldn't overdo it.

This led to a long series of double entendres that always got giggles in the newsroom.

George would start, "Hey Carol, are you holding my nuts?"

Carol played along. "I've got your nuts in a jar."

George: "Can I have my nuts back?"

Carol: "Hey, just so you know you've only got two nuts and I got my hands on them."

George: "Just don't shake my nuts."

You get the picture.

In the same newsroom there was a computer screen with all the stocks of interest and what they were doing on that day. Exxon up three percent, Proctor and Gamble down two and a half, and so on. You'd type in the ticker symbol and get the latest numbers.

As the day went on some of the stocks were erased from the screen in favor of more active issues. One day George walked up to the computer screen and with no room to add any more stocks turned to Carol and asked if she needed any stock prices in particular so he could make room for one or two he had to add.

"Carol, do you need Saks?" as in the department store chain Saks 5th Avenue.

Carol doesn't hear Saks – she hears "sex."

In a sultry voice and pretending to be offended she said, ""Excuse me?"

George quickly recovered, "No, Saks! Saks 5th Avenue... Saks... !"

I thought it all very innocent until about four months later when Carol got back at him. This time the computer screen was bunched up with all the major big box store stocks. Costco, Sam's Club, and others, and she needed room to add her stocks.

Carol, seeing an opening, glanced over to George with bedroom eyes and said, "George, do you want BJ's?

Chapter 18
TRAVELS WITH JIM

Away from the field and back at Channel 9 things were happening. One news director was gone, another hired out of Detroit. A whiz kid who was gone in short order.

In my five years at UPN 9, I went through four news directors. There are plenty of stories about how news directors come and go, but let's just say that if you're looking for long-term job security, you might consider buying a lunch truck.

My stories were still leading a lot of the newscasts. Once I had proven myself, I understood the same strategy applied as before—find who it was that had their hand on the power switch and schmooze the heck out of that person.

I may have been having a ball reporting in the field, but my ultimate goal was to anchor in New York. UPN 9 offered that opportunity, but I had to be aggressive.

A lot of what I learned about navigating those tricky waters came from Jim Sabastian. Sabastian is one of the finest shooters in New York, and he and I clicked right away.

We'd spend hours cruising the streets of the New York metropolitan area chasing stories, and in doing so managed to solve all the problems of the world.

Jim had known the executive producer at Channel 9 for years. Both had been at the station when Jim first started and the EP was a desk assistant.

"So how do I handle this Jim? I don't want to come on too strong but I have to get in position so he knows I'm capable and want to do it."

"Call him now."

"Now?"

"Yeah."

It seemed easy enough. So while I was waiting out in the field to go live I grabbed my phone and left a message on his voice mail. I basically said, "You know, I can anchor and if you need someone to cover an anchor shift I'm there."

Apparently the powers that be were thinking the same thing. Within a month I was told I'd be anchoring a weekend shift. That's where the new anchors are tested out. I didn't need a test – I needed to show my stuff, so I approached the weekend shift with laser-like attention.

I got to the station early and went over every word in my script. There was little fooling around. Like many things in life, you get one chance and I was not going to blow it.

I was teamed up that night with a talented anchor named Cathleen Trigg. Cathleen was not only great on the air, but also a super person behind the scenes. I might have been just a bit tight on the air but there were no mistakes and lots of easy throws to the sports and weather guys. I got a lot of upbeat praise from the tech guys when the hour was over.

I remember thinking that even if it ended tomorrow I was totally satisfied that I had achieved my goal. I remember telling Jim, "No matter what happens from here on in, no one can ever say I didn't do what I always wanted to do – anchor a TV newscast in my home city of New York. And no one can ever take that away from me."

Before long the regular weekend anchor was moved to the reporter ranks – an indication that the EP liked my work and chemistry on the air with Cathleen. I liked it too. After that I was occasionally put in the vacation anchor rotation and once in a while I got a weekday anchor shift.

In the fall of 2002 I anchored nine days in a row including Labor Day weekend. It was a real thrill for me. Across the hall they were doing the Labor Day Jerry Lewis Telethon. In the makeup room I met and talked for about twenty minutes with Tony Orlando.

I was also doing what I could to be seen more and more in the company of the regular anchors Brenda Blackmon and Rolland Smith. When you want to step up to the next job you must be seen in the company of those who are at that level. At staff meetings I'd sit next to Brenda and Rolland. But it was more than that.

Rolland was a TV news hero to me. He had no idea that I had idolized him as a kid and now here I was in his company, watching his on-air technique, chatting about his career.

Occasionally I would be asked to fill in for Rolland. Sit in his chair and anchor for him. It's funny how if you visualize – even as a kid – what it is that you want, the universe works to give it to you. I mentioned this earlier in the book and this was just another example of how hard work and focus equals success.

My greatest night on the anchor desk was yet to come. In the meantime I had to keep producing in the field.

Jim Sabastian and I were working together more and more. I was with Jim in Times Square when the first bombs fell on Iraq in March of 2003. He and I, like everyone else, saw it coming but we were still shocked by the pictures. In the lead-up to the war we analyzed every aspect of it. Jim, like I did, realized there was so much more to news than covering the random acts of violence. We often pleaded with the assignment editors to let us do something of more significance, maybe about the march to war, but were brushed aside and sent instead to cover some minor local council dispute or yet another tragedy involving inner city kids killed by stray gunfire.

Jim was opinionated and a perfectionist when it came to his work. Because of that a lot of reporters did not want to travel with him. I enjoy Jim's intellect and stimulating conversation.

His professionalism made me better. It was a collaborative effort. The questions I would forget to ask during interviews he would remember, chiming in with one eye in the viewfinder of the camera and the other looking at the subject of the interview.

Jim also had the New York edge. He ferociously fought for our right to be where we were allowed to be.

I stood by Jim as he argued with a police officer who told us we couldn't wait on the street or sidewalk outside a funeral home. The cop knew better, and so did we. Jim flat-out told him he was wrong, that the sidewalk and street belonged to the public, and as a photojournalist he was entitled to stand there. Often he'd grab his press pass and say to the cop, "Read it… this says I can stand here!"

One night while covering news of a suspected terrorist who was taken off a flight from India to JFK Airport Jim and I were approached by an airport security guard who wanted us to clear out and not speak with any passengers exiting the jet.

Jim and I ignored the guard and I continued to interview the passengers, but like a buzzing bee he would not leave us alone. Jim had the right to be there, and so did I, but this guy thought we did not. As the guard babbled on and I continued my interview, Jim, his right hand holding the camera on his shoulder, took his left hand and smushed it into the guy's face.

The guard staggered back. He got the message and left us alone.

Doing our job within the law and working as journalists free from harassment was an ongoing battle. Many police officers know what our rights are. Sadly, too many do not. Often police, without knowledge of what is permitted under the First Amendment, would tell journalists like us what they thought the First Amendment meant. Jim's studious and persistent protection of our rights as journalists rubbed off on me.

One Saturday afternoon Patrick Horan and I were sent to cover a fire in the home of a hoarder up in northern New Jersey. The blaze burned out the back of the house. The damage was not visible from the front of the structure so the only way to get the video we needed was to go around back.

The property was secured with police tape, but there was easy entry and a view of the burned out house from the backyard of the house next door. Knowing the law I asked the owner of the house who was standing outside if Patrick I could go in his backyard with our camera and get some video of his neighbor's burned-out house. He said yes.

As Patrick rolled an irate police officer came charging at us and said we had to get out of the backyard and back into the street.

"This is private property officer and this is the owner," I said. "He has given me permission to be here." Patrick kept rolling.

"I am telling you to get out of this backyard now."

At this point I calmly looked over to the homeowner. "Sir, I said, "Do you own this house?"

"Yes," he said.

"Can I remain on this property and continue to have my photographer shoot video?"

The man looked at me, looked at the officer and said, "Yes."

Busted!

All my bases were covered. I was on the property legally, and this particular cop – whose job it was to uphold the law, had no idea what the law was. He stomped off; hopefully to go read the Constitution.

In these cases the camera is your most powerful tool. When a police officer or an especially ornery private security guard gave me trouble I would tell my shooter, "Turn the camera on this guy. Now sir, tell me again why I am not supposed to be here. I want to make sure I have that on camera."

You'd be surprised how many know-it-alls would just slink away.

No one I ever worked with cared more about accuracy and access than Jim. He and I would often analyze stories before we arrived and then work collaboratively on how it would look. We'd also laugh at the dumb ones we were forced to cover.

Jim has this way of getting right to the heart of the story and cutting through the crap. He'd chuckle at yet another story about a "star" we were forced to talk to, some twenty-three-year-old bimbo who was upset that she had been voted off some reality show. This kind of "journalism" leads to a celebrity culture where everyone thinks they're special.

One afternoon Jim and I were sent to cover a string of bank robberies on the upper East Side of Manhattan. If you know anything about Manhattan this is the home to the ultra-rich. Those who can afford to light their cigars with hundred dollar bills.

As Jim and I stood on the street and prepared to videotape my stand-up we saw what was a very common sight; a Caribbean woman – clearly a nanny – holding the hand of a milk-white, blond haired, blue-eyed ten-year-old boy.

As I recounted the details of this latest bank robbery the ten-year-old went into the "I'm Special" mode.

"Oh… Oh… let me talk on camera… let me on camera… Oh… oh…"

Now, Jim and I were trying to work. We were on deadline. There was a lot to do and the last thing we needed is for some Harvard-bound rich brat to get in the way.

I humored him as best I could and asked him and his nanny to please let us work. The kid wouldn't stop.

"Oh… please… I want to talk on camera."

I could see that Jim was thisclose to snapping. He had no tolerance for this kind of nonsense and this kid – who'd been told by his parents since he was a sperm that he was special – was not getting the message.

He started up again, jumping and posing behind me.

"Could you please move young man?" Jim said between gritted teeth.

"But I can do lots of things… what's the story… I want to talk on camera."

This was all Jim could take. "NO," he shouted. The kid's face turned dark. It might have been the very first time he had heard the word in his life.

"Why… why?" he mumbled.

"Because it's not about you!" Jim shouted.

The look on the kid's face was priceless. It was as though life had finally intervened and told him he was just a kid-like any other kid – and not anyone special.

I looked at the kid as this realization sank in. Remember: I grew up in a lower middle class home in South Queens with three siblings, wearing hand-me-downs, a million miles away from this kid and his endless opportunities. I learned it was not 'about me' from day one. He was getting the message for the first time.

Jim chuckled as the world caved in on this kid. I giggled later after spying the nanny. As soon as Jim dropped his "It's not about you" bomb, the nanny covered her mouth and laughed along with Jim.

Apparently she had had enough of the kid's nonsense as well and was pleased this brat had finally gotten his comeuppance. If his parents were there they probably would have hugged him a zillion times and told him the "bad man" was wrong and that he was indeed "special."

Later Jim, still giggling at rocking this kid's world said, "I probably cost that kid's parents thousands of dollars in psychiatric fees. The poor bastard will never be the same."

Lots of people of all ages jump behind and in front of the camera while reporters are doing live shots. Or come up to us while we're busy and ask to be on camera. It's annoying. It's like me showing up at your job and jumping around while you're trying to concentrate.

One night while working on an especially complex story, a shooter and I were getting ready to go live in an urban area in northern New Jersey. Moments before we were set to go a couple of kids pulled up in a low souped-up sports car, rap music blaring out of every opening.

The kid on the passenger side pulled down the window and said, "I want to talk about the story you're working on… I want the world to know what I have to say."

I couldn't be bothered at this point, as three people were talking to me in my earpiece at the same time and I was concentrating on what I would say to open the story.

The kid continued – only louder – "Hey man, you probably didn't hear me… I want to talk on camera."

My shooter, who grew up in the inner city, tried to be polite.

"We're working over here," he shouted back. "Can you give us a break?"

"But I want to talk about what cha doin'… I want to be on TV… tell me about the story so I can give you *MY* view…"

"Please, just give us a moment," my shooter said, "and can you lower that rap music? It's drowning us out."

"Yeah man… I will… just let me talk on camera."

In my ear I heard the director say, "Fifteen-seconds to live, Frank."

The kid wouldn't let up. "Hey man – you didn't hear what I said… I have things to say." The music blared.

"Ten seconds, Frank," said the director.

"I'm the prince of this town – I must be on TV…"

"Five… four… three… two… "

At the very last second my shooter took control of the situation.

"SHUT THE FUCK UP!"

I started, "Police in Irvington tonight…"

The latest trend is people who call their friends to tell them to watch the news and then stand behind the reporter, cell phone jammed in their ears, dancing and mugging for the camera. Paul Garrett, one of the shooters at Channel 9, actually came up with a term for these yahoos, "Phonicators."

As Jim and I became something of a team we were asked to do special reports. The EP cooked one up that almost got us killed.

"I need you guys to do a special for sweeps month." ("Sweeps" are the four months out of the year when ratings are determined at each station and advertising rates are set based on those ratings.)

"Sure," I said, eager to please.

"I want you guys to cruise the city at night trying to find workers sleeping on the job. Cops, doormen, bus drivers, anyone sleeping who's supposed to be working."

"I'm sorry—you want us to go find sleeping police officers? In their cars? Isn't that a little dangerous, not to mention opening a can of worms that could have them harassing us for years to come?"

Cops in New York don't forget when you make them look bad. The story of one reporter at WABC in New York is telling: He went to a police station in downtown Manhattan and did a story on how all the cop's personal cars were parked illegally in front of the station. How ironic – he reported – that they were giving New Yorkers tickets for the same parking violations they blatantly violated every day.

For weeks after that report aired every news vehicle, live truck or anything with New York Press license plates on it was slapped with a parking ticket. It cost WABC and other stations that were guilty by association thousands of dollars in parking fines.

My protestations at this latest "special report" caper didn't matter. The EP was under pressure from the new news director to do some "edgier" stuff.

Jim and I were pulled off our regular schedules. We'd come in near midnight, load up gear and hit the road.

The first person we found sleeping on the job was a New York bus driver. He was parked in a remote area of Staten Island, about a quarter mile from Staten Island Cable where I did my old talk show. It was pitch black.

The bus was running and he was slumped over the wheel. This area of Staten Island was so remote and so dark I was afraid the guy might be dead.

Jim and I parked about a half block away and stepped out of our black SUV. Jim fired up the camera with a special nighttime lens and we quietly approached the bus. When Jim was set and the camera aimed at the cab, I knocked on the window.

The guy's head snapped back.

"Hello, I'm Frank Cipolla from UPN 9 News. We were just watching you. Looks like you're asleep."

"Aahhhhhhhh…. I… I… wasn't sleeping. I was… I was praying."

Praying? This guy was good! He'd probably been told by his union rep "If they ever find you asleep at the wheel tell them you're praying." There's really no place to go after that. What are we going to say, "No, you were not praying? You're not a religious man?"

After I tried a few times to get him to admit he was sleeping we moved on. The north shore of Staten Island at two in the morning is a creepy place. It has long been known for unsavory characters, and we met at least one night crawler who yelled at us as we passed, but neither one of us was in the mood for some dirty sex with a streetwalker.

The next night we hit Manhattan, peered into a couple of buildings and spied a few doormen with their eyelids half closed. Nothing spectacular, and surely not yet one of those "shocking" reports that local TV news stations scream about in promos leading up to the 11 o'clock news.

Two nights later we were back on Staten Island. Jim and I were again rolling along Staten Island's seedy north shore when we saw it: A police car, lights out, parked between two tall concrete walls next to a gas station. The car was running and there was a small cabin light on but even with a special lens we couldn't quite make out who was in there or what was going on.

The way it was parked we couldn't approach the car from the sides or the back. The only conclusion we could reach was that this spot has been scoped out by the cops long ago as a place to get some sleep without getting caught.

We parked across the street for about twenty minutes trying to see if there was anyone in the car and if it was – was he or she sleeping? Taking a break? Awake and watching us?

"The only way we're going to find out," said Jim, "is if we approach the car from the front with camera rolling and you holding the microphone, knock on the window."

Even as he said it he knew it was idiotic. We were going to walk up at three in the morning to a parked police car and knock on the window with a shoulder-mounted camera that could be mistaken for a rifle and a microphone that could be mistaken for a pistol?

It had disaster written all over it.

"You're out of your mind," I said. "And who's going to come visit me when I'm in the hospital?"

We pulled away and kept looking.

At this point I got behind the wheel and Jim sat in the passenger seat with the camera on his shoulder. About two miles away we saw a small road heading to the Staten Island waterfront. The road was right next to the state prison on Staten Island.

"If I was cop and wanted to catch a few Zs this is where I would head – a remote road down to a dark shoreline," said Jim

"Okay," I said.

Jim and I went rumbling down this small road. Somewhere along the way three black vans swung out from behind and started following us. This was not good. We were headed to a dead end in the middle of the night and now we were being followed.

The vans sped up to get a closer look at us. "Hey, I've got a bad feeling about this," I said. Jim did too but he kept rolling.

The road didn't go to the shoreline but instead a dead end. Now the only way out was the way we came in. I made a wide turn and as a headed the other way the vans that were following flared out in a position in front of us that blocked our escape.

"What the hell?"

Six guys with guns drawn jumped out.

I whispered, "Just keep rolling." If we're going to get killed I wanted to make sure it was caught on tape.

"Put that fucking thing down right now," one of them screamed. Jim ignored the command and kept rolling.

At this point I whispered to Jim, "Maybe you should put the… "

"PUT THAT GODDAMN THING DOWN NOW!" someone outside shouted. Jim stopped rolling and put the camera on his lap.

"GET THE HELL OUT RIGHT NOW. RIGHT NOW."

"Whoa! We're with the press! Channel 9." I shouted back.

In a second they surrounded the car. We got out, hands up. The cops frisked us, and then had us stand aside while they rifled through everything in the car. They even had small mirrors on wheels to search under our vehicle for explosives. They told us they thought the camera was a rifle.

For the next hour we answered questions and showed all sorts of ID.

Apparently, we had wandered down a private road that led to the prison entrance. Suspecting it was some kind of planned middle-of-the-night prison break corrections officers pounced on us.

After they had scared the shit out of us they told us about a sign at the front of the entrance that warned anyone from entering that road. The sign was the size of dishcloth and not illuminated. How the hell were we supposed to see it?

Before we were released one of the guards pulled me aside. I figured I'd get a lecture about being more careful and how the press oversteps the boundaries of what's safe.

"Hey," the guard said softly so his colleagues wouldn't hear him. "I have an idea for a reality show. Can I give you my card? Maybe you can help."

Sure, I thought, *just as soon as I get home and clean up the caked-up crap in my pants I'll call ya.*

The video of us being chased and stopping the camera as the prison guards yelled at us made it to air. It had to. It was the second most compelling piece of video of this misguided "Special Report."

The absolute best shot in our report was one of a security guard, in a car, head on the steering wheel, sound asleep with drool coming out of the corner of his mouth.

We didn't have to go far.

He was the Channel 9 security guard on duty as we pulled into the parking lot on the last night of shooting.

Chapter 19
THE LAST DAYS

With most jobs in broadcasting you usually see the end coming. I have boxes in my garage with mementos from all of my jobs. On the side of each one it says, "The Last Days of (fill in the blank)." In this business your grave is usually dug months in advance – a gaping hole waiting for the news director to give you the elbow.

In the summer of 2005 new management took over at Channel 9. I'm very much into body language so when the new station GM and his underlings came over to speak with the staff as a group I was watching closely for any "tells": a shift in the eyes, a look down, a side shuffle while talking, anything to give me an idea if they were here to make things better – or worse.

The first bad sign were the famous words every new manager says when he takes over and the one thing that absolutely guarantees there will be changes. Ask any TV or radio talent. They are as follows:

"We love everything you guys are doing and don't foresee any changes in the staff."

Let me translate.

"We want you to remain calm and secure while we formulate a plan to slowly but surely dump your sorry asses out of here one by one."

I already had one strike against me since the folks who took over had already rejected me years ago. I had applied for a job years before at a rival station they were running and was told straight out that they didn't care for my work. Any hope that they may have changed their minds came at the end of the meeting.

When there are meet-and-greet meetings I usually go out of my way to introduce myself. A handshake and a look in the eye can tell you plenty.

"Hi, I don't know if we've even really met, I'm Frank Cipolla."
The new GM gave me a grunt, looked away, and released my hand
more quickly that usual.

Bad sign.

When that happens the next step is to start cleaning out your stuff. It
means the "hit" has been ordered and now it's just a matter of time.
The most important thing you can do is try to control, if you can, the
events of the next few weeks. Or days.

So I did what I usually do: Over the next few weeks I slowly and
efficiently began emptying my desk. I kept everything on top of my
desk the same but in due time every drawer was empty.

You do this for several reasons. First, you don't want to be hauling a
bunch of boxes when you're blown out and have to come in and out of
the building several times to the frowns and embarrassing looks of
your colleagues.

Second, you want to make sure that you get everything on your
schedule because the "hit" usually comes in the blink of an eye. When
that was completed I shoved an empty box underneath my desk where
no one could see it. That box was for whatever was left on top of my
desk when the time came.

Word quickly started trickling in that the older reporters who were
making the most money would be let go first. The change to the
younger, perky blondes to chase the elusive male 18-to-34
demographic – and of course to save money – had begun.

Folks ask me now, "Why'd you quit TV?" First, I say I didn't. "My
contract came to an end and I was invited to leave. Anyway they
wanted to go younger, Hispanic and female – none of which I can do."

Within weeks of that meeting one of the great reporters of this city,
Bob O'Brien, who had been beating the streets of the Big Apple for
thirty-eight years, got a call.

"Bob, can you come in and speak with the GM before you go out on your story today?"

We never saw Bob again. I don't know if he saw it coming, but like a fading tombstone his personal items stayed on his desk for weeks after until he had a chance to come by when no one was around and clean everything out.

With blood in the water my colleagues began reading the tealeaves, looking for clues to who was going to get whacked next. The call came for me on December 9, 2005. That was the date Channel 9 had set to either renew my contract for another year or let me go. My agent called me at home. I can't I was surprised.

My contract required me to work the next thirteen weeks and leave on the end date of my contract, March 11, 2006.

I wasn't going to listen to the powers that be. I felt like the jilted wife whose husband had left for a younger woman and I sure as hell wasn't going to sit around for three months before the divorce came through. I remember saying to a friend, "I'll be damned if I'm going to show up for my funeral every day. I want to get out of here so I can get another job."

"Stick around till the end," my agent told me, but that's just not the way I operate. If a station no longer wants my services I no longer want to provide them.

I stuck to my guns and we worked out a compromise with management. I would work for six of the last thirteen weeks, they would allow me to leave and pay me for the last seven.

On that score they did the right thing and I appreciated it. The next time I saw the guy who axed me I went into his office and shook his hand. No hard feelings, I said, business is business and I never take it personally. Over the years I have seen reporters and anchors – most of them young – take it personally and have their spirits crushed. I tell them, and all reading this book, that in the news field it's just business. And news is business and most importantly, entertainment.

After a long night of anchoring one summer weekend I got to talking with our weather guy Storm Field. Storm is one of he nicest guys in this business. He earned lots of cash working at rival stations in the city over the years and now in his fifties he had the financial independence to tell management to take a walk. He planned it that way. One day he said, "Frank, whatever you do, move quickly to put together an FUF."

"An FUF? What the heck is an FUF?"

"A Fuck You Fund," Storm said. That meant, have the money you need socked away so you can tell management how you really feel and if they don't want your services you can retire early.

I witnessed his power one day when the news director said, "Storm, we'd like you to come in about three or four hours earlier tomorrow because we have a couple of meetings and want to go over a few things with you."

Storm without missing a beat said, "No. You pay me to be in here between two p.m. and eleven p.m. I'll be here at two p.m." Case closed.

Storm, an icon in this business, really did what he wanted. He also had a great sense of humor. One night when I was on the set recording a one-minute promo for the upcoming newscast, my fellow anchor and I, and all the technicians in the control room, were waiting for Storm so we could quickly read the headlines, have Storm do a weather tease and wrap up the promo.

In walked Storm. He had on a beautiful jacket, shirt and tie on along with boxer shorts, no socks and sneakers. I cracked up. For Storm it was no big deal. No one was going to see him from the waist down during the promo anyway, so why sweat it?

There were still a couple of things to do before I left. One was not planned. In a quirk of fate several weeks after I got the word I was being let go the weekend anchor shift had to be juggled and I had to fill in. That was pretty standard by now but this time it was different.

As if I was getting a parting gift, my co-anchor that night would be Rolland Smith.

This was the man I had emulated and imitated as a boy in front of a make believe camera, and later in front of my high school buddies, who in 1977 recorded it for posterity on the crude videotape of the day. That same Rolland Smith of my youth, who I was thrilled to be around at Channel 9 and am proud to say is now a friend – would be sitting by my side.

The newscast was yet another inexplicable gift in my life. I can't explain what it was to live another dream for that hour. Imagine this kid from Queens sitting next to the guy who made him sit up and pay attention to the news.

Toward the end of the show there was a fluff piece on some rapper. I whispered to Rolland while the mics were off that I was going to mention that he was a big fan of this particular rapper. The incongruity of the dignified Rolland Smith listening to rap was what made the comment funny.

To my surprise Rolland said, "Go for it."

We came back on camera and I did. "I know Rolland, YOU are a big fan of Snoop Doggy Dogg."

"You bet," Rolland said, "I've got him in my vinyl collection."

Rolland, the sports guy, the weather person and I laughed, said good-bye and the show was over.

About two weeks after that Rolland searched me out in the newsroom because he heard a rumor I was being let go. He was much too polite to ask directly but I owed it to him.

"Rolland, Saturday is my last day. I want you to know that I have always admired your work. In fact somewhere on videotape, or maybe even on YouTube by now, is a very young Frank Cipolla imitating you doing a newscast. That's the kind of impact you had on my career – and I wanted to thank you."

Rolland seemed touched. He was also annoyed that someone he felt did a good job on the air was being let go for financial reasons.

Soon after my colleagues held a small party in the newsroom for me. There was a cake, heart-warming applause, and hugs and kisses. There in the back stood Rolland, hand on chin. I'll never forget his face. Rolland, a very spiritual man, knew this was a passage for me to something else and he seemed to be beckoning the universe to guide me in my journey.

My last night on the air at Channel 9 was January 29th, 2006. I was lucky one more time to work with Jim Sabastian, on a fairly innocuous story about some screw up at Fort Monmouth, a military base in central New Jersey.

The lights went on across the street from the base, the camera powered up and I was ready to go live and guess what? It happened again; a rowdy kid in a car.

"Hey man… yo… YO! I want to be on TV!"

Jim peeked his head out from behind the camera and rolled his eyes at me.

"One minute to air," the director said in my earpiece.

"Hey, look at me! I have somethin' to say… why won't you answer me? Why won't you put me on TV?"

Together, and without missing a beat, Jim and I turned to this knucklehead and said in unison, "Because it's not about you!

EPILOGUE

It's three a.m. on March 15, 2010, and there's an elephant sitting on my chest. I struggle to catch my breath and then quietly get the attention of the Bride who's sleeping next to me. The pressure on my chest is accompanied by the feeling of a knife sticking through the center of my back.

Then the radiating pain starts from shoulder blade to shoulder blade.

To make matters worse the fingers on my left hand are tingling and I have a throbbing pain in my jaw.

I've done enough medical stories in thirty years to know the classic signs of a heart attack.

I've had similar kind of pain on and off in varying degrees for the past two years but really never said anything. But now I'm sure, as Fred Sanford used to say on that old Seventies show 'Sanford and Son'

"This is the big one."

I'm also amazingly calm.

That's odd, I think. I could be ready to check out in a few minutes and I'm cool with it. I realized why and it was liberating.

I'm secure in knowing I leave this world having met my soul mate, my wife Lauren, and having brought up two healthy kids, Charles and Taryn. Most importantly I have done what I always wanted to do and pretty much as I planned. I also have the awards to show it and have even been honored by my alma mater Christ the King High School by being inducted into their Hall Of Fame in 2005. All the checks that I wrote as a twenty-one-year old leaving college and headed into my chosen profession have been cashed. All the boxes checked.

After leaving Channel 9 I knocked around in a rapidly changing industry, and after doing some documentaries for a Family Net, a cable network, and some behind the scenes work for the launch of the Fox Business Network, I am back in the radio where it all started. I now am working with a great group of broadcasters doing network radio business news reports on 300 plus stations, coast to coast.

In fact, a few months earlier I enjoyed the great honor of working with the last of my three news idols.

I listened to Gary Nunn when I first started in radio. He spent years as a network news anchor at the NBC and ABC Radio Networks and now like so many of us, he had been let go in the latest round of budget cuts. Today he was in my radio newsroom training.

I didn't want to freak him out so I waited a few minutes after shaking hands and chatting with him before reminding him that on March 6, 1981 Wayne Cabot and I took the eighty-eight-mile ride from WCRV in Washington, New Jersey where we were working to visit him at 30-Rockefeller Center. Gary was the afternoon network news anchor on the NBC Radio Network and we loved listening to him.

In was a classic "Frank in-your-face phone call." Wayne said one day, "I'd like to meet Gary Nunn." So without missing a beat I picked up the phone, dialed NBC, asked for Gary, and got him on the phone. Wayne sat there shocked. I essentially invited both of us to come see him and Gary graciously agreed.

Two weeks later we drove to 30-Rock and hung out with Gary for about an hour or so. He showed us around. We played some goofball novelty tapes we had put together for him. He gave Wayne and me headshots of himself and off we went. Wayne and I were so excited we never forgot it.

Now here I was twenty-nine years later shaking his hand. This time though Gary and I were equals. I had survived all the changes in the business, the layoffs, the corporate nonsense and now we were just two radio guys bitching about the vagaries of the crazy news business.

Gary returned a week or so later to train on my shift. On my shift! This blew my mind. I told the Bride but she couldn't grasp what it meant to me. It meant that if it all ended tomorrow the circle was complete.

Charles McCord – Imus's sidekick another of my news idols – had worked by my side at WNBC first when I was an intern there and then seven years later when my shift on the Soupy Sales' show followed his shift on the Imus in the Morning Show. I had also anchored alongside and befriended Rolland Smith my TV news icon and now I was standing behind Gary Nunn – in the studio – training him to fill in *for me*!

After he got a bit more comfortable in his new setting I brought Gary a photo from 1982. It featured a mustachioed Frank Cipolla sitting at a dumpy newsroom desk at WCRV with a manual typewriter at my elbow and on the wall above me the Gary Nunn headshot he gave me in 1981. Gary looked at the photo and smiled.

What working with and beside Charles, Rolland and Gary meant was that I could go to the grave knowing I had accomplished everything in my career I ever set out to do. The chest pain got stronger but that was okay. I was happy. I left nothing on the table.

Could I have made more money doing something else? Sure. But then there would be no Soupy stories, no Frank newsman stories, no laughing on the set during the TV commercials at News 12 and coming home with my sides hurting. No book. Nothing.

The chest pain is stinging now.

Bride throws on her clothes and we drive in the dead of night to the emergency room. It is a Monday morning and there are no other patients around.

In an instant everyone is on me.

They take my shirt off and jam an IV in my arm, put suction cups on my chest to get a look at what my heart is doing. One nurse hands me a nitroglycerin pill and tells me to let it dissolve under my tongue.

Then she calls the doctor on duty.

I've never been seriously ill in my life, so this is all new for me. I think maybe this is the payoff for that, the heart attack that comes quickly and with lethal results.

Not long before I'd been writing stories at three in the morning and getting ready to go on the set. Now I'm fifty-one years old, wondering if the time has come for me to check out.

I do another quick inventory of my life. Several things I am sure of:

First, I am confident that there is some kind of spiritual being that helps us along. Call it what or who you want – but the desire that came from me to live my dreams was helped along by *something*.

Second, having someone who loves you makes the journey infinitely better.

Third, having kids who are healthy and happy like Charles and Taryn means you leave a piece of yourself behind.

Blood is taken. More tests are done and then I'm rolled down the hallway for a Coney Island amusement park style ride through a giant MRI machine.

These are the times you realize you really don't have control over life. Someone else is driving the car. Who's driving the car depends on what or whom you believe in.

I have had friends over the years say to me, "As soon as I get this paid off, or when this happen or that happens, I'm going to finally make that move. Or change my career."

The one thing I have learned is that it doesn't work that way. You make the decision first: you ask the driver to take you where you'd like to go. Then you work hard and rely on the "driver" to get you there. You do that because tomorrow is promised to no one – and the day when all things are perfect never comes.

It hurts now when I breathe.

In the end the tests show the pain is caused by an infected and scarred gallbladder. It's something that is fairly common and causes the kind of pain that mimics a heart attack. Something I didn't know.

Five months later a middle-aged doctor with hands like butter removes it laparoscopically and aside from three small holes in my chest (which, to give me 'street cred', I tell my friends are bullet holes from a drive by shooting) I'm as good as new.

So the career continues.

But who knows what life holds? There have been offers to do some other things outside of radio and TV, but once broadcasting is in your blood it's impossible to get it out.

We talk and play for a living. And I wouldn't trade that for anything.

CPSIA information can be obtained at www.ICGtesting.com
Printed in the USA
LVOW061144161212

311876LV00004B/428/P